S0-AYC-079

ACKNOWLEDGEMENTS

I give my humble thanks to my brother and sister who shared their memories and thoughts with me so that our story could be written. I so hope that you enjoy the book and that they find healing of the emotional scars that we all carry and that cannot be seen by others.

To my Mum and Dad who sacrificed so much for us so that we might live. Our family relationships were never the same after we returned from our second evacuation. I never felt like I was ever truly home. I didn't know where home was. After my beautiful father, whom I loved so much, passed away I would return to London to visit my Mother and I got to know her all over again. Our long talks and sharing and not being afraid to show love to one another created moments together that we cherish. She was my Mum in the end and I was finally Home again. I am home at last and now wherever I may be I realize a house is not a home. A home is wherever your heart and loved ones are.

To my ever patient husband, Robert, who worked alongside me and put up with all the tears, emotions and conflict. This book would never have been written if he had not encouraged and dragged me screaming on many days to put pen to paper for a book about a time that I didn't want to relive in order to write. I am now glad that I did. Thank you for standing by me and believing in me through the work, the laughter and the tears.

SOMERSET COUNTY LIBRARY
BRIDGEWATER, NJ 08807

Prologue

This book is based on my life as a child growing up with war. I was born in 1935 in London. When WWII started in 1939 I was four years old and I lived with war in my life for the next six years. It has taken me four years to recall, relive and write about the experiences as I lived them and the effect they had on me, my family, friends and countrymen. This has been a difficult task as the emotions are relived as they are recalled. I hope that readers of this book take away from this story a remembrance of the wide reaching effects of war and credit the strength and tenacity of the English people, children and grown-ups, who lived through this experience with me for enduring. I hope that English readers will appreciate being able to read the story as in those times it was not the British way to talk about these things because showing emotion was a sign of weakness. We all just got on with it.

SOMERSET COUNTY LIBRARY
BRIDGEWATER, NJ 08807

MY FAMILY

Before my story begins, I believe it is very important to introduce you to my relatives. It is important as they are very pertinent to my story. My father Henry was born and grew up on the streets of the Elephant and Castle. At that time not the best place to grow up. He spent much of his childhood waiting outside the pubs for his mother, my grandmother, who would be in there drinking as long as the pub doors were open. She spent every penny her husband, my grandfather, earned. He worked. She drank. My dad had no place to go but to wait outside the pubs for her to throw him and his sister Win a packet of crisps for their dinner and maybe a lemonade if they were lucky. As a child he was always hungry and cold with threadbare clothes that he had long outgrown. He and his dear sweet older sister Winnie had a terrible life. They would beg on street corners so they could eat if she, my grandmother, didn't take their money from them first. She would hock everything in sight at the pawn shop in order to drink. At thirteen my father worked as an apprentice to a building contractor and he would have to hide anything that he wanted to keep. He would stow it away under lock and key in a trunk that he kept. When he and my mother to be decided to get married he bought the first new suit and shirt that he had ever owned. He was so proud of that suit, and he locked it in that trunk. The day before the wedding he unlocked the trunk to take the suit out and press it, ready for the big day. But sadly it was gone. The trunk was empty. The lock picked. He knew then and there that my grandmother must have taken it and indeed she had. She had hocked the suit, shirt, tie and everything else he had

3

and then she had drunk away the money she got for his things. My poor dad had to wear his old shabby suit. He bought a shirt front that had no sleeves and celluloid collar and cuffs to wear under his suit coat, the sleeves of which were short and showed his bare wrists. I look at the wedding pictures today, lovingly and sadly, and wonder how my grandmother had the bloody cheek to show up at the wedding and be in the wedding photograph. I am sure that she was hoping that there would be booze at the wedding. When my grandfather became ill and was dying my grandmother ripped the sheets off the bed underneath him and the blankets too. She took them to the pawn shop. Ah, but revenge is sweet. The day he died he got sweet relief from his life and my grandmother. She took his life insurance policy that very same day and climbed up ten flights of a curving stairway at the insurance office and got paid for the policy. She then climbed back down the stairs heading for the pub before his body was even cold. Ah but; this is where revenge is sweet comes in. There were tram lines all around the Elephant and Castle where the double decker trams rumbled along on their big steel wheels. In her extreme hurry to get to her favorite pub and drink, she accidentally caught the heel of her shoe in the tracks and took a severe fall and broke her leg badly. She spent the rest of her days in a leg iron that fit into the heel of her shoe. With that and a cane she was still able to make it to her favorite pub. I really think that the booze must have pickled and preserved her because she outlived most of her family to a right old age of 90. She was a real character indeed. My grandfather, her husband, Henry, was a real gentleman, very quiet, well-spoken and had a good word for everyone. By trade he was a French polisher which today I believe is a lost art. He also taught my father that craft. From what my dad told me, my grandfather had tried to protect him and my auntie Win from my grandmother, but he was a much weaker person than she and to keep peace in the

4

family he turned a deaf ear to it. It made life a little easier for him. My dad was so much like his father, a very hard working man. He worked tirelessly to support our family. Whatever it took he was always there for us. We were poor but we always had food on the table and clean clothes, however old and hand me down they were. We as kids didn't know that we were poor. My auntie Win died of a broken heart after her young husband of two months went to war and was killed in Flanders field in 1917. I wish I could have known them both. Keeping true to form my grandmother sold all of Win's belongings before the poor girl's body was picked up by the undertaker. In my early years my father would take my brother, sister and I on Sundays to see my grandparents. My Mother refused to go. She couldn't forgive my grandmother for stealing my father's wedding suit. They lived in a two room cold water flat located in the Elephant and Castle. My memories will never fade of the smelly dark greasy noisy hallways and stairwells. You could smell everyone's Sunday dinners cooking and the pervasive odors of long past dinners as well as the strong aroma of overcooked cabbage and the smell of urine from men urinating in dark corners. I can still remember climbing the steep dark creaking wooden staircase, up six flights, to their flat and hearing the sounds of screaming kids coming from behind closed doors, grownups arguing and fighting and lavatories being flushed by the long chain handles. There was only one bathroom on each landing for the six families on each floor. The slop from families' chamber pots being carried to the lavies made an unimaginable pong and the filth in those bathrooms would have deterred most people from using them, but use them they did as there was no other recourse. Father never let us use them. He would tell us to hold it till we got somewhere he thought clean enough for us to use. My grandparent's flat was dark because the one window in the kitchen looked out onto a brick wall. It didn't open. They cooked on an iron coal stove in the kitchen. The cook stove also served for warmth in the winter. There was one sink with a cold water tap. In the summer it was stifling in there. The air smelled fetid. There was nowhere for cooking and body odors to go. One small bedroom completed their living quarters. My grandfather was so ill one time when we visited and he was in a dirty disheveled unmade bed, unwashed and unshaven. My heart broke for him. My dad would do what he could to make him comfortable and always left them money which he knew would end up at the pub. At the same time my grandmother would be in the kitchen swigging from a bottle of gin that she kept in her bloomer pocket. Grandfather died shortly after that last visit. May he rest in peace? I know what it means to be poor but that was drunken poverty. My grandmother died many years later, living her years out in a nursing home. I never saw her again after my grandfather died. My mother's family was quite different. My mother Ruby was the eldest of seven children, two girls and five boys. One boy child was scalded to death at the age of three. He had pulled a chair over to the stove and toppled a large pot of boiling water over and scalded himself to death. My mother who was barely five at the time was in charge of watching him. I don't think she ever really recovered from the shock of his death. Who could? Then there was my uncle Pinky, known as such for his always ruddy face. I never knew what his real name was. Uncle Lenny was the next child. I was too young to remember them and eventually they both immigrated to Australia and New Zealand so I never saw them again. Next was my Uncle Eric who I adored. He was so full of fun and laughter. His sense of humour was so well known. He was also a great tease. I always told myself that I would marry him when I grew up. Then there was Aunt Doris whom I will speak of later. Then last but not least is the baby of the family, my Uncle Ivan. According to my mum he was a gorgeous baby. As her baby brother they

6

were very close. She had been there for all the children, helping to raise them, especially Ivan, because my grandfather William Thomas Edwin Didmon and my grandmother Emily were seldom at the house. Grandmother worked at the pub pulling pints and my grandfather was away serving with the royal horse field artillery. He was later posted to France fighting in the trenches at the battle of the Somme 1916 World War I. Fifty eight thousand British troops died on the first day of the offensive, July 1, 1916. The most soldiers to die on the first day of any battle in history. By the end of the war in the Somme, November 1916, four hundred twenty thousand British souls had perished. But, amazingly, my grandfather survived and lived until his death in 1932. Regrettably, I never got to meet him. Thank God he was to miss the horrors of another war, 1939 to 1945, World War II, the war to end all wars. As a young man he had worked as a solicitor's clerk. He liked the theatre and music but vaudeville was his love. He was very active in a theatrical troop called the Victory Boys. They were a cheeky bunch in their straw boater hats, red bow ties, white pleated shirts and arm garters. They sang barbershop and were quite successful locally. He wanted to make music part of my brother and sister's life as well. When he was ill he would have them stand at the foot of his bed and sing in their very young voices, "All things bright and beautiful", over and over till they got it right. Their reward for all their vocalizing was a brand new penny, but only if they got the words right. I am sure that he loved them very much but like many Englishmen of that era to show emotion would have been a sign of weakness. How sad to have missed out on all that love. My mother inherited grandfather's love of music. She had a beautiful voice and played the piano by ear. My nanny Emily Lodge was a very attractive bar maid at a pub in Peckham when she met William and they fell in love and later bore seven children. I did meet my Nanny. I knew her for four years before she passed away in 1939 from cancer. I will never forget her. She always wore her hair up in a snood and wore a beautiful pin at the throat of her high necked silk blouses. She always smelled of sweet lavender. She was always a very regal lady. I admired and loved her from afar and missed her so much when she went away to Heaven. My mother didn't have an easy life growing up. My Nana was always working at the pub to help feed and support their seven children. My grandfather was away serving his country. After returning from France he exhibited a Victorian strictness. There was never any talking at the dinner table, as the saying goes, "Don't talk unless spoken to". You were to be seen and not heard. There were beatings with the switch for miniscule misbehaviors. My mum said he was changed quite dramatically when he came home from the war. My mother who was a nurse probationer was never allowed to go out with friends, let alone boys. When my aunt Doris, her sister, wanted to be a dancer I think the roof fell in even though he had at one time loved musical theatre. It was, "Do as I say not as I do". In my parents case love would not be denied and my dad's sister Winnie secretly introduced my dad Henry (Harry) to my mother Ruby. My dad was instantly besotted with her dark beauty and fell in love instantly. They had many clandestine meetings. My mother was so fearful that her father would find out she confided only in her mother and my aunt Win. Mum was in love but when she found out that my dad was five years her junior she was shocked and embarrassed. It just wasn't done in those days to be courted by a man five years your junior. How could she possibly love him? But he pursued her mercilessly until she finally agreed to marry him. He was a man who knew what he wanted and even though she told him he still had the marks of the cradle on him it never deterred him. He was in love. My mother was more reserved with her feelings but love him she did. Their next big hurdle was for my

8

father to ask my grandfather for her hand in marriage. He would have to face the lion in his den. A one on one appointment was made for a Friday evening at my mother's house. Her father did not even know that she had been seeing a beau so he assumed the private talk was for my dad to ask if he could have permission to court my mother. Marriage was not even a speck on the horizon for my grandfather. Oh, my father was a brave man indeed. On that Friday evening at the appointed time a loud roar erupted from the parlor. All the children scattered from the parlor door where their ears had become adhered to the door frame permanently. My grandmother and mother were summoned into the inner sanctum for a melee of questioning. I understand that my grandfather stomped around the house harrumphing here, there and everywhere for a week. Everyone stayed out of his way, especially my mom but eventually he gave in and gave his consent for them to court for two months and then the nuptials could commence and consequently they did. They were married for 35 years. They were a working class family. There were five of them. My beautiful mother Ruby and my forever gentle patient father Henry Leonard. First born was a still born little girl. Second born was my older sister Rita who has the most beautiful copper curly hair. Next born was their most wished for bonny boy whom they named Leonard Henry but who became affectionately known as Boysey by all of the family. Boysey is a term of endearment which unfortunately stuck. He hated it as he grew up and it caused problems. After several years our mother insisted that they use his birth given name but it was a hard habit for everyone to break. It was the only name that he was known as. My Mum and Dad's family was now complete. Who could want for more, one girl and one boy. But in early August of 1934 my mother came down with a severe cold or so she thought that was what it was. But guess what; eight months later, in April of 1935 a bouncing baby girl was born. I thought many times in later years that she wished that it had been just a cold. I certainly was not planned but there I was, Sheila Ruby Harvey greeting the world and bawling with gusto, gutsy, red faced and determined. I would need that determination and guts for what life was going to offer me and that is where my story begins.

MY WORLD

We are living in London in a downstairs cold-water flat with old George our cat and Polly the parrot. My father is a paper hanger struggling to make a living. Times are economically bad and jobs hard to come by. Dad is out every day searching for work. He never gives up. We don't have much but Dad always provides food for the table. No luxuries but we eat. We have a hot dinner every day. We have beds to sleep in and my Mother keeps us clean and fed. Mums don't go out to work much. Working in the house with three kids and a husband is a full time job. She keeps the home fires burning. Our flat is so cold, we have only one small fireplace in the kitchen for heat in the winter and to boil a kettle for tea or make toast. No radiators or central heating. The flat is frigid in the winter months. We have to put our coats on the bed as blankets to stay warm with a rubber hot water bottle for heat. My Dad wraps all of the outside pipes with sacking to keep them from freezing but that doesn't always work the lavatory outside sometimes freezes up. Life is hard for my Mum. On Mondays she has to set a wood fire under an old stone copper in the scullery, fill it with buckets of cold water from the tap, light the fire and wait for it to come to a boil. She puts all of the sheets, underwear and hankies in the sink in cold water scrubs them on a scrub board with a bar of soap and then puts them in the copper to boil. She swishes the clothes around with a wooden copper-stick. The sink is then filled with cold water, the clothes taken out of the copper with the copper-stick steaming and dripping and plunged into the cold water and rinsed. Then they are put into metal pails and taken outside the back door of the scullery to be wrung out with the old rubber roller mangle. A pail underneath catches the water that is then used to water a few scrubby plants out back. Waste not, want not. The clothes are then hung on the lines with pegs to dry. In summer this goes quite well unless it rains and then a mad dash is made to bring the clothes indoors but in winter it is hell. The freezing temperature, the snow and ice, clothes freeze solid on the lines and are hard to fold when taken down. Hands become red and frozen from the cold water. Painful itchy chilblains from the cold are a common occurrence. Clothes are brought in in the evenings, dry or not and folded and put into baskets. The wet ones are draped around the open fire in the kitchen to finish drying. The kitchen is always steaming and damp as clothes began to dry. It is always a cold supper on Mondays, leftovers from Sunday dinner. I don't like Mondays. I am sure my Mum doesn't either but she never complains. She comes in from the freezing cold and huddles over the small fire to warm her legs feet and hands before she has to go back out again. She has these red circles over her lower legs caused I understand from being in extreme cold and then exposing them to direct heat from the open fire in the fireplace. I also dislike Tuesdays. Mum heats up flatirons on the gas cooker or an open fire and irons for hours on a blanket covered kitchen table. Sheets, shirts and underwear, there is not a single item that escapes Mum's black flatirons. I am not allowed out of the house without a crisp, perfectly ironed, folded hanky. She always says that when her ship comes in she will get one of the new electric irons that plug into the overhead light socket. It may be many years before her ship finally docks. Our flat in East Dulwich has one bedroom, a front room for special occasions, a kitchen and a small dark scullery. We have no bathroom. There is an outside lavatory with a chain to flush and no electric light to see with at night. Stiff, stiff lav paper or squares of newspaper on a nail are used to wipe. On Friday nights Mum boils water on the gas cooker and pours it into the tin bathtub that is brought in from outside where it hangs on a post along the garden fence. You then get you're once a week bath. More hot water is added as each child or adult takes their turn. The scum around the tin tub grows with each person taking their turn and the water turns greyer and greyer. Mum scrubs us kids then gives us our weekly change of underwear and pajamas. Mum and Dad are last in the tub. After everyone is clean Dad then drags the tub out of the kitchen, dumps the dirty water into the garden and then rehangs the tub on the post till next week. Bath nights are so cold in the winter that Dad lights a paraffin stove in the kitchen to keep us warm. I like the smell of its fumes. It makes me feel warm in a cold world. As our downstairs flat only has one bedroom, Mrs. Harwood who lives in the flat above us rents a bedroom to my Mum and Dad for my sister, brother and I to sleep in. Mrs. Harwood is a very grumpy old spinster lady. We have never seen her without metal curlers in her hair and all tied up in a scarf. We are always wondering why she has a moustache. We ask my Mum why. She tells us to mind our own business and not to be so rude. But of course we don't do as she says. We talk and giggle and jump on the beds. Then we hear Mrs. Harwood screaming at us in her cockney voice. You bleedin kids shut your gobs. Don't make me have to come in there. That just makes it worse. We three get under the covers to muffle our laughter as we imitate her voice. Shut your gobs. Shut your gobs. Ooh we are terrible. Finally Mrs. Harwood yells down to my Mum. Shut your brats up or you will have to find them somewhere else to sleep. Mum comes thumping up the stairs. We know that we are in trouble. She pulls back the bed clothes and smacks us on our backsides. We all start sniveling and snuffling. Mum tells us to stop crying or she will give us something to really cry about. Not wanting for that to happen, we stop except for a few breathless sobs. My Mum is the one who always gives out the good hidings when

13

needed. My Dad never smacks us. He is the quiet gentle one. I love him so much. After getting our good hidings we pull the covers over our heads nursing our hurt pride and not another sound is heard. This was our world until September 1939 when things changed.

War was on the horizon and then became a frightening reality in September of 1939. In the four short years of my young life a king has abdicated the throne and a new king has been crowned King of England and the Commonwealth. Hitler has started his march through Poland and Neville Chamberlain has become our Prime Minister. On Sunday September 3, 1939 I don't think there is a wireless that isn't tuned to the live broadcast throughout the whole of England. On this Sunday people are outside enjoying the very last of the summer of 1939. You can smell the Sunday dinners cooking through the open windows and neighbors are working in their gardens. The cluttering sounds of push mowers can be heard over the children laughing and playing in the warm late summer sun. In a fleeting moment at 11:15 AM the mowers go silent. Men and children are called indoors. There is an uncanny silence all throughout England from countryside to city to ocean. People everywhere in Britain are in their kitchens and front rooms listening intently to Prime Minister Neville Chamberlain announcing on the wireless that we are at war with Germany. Whole lives are to be changed forever by the events in this broadcast. I think that mine and my families' will also be.

EVACUATION DAY

In September of 1939 a mass exodus of children is undertaken by the British Government. A four day task of evacuating three million children from all of the big cities of Britain begins. Nearly half of the three million are from greater London. Predictions of imminent, massive air attacks or gas attacks from Germany on all of the big cities prompted the plan for this exodus. The word went out. Get the kids out to the safety of the countryside and the sea. The scenes are chaotic. Train stations are packed with kids ages three to fifteen. Parents are being jostled by the crowds trying to keep up with their children, lines everywhere with Mums and Dads not wanting to let go of their children. Where are they going? No one seems to know.

My sister brother and I are part of that great evacuation and as I am only four my Mum asks for permission to accompany me. My older sister is just too young to take responsibility for my brother and me. She is nine and my brother is seven. Mothers with children under five years old are given permission to go with them. My Dad is very glad that she can go. He tells me that he will miss us but he at least thinks that we will be safe. He will write us and come to see us when we get settled. He will stay home and care for Nanny who is sick with stomach flu. Teachers from the schools will accompany all the older kids to their destinations and then will teach the evacuees in their assigned towns or villages. We are to be billeted with families who have volunteered to take in children from the large cities. We are worth seven shillings and sixpence per child to the host families. Not all people want us, the unwashed. They think of us as dirty London Cockneys, ill mannered, infested brats invading the tranquility of their small countryside villages. Most of the villagers have never met a Londoner so they don't really know what we are like but rumors are rampant. They are not quite ready for this mass invasion by city children. My Mum says that she can certainly understand their misgivings. They know nothing of us and to be asked to take in strange children, one child or maybe three, to take over the responsibility of young lives for who knows how long this ruddy war will last. Host families and evacuees from completely different worlds is a lot to expect from all of us.

Our evacuation day is an autumn day, warm with just a few fluffy clouds and a gentle breeze; we are up at first light. Mum has our luggage ready. One small suitcase per child is allowed, only what we can carry. One change of underwear, two pair of pajamas and one clean outfit go in the suitcase. Names are sewn into every article of clothing. One toy can be taken per child. I take my beautiful soft Heather doll. She is dressed in her dark green velvet dress. I love her so much. She is my friend. Most essential to be taken is one gas mask in a cardboard box with a strap that goes over your shoulder. The government is preparing us for gas attacks. Instructions are to take enough food to last 24 hours as there could be many stops along the way as trains pull into sidings for troop trains to pass or to be re-routed. Some stops might take up to three hours so extra food is necessary. With a mass exodus officials are not sure what to expect. We choose to say goodbye to our Dad, Nanny, George the cat and Polly at the flat. It makes it somewhat easier. Dad tells us not to cry and to be brave and hugs us close. I wonder why this is all happening. This is so hard. I don't like having to be so brave. I would rather cry but I don't. I just bite my lip and force the tears back. The four of us walk to Rita and Len's school. George starts to follow us. He is really Mum's cat and always wants to be where she is. Go Home George, go home now. I'll be back soon. He stops, looks at us dejectedly and finally turns and saunters off towards home. He knows that something is different. We will miss him. I will also miss my Nanny, she is so lovely and smells of lavender water and wears her grey hair back in a snood. She gives the most wonderful hugs and kisses to make things better. I am sorry that she has a tummy ache and can't come to the train station. Get well Nanny. Upon arriving at the school we are assigned to coaches. Every kid from the school is on scene with Mums, Dads and Grandparents in tow. Even crying babies in prams come to say goodbye. It is like a carnival scene but without the rides and calliope. Teachers are checking all evacuees to make sure each and every one is labeled. Two big labels, one denoting destination in an unintelligible code identifiable only to officials of the railroad and another that is either pink or yellow are attached to each child. Yellow labels attached to children unaccompanied and pink to children under five accompanied by their mothers. To some it is a festive and fun occasion. We are going on an unexpected holiday. Some children have their buckets and spades hoping that they are going to the seaside. Mums are telling their children don't worry dear, you'll be back soon, and you are just going on a short holiday. Older kids are laughing and joking on the coach. I don't know any of them. Rita and Len have their friends and go and sit with them. I hold my Mum's hand and ask her, Mummy where are we going. I just don't understand why all of the children are going away at once. I don't want to go Mummy. I want to stay home with you and Daddy. Why can't Nanny come too? Mum tells me, you will like it darling. It is going to be fun like going away on a holiday. Nanny couldn't come because she is not feeling well and she is going to help take care of Daddy while we are gone. There is that word holiday again. If this is what a holiday is, I don't like it. Arriving at the station the traffic is terrible with motor coaches all trying to park to unload their passengers. You can't get close to the entrances. We all alight. Teachers call out instructions, pay attention please, form lines four abreast and no talking. Impossible, the excitement is high, and everyone is talking at once. Numerous lines of children from many other schools throughout London are all waiting to get into the station. Parents are all huddling in groups just praying for this day to be over. After about an hour we are told to march into the station among hundreds of other kids. Stay in line. Stay in line. Teachers are blowing whistles to get our attention and to follow instructions. It is such a large train station with so many platforms and tall arches that seem to reach to the sky like in a cathedral. The loud speakers are calling out what schools are to go to which platforms. Our platform number, 10, is finally called. I feel so small in such a noisy sea of humanity, all surging to go where? I am struggling to keep up. I am so afraid of being separated from my Mum. I can see my Mum off to the side of my line. Rita and Len are on either side of me with one other older child on the end. I feel that if I lose sight of my Mum I will cry but that is not an option, in wartime England one has to always be brave and as the English say; keep a stiff upper lip so I bite my bottom lip and hold back the tears determined not to cry. Some small children like me can't hold them back. The situation is all so overwhelming. After we reach gate number 10 we are checked by our labels and allowed on the platform. There are hundreds of us. Who knows what our destination is. Only the officials know. Every platform is packed with lines and lines of children. Mums and Dads puffing on their fags are saying their goodbyes. Everyone is asking where the children are going? When can they come back? Will they be all right? Nobody seems to have any answers. It is indeed a sad morning for Londoners. I hated saying good bye to my Dad this morning at the flat. I asked why can't I stay here with you Daddy. Why can't you come too? Daddies can't go my child. They have to stay behind and take care of things at home. We are needed here. My Dad tried to join up with the armed forces to go to war but was rejected because of having flat feet. We all know that he will try again. Like all Englishmen he wants and needs to serve his King and his country. We are allowed to sit down on the benches or on our suitcases till the train comes. There are volunteer ladies giving out cups of stewed tea and dried up fish paste sandwiches. The bread is curling at the edges but it is a most welcome distraction. Everyone is devouring and drinking the offerings gratefully and of course, as kids do, everyone at once seems to have to go to the loo. There is only one toilet for girls and one for boys on the platform. But there is a problem after so much use by many other children on the platform this morning the toilets are overflowing and un-flushable. Small children can't hold it and are soiling themselves and crying in embarrassment. Teachers are suddenly thrust into the role of parents and are searching through the luggage for any dry clothes and trying to clean the children up. I am lucky, my Mum walks Rita, Boysey and I to the very end of the platform. I don't think I can make it. The platforms are so long and at four I will be humiliated if I wet my knickers. I run to keep up with my knees locked together. Finally my Mum holds me out over the end of the platform with my knickers around my ankles. I feel such instantaneous gratification. Other teachers and mothers have followed us with kids in tow. It is extremely humiliating for all of us going in front of one another but it can't be helped. A lot of children have red embarrassed faces but it's so much better than sitting in soiled underwear for hours. The boys are lucky because they just go around the corner to relieve themselves where nobody

19

can see them. A loud steam whistle startles us all. It heralds the arrival of our train. It is finally here. The train station is so noisy with porter's whistles, train's whistles and teacher's whistles. The train arrives huffing and puffing. A large black iron horse blowing hot steam out of its nostrils as it comes to a laboring stop with much screeching of metal wheels and brakes. We are told to be orderly and line up again four abreast. Children without mothers are to board first with their teachers. It is not a corridor train with toilets but all third class carriages which hold at a stretch ten adult passengers so at least twelve kids can be fitted in but then there has to be an adult to each carriage. Finally amongst much commotion it all gets sorted and we board. Cases are thrown up into the overhead luggage racks. The carriages are stuffy. Adults are smoking even though these are posted nonsmoking carriages but this is war and on this train it seems that no one pays attention to such notices. Children are pulling on the wide leather straps to pull down the windows to try to see their families. Carriage doors are banging as they are closed shut by the big brass handles one after another. There is such finality with the closing of these doors. It is done. There is no turning back. We are leaving. Will we be back? Kids are hanging out all the windows, waving and calling out their good byes to families left standing on the platform. There are so many scared and alone children trying to be so brave and to not cry. The train whistle blows loudly. The train has started to move as coal is shoveled into its ever hungry flaming mouth. Grinding metal against metal and slowly shifting its massive iron hulk. Adults running alongside trying to hold on to a child's hand out of an open window until it cruelly slips away from theirs as the train slowly gathers speed and moves out. Kids strain their necks to get a last look at loved ones left behind. Our adventurous journey has begun.

THE EVACUEES HAVE LANDED

At four in the afternoon the train pulls into Pullborough station straining at the seams with its consignment of evacuees. We are in the countryside well away from London and the anticipated bombings by Germany. All of us are tired and dirty after a long day of travel. Everyone is pushing and shoving, all anxious to get off the train at once. Teachers and school officials are calling out orders trying to calm everyone down and to restore some order. Kids are all running for the toilets. Kids, kids, are everywhere and teachers with whistles are blowing them to get everyone in line. I cling to my Mum's hand so afraid that I might get lost in this melee. She is trying to round up my sister and brother who are off running with the other kids. All the children are now feeling a new found freedom from constant parental supervision. Lines are finally and reluctantly formed. We are all loaded onto coaches and thirty minutes later arrive at the austere local village school hall. We are formed into lines to enter the stone Victorian looking building. Villagers are lined up in front of the building to observe what is happening. The evacuees have landed in their hamlet. We are from London. We are different. Do we have two legs and two arms? Are we human? Are we dirty? Are we dangerous? It feels like we have come from another planet. Most of the villagers have never seen a Londoner before. They whisper amongst themselves and one lady says out loud; "Dirty London evacuees, I hear most of them are lice ridden." Soon the headmaster of the Sussex school comes out to welcome us and to introduce himself to our teachers. He looks overwhelmed by the mass of tired dirty hungry labeled

21

children all carrying gas masks. We are ushered inside and all of us children are unusually quiet for once in our lives. We are all so scared of what is to come, a fear of the unknown. Thank goodness my Mum is here for me. The villagers follow us in. The village women's institute is on hand to serve cups of tea and currant buns which are welcome as we had finished our sandwiches hours ago and are thirsty and very hungry. We eat while the locals look on. Then there is a mad rush for the toilets again. Our teachers finally gather us all back into the school hall. I wonder they don't blow the pea out of their whistles. Their whistles hang on lanyards around their necks. It is the mark of a teacher. I wouldn't be surprised if they also wear them to bed. We are made to stand in lines. Brothers and sisters are told to stay together in hopes that they will not be separated by a billeting officer and go to live with different families. In some cases staying together is not possible. Some adoptee families only want one child. They don't have the room for more or can only put up with one evacuee. The villagers walk up and down the lines looking to see who they will pick. It seems that the good looking and well-dressed are always the first to be picked. Then maybe the strongest that can do chores or farm work and then lastly the not so clean or shabbily clothed get billeted. The meat market is open. There is no way on earth that my Mother will let her family be split up. We stand close together but other children are crying as they are separated from their siblings and taken off to live with their adoptee families to probably only see their brothers and sisters at school if they are of school age and on the weekends. It is miserable. I want to cry. I keep saying to myself, please don't look at me, and don't make me go with you. They try to separate us but my Mum says no or we will return to London on the next train. I doubt that she means it but it works. Finally after several hours a very stout older lady looks us over and says that we can all come with her. It turns out that she is a cook for a very wealthy upper class family. The gentleman of the house is a Harley Street specialist. Rita and Len wave goodbye to their friends. I don't have any yet as I am not yet in school. Rita, Len and my Mum are my only friends right now and of course my silent friend Heather. There is a large car waiting outside with a liveried chauffeur who opens the door for us in the back. He doesn't speak. He is in service. He gives us the feeling that he is better than us because we are disheveled evacuees and have no place to go. To him that means that we are working class. He has only ever worked with the upper class. I don't think that he can understand what is going on in the world outside of Sussex. After traveling about twenty minutes we pull up in front of a very large posh house. It stands proudly all on its own. It isn't like the row houses in London, all crowded in together. This house is very grand indeed with white columns the likes of which I have never seen before. We struggle out of the car with our suitcases. It is dusk now and the evening is beginning to draw in. The cook hurries us around to the back of the house to the tradesman's entrance. I am sure that she doesn't want neighbors to know that the family has taken in evacuees because it might bring down the neighborhood. For the first time in my young life I realize that there is a class system in England. I have believed that everyone is equal but now one doesn't' dare step out of where one belongs. You are born into either upper class, middle class or working class and must always be aware of who your betters are. As we are evacuees from London we are considered to be in the working class system. We are pigeonholed. We learn with abruptness that we are not to the manor born. Cook opens the back door of the house and hustles us all inside, lights a kerosene lamp and leads us up the back staircase. We climb up many gloomy stairs and landings to the attic room at the very top of the house. She tells us that this is where we will live. There are two iron bedsteads, one double and one single. My sister, Mum and I will sleep in the big bed and my brother in the single. There are tick mattresses on the springs with bedding, towels and flannels piled on top for us to make the beds up. Two old arm chairs with the springs popping up on one and a bare wood table with three old kitchen chairs, an old chest of drawers with a wash basin and jug and a threadbare carpet that barely covers the wood floor. Light is provided by two oil lamps. This completes our living quarters. Cook tells us that dinner will be served down in the basement kitchen where the servants eat and if we want water to wash ourselves; my Mum will have to go down the stairs and pump it from the scullery sink. Cook tells us that there is a toilet and bath down in the basement servants' quarters. We can use that toilet but the bathtub is to be used only once a week. There is, we are told, a schedule on the bathroom door and to please adhere to it as the whole downstairs staff uses it and they don't want any confusion in their daily routines. Cook turns to my mother and says, "Dinner is at 6:30 sharp and don't be late as the Doctor and his family are served dinner upstairs in the dining room at 8:00 PM and all of the staff have to be on hand to serve." With that said she leaves and we don't even know her name. Mum, Rita, Len and I look around us. This is it. The oil lamps are smoking. We can hardly see one another across the large attic room. Mum pulls back the curtains and opens out the only window to let some of the smoke out. A chill evening breeze blows in and seems to make the lamps smoke even more. We help Mum make up the two beds. I look under the bed springs to make sure that there are chamber pots. Yes they are complete with lids for the long climbs down the long stairs to the lavatory to empty them every morning. Mum says that we should go down right away and eat. We will bring up the water tonight and have a wash before bed. The three of us climb back down the narrow stairs for supper. We are all nervous, not knowing what to expect from the staff and from our host family. What will they all think of us and how will we be treated? We are soon to find out. The kitchen feels warm and cozy after the attic room. A long wooden scrubbed table is set for supper. The chauffeur is seated at the table reading the newspaper. He peers above his paper and says, "Evening, I am Fred Mason. You'll get used to how things work around here. Just keep your nose clean and you'll be fine." My Mum wants to introduce us but his face is already back in the paper. Cook is bustling around the stove. She tells us to sit. I hope your hands are clean she says. Mum had spit on her hanky before we came down to clean us up a bit as there is no water in the room. Put your hands on the table children and let me look at them. We know now that she is the boss. Well I guess they'll do for now she says. Dirty hands and you don't eat. If you need anything talk to me. The name is Beryl or Mrs. Bates to you. The master and his family want to see you. I'll take you up before we eat. We may as well get the house rules out of the way. On no account do you ever use the front door. Always use the back staircase. Never ever go up the front staircase and never go into the family's quarters unless invited by the family. Never ask them for anything. Always come to me. You kids are to be seen and not heard at any time. Remember at all times that the family is doing you a great service by taking you in. We are all trying to do our bit and that calls for sacrifices. I look up at my Mum. I know it has got to be hard for her to listen to all of these admonishments and to not be able to answer back but right now I feel that we are at their mercy and have no other place to go. Times have changed. The world is at war. The house staff comes in to get ready for supper. We are introduced. One tall very plain skinny girl known as the upstairs maid is introduced as Ethel. Ethel snickers. So you're the evacuees we have been hearing about in the village. My Alfie says none of you are very welcome here. It makes life harder on all of us. It is like a foreign invasion. We take Mum's queue and don't say a word. Ethel can't keep her mouth shut though. Did cook tell you to keep your own room clean and to do your own washing and ironing? The scullery maid Mavis does ours. But you are responsible for your own. I am petrified of Ethel. She seems so very mean. My Mum does find her tongue. I would not expect any one else to do it, I have been taking care of my family all their lives and will continue to do so while we are here. Hopefully for all concerned it will not be for too long. Mavis the scullery maid smiles at us. She cannot be more than thirteen years of age. She is a slight little thing. I think I'll like Mavis. Cook says, pay no mind to Ethel. Her bark is worse than her bite. I make the rules down here not you Ethel. When I need your help I'll ask for it, now get along with you. Ethel, red faced, glowers at cook. Now she really has something to dislike us for. Mrs. Bates says it is time for us to go upstairs to meet the family before we have supper. She escorts us from the large kitchen up the back stairs to a second landing, pushes through a green baize door and suddenly we are in a beautifully paneled dining room. It is so very posh. A long polished table set elegantly for dinner with high back upholstered chairs. The light from the fire in the fireplace shines through the crystals of the crystal chandelier and reflects on the beautiful china place settings. It is all so very awesome. My mouth hangs open. I never knew that there were such things of beauty and richness. We stand rooted to the spot. Cook summons us on through to the drawing room. I hold on tight to my Mums hand. I am feeling so unsure of myself. A fire burns in the beautifully tiled fireplace in the drawing room. The room is filled with brocaded couches, opulent cushions, highly waxed tables and beautiful lamps lit with electricity. Gilded framed portraits cover the walls. The silence is broken. The Cook says Mrs. Fletcher; these are the evacuees from London. Cook introduces us one by one. I don't know if I should curtsy when it comes to my turn, it feels so much like what I think royalty would be. Mr. Fletcher, the Harley street specialist, rises from his chair by the fire. He is a tall slender man with very black hair and piercing blue eyes. He says, "Welcome to our home." We hope you will be happy here. Is cook taking good care of you? My Mother answers, yes, thank you for having us, we are appreciative. A slightly overweight lady enters the room with two beautifully dressed children. My face turns green with envy at their lovely frocks with matching cardigans, black patent shoes and white ankle socks. They clutch two exquisite china dolls that are nothing like my Heather who I hold even tighter. I myself feel dirty and unkempt as I know Rita and Len must as well. I feel smaller than ever. I don't want to look up at them. The lady introduces them. This is Emily, she is ten and Angela my youngest who is five. I think to myself that maybe I will be able to play with Angela as she is only a year older than I. Say hello to our visitors, girls. I do look at them. They have big dishwater blonde sausage curls and fat faces. They look at us with their bored, better than you expressions. We must look a sad bunch, mussed and tired from the long trip. My brother keeps tugging at his grey knee socks, pulling them up to look better but to no avail. They hang baggily around his ankles and overlap onto his dirty black lace up shoes. Mrs. Fletcher comes forward. Mrs. Harvey, your children will be going into the village school with their own teachers from London. We think it best that the evacuated children stay with their own kind. A lot less burdensome for them, don't you think? Oh, I am sure that my children will be happier with their own kind as you say. We wouldn't want to usurp ourselves on the local children. Mrs. Fletcher smiles thinly and adds, of course now we know that Sheila is too young to go to school so I am sure that you will find things for her to do in the kitchen, helping down stairs and helping out in the staff's garden. Idle hands are the Devil's

27

workshop you know. My Mum answers grimly. She will not be a bother to anyone here. My children are my sole responsibility. Mrs. Fletcher adds, well, good I am glad that we have had this pleasant little chat. If there is anything that you are concerned about or need, always ask Cook first. She will convey it to us for approval. Goodnight to all of you. Enjoy your stay with us. Mr. Fletcher also wishes us goodnight. The girls ignore us, playing on the couch with their beautiful dolls. Cook hustles us back out through the green baize door to the reality of the back stone staircase and servants quarters. Back in the warmth of the kitchen, warmed by the wood burning stove, Cook serves us supper. I am so hungry. We all sit at the scrubbed table. No one talks to us, just among themselves, the chatter of the day. Mum, Rita, Len and I will have lots to talk of when back in our attic room. Until then we just eat. A lovely neck of lamb stew is served with hunks of a white cottage loaf to soak up all of that beautiful gravy and bits of dumpling. There are big glasses of milk for us children. Don't they know that milk is on short supply in London? The food helps heal some of the pain of the day. Mum helps with the washing up. We kids dry while the staff is busy serving dinner upstairs. No lambs stew for them. Only poor people eat that. They don't know what they are missing. Cook tells us to be down in the morning no later than seven for breakfast or we won't get to eat. She shows Mum where to pump water into a jug for us to be able to wash tonight. The big white china jug is so heavy that Mum struggles with it up the dark back stairs. My sister gets to hold the paraffin lamp to show us the way. Why is there no electricity in this back stairway? Finally, at last, we reach the top landing exhausted and with a little less water than we originally had. Mum closes the door on the world outside. It is just us at last. Mum gets me washed in the cold water while I shiver sitting on the bed in my liberty bodice and knickers. She dries me with a rough towel and pops my flannel nightie over my head. It feels good. I pick Heather back up. I love Heather. I never go to bed without her. I tell her all of my secrets and I have a lot to tell her about today. Mum tucks me and Heather into bed. She nuzzles my neck and kisses me goodnight. It will be all right my child, not to worry. We will be going home before you know it. I am sure of that. God bless and sleep tight. I listen to Len and Rita washing and getting ready for bed, Len telling Rita not to look at him. He goes behind the curtains to put his pajamas on. He is always fussy about things like that. Rita continues teasing and laughing at him. By the time Mum gets to have a wash I think the water must be grey, scummy and very cold. Poor Mum. She always gives everything up for us. I feel Rita climb into the big bed. I snuggle up to her. I am scared as I am sure she is. It is all so new and she has to go to school tomorrow in this strange village. I will miss her terribly. I hear my brother getting into his bed. It creaks every time he moves. Mum goes over to kiss him goodnight and he grumbles that he is too old for that. He is just eight years old but today he has grown up fast. How could he not. The room is dark now. I hear Mum strike a match and light a woodbine. I can see the glow of the cigarette in the dark as she sits there quietly in the broken arm chair. I wonder what she is thinking about this day. Is she hoping that the morrow will be better? She eventually comes to bed. Now I can give in to sleep. I hear her kiss Rita goodnight and the house is now quiet except for an owl hooting in a tree outside the window, all so very different from the sounds of night time in the city of London. I miss my Dad so much. For the first time in my life I don't get to kiss him goodnight. Is he thinking of us and missing us as well? I love you Daddy. Finally sleep takes over my world and I dream of home.

LIFE IN THE MANOR

The next morning, in our room at the very top of the big house it is busy and noisy. My Mum starts to roust us at 6AM when the big alarm clock sends out its ear splitting bells and we all yell, "Shut it off Mum. Shut it off". It's cold and we don't want to get out of our warm beds. Rita is the worst, she loves to sleep. Len grumbles don't look at me. He is always mean first thing in the morning. I think maybe we are all a little irritable and on edge. When Len tells me not to look at him it makes me want to look at him all the more. He cries out, Mum Sheila is looking at me. Make her stop. I get a smack around the head from my mother. Stop it Sheila. It is bad enough as it is. He sits in his vest and under pants on the bed shivering and grumbling. He pokes his tongue out at me in revenge. Suddenly I feel sad for him. Len is small for his age and he is thrust into a world of females. Not by his choice. He has got to miss Daddy very much. Rita crouches behind the arm chair and gets dressed and tells my Mum that because she is older she needs some privacy. I hate this room she says. I hate when I hear everyone peeing in the Poe during the night. It is so rude. I just want to go home. Be quiet or I will make you carry it down stairs on your own and believe me my Mum means it. We brush our teeth in the little bit of water left from last night and all spit into the china wash bowl. It looks disgusting. The water looks like a cold grey sludge and now tooth spits are floating around in it. Thank God Mum will take it down the stairs later today and not me. My hair has to be brushed and combed. I always cry when Mum brushes my hair. It is curly and she pulls hard. I think she takes out her frustration of the situation we are in on me. Finally we are mostly presentable to go down the stairs for breakfast. Mum takes the Poe with the lid on it and tries not to slop as we descend the stairs. Thank goodness she makes it safely and dumps it into the pull chain toilet in the downstairs bathroom. Am I going to have to do this when I become a mother? Oh God I hope not. When we arrive in the kitchen we see Mavis is stoking the fire. There is a big brass pot and a kettle on the stove top. Cook doesn't say Good Morning just Mrs. Harvey make the tea. I have never seen such a huge brown tea pot in my life. It takes two hands to pick it up. Mum struggles getting the huge brass tea kettle off of the auger. She warms the big tea pot and makes the tea. No Englishman worth his salt would ever start his day without his first cup of tea. When I was six months old my Dad would mix milk and a little tea from the pot with a teaspoon of sugar and combine it into my bottle. I would sit in my high chair so very contented. I loved it. Daddy called me his little tea pot sucker. All I can say to that is tea in England is a way of life. Whenever there is a crisis a cup of hot sweet tea will solve it. The staff shows up in the kitchen for breakfast. They have all been up in the family quarters cleaning fireplaces, setting new fires, dusting, running carpet sweepers and setting the day room for breakfast. They do all of this is the cold early dawn hours. Up at 5 AM. At least we don't have to get up till 6. Cook serves us our breakfast of porridge, toast, marmalade and soft boiled eggs. I hate marmalade. It is bitter. I want jam but I know better than to ask for it and I dislike the soft yolks in eggs. Thing is though I have never eaten a soft boiled egg, so how would I know. It just looks disgusting. My Mum says no child of four should have so many dislikes. She says that I am such a difficult child and she is right, I am. She tells me to eat my breakfast or go without. My Mum, brother and sister love the breakfast and dip their toast soldiers in the egg yolk. Yuck. I do begrudgingly eat my porridge. I put two teaspoons of sugar on it and cream to disguise it. Thank goodness sugar is plentiful here. Can you just imagine porridge or tea without sugar? It just can't happen, or can it? After we eat I help my Mum wash up and dry the dishes. I can smell the sausage and bacon cooking that Mrs. Bates is making for the upstairs family's breakfast. I wonder if she is going to cook fried bread as well. My little belly growls as the sizzling savory aroma assails my nostrils. Now that's proper food. Back home in London we used to have a good old fry up on Sunday mornings. I miss that. Rita and Len are ready to leave for their first day of school. Mum and I walk out to the front of the house with them to wait for the evacuee's school bus. It is due at 8:30 and for the first day it is on time. It rumbles down the street, black smoke coughing out of the exhaust. This rusty dark green single decker bus has seen its day. But it is better than walking the six miles to the school that has been allocated for the evacuees. The bus is full of the kids from the London schools all picked up at their various billets. Some of the boys are hanging out of the windows waving their school caps and yelling, rudely breaking the quietness of this very posh upscale neighborhood. I am sure that there are many twitching lace curtains on the street. Mum and I wave goodbye to Rita and Len as they get on the bus. I don't want them to go. It will be a long day for me without them. They won't be back till late afternoon. To me that seems like it will be forever. After the bus is out of sight Mum and I go around the back and into the scullery. There is laundry in the big stone sink to be done. Mum lets me help her mangle the washed clothes and hand her the pegs for the line as she hangs the clothes out to dry. Mavis the scullery maid is outside hanging up clothes too. Cook screams out the back door for her to come in. She bobs to my Mum and I and then scurries back into the house like she is scared of her own shadow. The day passes slowly. Making beds, tidying up, bringing in laundry and folding it. Finally Mum lets me go outside to play in the back garden. I am reminded to not go into the family's gardens and do not wander away. I am so ready to explore. There is a big vegetable garden on one side. It looks like it is well tended. Bean poles and some winter vegetables soaking up the winter sun. There is a stiff cool breeze today telling us that the long cold winter is on its way. The trees are already shedding their leaves in vast numbers. I jump in them, lay in them and toss them up in the air. Then I watch them drift and float back to the ground. I pick out the most beautiful red ones to press in a book and take back to London with me for my Dad and Nanny. What to do now? An old shed at the end of the garden looks very tempting. I try to open the door. It scrapes on the dusty ground. I push really hard and it finally gives way with a grating sound. Inside it is dusty and cob webby. A shiver runs up my spine. I know I am where I shouldn't be but it is so exciting. Inside a bright shaft of sunlight comes through the small grimy window showing rakes, a push lawn mower, striped canvas lawn chairs and other garden tools. Garden shears hang from the crude beams of the ceiling. Old plank shelves are filled with clay pots of all sizes. Old dusty bottles some filled with colored liquids and old garden ornaments. I reach out gingerly and touch a dusty old discarded gnome. I trace his craggy old face with my fingers. I wish I could keep him. I am suddenly jolted out of my reverie. What is that sound? The hair on the back of my neck stands up. I am not alone. I feel like I am being watched but by what or by whom? I nervously look around and then I see big yellow eyes peering out between some canning jars. The eyes are huge and ferocious. In fear I drop the garden gnome and it breaks. The head comes off and rolls over the hard ground. The noise scares the big yellow eyes out of their lair. It is the largest, fattest ginger cat I have ever seen in my young life. The cat jumps down with a heavy thud on all four feet and sits down. We look at one another and size one another up. I break the silence. Hello Mr. Cat I am sorry I scared you. He gets up and walks toward me meowing. His ringed tail straight up in the air. I stand and wait as he approaches me and entwines himself around my legs purring loudly. It is unanimous. We are friends. I try to pick him up but he is so very heavy that I can only get his front paws off the ground. I crouch down on the dirt floor and pet him under the chin. He swoons. He is mine. I am going to keep him. I have a friend. And then I hear Mrs. Bates the cook calling out my name. Sheila where are you? Come here right now. It is time for your tea. Your mother is looking for you. I hold my breath fearing the worst. I am in trouble. The cat feels my fear and bolts for the open door. That does it. The next moment cook's large girth fills the doorway. I am done for. Get up off the floor you little street urchin. You children might behave like little hooligans back in London but not here. Do you hear me? What are you doing in here anyway? Why do you think the door was shut? That means stay out. No nosy children. There are way too many things in here to cause you harm. The only one allowed in here is Jones the gardener. You are so very lucky that he is not here today. If he were to catch you in his shed you might never be seen again. I keep my head down shamefully. I am scared and there on the floor is the broken gnome. Oh please don't let her see it. Maybe she will think the cat did it. I could say the cat did it. After all he can't talk. But thank goodness cook is on such a rant that she doesn't see it. Now get on up to the house and explain to your mother where you were. Four years old and causing so much trouble, I ask you, evacuees who needs them? I am duly punished by Mum for my sins and am put to bed at 6PM and no supper. Rita isn't allowed to read to me before I go to sleep either. The worst part of the punishment is being left alone up in the attic room while they go down to supper. It is dark except for the flicker of a candle that Mum left for me. It casts scary moving shadows on the wall. With my vivid imagination there are suddenly monsters. I pull the covers over my head, clutch Heather tightly and pray for my family to come back up the stone staircase. I miss my Dad so much. I

34

cry for him to be here this night but I know that he can't be. I hear footsteps coming up the stairs and I pretend that I am asleep. I don't want anyone to see that I am afraid or to see my tear stained face. Even at four years old I have to be strong.

A SECRET IS KEPT

It is November. Winter is setting in and it is brutally cold. We have no fireplace in our room and no hot water, just cold water in the large china jug to wash in. Sometimes there is ice on top and we have to break it to be able to wash. Cook takes pity on us and gives Mum three rubber hot water bottles for our beds which my Mum fills from the hot kettle downstairs. She warms the sheets with them but in the morning the bottles will be cold but warmer than the water in the jug so we will empty the water out of them to wash in. We are given an old black rusty paraffin stove to be lit only in the evenings to conserve money. I love the smell of the paraffin burning. Just like at home, it means warmth and that is comfort. Rita and I wear our wool pixie hats to bed. Len wears his wool balaclava. All of us are desperately trying to stay warm. We put our coats on the beds and it helps a lot. I love the early evenings when Rita tells me all about her school. She tells me that they have country dancing and that that is her favourite subject and she has her first crush on a boy. He always picks her for his partner. She says he swings her around like a rag doll and her feet hardly touch the floor and she loves it. She shows me how to do it. I wish I was old like her. I can't wait to go to school next year. Len doesn't tell me much about his school. Most boys of his age don't talk to their baby sisters. He is only interested in trains, toy soldiers and forts but he does play with Rita and I on the weekend's because Mum makes him. I just crave someone to play with. Friday nights and weekends are my favourites because Rita and Len are home and Mum lets us stay up until 8 PM on Friday and Saturday night. During the weekend the three of us play outside in the servants' garden. Today I will show them the gardeners shed, my secret place. They are not too impressed so I introduce them to big cat with the yellow eyes. Len says;" He's just a cat". They suddenly become interested in him when they discover that he is a ratter. They find some of his victims behind the shed and poke at them with sticks until they are staring up at us with their dead black beady eyes. Len even picks up one by its long skinny tail swinging it back and forth and teasing Rita and I with it until we take off screaming and he lays about, laughing. That's what he does whenever there is a crisis, someone is hurt or falling over he always seems to see the funny side of it. We get bored with the rats and venture out of the servants' yard around to the other side of the house, to the forbidden, off limits restricted garden of the owners. Len leads the way followed by Rita and little old me. Oh, I can feel the trouble we can be in for but a strong curiosity and excitement overcomes my fears. There is a loose gravel pathway that leads us around to the gated garden. The gate is unlatched and we quietly let ourselves in and there on the side of the house propped up against the wall just like out of a fairy tale are two brand new two wheel girls' bicycles. We have never seen a new shiny bicycle before with a bell and a basket. This is posh. We three stand there silently in awe our mouths open absolutely gob smacked. There isn't a soul around and this is just way too tempting for my sister and brother. They just have to try them out. Who wouldn't? In our minds we know that we can be in hot water but all caution is thrown to the wind. The temptation is just too much not to ride them. After all they are just waiting to be ridden. Oh my God, are we ever going to be in trouble. I can only stand there and watch. Besides I can't ride a two wheeler and I don't see any tricycles around. Rita and Len each take a bicycle away from the wall. They have big grins on their faces as they climb on. They have to push off on all the gravel which makes it all the more difficult to balance themselves. As the wheels start to go around gravel flies everywhere but they daren't go out on the street otherwise they will be seen by neighbours or the family. My brother and sister finally wobble off up the driveway yelling with joy. They circle around nearly hitting each other. Len is laughing hysterically. He loves it. They decide to race down the driveway and back to the back gate. I sit on the gravel to watch and call out, on the mark, get set and go. They take off with Len in the lead ringing his bell constantly. I wish I was them. Rita is close behind. On the turn coming back they get too close and lock their front wheels. They brake too hard and Rita comes off over the front wheel and Len falls off to the side and the new bikes lay on the ground with the wheels still spinning. My sister gets up on her hands and knees crying. Her cheeks and chin are bleeding and scraped and her bare knees are a mess. Len is shaken but seems to be okay, no broken bones just a very bruised ego and a few grazes. I run over to Rita's side and Len and I help her up. She is shaken. Leave me alone she says and go pick up the bikes and put them back where they were. Quick, quick before someone comes. Len and I pick the bikes up together. Oh this is not good. The chain is off on one and the front wheel on the other is bent. The new red paint is scratched and one of the bells has a big dent in it. We manage to put them up against the wall where they were in the first place. Len says I think we should run away now before anyone finds out. All of the exhilaration of this afternoon is gone and now fear and foreboding cast their cloud over us. Do you think they will notice I ask? Rita says don't be dopy of course they will notice. But they won't know it was us I insist. None of us want a good hiding. Rita says, we can't tell, we just can't. We better get back over to the servants side before we are caught. My sister is limping and in pain. We'll just have to tell Mum that Len and I fell over playing Rounders". Oh

Lordy, I wish I was back in London and that this was just a bad dream. I have never been able to lie to my Mum. My face goes bright red when I do. Rita says; Sheila you don't say anything at all or I will kill you when we go to bed. This has to be the worst weekend of my young life. I know she won't kill me but she could give me a good thumping. My lips are glued together permanently. It is now dusk and cold as we arrive back on our side of the fence. There is nothing for it but to go straight away indoors. We pass the gardeners shed when we hear. Oi! You kids! I realize that it must be Jones the gardener. You stay out of my shed. You may behave like hooligans up in Lunnon but we don't tolerate it down here in the country. From the looks of you it looks to me like you have been up to no good today. Better not let the Master find out. Now, hop it! The three of us are really scared. Does he suspect anything? Len starts to grizzle. It is all your fault Rita he says. She retorts it is not my fault; you wanted to do it too. Don't blame it all on me. At least for once I can't get blamed. I like that. I feel a kind of naughty satisfaction in that. I might see them getting a good hiding for a change. We have to go in before Mum comes looking for us. Len cautiously pushes the back door open into the kitchen. Luckily there are no servants around. It is Saturday evening and they are off and out. A cold supper is set out for the four of us. We quietly enter and head for the bathroom to wash up. It is bath night but we can't wait until then. Rita puts her hand on the china door knob and turns it very softly so as not to make noise. Too late! And where do you think you three are going? It is Mum, coming down the back stairs. We slowly turn around. We are like scared rabbits running into a trap and waiting for it to snap shut. Rita nervously pipes up. We fell over outside playing "Rounders and we were just going to wash before super. It is going to take more than a wash to fix your face and knees my girl and why is Sheila not hurt. It seems that it is just you and Len. Now get into that bathroom

39

and let me take a look at you. Mum cannot understand why there is gravel in Rita's face and knees. She is scraped pretty badly but Mum doesn't say more. She has that look on her face, grim, tight lipped and quiet. She senses something is not quite right about our story. Mothers are like that you know. Rita gets her bath first to soak the gravel out. Her knees are then coated with iodine and bandaged and iodine applied to her face and that causes a screaming match. I can only thank God that it isn't me. Next Len gets scrubbed and the deadly burning iodine applied to his scratches. They are both crying. I stand smugly outside the door waiting for my turn to be bathed. I am good. I am not going to get that brown stinging stuff on me. They are finally done and are sent into the kitchen in their dressing gowns. Mum bathes me and asks me why I don't have any scrapes? They wouldn't let me play with them I reply looking away from her. But Sheila she replies it takes more than two people to play Rounders. I know I am going to turn red any minute. I look down and feel a flush coming up into my cheeks. I won't tell. I just won't. Don't lie to me my Mum says or you will be the worse for wear. She doesn't say more. She doesn't have to. We eat our cold supper in silence. The three of us sort of push our food around on the plate as overwhelming guilt takes our hunger away. Mum is silent. She washes up the dishes, lights the oil lamp and leads us up the stairs to the attic. She tucks us up into bed. She is going back down stairs to take her bath. She says; Say your prayers and night, night my children. She shuts the door. We are alone. Len whispers, did you say anything Sheila? No I promised I wouldn't. Well, spit on it, he says. I think Mum suspects something Rita says. Say your prayers and pray she doesn't find out. Now go to sleep. Good night both of you. What will tomorrow bring I wonder. Will we be caught in our lie? I lay and think about how lucky Emily and Angela are to be able to have new bicycles even though they are now scratched and broken. I feel that I am different from them and why does Angela hate me? This morning I saw her out in the front garden pushing her beautiful doll's pram. I asked my Mum if I could go down and say hello and play with her. She had said yes but be very good because I don't want any trouble. Once outside I asked Angela if I could push her pram and play with her. She wouldn't let me. She told me no and told me to go away. I wouldn't so she poked her tongue out at me, started pulling my hair and calling me names. You're a dirty evacuee she said and my mother doesn't want me playing with you. Now go away and go back to the servants' quarters where you belong. I am confused. So many things are wrong in my young life. I await sleep and for the trap to snap shut?

THE TRUTH IS REVEALED

It is Sunday. I hate Sundays. I hate it even more today because of what happened yesterday and today we could get found out and be in a lot of trouble. On Sunday mornings evacuees have to go to church with teachers and parents. Mum tells us to buck up and get dressed and go down to breakfast so that we won't be late for church. I don't think I have been to church since I was christened. I mean I know my prayers and I know who God and Jesus are but I am not so sure who the Holy Ghost is and I don't think I want to. Do you know what I mean? Ghosts are scary right? On Sundays back in London Mum used to read us stories of Jesus's birth, life and death and teach us hymns so we do know of a higher being. The church in Sussex is big and very holy with beautiful pictures in colored glass windows, a big gold cross with Jesus nailed to it is at the altar. People entering the church are going down on one knee and making the sign of the cross. I want to do that. I want to be like them but my Mum pushes us into a pew and tells us to kneel down and pray for forgiveness of our sins. Others are in the pews kneeling on their hassocks, eyes closed either praying or sleeping. I find my hassock and kneel. Mum tells me to put my hands together close my eyes and pray. I can't close my eyes; I have to see everything that is going on. I might miss something. People are very interesting to watch, all shapes and sizes, some women with funny hats. I notice all the ladies and young girls are wearing hats. Oh, No! I suddenly feel very self-conscious. We didn't know that women are to wear hats in church. We don't have hats anyway. Suddenly I am jolted out of my musings when a tall man in a red and black frock is trying to get my mother's attention. I nudge her shoulder and she opens her eyes and frowns at me. What is it she asks? I tell her that this man wants to talk to you. The man in the frock in a deep voice says Mum I am going to have to ask you and your young family to move to the other side of the aisle. This side is reserved for village families. Evacuees are across the aisle and ladies next time please wear hats. Mum yanks us up off our knees. We shuffle, embarrassed, out of the pew and find room on the other side. Other evacuees who made the same mistake are being removed from the locals' pews as well. I wonder if God knows or cares if we are evacuees. Maybe we should start wearing signs on our backs stating who we are. But this is all soon forgotten in the swell of the organ and people's voices raised in song singing the first Hymn, Oh God our help in ages past. I love it. You can sing as loud as you want. I look across the aisle at the village people and my eyes catch the gaze of our host children Emily and Angela. They are glaring at me and sneakily poking their tongues out. How rude but how posh they look in their beautiful dresses and coats, straw hats with ribbons. I can just fancy myself in a hat and a dress like that. I am jealous of them. I can feel the color coming into my face, getting redder and redder. Liar, liar pants on fire. Do they know my secret? I feel they can see right into my brain. I look straight ahead. Mum is between me, Rita and Len so she doesn't see their rude fat faces. When church is out I will have to tell my brother and sister that maybe Emily and Angela know our unspoken secret but now the collection plate is being passed. Mum has given us all a penny to put in. I would love to keep that penny to buy Pontefract cakes at the sweet shop but Mum is watching and will rap my knuckles for it. It just isn't worth the chance. The service finally comes to a close. Luckily the regular normal village people get to leave first. No confrontation right now. We are safe for a while longer.

Walking home I tell Rita and Len that I think Emily and her sister suspect us and I don't think that I can keep our secret any longer. I would rather take the good hiding than have this awful feeling of guilt. They are both angry with me and threaten to call me smelly knickers. I hate that and they know it. On arriving back at the house we go down into the kitchen to have lunch. Cook tells us that the Master wants to see us in the family quarters as soon as we are through eating. She doesn't say why but we three kids look at one another and we know the game is up and heavy punishment will be meted out accordingly. I know Mum is wondering why we are being summoned. I feel guilty for not telling her and just letting her walk into it. Oh this is going to be so bad. I am positive that at this point Len and Rita feel really bad too. I mean after all it was an accident. It wasn't done maliciously but will Dr. and Mrs. Fletcher see it that way. In hind sight we should have told Mum when it happened and taken our lumps. As for me, all I have to say is that it is all Adolph's fault. If he hadn't started a war this would never have happened. It's all his bloody fault and now we are going to have to take the blame and suffer the consequences. It is time. Cook takes us up the back stairs and through the ugly green baize door and into the family quarters. We kids are scared stiff of what is to come. I am shivering and want to be sick all over their Persian rugs. I can see fear in Rita and Len's faces. They don't look so good either but in truth they are the ones who rode the bikes, not I. Would my punishment be any the less? I doubt it. If you know what I mean I haven't confessed, have I? We nervously follow cook into the opulent living room. A warm fire is burning in the grate and it is lovely and warm. Not like our cold upstairs attic room. Mrs. Bale pushes us up front and takes her place behind us with her arms akimbo. The family is seated on the settee and in arm chairs. Emily and Angela are stretched out on the settee stuffing sweets and chocolate biscuits in their mouths.

Ooh, Er! Back home chocolate biscuits are my favorites. I can just taste them. Dipping them in a cup of tea on a Sunday morning is my idea of heaven. We haven't had any since being evacuated. Mum can't afford them. Dad has very little work but he sends us what money he can to cover the basics. The girls stare at us haughtily with smug looks on their faces, eagerly waiting for the show to start. Dr. Fletcher and his wife are seated in their arm chairs drinking tea out of beautiful China cups and saucers. Sometimes when I have tea and it is too hot to drink I will pour it in the saucer and blow on it to cool it. They would find that common. The doctor speaks gently addressing my mother. Mrs. Harvey we seem to have a problem with our girl's new bicycles and we are not sure as to who is to blame. I don't dare look up or at Rita or Len. I keep my eyes glued to the carpet. Oh, my God, here it comes. He goes on. Someone has ridden the bikes and obviously fallen off and the bikes have been damaged. They were both down in the gravel with a bent wheel, bike chains off and badly scratched. My girls of course are very upset and crying about their new bicycles. We will have to send the two bicycles to the bike shop to be repaired so my wife and I are wondering if your children have possibly seen or heard anything that could throw a light on this disturbing situation. My mother looks at us. Do you children know what happened to the new bicycles? I need to know now. There is an unbearable silence and then my brother blurts out. Rita and I did it. We didn't mean to. The words come tumbling out. We were just having fun. I am sorry. I am so very sorry. We knew we shouldn't have been over in your garden riding the bicycles but we just couldn't help ourselves. We will never touch them ever again and we will stay on our side of the fence. I hear Mum say, Rita what do you have to say for yourself? Is this what happened and is this how you both got hurt? Yes, Mum. I'm sorry. I can barely hear her voice. It is low and trembling. Well don't say you're sorry to me.

45

Apologize to Dr. Fletcher and the girls. Do it now! In unison we speak. We're sorry Emily. We're sorry Angela. We're sorry Dr. Fletcher. We'll never ever touch them again and never come into your garden. Mrs. Fletcher says in her tight lipped way, Mrs. Harvey you must watch your children and keep them to the servants' side of the house so things like this will never happen again. My girls have been traumatized from this whole horrid situation. Emily and Angela sit there with a wicked look of satisfaction on their fat faces. She goes on to say, I am sure you will hand out the punishment to adequately pay for this egregiousness and we will not have to mention this again. I look at the girls faces framed in their big fat stiff ringlets. They just smirk and look happy that we will be punished. There will be only one thing that could make them happier and that would be to watch the punishment given out. Mrs. Fletcher dismisses us back to our quarters. Not a word is said on our way back to the kitchen. The three of us are doomed. My mother's face is tight lipped and angry. We are told to get up the stairs to the attic. Len snivels all the way up fearing what is to come. Once in the attic room Mum says, how dare you all embarrass and humiliate me by not telling me what happened. Oh, is she mad. She tans all of our hides within an inch of our lives, even me. I don't think that is fair. All I did was keep a secret. Mum has very hard hands and her wedding ring stings our legs and bottoms. When her hand tires she uses the wooden hair brush. We are put to bed all crying. She doesn't tuck us in. I think that hurts more than the spanking. Len and Rita are sobbing and blaming one another. My Mum leaves and goes down to the kitchen. She doesn't want to look at us any more tonight. She says that she can't stand to look at us. This night I cry myself to sleep.

THE MOVE

It is November. Winter has really set in. The weather is brutal with heavy snow and bitter cold. In the mornings none of us want to ever get out of our warm beds. In order for us to be able to wash Mum has to break the ice in the water pitcher and Len and Rita can't wait to get to school. They have coal fireplaces in their classrooms so they are able to get warm. Mum bundles me up in everything she can find. Pixie hat, scarf, gloves, sweater and coat. My feet are always so cold and feel like ice. They are never warm. Mum puts me in front of the paraffin heater and I try to warm my feet with them nearly touching the hot metal. Later my feet start itching. They feel like they are on fire. Mum looks at them and says, you have chilblains and that she will get some ointment from the chemist to make them feel better. I am so miserable but today is a happy day. Mummy gets a letter from Daddy. I can't wait for her to read it to me but she won't open it till my brother and sister get home from school so we can all share together in his news from home. It seems that the hours drag by slowly until I hear the door bang in the kitchen. They are home. I run down the stairs two at a time to tell them to hurry and get upstairs. We have a letter from Daddy. Come on. Hurry up. Mum is waiting. They throw their satchels on the bed and we all sit down in anticipation, pleading now Mum now. My Mum opens the envelope and takes out the blue sheets of paper and starts to read out loud. To my Dearest wife Ruby, How are you and the children? I am well. I go out looking for work every day. I pick up a few jobs here and there, just enough to be able to pay the rent and to send a few shillings to you. I wish it was more. Every laborer is looking for work. I go out very early and line up for whatever I can get. It seems because of the war that nobody is having much work done on their houses and no building is going on. The threat of the bombs looms over us but in that regard it has been very quiet here. No real raids. Just practice runs. We hear the sirens and all clear going off. They make a terrible racket. It certainly wakes you up at night. I guess that is its purpose and it works. It is strange to walk the streets in the daytime. The quietness is overpowering. The school playgrounds are empty. No children laughing or playing. No skipping rope, playing soccer or spinning tops. No whistles being blown by teachers to bring the children back into the classroom after play time. The park down the road is still. The swings are empty and squeak as they sway back and forth in the breeze. The slides are vacant, just waiting for happy children's' bottoms to polish them back to that brilliant shine. If we didn't know we might well ask one another, where have all the children gone? Kids, the house is always too quiet. No yelling, fighting, tears or laughter. Funny but I miss that. I want all of you back so badly. I miss you so much. I pray that this will be over soon and we will be reunited. They say it won't last out the year and you can come home. Let's hope that is true. George looks for all of you everywhere. He sleeps on everyone's bed in turn. He wraps around my legs in the morning, looks up at me and meows. It is like he is saying, Where are they Dad I can't find them anywhere. Poor old George! Nanny sends lots of love to you. We are taking good care of one another but it seems that she still hasn't gotten over the tummy problems she had when you left. She has lost a lot of her energy but then some days are better than others. I am going to take her around to the Doctors' surgery if she doesn't improve but you know Nanny. She doesn't want to go. She says that a bottle of Guinness every night will fix her up. All the aunts and uncles miss you and send their love. They come around to the house regularly for a cup of tea and a round of cards. But Ruby they miss you because you are the card master and I am not. I lose my three pence regularly but it helps with the loneliness having them here. Well children, I hope you are behaving for your Mother. She needs you to be strong for her. Len and Rita, I hope that you like your school and are good at your sums and reading. Len, you are the man of the house now so help Mummy all you can. I miss you my son so much. Rita my child as the oldest I know that this is extra hard for you trying to take on all the responsibility and helping with your sister Sheila at such a young age but I know that you can do it. I love you my child. Sheila, my very own little sunshine, I miss your smile and laughter. Every day without you is like a day without sunshine. Please be my good little girl for Mummy and say hello to your doll Heather. I love you. Ruby, I am so lonely without you. I must admit I miss your cooking too, especially your shepherds' pie. I am going to try and come down and see you and the children as soon as I am working regularly. I will cycle down on Friday nights and come back on Sundays. Would you like that? Sorry but I have to run now to get this in the post. I miss all of you. Bye, Bye, Daddy. PS; Ruby, you are my love and light of my life. Harry. We sit there quietly. Mum has tears in her eyes. It is so hard for her, alone, with the three of us. Do you think Daddy will really come to see us I ask? I am sure he will try to Mummy says. We just all have to be patient and in time things will all work out. Now I want to tell the three of you something of importance. As you know, living in one room has been tiresome and at times really difficult for all of us so I requested a change of residence with the billeting officer and today our request was granted. We are going to be moving to a new billet this coming Saturday. I hope that you will like it. It is on a farm outside of the village. Rita and Len moan but what about school? How will we get there? Mum says, you will have to walk. I am afraid the old school bus won't come out that far for you. Oh, No they groan. They are not very happy. I am overjoyed. There will be lots to explore there. Mum says we will have the run of the house and a fireplace for heat and that she will get to cook for us too. I like that. I can't wait for Saturday. Saturday is get away day. Mum tells us that farmer Turner is going to come and get us with his horse and cart so that we can load up our few meager possessions. I am thinking that this will make Emily and Angela jealous. I hope that they will be looking out of the upstairs windows to see us riding away in that horse and cart. This will be more fun than their crummy old bikes. I shall give them the royal wave like our King and Queen do to the adoring crowds while passing by in their coach and horses and I shall say Ta! Ta!. We won't be back. I have such a vivid imagination as you can tell but it takes me away to safe happy places.

THE JOURNEY TO THE FARM

It is finally Saturday morning. I awake early. We are going to a farm called Turner's Mill today. I don't know what to expect. I have seen pictures of farms in books with cows and chickens. Maybe I can have a pet chicken. I ask my doll Heather if she would like that. I get out of bed and shiver. It is cold. I pull the curtains away from the windows quietly. The panes of the window are frosty inside and out. I blow softly onto the frosty pane. My warm breath makes it melt in one small area and drizzle down the window. I wipe it with my hand. It is so cold but I can see outside and it is an all-white world. Yippee! It has snowed. That means snow men and snowball fights. I am so happy. I run back to the bed and shake Rita and Mum awake. It snowed! It snowed! Come see. Len hears me and is at the window immediately as he is pulling on his clothes. He has to go see outside. I want to as well but Mum says no. We have to be ready to go when farmer Turner gets here. Oh, Please I beg. I'll come right back. I promise. Mum says Go! Go! Ten minutes and no more, then back in here. Len, wait for your sister. It is glorious outside. This is going to be a perfect day. I just know it. At noon we are watching from the upstairs window when the horse and cart arrive in the Fletcher's driveway. Mr. Turner gets down off of the cart and goes around to the back door. He is bundled up warmly against the cold with a scarf wrapped around his peaked tweed hat to keep his ears warm. He looks short and roly-poly just like roly-poly pudding. We are all so excited, even Rita and Len at this point. We run around to pick up all of our stuff. My main concern is to make sure that I have Heather and then we start to lug all of our cases down the narrow stairs. Cases and gas masks that is all we have. That is what we came with and that's what we are leaving with. The cook and Mavis meet us at the bottom of the stairs. They want to wish us well. Cook thrusts a brown paper bag into my hands. Sheila, it is your favourite bread pudding. Don't eat it all at once and share with your brother and sister. I can feel the warmth of the pudding through the bag. I open it and it is all dark brown and crusty with raisins. The smell is heavenly. She must have liked us at least a little bit. Thank you cook, that is so kind. Mavis shyly takes our hands and says goodbye. Mr. Turner comes over to help us with our cases. Mum introduces us to him. He seems very nice. He says that he is very happy that we are coming to live with him and hopes that we will be happy and not too lonely on the farm. He has a nice kind face with grey and white whiskers and blue eyes. When he smiles you can see the merriment in them. I know that we are going to like him. I can tell. He puts our belongings into the back of the cart. He lifts me up onto the seat. His arms feel warm and strong. He puts me into the middle of the front seat. What is your dolly's name he asks? Heather. She is my best friend ever. He helps Mum up into the back and she sits on the side seat. Rita is next. She sits next to me. Mr. Turner is to my left and Len is next to him. Are we ready he says? Okay. Come on Daisy. He clicks his tongue, flicks the reins and Daisy the horse looks around at us as if to say glad to have you aboard and slowly makes her way out of the driveway. I look up to the windows of the family's quarters to see if Emily and Angela are watching. I can't see them but I wave like the Queen just in case. I am sure that they are there and I want them to be envious but little do they know that some of my bravado has lessened. My face is hurting from the bitter cold and I am secretly scared of going to a new place. I hold onto Heather tightly and wave again. Ta! Ta! Soon we are out onto the country roads. The land looks barren and frozen. The trees are bare and a cold wind whistles through their branches. Daisy picks her way carefully through the snow covered lanes. It seems that the road goes on forever. It curves around and around. There are cows and sheep out in the frozen pastures. Ricks of hay lay in the fields for them to eat. Farmer Turner suddenly hands over the reins to my brother. Here, get the feel of it young man. That cheers up Len's frozen little face instantly. He has never done anything like this in his whole life. He loves it. I can see the joy in his eyes. I am very happy for him. I tuck my face down into my coat trying to avoid the biting wind. I feel like my face will crack into a hundred pieces. My knitted pixie hat doesn't cover my face. I wish I could wear a balaclava like the boys and my brother do but Mum says that girls can't wear boy's clothes. I don't understand why as it has more protection for the face. Within another five minutes we approach wooden fences and gates. Without any hesitation Daisy turns into a driveway through open gates and continues up the long tree lined drive. A big grey stone barn is up ahead. Mr. Turner takes over the reins and pulls up to the barn doors. Whoa Daisy! He takes off one mitten and puts two fingers to his lips and blows out a loud whistle. Oh, I have to learn to do that. Two farm hands come out of the barn. Fred and Sam, meet our new friends. They will be staying up at the big house until it is safe for them to return to London. Fred and Sam help us down from the cart. Welcome littleuns. Sam and farmer Turner take our cases and start to trudge up the drive to the house. Fred leads Daisy into the barn to get warm and to have her dinner. Bye Daisy! We all call out. The stone farmhouse looks big. It looms big ahead of us with lots of windows and a big front door. It looks very lonely standing there in the deep snow. The front door opens and a tall grey haired lady in a long grey cardy and a wool skirt down to just above her ankles, lisle stockings and black lace up brogues appears in the doorway. Mrs. Harvey, children, this is Miss

Johnson my housekeeper. She will take care of you and show you to your rooms. Come in! Come in! She warbles in a high falsetto voice. Supper is almost ready. That's all we needed to hear. A warm supper and a comfortable bed waiting for us, but that would be the last supper she ever fixed for us. After all she is Farmer Turner's house keeper, not ours. From tomorrow Mum will be in charge of our food but we are happy with that arrangement. Tonight all we need is a bed to sleep in as we are all so tired from the events of the day. In the morning we will face a new chapter in our lives.

OUR LIFE AT THE FARM

If we think that we are going to be warmer at the farm and that life will be a bed of roses that dream is crushed very early on. The house is big and drafty. The wind whistles under the doors and rattles the windows. There are bare stone floors downstairs and bare floorboards upstairs. The kitchen is the warmest place and a haven. There is a big open fireplace that has a fire going all day until bedtime. Mum boils water on the fire for washing up, for tea and for bathing us. She also has to cook over it. There is no electricity just paraffin lamps that smoke so much that we can hardly see one another across the room at night. To get water we have to pump it out of a well but in all it could be worse. Farmer Turner is very kind to us. He has never been married but he has Miss Jones the housekeeper to take care of him. He is always busy out on the farm. He has lots of chickens so we always have warm brown fresh eggs. He sells a lot of the eggs at the village market. He also kills a lot of chickens out in the barn to sell at the weekly market. Sometimes he takes Rita and Len out with him in the late afternoon to tend to the chicken coops. The chickens are locked up at night to protect them from foxes. Len and Rita rake under the coops with big sticks to rake out any foxes hiding there who are waiting for dark so they can come in and kill the chickens. Farmer Turner also has another passion, rabbits. Two hunting guns hang on the stone kitchen wall. I have never seen a gun before and have no concept that guns can kill. He takes one down to load it. I hear the bullets click into place. Mr. Turner asks for my Mum's permission to take my brother to hunt rabbits with him. It is time for him to be a man he says. He has to learn the ways of the countryside. My Mother is not thrilled about Len becoming a man so soon but she gives in. They go off on a Saturday morning out into the frozen fields. There are still some rutted turnips rotting in the ground and the rabbits are looking for anything they can eat in the frozen hard fields. Inside the farmhouse kitchen we hear the shotgun going off and we know that a rabbit has died. I cover my ears. I don't want to know. I hate it. My brother also hates it. He has to pick up their furry bloody bodies, put them in a cloth sack and drag them home. When he gets home he is very sad. His face is white and pinched from cold and fear. He begs my Mom to not make him go again. In secret Len tells me and Rita how they die. Farmer Turner aims, pulls the trigger and shoots them. They fly off the ground, squeal, thud back to earth twitching and die. Oh no, I sob. This is awful. Don't tell me anymore. I don't want to hear it. It is wicked. My brother insists on telling us the rest. He says their bodies are still warm when he picks them up bleeding and sometimes their little heart is still beating in their furry bodies. They are in the last throes of death, eyes looking piteously at him. My sister insists that she tell Mum about the events and how upset Len is. My Mother puts her foot down and stops Len from going out with the farmer once and for all. To us children it is like killing the storybook characters of Flopsy, Mopsy and Cottontail. I hate the farmer for what he does to those rabbits but I am just a child and really he is only doing what he has to. He is a farmer. This is life on a farm. These are the ways of life in the countryside. The rabbits are damaging to his farm and multiply freely. They are also a food source. The villagers love to have fresh rabbit meat. He skins them and hangs them up on a taught line by their back feet draining their life's' blood. I see these stiff dead skinned bodies hanging in the kitchen waiting to go to market. I loathe going into the kitchen on hunting day. Have you ever heard the song "Run rabbit, Run rabbit, Run, run, run. Bang, bang, bang goes the farmer's gun".

That sums it all up. Some nights I hate suppertime. It seems that all we have to eat is rabbit. Rabbit stew, rabbit pie, rabbit every way possible and every night a crying match ensues over eating the rabbit. I just won't eat it. I can't. Neither can my brother. I know I will be sick all over the place if I do eat it. Mum makes me try it but I just choke on it and spit it out. I will never eat it. Mum and Rita quite like it. Rita loves her food. Len and I will eat the dumplings and the vegetables from the rabbit stew but that's all. Every night it is either rabbit or chicken. I won't eat chicken either. I mean after all it was just strutting around the barnyard, clucking a couple of days ago. As I have no one to play with here in the countryside I have named all of the chickens in the barnyard. They are my only friends. I mean how can you eat something that has the name Josephine. It is like eating your best friend. Once a week my Mum and I walk about five miles to the village to buy food. Our first stop is always the butchers shop. Once in a while the butcher will give us a few sausages or a couple of chops. I do love my bangers and mash. The butcher of course gives his best meat to his regulars. We line up with the villagers but when he waits on us he usually tells us that he is out of sausages and chops. He only has rabbit left. What else can we expect? We are Londoners and evacuees. I am sure that if the roles were reversed it would be the same in London for them as it is for us here in the countryside. War forces people into roles I am sure they don't want to play and it will get even worse if rationing comes to England as it is rumored to very soon. Mum always buys a newspaper when we go into the village so she can see what is happening with the war. She feels very shut off with no wireless and no telephones. Very rarely do people have their own telephones. In an emergency you will have to find a big red telephone box. I think there is only one phone box in the whole of the village. Mum reads to us from the newspaper in the evening, straining her eyes to see the words through the smoke of the paraffin lamps. It is said that people in London are waiting for the many bombs to drop and destroy the city. They are repeatedly told on the wireless and in the many newspapers that the Germans are coming. But they don't come. There is a hue and cry from the general public in London. Why can't we bring our children back? Why can't we bring them home? Rita, Len and I are very excited over that news. We can go home. It is not going to happen. The bombs aren't coming. The war will be over soon. Mum tells us to be patient. We have to wait and see. What she doesn't read to us is that the threat of invasion of this beautiful isle by Germany is imminent but my sister reads it and tells my brother and me. People are preparing throughout England. All street signs, city and village signs, train station signs and anything that could help direct Hitler's troops to us are removed. Beaches throughout England are barricaded and mined. Gun turrets go up on the cliffs on the coast. England will fight for her life. She will never give up. Our people are strong and united. We will never fall. There will always be an England. Even the farmers throughout the land are ready to fight and defend. They have no arms or ammunition just pitchforks and shovels but they band together and have exercises in the fields to plan their defense. We will prevail. For the first time this week I go to bed happy. Rita isn't always right and I think that she just tries to scare me so I believe my Mum. The bombs aren't coming. We can go home. Bed is my best friend. I snuggle down under the eiderdown with Heather. Heather, I say, the bombs aren't coming and we can go home. Maybe we can go home for Christmas. I hold her close. Mum gives me a hot water bottle tonight. I am so cold throughout the day that my bed is the only place that I feel warm. I put my feet on the bottle and feel that wonderful heat through my bed socks but the heat makes my chilblains start to itch and of course I start scratching them. The more I scratch them the worse they get. Over the last few days my feet have begun to swell badly as they have become infected from the chilblains. In the morning my feet are so bad that I can't wear my shoes anymore and my Mum says that I have to stay in bed. I am upstairs all by myself except for Heather. I am so lonely. I want to go home. I cry because the chilblains itch and hurt so bad. Mum comes up to wash them. I scream. It is agony. Mum is at her wits end because she is so worried about my feet. Miss Jones the housekeeper tells her to put iodine on them. That is the way to do it she says or the child could lose a foot from infection. Mum wants to get a doctor out to the farm but there is no phone to call the only doctor in the village and there is no way that I can walk the five miles to get there. Mummy says that she will walk into the village in the morning and try to bring the doctor back with her but tonight she will try the iodine or maybe hot poultices to stop the infection. Now, I am no novice to hot poultices because sometimes I fall and scrape or cut my knees. The wounds sometimes become red and pussy or infected. My mother cuts a square of pink lint, tears up an old holey white sheet, takes a strip of it and rolls up a sheet of the lint inside of it and then dips it into a saucepan of boiling bubbling water, lets it sit for a minute in the bubbling water, removes it, unrolls the strip of sheet and slaps the pink boiling lint on my wound and then binds it quickly with another strip of old sheet. It sounds barbaric I know and my screams can be heard for miles but after several applications it works. The heat draws the poison out and the wound heals. But tonight Mum thinks the iodine will be easier to do so she gets out the brown bottle of iodine. She soaks two cotton battens with it and applies them to my feet. How can I describe the pain? I can hear someone screaming in my skull.

It is me. I am in agony as the iodine burns and eats the skin. I writhe in pain. The cotton battens are stuck to my skin. My Mum can't get them off. She tries to hold me down to remove them but she can't. The whole household comes running to see what all the screaming is about. Rita and Len stand rooted to the spot with fear written all over their faces. Farmer Turner tries to calm the situation down. He tells my Mum to get a pan of cold dishwater right away. No time to warm any. When my Mum comes back the farmer helps me up to a sitting position to put my feet in the dishpan. I am sobbing. Take it away, take the pain away. I don't want my feet any more. Slowly the cold water eases the burning of the skin and the cotton comes off. Please Mummy I beg. Don't do it anymore. I won't my child I won't. It is all over now. Don't cry any more. We will get the doctor in tomorrow. My Mum puts thick Vaseline on some torn rags and binds my badly burned feet. The Vaseline soothes the burning somewhat. Mum tucks me into bed. Len and Rita feel sad for me and offer to read me a story till I fall asleep. I love that so much. Mummy says, as she sits on the bed, that she has a nice surprise for all three of us. Who would you like to see most of all in the whole wide world? The three of us chorus, Daddy and Nana. Well your Daddy is coming down on Friday evening and will stay with us through Sunday afternoon. We all keep saying; Daddy is coming! Daddy is coming! The excitement nearly overcomes my pain. We are all so very happy at this moment. I finally do drift off to sleep but it is a night of pain and wakefulness. My Mum is by me all night changing the dressings, comforting me and trying to get me to go to sleep. In the morning my Mum takes the long walk into the village to get the doctor. I watch her from the upstairs window trudging through the snow on that long winding road that seems to go on forever. I watch her until the trees and the hedgerows hide her from view. I pray she will be back soon. I am scared to be alone but at my age that is to be expected.

What if she never comes back? Whatever will I do? Miss Jones the housekeeper comes into the bedroom with some warm bread and milk for me and as a treat has topped it with brown sugar. Please stay I beg her. I just don't want to be alone. You sleep my child; I have way too many things to do for Farmer Turner. You will be fine. Your mother will be back soon. She always puts on an air of being prim and proper but I have a feeling that she really does care. She just tries not to show it. I even saw a half a smile on her face. I don't think she really likes children. Maybe she likes little girls but definitely not little boys. She thinks they are always grubby and loud. Once Len showed her his matchboxes with caterpillars inside and she screamed and called him a nasty little boy. After she leaves I hide under the eiderdown with Heather and try to pretend that we're back at home and that when I put my head back out I will be back in Rita's and my bedroom with my Daddy tucking us in but it is not so. It is just the same walls and windows of the farmhouse. After many long lonely hours my Mum gets back from the doctor's and tells us he can't come out until the next day. He is so busy with a big break out of influenza. The next day he arrives. He gives my mother Germolene ointment and bandages to bind my feet and tells her to give me half an Aspro every four hours for the fever and to keep me warm. The Germolene is pink and smells very medicinal. I love the smell and the relief it gives me. It is so cooling and feels very healing. He comes every other day to the farmhouse and tells my mother that we are very lucky as it is one of the worst cases of infected chilblains he has ever seen. I love Dr. Mills. He reminds me of my Dad. He gives me comfort when I so need it. He says my feet will take at least two months to heal. Dressings are to be changed three times a day. He tells us that I might have some permanent scarring.

D-DAY DADDY ARRIVES

Daddy's first visit day has finally arrived. It is a Friday. It seemed like this day would never get here. The days have drug by interminably but finally the day is here. I can't wait for Rita and Len to get home from school because that means that his evening arrival time is even closer. This evening we sit at the kitchen table in silence listening to the wall clock. Tick Tock! Tick Tock! Bong! Bong! Bong! It strikes six o'clock and still no Daddy. The only sound we hear is the wind and rain lashing at the casement windows. What foul weather for Dad to be traveling in. I ask, Is Daddy coming on the train? Will Farmer Turner meet him at the station? Mum answers, no my luv. We can't afford the money for a ticket so Daddy is riding his bicycle down. He probably left London around twelve today so he should be here very soon. I just hope that he isn't lost. She continues, He could be having trouble finding his way in the black out and rain and as there are no street or village signs it must be a very difficult journey for him. Len and Rita go to the windows and pull back the thick curtains and stare out trying to see through the stair rod rain. It is so dark and wet out there and oh so cold but he will be here. We know it. They can't see anything out of the window except the rain bouncing off the long driveway. I shuffle over in my bandages. I can't wear shoes yet but I just have to see if he is coming. I am thinking of him riding that heavy bike with no gears, just brakes and no bike lamp because of the blackout. Mum had told us that he has a bike that he bought down at Petticoat Lane Market in London. He paid a few shillings for it but that is a lot of money for Dad as times are so hard and when he got the bike back home he found that the crossbar had been replaced with an old broom handle that had been painted black. Can you imagine sixty miles of dark lonely country roads and having to stop to ask for directions? He has some form of road map to go by and he knows when he reaches the village that everyone will know where Turners farm is. The hours of peddling to see his family must seem endless but he does it to have just a few hours of being with his loved ones that the war has so cruelly separated from him. Thanks Dad. This evening seems so long. Another excruciating hour goes slowly by when all of a sudden we hear a loud banging on the front door. Mum grabs a paraffin lamp and everyone runs down the stone flagged hallway. Daddy! Daddy! We are all screaming. I shuffle along as fast as I can behind the others. Mum gets there first and opens the heavy front door. There he is, my Dad, a dripping wet figure with his bicycle mac making a puddle on the front step. Rita and Len drag him in over the doorway. They are hugging him and screaming with delight at the same time. Mum puts the lamp down on the hallway table. Dad puts his arms around her and gives her a kiss. I hang onto my Mum's skirt. I am afraid that he has forgotten me but he hasn't. He picks me up and holds me close. Hello Sunshine! I rub my cheek on his. He is my Dad. He has come like he promised. Oh how much I love him.

The weekend flies by so fast. He tells us of home and family. Nanna is still not feeling well and is with my uncles at home. I know my mum is so worried and wants to go back to London to help with Nanna but Daddy says that we must wait a while longer. At least till after Christmas as the threat of invasion still exists and that it would be too dangerous to return to London at this time. At night I hear Mummy and Daddy talking about what they will do if the Germans invade. Dad thinks we will be safer out here in the country. I sit on the stairway and wonder, will we all die if they come? Will they shoot us like Farmer Turner shoots the rabbits? It is cold here on the stairway so I go back to bed and pull the covers up over my head. I don't want to think about it. The next morning Dad tells us that if no bombs or invasion happens there is a great possibility that in January we can go home and that he will work at any job to pay for our train tickets back to London. The British government paid to send us out of harm's way but will only pay for our return to the city when the war is over. They don't want to carry the responsibility of children dying in bombing raids. In the afternoon my brother and sister show Daddy all around the farm. He meets Farmer Turner and Miss Jones who both tell him that they are happy to have us to stay with them and that our noise and laughter make the house a happy place for them. Saturday night Daddy reads to Heather and me and tells us all about the crazy antics of George the cat and how all the aunts and uncles, especially Nanna miss us. I wish that Daddy would never have to leave. Mum is so happy having him here. They have long talks over cups of tea and they both spend Saturday evening playing games with us. It is all so much fun. The war seems so very far away. On Sunday Daddy says he has a nice surprise for us. He tells us that he will come every weekend to see us until we can come home. It hurts to see him leave on Sunday but we are assured that he will be back. Mum makes him a cheese sandwich and a thermos of tea for the long trip home. In the driveway we all cling to him as he kisses each of us goodbye. Glumly we watch him peddle off down the driveway. We wave until he is out of sight. Then as fast as we can we run up to the upstairs window and watch him some more until he is just a dot on the horizon. We are all misty eyed but he will be back. Nothing will keep him from us.

GOING HOME

It is now January 1940. True to his word Daddy comes every weekend snow, rain or shine. He never complains about the long extremely tiring trip but that is how he is. Dad is with us at Christmas and New Years and then in the middle of January Mummy gets a letter from Daddy saying that he will not be here for the weekend and that Nanny has just been admitted to King's College Hospital seriously ill and that we need to come home immediately. As yet there has been no bombing and he believes that it is safe for us to return. He includes money for our fares. We all know that it has been a hardship for him. He struggles each week to make enough money for rent and food. Pounding the pavements daily for any work he can get. Daddy says that there are thousands of men out of work and that it is a bad time for all. As kids, our feelings are so emotionally mixed. We want so desperately to go home and be with our family but our hearts are sad that the main cause of our return is that our beloved Nanny is so very ill. Mum needs to get home as soon as possible to be with her beautiful Mama. I know my Mum's heart is very heavy. We cling to each other for comfort.

It is arranged that we will leave on Sunday morning. Farmer Turner will take us to the station in the horse and buggy. Miss Jones offers to help us pack and get ready for our trip. Mum is very grateful to her. On the Saturday it is rush, rush. By eight AM Mum is hanging out washing. It is a cold windy day but the sun is shining in a cloudless sky. We kids play outside while Mum pegs the clothes onto the clothes line. We know she will have them dried and ironed by late afternoon and into the suitcases by evening. No way will she let us go home unless we are all clean and paid for. It can't be any other way. We watch as our Mum climbs up cautiously onto an old broken kitchen chair to reach the clothes line. The wooden rail is off on the back and only the rickety spokes remain. Mum reaches into the peg bag to get some pegs when oops; her feet go out from under her. The seat of the chair is wet. She struggles to stay upright but to no avail. She goes down with a loud gasp and intake of breath. She looks like she is impaled on the spokes by her midsection. We hear her groaning and look to see what is happening. She struggles back up. We can't see any blood on her apron so she must be all right and once again she steps back up on the wobbly old chair, stretches up her arms to peg a white sheet when she loses her footing again and lands on her back on the hard frozen ground. It knocks the breath out of her and she can't speak for a minute or two. Len is hysterical, doubled over on the ground with laughter. He thinks Mum is trying to entertain us and the more she tries to get up off the ground the more he laughs and it quickly becomes contagious. Rita and I start to giggle and in seconds it becomes full blown laughter. This is better than a circus. Our Mum is really funny. She likes to entertain us, or so we think. When she does finally get her breath back and is standing on her own two feet she sternly tells us, if you keep that up I will give the three of you something to cry about and you won't be laughing any more except on the other side of your faces. We know that means trouble for us. Rita's and my laughter subsides quickly but Len has to stuff his hanky in his mouth for him to stop laughing. I am pleased that she isn't seriously hurt just badly bruised and I am sure that her ego must be too. It is Sunday morning. The three of us are so excited. We are going home to our loved ones and our own beds and all of our prized possessions no matter how meager they are. To us it is all precious. We are packed and ready to go. Miss Jones makes us sandwiches for the trip and wishes us well. We tell her goodbye and thank her. I think that she will miss us but of course she will never admit to it. How quiet and empty the house will be after we are gone. Farmer Turner loads up the buggy with our suitcases. We all climb aboard except for me. I am still too small to climb up so Farmer Turner picks Heather and me up and sits us next to him. I shall miss him. He is always very gentle and kind to us. I wonder if he will take in any other evacuees. I am sure he will. He is a good Englishman wanting to do his part for his country. We can't all be at the front fighting. People are needed at home to protect the homeland. Everyone has their job. We arrive at the station and it is crowded. Lots of evacuees are returning to London going on the assumption that if the bombs aren't dropping it is safe to return. Mum queues up to get our tickets. We sit on the platform on our upturned suitcases waiting for the train to come in. Within half an hour it does. Huffing and Puffing its way along the platform with steam and wheels finally grinding to a slow halt. A few people alight but more are leaving than coming. We look for a third class smoking carriage. None of this crowd of returning happy evacuees can afford first class. Farmer Turner bids his good byes and tells us to be safe back in London and also says that maybe after this wretched war is over we can come and see him for a holiday. Mum thanks him and tells him how much she appreciates him taking us in. He helps us up onto the train with our suitcases. The porter blows his whistle for us to all be aboard. Doors are banging, windows being lowered to say our last fair wells. The trains whistle blows loudly. The long green train starts shunting forward slowly. We are hanging out of the windows calling out our last good byes. Waving as the train slowly gathers speed. We wave until we can no longer see Mr. Turner. He is now just a memory and we wonder if we will ever see him again. He is gone and we are on our way home to Daddy and Nanny. The train wheels seem to say we are going home, we are going home. At that moment this is our victory. We vow that our family will never be separated again but we children can't know what fate has in store for us.

LONDON 1940

I am so happy to be back in London amongst all of my family. I feel so loved and wanted. The loneliness in my heart has left. The house is filled with aunts and uncles, conversation and laughter. We are poor but we have love. At night time I say my prayers and thank Jesus for my very own cozy bed and my doll Heather and for bringing my Mum, brother, sister and I home safely. Times are not easy back here in London. Rationing has been instituted. Life is austere and the rationing just adds to the hardships of everyday living but we get on with it. Our strong spirit never wavers. Sadly for us, on a bitterly cold February day, after a long brave battle with stomach cancer, our beautiful Nanny dies in King's College Hospital. My Mum is with her to the very end. It is such a heart wrenching loss to all of us. She was the glue that held all of us together. The whole family mourns her deeply. My Mother's grief is interminable. I miss Nanny. I can still see her like it was yesterday. She will always be with me. The winter months in London are miserably cold and wet. Food is hard to get. Queues form for everything from bread to potatoes. To add to it the news on the continent is not good either. Hitler continues his march across Europe. The German jack boots just keep on marching. It seems that there is no stopping them. Spring has finally arrived. It is so very welcome especially this year, 1940, with our country at war. Spring is when new life emerges. Flowers and trees bloom. There is new birth everywhere, and in the countryside animals, lambs and calves. Everything is new again. There is a quickening in your step as you anticipate the coming warm days of summer. It has to be a good sign that the war will end and that the world can finally live as one people. Everyday Mum struggles to put food on the table and make ends meet. Dad still searches for work but thankfully we do have each other and we are alive.

The bombs have not come yet and it is now June 1940. The wireless broadcasts dire news daily. Europe has fallen and France has succumbed to the Blitzkrieg and on June the 14th the Germans proudly enter Paris. England is in great danger. England no longer has allies on the continent. The British army is trapped in Dunkirk and is bravely evacuated by an armada of British boats of all sizes from every English seaport. It is truly a great accomplishment to bring the troops back to England. Ordinary Englishmen from all walks of life take courageous risks to bring the soldiers back safely across the English Channel to home. England now stands alone. This beautiful island surrounded by the sea. We are next on Hitler's list of peoples to defeat but there will be one thing that he can never defeat the ever enduring unending spirit of the British people. We will defend this island to the death. We will survive. No German jack boots will ever be imprinted on our sands.

Many nights after my brother sister and I have been put to bed we get up and go sit on the stairs listening to the family talking through the open front room door. Their tones are grave as they talk of the presumed invasion by the Germans onto our soil. Boysey chants softly under his breath to scare Rita and me, The Germans are coming! The Germans are coming! I pull my dressing gown tightly around me as if to protect myself. Not from the cold but from really bad things happening. Sitting in the dark on the stairs only makes it worse. I know that Boysey only teases us because he, at eight years old, is scared but tries to show bravado. I know myself, having just turned five that something is going to happen to change our lives and I am worried and confused and then come the words and the reality of my fears. We hear one night from the stairway my Mum say; the children have to go Harry. We can't protect them here. It is too dangerous. We have to get them back out of London to the country where they will be safer. What a worry it is for parents wondering what will happen to all of us if the Germans invade. Rumors run rampant. There is a rumor about a pill that parents can give to their children in the event of invasion to keep them from suffering at the hands of the Germans and if there is a pill, can a parent have the strength to use it? Mind you, this is just a rumor.

Rita whispers, they are sending us away. How can they? Will Mummy be coming with us I ask? Not this time Sheila, you are a big girl now and you will be starting school in the autumn and Mummies are not allowed after you reach five. Boysey whispers you'll be all right Sheila, we'll be with you. We hear Mum's footsteps coming out of the front room and we bolt back to our beds. I lie curled up like a baby in my bed. I have a lump in my throat and I gulp. My chest grows heavy and I want to scream. Please don't send me away, I'll be good. I won't be naughty any more, I promise. Please Mum, Please. I have never in my short young life at any time ever felt so helpless and powerless. I can hear the soft muffled sobs from my brother's and sister's beds.

WHY DOES THIS HAVE TO HAPPEN, AGAIN?

It is the beginning of June 1940, there is another mass evacuation of children out of London after so many kids had returned home, their parents thinking the danger had passed. We are to leave right away. We don't know where we are travelling to. No one does except government officials and they are tight lipped because "Loose lips sink ships". One of the fears is that the Germans could drop their bombs on the departing trains if they knew departure times and destinations. What a world we live in.

We are to depart on Friday morning from Heber Road School. Mum has spent the last week sewing names onto all of our clothes and making sure we have everything the government list requires, no more and no less. I cling to my Mum this week. I won't let her out of my sight. I can't bear the thought that I might not see her or my Dad for a long time and I am always hoping against hope that at the last moment something will happen to prevent us from being sent away. On Tuesday I wake up in the night with an excruciating toothache. It throbs and the pain will not stop. My Mum stays up with me all night. She puts salt on the infected back tooth, guaranteed by some to stop the pain. She tries to soothe me but I am inconsolable. I think it is more the pain of being sent away than the toothache and I want her close to me. The next morning, on arising, my face is swollen. My brother and sister laugh when they see me. They call me fat face and giggle. Later that morning I am yanked off to the dentist for the very first visit of my young life. When I am seated in the chair the dentist tells me to open wide. He inserts his fat pudgy fingers into my mouth and he pokes at my tooth with a metal instrument so I bite down hard on his fingers and he quickly withdraws them, squealing loudly. Mum is so embarrassed but I am happy that I bit him. He doesn't attempt to do it again. He tells my Mum that I have an abscessed tooth and that he can't pull it until the abscess has receded and that when that happens my Mum should try another dentist. It takes two to three days until the abscess has drained and by that time it is too late to go to a different dentist before evacuation. My Mum writes a letter and gives it to my sister for safe keeping. It states that my daughter Sheila should see a dentist when the children are settled in their billets to attend to her bad back tooth. I am hoping that my Mum and Dad will not send me away because of my tooth but they believe the danger to London and to us is more important than my abscessed tooth.

I am dreading Friday's arrival. There are only two days left. Will my sister, brother and I be able to persuade them not to send us away? I cling to my Mum during the day and to my Dad at night. I hold onto them tightly when they kiss me goodnight. I don't ever want to let them go. Don't send me away I beg. You won't even know I am here. I won't make a lot of noise and make you cross. My Mum laughs softly. Tucking me up, she says, "Sheila, look at me. We are sending you, your brother and sister away because we love you so very much and we want you to have a life and be safe." It is so very hard for us to have to do this but we must. It is the most heart wrenching decision that Daddy and I have ever had to make. Now, when we find out where you are we will come and visit you. Please be my good girl and try to understand. You will all be safe away from London. She tucks me up and kisses me good night. I don't understand. I would never send Heather away. I will always take her with me wherever I go. But Mum, who will tuck me up at night? I ask. Your sister will. She will be there for you. Mummy, don't make me go I want to stay here with you. I'll be good, I promise. She smiles gently at me. I know Sheila, I know. I sit up and watch as she goes over to Rita's bed to kiss her good night but Rita turns her head away. She is angry at Mum and Dad for sending us away. Rita is eleven and suddenly is expected to understand and grow up overnight and to become Boysey and my adopted Mum. What a frightening and overwhelming responsibility it is for her. Rita is very confused and hurt. Mummy kisses her and tells her to be brave and that she loves her. Boysey tries to accept evacuation. My Dad tells him, I want you to be my strong little man and help take care of your sisters. Watch out for them at all times. Can you do that for me? I am relying on you to be there for them. This is not what your Mum and I want for you but we have no other choice at this time. Maybe the three of us kids could accept this dire situation if the forecasted bombs were dropping and destroying lives and cities but then what do we kids know. On the Thursday night before we are to leave aunts and uncles come over to the house to say goodbye. Many hugs and tears are exchanged and words of good cheer are given. You'll be back before you know it. It won't last long and we'll be here keeping the home fires burning. We have heard that all before. We three look at one another glumly. We smile falsely at them. What else can we do? We have no control whatsoever. We will miss everyone so much. They all bundle up the stairs to tuck us up and to say goodnight. I wonder, will we ever see them again? I pray so.

WE DON'T KNOW WHERE WE ARE GOING UNTIL WE'RE THERE

Our D-day has arrived. Mum wakes us out of our sleep and tells us to get washed and dressed. We are all sulky. I am being extra difficult and have a grumpy looking face. I fidget and complain when I am washed, cry when my hair is brushed, won't brush my teeth because my tooth hurts and I won't eat my porridge. I want sweets and I can't have them. Daddy tries to cheer us all up by acting all soppy. Come on children, smile. He makes funny faces and ties a dish towel around his head. We try not to laugh at him but we can't help it. He is really funny and we all end up giggling and call him silly Daddy. Our suitcases are packed and we each have a lunch. We are to collect our new gas masks at the school. We have great big labels pinned to our coats. Last time I had a pink label because Mum was coming with us. This time it is yellow for unaccompanied child. There is something not very nice about being labeled and sent away to who knows where. Trying to make me feel better Mum even puts a small label around my doll Heather's neck so she won't get lost. I will hold on to her very tightly during what Mum says is going to be a very long day. Heather will help to fill the ugly hole in my heart. It is time for us to leave the house. Daddy hugs all three of us tightly and kisses each of us goodbye. It is the only time in my short life that I have seen tears in those deep blue eyes. Girls, one last thing before you go, I want you to do Daddy a big favor for your brother. Mum and I would like you to not call him Boysey anymore. He is growing up and needs to be called

75

by his proper name, Leonard. Can you do this for us and more importantly for him? We will try Daddy, we promise. He says thank you girls. I see the pain in his eyes as he leaves for work. We all watch him walk away. I want him to look back and then to run to him and be picked up in his arms but that doesn't happen. He knows that he can't do that. He has to be stronger than he has ever been in his life for all of our sakes. My Mum holds onto our hands tightly. She knows that we want to run after him. You have to let him go children she says and so we do. I can never imagine how he must feel knowing as he walks away that we won't be there when he gets home tonight. Tonight our beds will be empty. Our pain is his. Mum and the three of us start walking up the street to the school. We are joined by many kids, mothers and babies all going to the same place, the departure point, Heber Road School playground. This is where we left from for the first evacuation. It is packed and noisy. Many officials are running around trying to organize the lines of kids. They are giving out gas masks and trying to answer the parents many questions. Even more labels are put around our necks and the most asked question by Mums is, where are our children going? They are told that notices will be hung on the gates of the school to notify parents where their children are within a week or two after we leave; also prepaid postcards are given out to the children to post to their parents to tell them where they ended up. We children are told to only write where we are and that we are happy and well. What if I am not happy? But, that is the rule. Our teachers, men and women, are assembled in one large group. Their labels identify them. Rita and Boysey know the teachers by name as they are enrolled in the school but I don't. This is all so overwhelming to me. There are a lot of children my age, five; all clinging to their Mums and not wanting to be parted from them but as painful as it is we five year olds are handed over to older brothers and sisters or teachers. My Mum gives me to my sister. Rita holds out her hand and I clasp it tightly. She is to be the one responsible for me and to whom I can always turn, to protect me, to defend me and to love me but who will be there for her? She has no one. Even Boysey needs her protection. He will never admit to it and always tries to push us girls away. We know that he loves us but it is considered sissified among his peers for an eight year old boy to show he cares. How sad. He is after all still just a little boy. Thankfully for Rita, she has a special friend, Betty Jones. They are so very close and have an exceptional understanding of each other and are always there for one another. I do have to admit that I feel resentful of their relationship. After all Rita is my older sister and I want all of her attention and to keep her to myself. I don't want to share her but they need each other and are there for one another at this emotional time.

The teachers whistles are blowing and we move into lines. We don't dare to disobey their commands. A whistle carries prestige and control. I wish that I could be a teacher so that I could have a lanyard and a whistle and then everyone would follow my orders. We are placed eight to ten abreast in our lines. A lot of little children are starting to cry and try to pull away to reach their Mums who are lined up on either side of us with our cases. Rita hangs on so tightly to me and me to her. I look at my Mother beseechingly. I say,"Please come with us Mummy, I am so scared and I don't want to go without you". Please, please come. Mummy says, "I know darling but I can't and I know that you will be my brave little girl". Rita grabs my hand and tells me that she is scared too and that Boysey is but that she will take care of me and I am not to be sad. There is no going back. This is it. It is happening. I will have to accept it. All of the girls in our group are sad and some in tears while the boys in my age group have stiff quivering upper lips and set faces. This is their test as little men. To pass they must grow up fast. The whistle blows again and we step out slowly moving forward. Our teachers struggle to keep one hundred or more of us in tidy lines. We march with our new gas masks boxes over our shoulders like children marching off to war. In reality I guess we are. The train station is about a ten minute march. People along the route are cheering, waving and smiling. A lot of the mothers are crying. Some of the children are confused. They have been told that they are going to the seaside or the country and that they will be home again soon. So why then are some of their mothers crying in the crowds? It is all very confusing to me. On our arrival at the station we meet up with hundreds of other children and parents from other schools who are also being evacuated, every one going somewhere but none of us knows where. There are boards posted with departures and platform numbers. It brings back to me memories of our last evacuation. Only this time it is different. Mum isn't coming with us. There are hundreds upon hundreds of children from all over greater London. Teachers, Mums and Dads are all there. It is a massive sea of humanity. We all have to hang onto one another to stay together. I can barely see the ground beneath my feet because there is no space. How can I feel so alone and confused in such a sea of humanity, but I do. Everyone is jostling to get to wherever they are supposed to be. Loud speakers are blaring out instructions over the heads of the crowds. Porters are running around with their luggage carts piled high with suitcases. A heavy pall of cigarette smoke hangs over everything. The queues are long for everything, tickets, tea, sandwiches, fags and sweets. Our school finally gets its marching orders and the teachers and parents are hustling us along with every one pushing and shoving to platform number twelve. On arrival at platform twelve registers are taken to make sure that no children have been lost along the way or have landed with another school group. It is pandemonium and emotions are running high. At five this seems like the longest day ever in my young life. The long corridor train has just pulled into the platform. Children from at least three other schools are with us on our platform. We are all going somewhere but who knows where that is. I know my parents are hoping that we won't be too far out of London, just far enough to be safe as it will be easier for them to come and see us. I know that every parent wishes for that but that may not happen. The teachers line us all up in front of the doors of the train. Parents are pushing forward to say their good byes and to give last minute instructions. Some parents even snatch their children back at the last minute which is very confusing to other children but their parents just can't bear to let them go. They will stay and take their chances together in the city. Who is to say who is right or wrong? Very difficult last minute emotional decisions are made at the very moment of departure. My Mum honors the decision that she and my father have pledged together. I am sure she is sorely tempted. She wants us to be with her and Daddy but she also wants us to live even if she and my Dad are to be killed in the bombing. She wants us to somehow survive and live in a free world. She wants us to have that chance. Mum hugs each of us tightly and tells us to be good, to remember our manners and to make Daddy and her proud. Let me know where you are as soon as possible and post your cards. Don't forget. Rita, be sure you put salt in Sheila's tooth if it starts aching and the two of you girls please try to remember to call your brother by his given name, Len. He is getting too old to be called Boysey and it just makes him very cross. We will Mum, we chorus. It is also very important that you three stay together. Do not let anybody split you up. Sheila please be good for your brother and sister. She knows what a hand full I can be. With that said she presses a sixpence into each of our palms and closes our fingers over them. It is a lot of money, a whole one and six. I know my parents went without something they needed that week. She helps Rita and Len up onto the train with their suitcases and hands me up to them. No, no Mum I don't want to go. Don't make me. My Mum says; I am sorry Sheila but this has to be as she hands me over to my sister. Everyone is getting on at once. There is no time for manners. Shoving and pushing is the motto of the moment. Children are crying and some of the boys are scuffling. We all want to get to a window to wave goodbye. Luckily, being a corridor train there are lots of windows but sadly only the windows in the doors come down to open so that you can reach out and touch your parents' hands but of course those windows are quickly filled. At least seven heads and fourteen hands are hanging out of each open window to say goodbye. The rest of us press our faces up against the closed windows. Rita lifts me up so that I can see. I find my Mum's face in the crowd. All of the parents are clamoring to get a last look at their children. The station masters whistle is blowing and the signal flags are waving to signal in advance of the train leaving. Doors are being banged shut. The trains steam whistle blows loudly. This is it. There is no turning back. Mum tries to keep us in her view. I can only imagine what she must be feeling. The train starts to shunt forward with steam rising from its funnel. Parents start running down the platform trying to hold on to outstretched hands. Mum is running alongside. She reaches her hands out to us and blows kisses. We try to reach out to her but can't. She runs alongside as long as she can to preserve these last images of us to keep in her heart and then she is gone. The platform has run out. All the parents are gone. I beg my sister to let me off, let me get off. No I won't go, I want my Mummy. Rita, please let me go, don't do this, please. She holds on to me tightly. No Sheila you can't. I sob in her arms. She is crying too and Len has tears running down his cheeks which he embarrassingly cuffs away with the sleeve of his blazer. All of us evacuees become very quiet. Many tears are being shed. The reality of this day hits home. Our parents are gone and we are on our own going to a faraway place to live with strangers. The teachers try to comfort us and get us all seated in our compartments. Their task is endless and their hearts go out to us.

REFLECTIONS:

The battle of Britain raged between August and September. Our RAF fought in the skies for our countries survival. Hitler wished to annihilate our airplanes, airfields and air force. He wanted to seize mastery of the skies over England in preparation for an invasion by the German armies onto our soil. The British pilots and planes were outnumbered in the air by four to one, day after day. The Germans came in waves, sometimes four to five times a day but our outnumbered forces never gave up shooting them out of the skies. It was touch and go many times but our defences never gave in. Our prime minister, Winston Churchill, said," Never before in human history was so much owed by so many to so few'. Amazingly in September Adolph Hitler lost his enthusiasm for the dog fights. He wasn't winning as he thought he would and he couldn't accept defeat. He was already working on another plan to try and bring England to her knees. Bomb her into submission. The bombs did indeed come. The blitz started September the seventh of 1940 and lasted through May of 1941. Night after night bombs rained down on all of England's major cities. Thousands lost their lives and homes. Seventy five percent of London was flattened and in that period over 5000 lives were lost but the British people dug in and held on to never giving in. Germany would never ever enslave us. Heir Hitler had obviously never heard the line, 'Britain's never ever will be slaves'. The cry went out, 'You want this country Adolph and you will try anything but you bloody well can't have her'. Sadly my Mum and Dad had made the right decision, to send us away, as they learned three months after we left when the bombing started.

After the children were evacuated most parents found the wait for news from their children was painfully long because a lot of the post cards given out were lost or never posted.

I would like to apologize for my jealousy regarding, Betty, Rita's closest friend. Although their relationship took my sister's attention from me it was good for my sister. During our evacuation I acted out on their relationship, none too kindly but I thank Betty for being there for my sister which helped them ease the pain of our evacuation. She was a good friend to her.

Teachers played a big part in our evacuation. They took over the huge responsibility of all of our young lives. We were children ranging in age from five years to fifteen years. I give much praise to these teachers who took on such a huge task, leaving family members behind, not knowing where they were going, where they were going to live, what to expect from this huge group of children, trying to be there for all of us in good times and bad, trying to heal home sickness, banged up knees, breaking up fights, giving love, not losing any of us and drying our many tears. They were such a brave strong group. They deserve medals of Honor. I say three cheers for all of these teachers who gave up so much to be evacuated with and to care for us children during World War II.

THE TRAIN TO ANYWHERE

The first wave of homesickness has passed and now this is slowly becoming an adventure that we have embarked upon. The dirty brick buildings of the city fly past our windows. Dear old London, we will miss you. The city begins to give way to the countryside. Green fields, hedge rows, farms dotted on the landscape, cows and sheep munching in the meadows and looking up at us lazily as the train flies by. War has no fear or anxiety for them. All of us kids are chattering about where we are going with everyone hoping for the seaside. A loud buzz of conversation arises from all compartments of the train. Will the people like us? Will there be more food there than in London? Will their kids be friendly to us? There are so many questions. I myself hope we are going to the seaside so that I can dig in the sand and paddle. I sit in my seat and clutch Heather close to me. She can't believe that we are going away again. Her little dark green velvet dress and hat have been tear stained so many times since this war started. She understands and is always here for me. I would be absolutely bereft without her. The train is suddenly plunged into blackness. Everyone starts screaming. What is happening? Are we going to die? I cling to Rita. Teachers are calling out to us to stay in our seats and to remain calm. It is all right. It is a tunnel. Within seconds dim lights above the seats come on. We all look at one another and start to laugh with relief. I don't believe any one of us has been in a tunnel in our lifetime. We are all acting brave now. This is fun. Will it happen again? If so, we will be ready for it. We emerge from the long tunnel into bright sunlight streaming into the windows. It is so bright that we have to rub our eyes to adjust to the brightness. This truly is becoming an adventure. An hour or so later there is another tunnel. The boys begin making spooky noises to scare us girls and kids begin scrambling into the corridors to open the windows and hang out of them screaming at the top of their lungs. The blackness echoing back at them as the train rushes along on its rails. The warm air of the tunnel is blowing back into their faces. The smell of sulphur or rotten eggs assails our nostrils. It is wonderful. The train whistle is blowing. It all adds to the excitement of this memorable day. As the train reemerges into the sunlight some of the boys that have been hanging out of the windows have black sooty smudges on their faces. It has us all laughing again, even the teachers. Even though they tell us that we really shouldn't hang out of the windows of the train in the tunnel because it could be dangerous a blind eye is turned on this game. If it takes our minds off of this evacuation day sadness, so be it. Rita and Betty take me to an open window when one becomes available. We hang our heads out of the window and scream as loudly as we can. It feels so good. The wind is blowing our hair into our faces and we can see the end of the long train as we go around a curve on the tracks. Other kids are hanging out of their windows in the back of the train and we all wave to one another. It is such fun. We wave at anything that moves such as sheep, cows and horses. Back in our compartment some kids read and others play games. Mr. Martin the head master gets the teachers to organize word games, stories and sing-alongs. Daisy, Daisy and Tipperary are my favorite songs. I know both of these and can belt them out with the best of them. It takes our minds off of home and family as the train speeds us farther and farther away from them. I am sure that in the quietness of the coming night the aching sorrow will return. Sandwiches and crisps are being pulled out of haversacks. Rita, Betty and I start to eat ours. Len is with his mates in another compartment so he will eat his with them. Rita tells me to eat. She opens up my crisp bag and loosens the dark blue grease proof packet of salt and shakes it into the bag. I love crisps. They are my favorite so I choose to eat them first. I bite down on the crisps and the familiar pain of my toothache comes back to me. It is a horrible dull throbbing ache. It hurts miserably. I want to cry but I know that Rita will get cross with me if I do. At her age this would be embarrassing with all of her friends sitting close by to have her little sister blubbering all over the place. Sheila, I told you to eat. I can't I reply. It is my tooth. It aches ever so much. Rita says, oh no and we just put our salt in the crisps. Does anyone have their salt left? Everyone is munching on their sandwiches and no one offers any salt packets. Rita tells me, you will have to wait here. I will be back in a tick. She comes back with six packets or more of salt. She has gone up and down the train asking for salt. She knows right then and there that I am going to be a source of worry to her. She makes me lie across her lap. I open my mouth gingerly. Please don't hurt me I cry. I'll try not to Sheila. She inserts a good pinch of salt into the tooth trying not to touch it. Why, oh why does this have to happen today? I am feeling utterly wretched. Try to go to sleep Sheila. You will feel better when you wake up. I will rub your head for you she says. Maybe it will help you go to sleep. I like that. I fall asleep listening to the rhythm of the wheels of the train as the wheels are clickety clacking along the track. Later, when I awake I am feeling better and I sit up. Rita and Betty are leaving to take a walk up the train corridor to see some of their friends. I don't want them to go because I don't know anyone else in my compartment. A teacher who is young and pretty comes into the compartment, introduces herself as Miss Green and tells me that she will sit with me for a while. She tells me about her family back in London. Her mother and father and a dog called Fred who sleeps on her bed at night. She is missing them. I can tell. I tell her about my Mummy and

Daddy and how much I miss them and about George our cat who follows us everywhere even following Rita and Len to school. But he always comes home I tell her. You will too Sheila, we will all go home someday soon. I immediately fall in love with her. I am five and anyone who pays me attention at this time in my life, I love. It is lovely to talk to her especially because she takes time for me today, a little girl from London. There are many children on the train all feeling like they have been torn away from their parents for no apparent reason. To them it is all too hard to understand. Miss Green helps many of us this day to try to make sense of it all. We have been on the train for what now seems like hours. The adventure is getting old and we children are restless, running up and down the corridors, yelling and letting off a lot of steam. The toilets are always occupied. Long lines of children are waiting to get in. Older kids are pushing in front of us younger ones. Some little girls of my age can't wait and wet their knickers. Puddles appear on the floor and slowly run down the corridor. I really have to wee too but I am holding my knees together tightly because I don't want to embarrass my sister and brother. The little girls who couldn't wait are crying because they are wet and uncomfortable. Teachers are trying to find dry underwear in suitcases and clean the kids up. Fights break out. Bad names are hurled. Mr. Martin's whistle can be heard over the fray. He is having a hard time keeping control. We need to get off of this train but that isn't going to happen. We fly past stations, not ever stopping. We pull into many sidings but we can't get out. Sometimes waits of thirty or sixty minutes occur before we are on the move again. No explanation is ever given. Possibly, we have to wait for other evacuee trains crossing the tracks. We are over tired having been up since 6AM and the emotional turmoil of the day only adds to the melee. Will this ever end?

We are all hungry again. Lunch was eaten hours ago and we don't have any more food. All was eaten at lunch. We are not prepared for such a long ride. A lot of us are thirsty. Our lemonade bottles are empty. The teachers tell us that it won't be much longer and to just try to be patient, please. Lots of the children have gone to the lavatories to get water from the taps to quench their thirst and it has run out. To make the situation worse the lavatories have backed up and overflowed into the corridors. The smell of urine and feces stinks. This is supposed to be a holiday train but it is a living nightmare. It is late afternoon when relief finally comes to our band of evacuees. The teachers are running up and down the train telling us that we are almost at our destination. They got word from an official who is on the train. Please, please children hold on for just a while longer. We are almost there, wherever there is. I have to go to the toilet so bad that I sit here holding on as tight as I can. Rita will never forgive me if I wet myself. She will be so embarrassed and I would never forgive myself either. I haven't wet myself since I was a baby in nappies. I could never live with that shame so I will cross my legs tightly and hold on for dear life. Please, God, let this train stop soon.

ARRIVAL AT LISKEARD

It is slowing. It is slowing. Three cheers. The train is finally slowing down. We all hope that we have arrived at our final destination. It has taken ten tiring, miserable hours. In peacetime this trip on the holiday train would only take five hours but now we are excited and all of the discomforts of this trip are forgotten and we are going to get to go to the lavatory and to eat. We are at the seaside for our holiday. At least that is what they are telling us but that is not what I overheard my parents saying. They said that the Germans were coming and that we had to get out of London for a period of time. I have never been on holiday without my Mum and Dad. All of a sudden I feel very grown up. It is early evening as our train slowly pulls into the station. Everyone is up and out of their seats and pushing to get to the windows in the corridor to try to see where we are. Every door window has been dropped down and is crowded with heads looking out to see where we are. I am being crushed by the bodies in the corridor and I can't see a thing. Being just five and short, all I can see are bare skinny dirty knees with dirty socks hanging around ankles. Everyone is chattering in high excited voices and asking, where are we? Are we getting off here? Are we really at the seaside? Everyone seems to be excited that at long last something is going to happen, be it good or bad. Mr. Martin and some of the teachers come running down the corridor of the train. He is furiously blowing his whistle to get everyone's attention. The teachers are calling out instructions and trying to create order. No one seems to be listening. Mr. Martin calls out, now children, please pay attention. Then there is another long blast from his whistle and spittle lands on my Heather. I glare at him. That is so rude. He tells us to collect all of our belongings and to make sure that we have everything that we brought with us and to please do not on any account use the lavatories even if we have the need. Does he think that we don't know that all of the toilets are overflowing and have flooded the corridors and that the stink has filled the air for the last five hours? Attention please. Be ready to get off the train when you are told to and only when the train comes to a complete stop and not before. The older children are starting to pull their suitcases down from the overhead racks. Some split open and spill their contents. Excitement reigns. Some surge toward the train doors. They are told to move back. Miss Green tells us to make sure that we put the straps of our gas masks over our shoulders. Why, I wonder? Will we need them here? Will the Germans try to gas us? Can the bombs reach us this far away? Miss Green adds; make very sure that your identity tags are still pinned to your coats. This is most important. I myself don't want anyone to know who I am but there is no getting away from it. The labels are way too big and all of our information is on them. I hate labels. Rita and her friend Betty Jones manage to get to a window and are leaning out. I ask; pulling on my sister's coat, where are we Rita? Are we really at the seaside? Are we getting off now? It looks like we are she yells over the excitement but I can't see the sea. The station sign is missing. The teachers tell us that this is Liskeard, wherever that is, but that is where we are. The train is puffing slowly and tiredly into the station and finally heaves and clanks to a stop. There is a huge commotion going on in the next compartment to ours. Everyone tries to surge into the corridor to see what is happening. Bobby Johnson, one of Boysey's mates is lying on the floor between the seats. His arms and legs are jerking uncontrollably and he has white foam all around his mouth like on top of a pulled beer from the pub. We all stand scared and frozen to the spot. What is the matter with him we are all asking? Some kids start to giggle nervously. I bet he has the St Vitas dance cries one. Miss Green and Mr. Horn, another teacher, push through the doorway. Everybody move back now. He leans over Bobby and takes a fountain pen out of his pocket and forces it between Bobby's teeth. He is still jerking violently and the front of his jumper is wet and covered in spit. We are all awfully scared and very quiet. The jerking slowly stops and then he is still. In a shaky voice Boysey asks; is Bobby dead? Everyone starts crying and screaming. Bobby is dead. Bobby is dead. More children start crowding around the doorway to see Bobby's dead body. Mr. Horn's voice is very stern as he asks us to be quiet and to settle down. Children, Bobby is not dead. He is all right. He has had an epileptic seizure. What is an epileptic seizure, I wonder? Is it catching? Will we all get it? I don't want to catch it and be jerking with everyone watching. I might show my knickers and Mum says that nice little girls don't show their knickers. Mr. Horn tells everyone to get back and give Bobby some air. Bobby sits up and asks; what is going on then and why is everyone staring? He doesn't know what happened to him. Everyone is quieting down. The fun is over and we all start to move back to our own compartments. Mr. Horn says, with a loud sigh; and this is only the first day, God help us all. We are now being readied to get off of the train. The teachers manage to squeeze past all of us to get the train doors open and step down from the train. Reclosing the doors by slamming them shut and telling us to wait until we are told to get off and that they will help the little ones off. We are all pushed up against the windows and doors just waiting to get off of this train. The teachers finally give the word. A whistle is blown and we are told not to push. One at a time please and be very careful as it is a long step down from the train to the platform. The carriage doors are reopened. Rita calls to me to stay with her but everyone surges forward pushing and shoving. All trying to get off at once, paying no heed to shouted orders or the many whistle sounds. The step down is way too steep for me. I can't see my brother or sister in the crowd. I look for someone to help but no one is paying attention to me in their eagerness to get off. I am having trouble keeping my footing. I just know that I am going to fall. I do. I miss the step and in vain I try to find it and reach for the platform. I am being pushed by too many from behind and it is too far for me to reach the ground. I cry out for my sister. I know that I am falling and that I don't want to. I put my arms out to stop myself. I try to clutch and hold onto Heather but she falls from my grasp and drops down in between the train and the platform onto the railway lines. I land on the platform face down with a thump. I am crying as several hands turn me over and help me up onto my feet. My left knee is bleeding and dirty. My face hurts. I bit my lip and tongue. Droplets of blood are on my new coat. Mum is going to be cross about that. I am more scared than hurt. I can taste the blood on my tongue. It is salty like the salt in the bags of crisps but more tragic than all of that I have lost my doll Heather, my best friend. Rita pulls me away from the people gathered around and tells me to stop bubbling. She tells me that if I had done as I was told to and stayed with her this would never have happened. She is very cross with me.

This responsibility thing is more than she bargained for. I try to tell her what happened but she won't listen. She reaches into her navy blue utility knickers pocket, pulls out her hanky, spits on it and wipes the blood, not very gently, off of my face and then very proficiently wraps it around my knee. Just look at you she says. You look like an orphan and look at the scene you caused. Right now I feel like an orphan. I sob as I try to catch my breath. Rita, I have lost my dolly Heather. We have got to find her. We can't look for her Sheila. It is too late. Our coaches will be leaving soon. If we look for her we will be left behind. We have to go. We will get you another dolly as soon as we can. But, I say to her; we can't replace Heather. There is no one else like her and she is my only friend. Rita takes my hand and pulls me into the lines leaving the platform. I have nothing. Mummy and Daddy are gone and now Heather is gone too. I try to pull away from her to look for Heather but as she should, she drags me back. I cry. I want Mummy. Don't touch me. I don't want you. I want my Mum. Why can't she be here? She would help me find Heather. Well, you can't have your Mummy any more. Mummy didn't want to come with us so be quiet and stop making such a scene. I want to go home, I cry. Why do we have to be here in this place? I hate it here already. Can't we get back on the train and go home, please? Poor Rita, she doesn't want to be here either. This is nobody's choice. She doesn't know how to handle all of this. At twelve years old she is suddenly thrust into the role of a substitute mother without any training. She is just not prepared for all of this. She looks at me with a mixture of pity and hate. I have never seen this look before today but this is what war brings. I know that she loves me but she is too confused and hurt at the role that she has been thrust into. She too feels abandoned. How could our parents do this to us? Her life of school friends and play has ended abruptly. I pout and cry quietly as we form into our lines. I don't think I can live without Heather but Rita tells me that I have to. Mr. Martin and the teachers are trying to get us to line up, two abreast. I know that Rita wants Betty as her partner but she is stuck with me. I am sure that she wishes that she could lose me right now but she is a good girl and will honor Mum's wishes, whatever the cost. Betty thinks that I am a nuisance and she pokes her tongue out at me and finds another partner. Boysey is in front of us with all of his mates. He turns and waves to us. We feel better now that we know that he too is safely off of the train. We straggle out of the station and everyone wants to use the loo. Calling out to the teachers; we have to go, bad. The lavatories are just up ahead of us. There is only one for girls and one for boys. This is going to take hours to get everyone through this line up. Only if you really have to go, we are told. Stay in the line. Some of the boys run down to the end of the platform and wee on the train lines. Some of the little kids don't make it to the loo before wetting their knickers and under pants. What a mess we are and like Mr. Horn said; this is only day one. However, an hour later we are back in our lines much relieved. Our stomachs are growling from hunger and we are all thirsty. We march slowly out of the station past the quaint station masters house with its lace curtains and red geraniums in the window boxes. It is a house, the first house that we have seen in Cornwall and someone lives there. I wonder if they have children. The station master and his wife are out working in the garden. They look up at us with curiosity. They know that we are evacuees from London. The word is out in the countryside. I doubt whether they have ever seen Londoners before. Londoners don't travel out afar these days. I think they must feel somewhat sad for us. We look a sight. Tired and dirty after nearly ten hours of traveling. Socks bagging around our ankles, hair ribbons untied, un-brushed hair, tear stained faces, food stains on shirts from our long ago eaten lunch. We trudge laden down with our battered suitcases and gas masks out onto the empty tree lined road. The sun is starting to cast its evening shadows and a cool breeze has sprung up. Rita buttons my coat against the early evening chill. She really does care about me and all we need right now is a warm supper and a place to sleep. We stop by the side of the road and Mr. Martin tells us that we will have to wait here until we board the green coaches that will take us into the village where we will be staying until the war is over which he says, to encourage us, could be in just a few weeks. I know that is true because I heard Mum and Dad telling that the war could be over in a month if the Germans don't come. A month seems like a long time to me. But if my Mum and Dad said it is so it has got to be true. We are waiting on a grassy verge. I am so cold and I start to cry again for Heather. I just can't go on the coach without her. She is back somewhere on the railway line. She is dead. I know it. I am trying very hard not to keep crying. I don't want Rita to be cross with me again. She asks me, what is it now? I tell her it is Heather. Can I go back and get her? She will be so lonely and cold without me. Oh what a nuisance you are she says, tying to sound like Mum. I get up off the grass and start to run the short distance back to the train station. I will not leave her there. Boysey comes running after me and Rita is yelling, get her. Come back here right now, but I don't listen as I run into a figure that looms up in front of me. Well, well, well what is going on here? Running away are we? I have run headlong into an unmoving object which brings me to a complete stop in front of the man's voice I hear. I look up from his black polished boots and recognize the station master in his dark blue uniform. His blue eyes are twinkling beneath his station master's cap. He reminds me a little bit of Father Christmas with his white hair. My eyes linger on the gold watch chain that stretches across his tightly buttoned vest. The buttons look like they could pop off at any minute. You come with me my little lady, he says. But I can't I explain, I have got to find my dolly. She is lost and she will cry if I don't find her. Will you help me please? Well now you must be the little girl that I was coming to find. I am, I ask? A lot of evacuees have wandered over to see what is going on. Rita pushes through to the front. Sheila, what are you doing? Come away and stop being a little nuisance. I am so sorry sir, this is my little sister. She doesn't mean to bother you. She takes my hand to pull me away. Now hold on there a moment he says. Don't run off. Oive got summat that I think you'll want to take with you. He reaches into his big jacket pocket. I think that this might be yours, young lady and with that he pulls Heather out of his pocket. She is mine. I take her from him. Thank you, thank you, thank you. She is mine, she is mine. Oh, Heather. I am so sorry that I lost you. I kiss her and hug her to me. She looks none the worse for wear except for a little soot on her clothes and one of her little black shoes is torn but she is back with me and she is safe. I hug her tightly. I will never lose you again, Heather. I promise. Rita says; remember your manners, what do you say to the nice man, Sheila? Thank you Mr. Station master. I will never forget you. You are very welcome my little luvvy. You take good care of your dolly. I am so glad I could bring you two back together again. He turns and walks back to the station. I will never forget him. He really is Father Christmas and for me Christmas has come early this year. One of the noisy boys standing in the group says; I thought somefink exciting was happening but it was just her dopey old doll. What a cry baby. The boys join in the chorus. Cry baby. Cry baby, bunting. Mr. Martin tells the boys to be quiet and that we have to hurry up. The green coaches are waiting. Everyone starts back to the side of the road. Rita pulls Boysey and me with her but he breaks away and joins his friends. He doesn't want to be with us girls. I can't blame him. Rita admonishes me and says; don't lose Heather again. I don't want any more trouble today or I will give you a thick ear. She drags me along with the crowd. Boysey runs back to me and whispers in my ear, I am glad that you have Heather back and he takes off to rejoin his mates. Thanks, Boysey, I whisper. I know that I am supposed to call him Len but he is my Boysey and I can't stop calling him that even though someday I may have to. It is now dusk as we pull away from Liskeard station on the coaches that are taking us into the village of Pelynt. Our bus seems eerily quiet after the excitement, noise and commotion of the day on the train. Tiredness is taking over in most of us. The exuberance of the day is leaving and each one is alone with their thoughts. On the train it was like a game we were playing. We were going for a day to the beach and would be going home in the evening and Mums and Dads would be waiting for our return on the platform at the station. And so it was alright. But now reality is beginning to sink in as I hear soft crying and a few sniffles from different seats on the darkened bus. I now know for sure that we are not going home tonight and no one is going to make us hot cocoa or tuck us in and kiss us goodnight. The platform at London's Paddington station is empty, cold and quiet. What is going to happen to us? After about thirty minutes our coach stops. Mr. Horn walks up the aisle and tells us to collect all of our belongings and be ready to get off. It is now dark outside. We wearily get out of our seats wondering what is going to happen to us next. We put our knapsacks and gas masks over our shoulders. We tiredly reach for our suitcases. We are just too tired with our suitcases feeling heavier by the moment for any games or teasing. We are told to line up two by two but Rita, Betty and I stand together. We see Len with one of his mates. He looks over his shoulder to see where we are in the line. I wave to him. Where are we going, Rita? Are we going to bed soon? Soon, Sheila, soon she answers. She takes my hand. It feels warm and comforting. I hold on tightly not wanting to let go. I look around to see where we are. There is a single story white stone building with many tall windows. A steeple points up from the peak of the roof and there is a big bell hanging from the rafters. Mr. Martin tells it is the Pelynt Village School. Through the lighted windows of the building I can see many people moving around. What are they all doing there this time of the evening? Mr. Martin and Mr. Horn tell us to follow them. We move forward in our lines with much apprehension. I hold on more tightly to Rita. I am confused and frightened. A big wooden green door with a huge brass doorknob is opened.

We pass through it into a dimly lit hallway. There are old pictures of past teachers, headmasters and headmistresses looking grimly down on us from the paint peeling walls. We are lead into a cloakroom off of the hallway and are told to wait here and to be very quiet. All of us huddle together for comfort. We realize that we are all in this together but we are the strangers. A few of us whisper amongst ourselves as to what is happening. Mr. Martin's footsteps are heard in the hallway as he comes in to tell us. All right children, listen to me, we are all going into the assembly hall where some very nice people are going to look you over and kindly take you into their homes. I want you to look happy. They are going to be your new families. I mumble under my breath, new family, I don't want a new family. I just want the one I have. Mr. Martin says no crying please and don't speak unless you are spoken to and mind your manners. Now then, follow me, chins up, best foot forward. Let's make your parents proud. We all clamber around him all trying to speak at once. He is our only lifeline. Mr. Martin, Mr. Martin. Questions fly. Why aren't we going home? Will we all be separated? Will we get to stay with our brothers and sisters and are we going to have any supper and also how long are we going to have to be here? He shushes us. You are going to be all right. They'll try to keep from separating you. If you have sisters or brothers, please stay together in a group and no, I don't know how long we will be here. As soon as this bloomin war is over we will all be going home. It shouldn't be too long so just keep your chins up and be brave and yes you will get some supper. They have set up tables with sandwiches and hot cocoa for you so now follow me. I am going to be right there with you. We all follow behind Mr. Martin, Mr. Horn, Miss Green and all the other teachers following them as close as possible as if we are all joined together. It is as if we are a chain and if we lose a link the chain will be broken and we will lose our strength. We proceed down the hallway and through the open double doors into the assembly hall. After the semi-darkness of the hallway we are suddenly plunged into the brightness of the many hanging white overhead lights. Our eyes are scrunched up against the sudden glare and a quietness descends all around us as the inquisitive eyes of the assembled adult crowd that are seated all around in a big circle are focused in on us. We move as one to the center of the hall. The only sounds are our heels echoing on the old planked floors. I wish right now that I could walk on my toes so that they wouldn't hear me. Against one wall I see tables and chairs set up. There are sandwiches and cakes set out. There are lots of them. The cakes are piled high. I haven't seen that much food in my short lifetime. My belly feels empty and is making strange gurgling sounds which sound so loud in the forced quietness. Rita rolls her eyes at me. I hate that look but she doesn't fool me because I know that she and every other child is as hungry as I am and all our eyes are on the grub laden tables. Mr. Martin tells us to put our suitcases and knapsacks down and to take our gas masks off of our shoulders and to put them on the floor in front of us. We are glad to be free of them for a while but I hold Heather tightly to my chest. I can't lose her again. Mr. Martin tells us to leave our coats on as our name tags are attached to them still and he says he doesn't want any unnecessary confusion. Children, you may proceed to the tables and sit down to eat. Please do so quietly and wait till everyone is seated before you begin eating and please no talking while you are having your meal. We move over to the tables and find our chairs. The chairs are rather big and my sister has to lift me up onto mine and my feet don't touch the floor. She pushes me up to the table. Rita and Betty sit on either side of me. I can barely see over the top of the table but the sandwiches and cakes are still in sight. I love cake. While we wait to eat ladies who are apparently from the village come into the hall carrying white enameled jugs that are steaming. They fill the big tin mugs on the tables with hot brown cocoa and start to pass the sandwiches. Many grubby hands are stretched out to grab the food. I don't think they can see me in the sea of hands. Are you hungry my wee bairn? Would you like a sandwich? I look up toward the voice. It is one of the ladies. She has the rosiest round cheeks, sparkling blue eyes and silver gray hair pulled up tightly in a bun on top of her head. You look like you have been in a war my child. Would you like a sandwich? Yes, please, I answer. She puts one on my plate. After you eat all of it you can have a cake, she replies. I would love to have the cake now. I look longingly at the plate with all of the lovely cakes on it. Jam Swiss roll, rock cakes and tea cakes with white icing and glace cherries on the top but I know that I have to eat my cheese and pickle sandwich first. It is so hard to eat when it is so quiet and many people are watching you. But hunger takes over embarrassment and soon we are stuffing the grub into our mouths as quickly as possible. The boy across from me is making faces and he is eating with his mouth open and he makes an ugly smacking sound. The villagers must think we have been brought up in the gutter. I hear one of the serving ladies say to another; just look at them, so dirty. I told you these evacuees have no manners. You mark my words. They are going to be nothing but trouble. They should have kept them back in London. I feel sick hearing that. I don't think I want cake anymore. Finally supper is over and all of our stomachs have been filled. Mr. Martin tells us to leave the table. Rita and Betty help me down. My tooth is hurting again. I dare not tell Rita. We are told to move to the center of the assembly hall so that the villagers can see us. They get up from their chairs, from where they have been observing us, then slowly if not a bit sheepishly start to walk around us looking us up and down and trying not to meet our eyes. I really don't want to look at them either so I hang my head down and stare at my shoes and socks, the shoes and socks that my Mum had put on me this morning. Sadly she won't be taking them off for me tonight. I miss her so much. I want my Mum. My chin is suddenly jerked upwards. You have to look up child. We may want to take you home with us. Would you like that? I look up into the eyes of a tall angular woman with a rather horsey face. I would like to poke my tongue out at her. I have always had a bad habit of imitating strange looking people but I know that it gets me into trouble with everyone so I think better of it. Instead I twist my face away from her bony grasp. Thankfully she moves on. Others ask us if we will agree to be separated. If so they will take us. Rita adamantly says no, that we have to stay together. Betty is standing with us and wants to stay with us too. All around us children are slowly leaving with their new families after a lot of them agree to being parted from their brothers and sisters, but with many tears. They sadly and quietly say good bye to one another looking very scared and looking back over their shoulders. Will they see one another again soon? Mr. Martin tries to comfort them by telling them that they will see one another again in a couple of days when school starts. Within the next fifteen minutes the hall becomes quiet as the hubbub subsides. Unwillingly, Betty has to go with another family. She and Rita say their painful goodbyes. We three stand alone. I wonder who will take care of us now. Maybe they will put us back on the train to London if no one wants to take us in. The double doors to the assembly hall bang loudly as a lady and gentleman enter hurriedly. They cross the floor going toward Mr. Martin smiling and making apologies for being late. They talk briefly with him and make their way over to three grubby looking children who are exhausted and willing to go anywhere with anybody at this point. How would you like to come home with us, the lady asks? She is very pretty. She looks about the same age as our Mum. Her short dark blonde hair looks very soft and curly and her eyes are the bluest of blue like bluebells and she is smiling. I like her instantly. The gentleman standing beside her introduces himself. Hello children, I am Squire Trewlawny and this is my wife Margaret. He speaks with a very posh voice. He has a long stiff mustache that is curled upwards on the ends and it wiggles when he talks. I am fascinated. I wonder to myself if it would tickle you if he kissed you. The thought of it makes me giggle. Margaret and I would like very much to have you come and stay with us at our farm. Do you think that would be all right with you he asks? Rita nods her head in agreement. That would be very nice, Thank you. Boysey shakes his head yes. Rita yanks on my hand. What do you say, Sheila? Thank you, Mr. and Mrs. Squire. Everyone laughs. I think it is going to be all right for us four, including Heather. We gather up our belongings and leave the school. The school doors bang behind us. We have found the family that will take care of us till we can return to London.

TREWLAWNY

Outside is an old farm truck. The Squire helps us in and loads our luggage in the back. We hang on tightly to our gas masks. It is all right children; you won't need them here, not to worry. We cautiously give them to him with some misgivings as they have become part of who we are. I will take care of them for you he says. The Squire gets into the truck behind the wheel and Margaret sits next to him. Well John she says; let's take these children home, clean them up and put them to bed. They must be exhausted. I have never been in a truck or a car before. It is exciting. It overcomes the tiredness. We are rattling along country lanes in pitch blackness with just the halos of the trucks lights piercing the ink black of night. Suddenly I am overcome with tiredness and struggle to stay awake. I am afraid if I do fall asleep that I might awake to find that Rita and Boysey are gone and I will be all alone in the world, so fear cancels out my feeling of lethargy. The truck comes to a stop. The Squire honks its horn and I can see in the headlights two closed gates. In a few minutes, from behind the gates, an older man appears with a lantern. He opens up the gates and they make a squeaking sound as he pulls them back. Evening, Frobisher, the Squire calls through the open window as he drives through. We stop again on the other side of the gates. We wait with the motor running while the gates are being closed. The older man comes back to the car. Frobisher, we have a guest for you to take care of. The Squire turns in his seat to face my brother. Young man you are going to be staying at the lodge house with Frobisher, our grounds keeper and Bess his wife. She is the cook up at the main house. They will take good care of you and not to worry. You will see your sisters tomorrow. Tell them goodnight now. Frobisher opens the door. He is smiling and reaches in to help Boysey to get out. I hold onto Boysey's hand. I know that he is going to cry. They said that they would keep us together but it is not so. Bravely, he lets go of my hand. I'll see you in the morning he says. Don't forget to say your prayers before you go to bed, Sheila, like Mum says. Ta-Ta Rita. Ta-Ta Sheila. Frobisher gets his suitcase from the back. The truck door shuts. I look back as the truck slowly moves away and I see Boysey standing in the dim beam of the lantern watching the truck as it slowly moves, crunching up the long gravel driveway. He looks so forlorn, just a little boy left on his own. As he goes off with the grounds keeper it feels like a bond has been broken that may never be mended or put back together. I am sad. He slowly disappears into the darkness. Rita and I already miss him. There are lights up ahead. I look out the window and see a huge three story brick house with many windows and ivy creeping all over the front of the house. I have never seen such a big house in all my life with so many chimney pots. Rita looks at me with surprised eyes. It is very posh; she whispers to me they are above our station so don't do anything to embarrass me. I give her a look. As if I would. The truck pulls up to the front of the house. The Squire and his wife get out. She goes up to the front door and the Squire helps Rita and me out of the back seat and walks with us to the entrance. The big heavy front door swings open as if on command. Welcome, children, to Trewlawny. Rita and I stand there with dropped jaws. Good evening Ambrose, the Squire says. Good evening Sir. Good evening Madam. The Squire continues, Children, this is Ambrose, our butler. We look up at Ambrose. His upper lip seems to curl up on one side. He looks down on us as if with utter disdain. You can hear him thinking and saying; where did you get these dirty little gutter snipes? I look him up and down. He reminds

103

me of a penguin I once saw in the Regents Park Zoo. His black coat has long tails and he wears white gloves with a white stiff high collared shirt, a black bow tie, black and white pinstriped trousers and the shiniest black patent shoes that I have ever seen. Yes, definitely, a large penguin. I look up to his head which has no hair except for little white tufts on either side of his head. He even has a large bony beak which wrinkles like it has a rather bad smell under it. Ambrose, let me introduce you to Rita and Sheila. They will be staying with us till it is safe for them to go back to London. Good evening, Rita and I chorus in union. He utters a mumbled, harrumph. This is not very welcoming to me. Already I don't think he likes us. I know that we do look like orphans. I wonder; what is a butler and why don't we have one at home? I am brought back to the moment with the Squire asking Ambrose, would he be so good as to have Janet and cook come upstairs. The butler disappears from the doorway down a long hallway. Rita holds onto my hand tightly as we enter the vast vestibule. We look around in wonderment. We are standing on black and white marble floors. There are many big oak doors leading to who knows where. Tudor paneling adorns the walls that hold immense gilt old framed portraits of military men in curled white wigs, red and gold braided uniforms some carrying sabers other with plumed hats and all of them with many, many medals but not one of them is smiling. They look very grumpy and cross. We were given cod liver oil once a week so we wouldn't get grumpy. Maybe they didn't get theirs. There is a wide grand curving staircase going upstairs. It is indeed a very grand house. I am afraid to move for fear of doing something terribly wrong. Rita and I stand there like statues. Within a matter of minutes Ambrose reappears with two other people who I assume are the cook and Janet. Good evening Madam. Good evening, Sir they echo and quickly bob up and down as if in a curtsy. Bess and Janet, I want you to meet your new charges,

Rita and Sheila, from London. Children, let me introduce you to Bess our cook and a jolly good one at that he chortles and Janet our maid who takes very good care of us in these very hard times. We stand there afraid to speak. The Squires wife asks; what's the matter, the cat got your tongue? How do you do, Rita answers. She is squeezing my hand very tightly and I feel her fingernails digging into my palm. I do a little curtsy as that seems to be the thing to do in this big house. Bess and Janet giggle. No need for that my little one, says cook. You can call me Bess. Hello, Bess. Hello, Janet, I utter timidly, looking up at both of them. Bess looks like a cook who enjoys her own cooking. She has a wide girth that is covered with a blue uniform, straining at the seams across her bosom and bottom, covering her uniform is a white starched pinafore and on her head a round white starched cap with tendrils of grey hair peeping out. She has a round rosy face. She looks like she could give big warm cozy hugs. Janet is quite young and pretty with the reddest hair and freckles on her nose. Her black dress, white apron and the little white cap on her head look very smart. Bess and Janet are going to take very good care of you remarks the Squire's wife. Now, run along with them children, they will attend to your needs. The Squire and his wife walk across the marble floor and ascend the marble staircase. Margaret stops part way up and leans on the balustrade. Good night, children. It is a pleasure having you here with us. Sleep well. We mumble sleepily, good night. I feel so small in such a vast space. Bess says, 'Come along then my wee ones, I think a good night's sleep is in order and by the looks of you a good hot bath would come to no harm'. You both look like you have been in a war of your own on that train, but not to worry; we will fix you up in no time. Ambrose brings in our luggage. Bess and Janet pick up our belongings and tell us to follow them and start towards a doorway through which Ambrose had passed a while ago. On the other side of the doorway is a steep stairway descending down to the bottom floor of the house which we soon learned was to be our living area and is the servant's quarters. This stairway is nowhere as grand as the other side of the door. There is no hanging chandelier to light the way, just bare light bulbs to guide us. In Sussex the stone stairway to our quarters went up but this one goes down. I clutch tightly at the banister as I descend. My feet feel like lead. I don't want to fall again. I hold Heather tightly in my other arm. Whatever is at the bottom of these stairs, she and I will face it together. Toward the bottom of the stairs you feel a heat radiating upward and see a brightness penetrating the dull light of the stairwell. The steps end and suddenly we are standing on the flagstone floor of a large cozy kitchen. A bright fire is crackling in the large black leaded grate of the fireplace. Oil lamps cast a warm glow on all of the brass and copper pots that hang above a large Rayburn cooker from which are emanating wonderful smells of bread baking. The whitewashed stone walls have pictures of old farm country scenes, some with horses being ridden on a hunt. Beside the pictures hang highly polished horse brasses. It is hard to take it all in at once. In the middle of the stone floor is a large, square scrubbed table. The wood is nearly white from many past scrubbings. Six farmhouse chairs surround the table. Across from that a big Welsh cupboard with shiny white plates and bowls on its shelves and hanging from hooks under the shelves are large white mugs. Heavy brown wool curtains are drawn over the windows, keeping out the chill and the damp. The best part of all, however, is lying curled up in front of the cozy fire. It is a huge marmalade cat. He opens his opal coloured eyes and looks at us strangers with complete disdain and disinterest. Bess says that his name is Marmaduke and that he thinks that he rules the house. I will try to make friends with him tomorrow. Bess tells us to follow her through to the hallway on the other side of the kitchen. She opens one of several doors leading off of the passageway and ushers us into a large bedroom. This is to be your room for as long as you are here, remarks Janet. We look around at the double bed covered in an Eiderdown and sizable goose feather pillows. It is going to be so lovely to snuggle down into that bed tonight. Janet shows us where we can hang our clothes. She points to a large mahogany wardrobe with a full length beveled edge mirror. I can see all of us reflected in it in the flickering light of the oil lamps. Our shapes are somewhat distorted and elongated. Have I changed since this morning? Did I grow? My usually short legs looked long and spindly. It is sort of scary but I am just too tired to be bothered much at this moment. There is also a tall chest of drawers. The top two drawers I will never be able to reach unless I stand on the brown velvet overstuffed chair that is next to it even though I get smacked for standing on furniture at home. Cook sets our suitcases on one of the sparse hooked cotton mats next to a marble topped wash stand. It has a brown and white china wash basin and a matching jug and soap dish. Janet points to under the high bed where there sits a considerable sized identical china chamber pot topped with a matching knobbed lid. It is all very posh. Cook tells us that Janet will bring hot water early in the mornings for us to wash ourselves in and that baths are at night. Surely she can't mean every night. Don't they know that water is rationed? I mean once a week was all that was allowed at home and that's when you changed your underwear too. I can see that this is to be very different. Now let's get your night clothes, Bess says and Janet will go run the water for your baths. Run along now Janet. Rita opens our small tattered suitcases and gets out our Flannel night gowns. Rita apologizes to Bess because we don't have dressing gowns. Well my wee bairns we will have to do something about that she answers. We can't have you shivering in your night shifts. Maybe Ambrose has some old wool shirts that you can use.

Come along; let's get you in the bath. I am sure that Janet is ready for us. Rita clears her throat and timidly asks if she can take her bath on her own as she is twelve years old and doesn't want to sit in the bath with me with no clothes on. Bess chuckles and asks, shy are we? Well young lady I think that can be arranged. Just make sure to wash the potato patches out from behind your ears. Bess adds, I don't let anybody have no supper unless they are squeaky clean. Rita is told to start unpacking while I am being bathed. Bess takes my hand. Come along child you can leave your dolly on the bed until you come back. My dolly's name is Heather, I declare, and I won't leave her anywhere again. I just can't leave her, I cry. Please let me take her with me. She might go away if I leave her here. I clutch her close to me. I will not give her up. Nobody is going to take her away from you my little one. You just keep Heather with you if she means that much to you. She can go with you wherever you go. Much relieved, I follow Bess out the door. I look back at Rita. She glares at me. Behave yourself, she whispers under her breath. Several doors down is the bathroom. I tell Bess we don't have a bathroom at home. We have an old tin tub in the scullery and a sink. Bess pushes open the door. Here we are Janet. Let's get this wee child cleaned up. The room is filled with steam and smells like pink roses. A claw foot tub sits on the black and white tiled floor against the wall underneath a closed, fogged up window. At the foot of the tub on the wall there is a big brass contraption that is gasping and rumbling. It reminds me of like when you are in church and everyone is praying quietly and your stomach suddenly makes those gurgling sounds and you peer up from closed eyes to see if anyone is looking but praying that they aren't. The contraption coughs and sputters. Steaming water is pouring from it into the bath. What is that I ask? It frightens me. Janet laughs. It won't bite you my wee bairn. It is just a gas geyser. I have never seen such a thing. It is truly unbelievable. I tell them that at home Mum has to heat water in kettles and saucepans on the stove in the scullery and you can only have three inches of water once a week. I want to take it all in so I can tell Mum about it when I get home. She will never believe it. I look around more and see through the steam a big china sink with two taps. One is for hot and one is for cold. Two sinks in one house, one in the kitchen and one in the bathroom. Can you believe it? Janet beckons me to come over. Let's get you undressed and into the bath, she says. I don't mind getting undressed in here. It is nice and warm. At home, in the winter, Mummy has to light the paraffin stove to warm up the scullery when we take our baths but it doesn't do a very good job. Bess remarks, we need to fatten these children up. They are nothing but skin and bone. I am suddenly overcome with a tremendous urge to go to the lavatory. I haven't been since the train station. The urgency is great. Please Bess I have to get my clothes back on I cry. Whatever for says Bess? I need to wee wee badly right now. I need to go outside to the lavvy. Come with me says Janet, wrapping me in a big white towel. She opens a door one down from the bathroom and oh my goodness. Would you believe, there in its own little room stands a big white china lavatory with a wooden cistern and a hanging brass chain with a white china handle? I am absolutely flabbergasted. I have never seen anything so beautiful, so grand. I whisper to Heather, guess what Heather, you don't have to go outside in the dark, the cold and the rain anymore. Oh if Mum could just see this. She would be amazed. A lavvy is in the house. I won't have to hold it for hours anymore for fear of going outdoors in the cold and the dark. Nature's needs attended to, Janet and I return to the bathroom and to my ablutions. The bath water is very warm and soapy and I am scrubbed from head to toe with a long handled brush until I am all pink and pruny. Janet helps me out of the tub and Bess envelopes me in a large warm fluffy

109

white towel. If this is to be a nightly ritual I love it but I do miss my Mum and Dad. I would rather be with them and have cold water and a single tap than in this posh bathroom. Are they thinking of us right now, I wonder? Bess pulls my nightgown over my head and wraps a large wool shirt around me which comes down to my ankles. I pick Heather up. She is sitting on an all whitewashed chair closely watching the activities. I know that she is as amazed as I am at so many new happenings in our lives. Janet walks me back to Rita and my room. I pass my sister in the hallway. She is off to take her bath which Bess is preparing for her. I will be back shortly to hear your prayers she says. Janet helps me up into the big bed. It is very high off the ground and has a little footstool at one side to help me climb up. She tucks Heather and me in and says that she will be back straight away. I lay there thinking back over all that has happened today. Who could believe that within twelve hours your whole life could completely and totally change? Maybe tonight I will go to sleep, wake up in the morning and it will have all been a strange dream but right now it seems so real. Janet interrupts my reverie coming in with two steaming mugs of hot milk. Now drink this up, it is good for you. It will help you sleep. I will leave this one for your sister. She puts it on the bedside table. Within at least half an hour Bess and Rita return from the bathroom. I can see in the glow of the oil lamp, Rita's cheeks are red and rosy, flushed from her bath and her dark hair is curled all over her head from the dampness of the bathroom. She is so pretty. I wish I had dark curly hair instead of yellow. She climbs into bed and I am so glad that she is back. Not that I would tell her so. We drink our milk up. I am so sleepy and snuggle down under the eiderdown. Bess and Janet pull the heavy curtains back from the window and turn out the lamps. Janet says, if you have to get up there is a torch on the bedside table. Bess says, as for me, I am off to my husband and your wee brother down at the lodge house. Good night my darlings God bless. Sleep tight. See you in the morning, they echo as they leave and close the door behind them. We are alone at last. The room is suddenly dark and very quiet except for an occasional stirring of the leaves in the wind amongst the branches of the tree outside our window. From our bed we can see the moon scudding across the black sky and all of a sudden I am heart wrenchingly lonely. I try not to cry but the tears won't stop. They are scalding my cheeks. I try to muffle my cries into the pillow. I feel an arm reach around me. It's all right Sheila, I am here with you. I won't leave you. You mustn't cry. Her voice quivers and we both start crying together, hugging each other. It is hard to be brave in the dark, even for my older sister. Our sobs gradually subside with exhaustion and soon after I hear the steady breathing of my sister who has fallen asleep. I don't want her to go to sleep and leave me alone. I am lonely with my sad thoughts of home. I see my Mum and Dad in our kitchen sitting in their arm chairs listening to the news on the wireless as they drink their hot cocoa. The news is filled with stories of a world at war. George is purring on Mum's lap while she is knitting. I can hear the comforting click of her needles. Dad is reading his Evening Star newspaper. Each of them is with their thoughts of us. Where are the children tonight? Are they with a good family? Did someone tuck them in and hear their prayers? More warm tears roll down my cheeks. I see the tears start to run down the curve of my Mum's cheek. From behind his newspaper so that my Mum won't see him my Dad blows his nose and sniffles into his hankie. I cannot watch them longer. I must go. The pain is too much. I will close my eyes and try to not think of them but I know that each night when in the solitude of my bed I will pull them back to me.

THE COLD REALITY OF DAY

I hear my Mum calling me, Sheila! Sheila! It is time to get up. I feel her shaking me. I turn over. Is this a dream? Thank you, God. I am so happy. I start to open my eyes slowly, waiting to be taken up in my Mum's arms, hugged and nuzzled. I rub my eyes, struggling to wake up. I open them wide and it isn't Mummy shaking and calling me. It is Rita. Get up lazy bones. Get washed and dressed. It is time for breakfast. Where has Mummy gone, I ask? She was just here. You were just dreaming, silly. She is not here. She and Daddy are still in London and they are not coming to get us. I just want to hide my head under the covers and never come out. Rita pulls back the bed clothes and I curl up in a ball. I won't get up. I won't. Not until Mummy and Daddy come to get us. Then you will have to starve to death, Rita retorts, because they are not coming. Do you not understand English? I will say it one more time, they are not coming. Her voice is raised. I still don't believe her. I never will. I struggle out of bed. The aroma of bacon frying cancels out wanting to starve. I reach for Heather under the blankets. Heather doesn't believe my sister, either. Rita is washed and dressed. She helps me pour the water from the pitcher into the washbowl. She soaps up the flannel and scrubs my face, arms and hands vigorously. She dries me off roughly with the towel and tells me to clean my teeth. I brush gingerly around them. I don't want to have that terrible toothache again. Even if I do, I won't tell. I don't want to go to the dentist. My sister brushes my hair and plaits it. She pulls some clothes out of my suitcase for me to wear. I don't want to wear what she picks out. I want to wear what I want. I am stubbornly determined to win this battle. I start screaming angrily at her. No, what I want. Leave me alone. I hate you.

Rita finally gives in. She just can't take my temper tantrum any more. I feel like I have won more than just the jumper fight. I have had no control of anything in my life. Everyone else controls what I do, where I go and who I live with. I am an angry little girl. Angry at the world and the situations it has thrust us into, not at my sister. She just happens to be the one closest to me. Hate is an ugly thing. I will tell her that I am sorry but not right now because right now, I am proudly wearing my choice of outfits. Fully dressed, we venture out of the bedroom, down the hall toward the kitchen from where the appetizing, savory aroma of frying bacon and eggs assail our nostrils. This is only Saturday. In London you only had a fry up on Sundays and that was before the war when bacon and eggs were in plentiful supply. We are so hungry. We shyly hang back by the kitchen door. On the wall across from the door there are at least six bells with numbers on them and they all seem to be ringing at once, demanding attention. Bess is standing at the stove breaking eggs into the largest black iron frying pan in the world. Come on in me lovelies and sit you down at the table and oi'll have a handsome breakfast for you in just a tick. We are feeling very shy in this new home. Janet descends the stairs with a large tray in her hands. The master would like soft boiled eggs and porridge this morning. Everyone wants something this morning all of them bells ringing at once. The mistress has already eaten in her room, says Janet. Right says cook, three minute eggs it is. Now sit down my wee bairns. As soon as the family is served we will all eat together. Ambrose the butler comes running down the stairs with his long sad face and with a gentleman's jacket in his hand. The master needs this steam pressed right away. I will have Gladys do it she answers. She picks up a hand bell and rings it and within one minute a young chubby woman with straight short brown hair dressed in a black dress and white apron like Janet's, appears through a door off the kitchen. What have you been up to Gladys, Bess asks? Oi be cleaning silver in the butler's pantry. She replies in her broad, west of England dialect. Well stop that for now and get busy pressing the master's jacket and Gladys say hello to Rita and Sheila. They are the evacuees up from London. They be going to stay with us for a while till we catch old Adolph and teach those Gerrys what for. Gladys stands there with her stocky, droopy wool clad legs encased in black lace up shoes firmly planted on the flagstone floor. Be you really from Lunnon she asks with a smile going from ear to ear? Oive never met anybody from the big city fore this. Ave you met King George and Queen Elizabeth? We shake our heads, no in unison. Rita whispers to me, I think she is a bit thick. Bess says; "Gladys, stop standing there gawking and asking soppy questions". The King and Queen indeed! God bless them! You get on with that jacket my girl, right now or the war will be over before you get it done. Get along with you, girl. Now! Janet, here are the master's eggs and porridge. Take them up and clear the trays from upstairs. Then we can all sit down and eat. She shakes her head and clucks her tongue. When Bess speaks, everyone scuttles to obey. I feel lost and scared in the crowd amidst the hustle and bustle of the kitchen. Everyone seems to have a job to do and they know how to do them. Rita and I on the other hand don't belong and seem to be in the way. We want to fit in so badly. The rush of breakfast seems to be over for a while and we are all seated at the long scrubbed kitchen table except for cook and Janet who are serving up breakfast. There is a lot of chatter and laughing. Inside family jokes of which we are not privy are bandied about. Cook sits in her rightful place at the head of the table and Ambrose holds court at the other end. Janet and Gladys sit on either side of cook. Rita sits to the butler's left and me to his right. There is a large warmed white china plate in front of me with a big fried egg, a glistening brown fried sausage, lovely fried tomatoes and a golden slab of fried bread. I cannot believe that this is really all for me. My mouth is salivating at the sight. Maybe I have to share it with Rita but I look across the table and see she has a big plate of food in front of her too as does everyone else; therefore all this must be mine. I pick up my knife and fork and cut into the fried egg. Suddenly the rich dark yellow yolk runs over onto the white plate. I take a piece of cottage loaf from the bread board and dip it into the yolk. I put it into my mouth and hold it there for a while, savoring the wonderful taste. I try each wonderful serving of food on my plate. The sausage is savory and the fried bread is greasy and absolutely delicious with bottled sauce poured on it. I hope Boysey is having as good a breakfast as we are. Bess tells us that Boysey will be coming up to the house later. In that case I'll save some of my food. Bess tells us to listen, she has something to say. I look at cook with her white starched hat. Her face is red and wet with perspiration from cooking over the Rayburn. She has a kind face. I like her. The Squire informed me this morning, she says, that Rita and your brother will be starting at the Plynt School on Monday. Ambrose grumbles and none too soon either. Bess says, won't that be nice. You will be able to see all of your school friends from London. Rita nods in agreement but the look on her face doesn't look happy at the prospect of going to school in a strange place. But what about me, I ask? I want to go too. Mum said I would start school. But cook says, there isn't enough room in the infant school. Too many local children are enrolled and as an evacuee you will have to wait. I was supposed to start this year in London. I don't want Rita and Boysey to go and leave me by myself. I can feel the scalding tears starting to sting my eyes. Rita kicks me under the table and glares at me as if to say, don't you dare. Bess says she will find things for me to do. She says she has very important jobs that she needs me to help her with. I feel better about that. One other thing, she adds, is that at no time do we go upstairs into the Master and Mistresses main house unless invited by the Squire or the Mistress. Just remember your place and everything will be all right, she says, with a smile. Of course, we learned that lesson in Sussex. Anything you need or don't understand, come to either me, Gladys or Janet. One more thing, grumbles Ambrose from his end of the table. Stay out of my way. I can't think for the life of me why we have to put up with somebody else's children. Whatever was the Squire thinking, taking in strays. I am not a stray, I retort. A stray is a dog. Bess says, hold your tongue child and mind your manners. I didn't think he liked us. Now, I know he doesn't. In the future I will try very hard not to incur his wrath. That is enough, Ambrose. As long as these poor wee bairns are here with us and in my care we will try to make them feel welcome. Not to worry, you two, says Cook, straightening her apron. His bark is worse than his bite. Janet and Gladys nod their heads in agreement. Let it be on your heads then, Ambrose mutters, as he pushes his chair way from the table. If it was up to me, well it isn't says Cook, so get to your duties and I'll hear no more. He looks down his long narrow nose at my sister and me and sniffs with disdain as he struts out of the kitchen. He looks like a dusty old penguin in his black tailed butler's coat. I wish I could make him smile, just once.

We pass the weekend pleasantly considering the newness of everything. Boysey spends a lot of time with us up at the main house. He says he likes it at the lodge house and that Frobisher and Bess are very kind. Frobisher is going to show him around the estate on Sunday and take him fishing and if we want we can go along. Rita and I jump at the idea. We are left to our own devices and spend Saturday exploring the downstairs of the house. There are at least seven bedrooms. Three of which aren't used. We play hide and seek between the three of them. We hide under the high old beds, trying not to sneeze at the dust balls that irritate our nostrils, or to bump our heads on the chamber pots and give ourselves away. There are large tall wardrobes to hide in with old musty clothes hanging in them. I won't hide in them. I am afraid that I will get locked in and not be able to get out. At first it is a lot of fun and we laugh and shout, forgetting for a little while how homesick we are and how much we want to go home but maybe we never will go home. None of us speaks about it. It is too painful. It is easier to play make believe. It is my turn to search for Rita and Boysey. I hear them giggling and call out, Ready. I start out to look for them, under the beds and behind the heavy curtains. I have to drag a chair over to the wardrobes as they are too tall for me to open. I look behind the dark heavy wooden doors and poke at the clothes. I am afraid that something scary will jump out at me. I start calling out for Rita and Boysey. No one answers. The house seems strangely quiet and still. Come out, come out, I call. I don't like this game anymore. I feel frightened and abandoned. Rita and Boysey have always been close to one another and are much closer in age than I. Sometimes there is a bond between them that I do not share. I am the baby sister that they have to drag along with them and who sometimes spoils there fun. I go over to the window. It is getting dusk already. I look behind the heavy curtains once more. I hear a door close. I turn and start to run to the door and try to turn the big brass handle but it won't open. I try and try. My hands are so small that I can't clasp the brass knob. I can't open the door. Let me out, I cry. Rita, Boysey let me out. I hear them laughing and chanting, 'Cry baby bunting daddy's gone a hunting to fetch a little rabbit skin to wrap his baby bunting in'. They used to taunt me with that back in London because I would always run to my Daddy when they teased me, to be comforted. I can't now because he is not here. No one is, not even Heather. She is back in my room. I wish she was here, she would understand my fear. My brother and sister's voices fade away. If I sit here really quiet they will think I am not here and they will come back. I sit on the floor by the door for what seems like an eternity but nobody comes. It is getting cold and starting to get dark. I am not allowed to light the oil lamps and even if I was big enough I couldn't because there are no matches. I am never allowed to light matches anyway. I am trying not to cry but I am afraid of the room and the long shadows that are being cast by the dying autumn sun. I walk over to the window trembling and hiccupping at the same time. Crying does that to me. I try holding my breath but that seems to make it worse. I see out of the window a large vegetable garden. There are runner beans climbing up the wooden stakes, some winter cabbages on the ground and tomatoes on the vines. I see a quick movement amongst the runner beans. There it is. It is a beautiful grey furry rabbit with long ears. He stops. I can see his whiskers twitching. His eyes are darting quickly, looking all around. I want to knock on the window to let him know that I am here but I am afraid that I will startle him and he will run away and I will be all alone again. He has found the winter cabbage on the ground and is sitting on his haunches trying to devour it. I am glad that he likes cabbage. I hate it. Mum says, cabbage is good for you. I wish I could keep the bunny. When I get out of here I will ask cook if I can keep him. Maybe Boysey can make a cage for him. Tomorrow I will look for him again. As I watch him the total silence in the room is suddenly shattered by a loud crack. The rabbit hurtles off of the ground and thuds back onto the soil, twitching and bleeding around his mouth. His eyes are turned to me beseechingly but I can't help him. No, no, why, why. Please, please help him I scream. I want to reach him. I try to open the large window. It is so heavy that I can't move it. I pound with my fists on the window. I hate you. I hate you, I cry as a man dressed in a peaked cap, gaiters and an old dirty tweed suit with a gun under his arm walks up to and bends

118

over the rabbit and picks him up by his back legs. I see blood spattered over his white furry chest. Oil teach you to go in my garden you varmint he yells in a gravelly voice. You'll make a good rabbit pie. You killed him. Why did you kill him, I sob? My face is pressed up to the window, wet with my tears. I couldn't help him. I wanted to. Why do they always kill the rabbits? Why, why? I asked that at Turner's farm in Sussex. It was always the same answer, for food. I understand now what upset Boysey so much in Sussex. A man peers into the window looking very surprised to see a child looking back at him in the early gloom. What you be doing in there he calls through the window. I am locked in, I sob. You hang on and I'll go tell Bess. We'll have you out of there in half a tick. He walks away and goes out of sight around the corner of the house. I am scared. Night time is settling in and it is cold and dark in the room. I can just make out the shapes of the heavy furniture but instead of furniture my imagination sees them as lions and tigers that could jump out of the darkness and eat me. I hide behind the heavy curtains at the window and cover my eyes. I wish I was back at home. I don't want to be here. I want Mummy and Daddy. Please come and get me. I am here. I am here. Don't let the animals eat me. But they don't know where I am, so how can they find me. Why did they send us away? Did they stop loving us? I ponder this for several seconds. Outside in the hallway I hear a lot of commotion, loud voices and running. There is someone pounding on the heavy door. Sheila, me bonny lass, are you in there. It is Bess's voice that I hear. I am here I call back. Please let me out. The welcome sound of a key in the lock tells me that I am about to be saved from the ferocious animals poised for attack. Just in the nick of time. Bess and Janet burst into the room. Janet is holding an oil lamp that dimly lights the room and the animals recede to where they came from (my imagination)? Lawks a mussy. What are you doing locked in this room, asks a red faced Bess groaning as she squats down on her thick stockinged haunches so that she is at my level? I try to explain to her between sighs and sobs of relief, that we were playing hide and seek and that I got locked in. She folds her arms around me and smothers me to her chest. There, there, it is all over my wee chile and I suppose your brother and sister had naught to do with this? My cheeks are rubbing up against the starched bib of her apron but it feels warm and safe there and she smells like new baked bread. Rita and Boysey always say that I tell tales out of school and punch me for it so I look up at Bess and tell her I don't think they had anything to do with it. Well, we'll see about that says cook struggling to stand back up with the help of Janet. Janet takes my hand and says; let's go have our tea but I tell her that I have to go get Heather from my bedroom first. I have so much to tell her and I need her right now. Rita and Boysey were duly admonished and an hour later owned up to the deed when they were threatened with no cream buns for tea. Just think I could have had three cream buns and if so I would have licked the thick Cornish cream out of the split first and then eaten the glazed bun afterwards. Oh well, I probably would have had a stomach ache and been sick. I guess honesty is the best policy. After tea we sit around the big table in the kitchen. A bright fire is burning in the grate; the logs are crackling and popping. Rita and Boysey are playing the board game, Snakes and Ladders. They won't let me play because I can only count to ten. Marmalade, the cat, unwinds himself from his place in front of the fire and jumps up onto the kitchen chair next to me and condescends to let me stroke him while he looks at me disdainfully and warily with those narrow orange eyes. I introduce him to Heather. He sniffs her and wrinkles his nose in dislike. He probably can still smell the soot from her accident on the railroad lines. Bess comes bustling into the kitchen and says it is time for her to leave and get back to the lodge house as her husband Bert will be wanting his tea and that Boysey should get his coat and go along with her.

She tells Janet to make sure that Rita and I get to bed on time and that she herself will see us in the morning. Night, Night, sleep tight my lovelies she calls out as she helps Boysey on with his coat. I don't think he wants to go. It is safe in the kitchen. He reluctantly says his goodbyes and that he will be up first thing in the morning as we are all going to see the grounds of the estate with Frobisher. Good nights are exchanged once more and the back door bangs behind them, caught in the wind. Janet has made cocoa for us and we sit around the table drinking it. It is sweet, dark, chocolaty and hot. I dawdle with mine. I want it to last forever as I don't want to go to bed. Rita gets to stay up an hour later than I as she is older. Sometimes it is hateful being the youngest. Marmalade jumps down from the chair next to me and wanders back over to the fire. He is lucky, he can do what he wants whenever he wants and nobody tells him what to do. He doesn't even have to be evacuated. Janet helps me take my bath and get into my warm nightgown. I climb up into the high bed. Let's hear your prayers now and be quick about it, Janet says, but she says it kindly. Dear Father God, thank you for this lovely day and the cream bun. Take care of cook and make her good and Janet and Gladys even though they talk funny. I hope the rabbit is in heaven with you as he was a very good rabbit and forgive the bloke who killed him. God bless Rita and Boysey and forgive me for telling Rita that I hated her, this morning even though they were mean to me this afternoon. I love them. I don't want them to go away. I will be very good and try not to be a snivel bonce and please, please father God let Mummy and Daddy come to get us soon. You will have to tell them where we are because they don't know how to get here. Please let the war be over soon and don't let Mummy and Daddy die in the bombs. Oh and yes I forgot; let me grow up fast so that I can play

Snakes and Ladders and go to bed late. Night, night father God. I'll give you, talk funny, says Janet. Father God indeed, you are a one. She tickles me until I giggle and then gives me a quick cuddle. Nighty, night, my child she says and Night, night, Janet, I say. See you in the morning. She starts to leave. The oil lamp casts her shadow on the bare walls. Please Janet, can you leave the lamp. I get scared in the dark. Well, just until your sister comes to bed. She sets it on the high chest of drawers. Thank you, I whisper. She goes out into the dark hallway and closes the door. I watch the flickering shadows from the lamp. The lions and tigers are coming back. I won't let them. I close my eyes tightly and clutch Heather closely. She will protect me. After what seems an eternity I hear the bedroom door creakily open. I pretend that I am asleep. Sheila, Sheila, are you awake. No, I answer. Sheila I am truly sorry that we scared you this afternoon. We really didn't mean to frighten you. We really did mean to come back and get you. Honest we did. I turn over and open my eyes to look at her. It is all right I say. I am so glad that you are here now. The lions and tigers will go away. You silly goose she says. She blows the lamp out and climbs into bed. She puts her arms around me. Will we really go home soon, Rita? Yes, Sheila, soon she says, very soon. She turns away from me so that I can't see the tears rolling down her cheeks.

A FEW WORDS FROM THE GOOD BOOK

Sunday dawns brightly. We hurry with our dressing and ablutions and scurry off to the kitchen for breakfast. We are so excited to be going out to see the estate today. We can't wait for Boysey to come up from the gate house and join us. Rita and I help set the table. Janet comes down from upstairs with a tray. She sits it down on the draining board by the big sink. The Squire says to tell you that you will be riding to church with him and the Missus this morning so after breakfast you had better be going to your room to change into your Sunday go to meeting clothes. Mind you don't forget your straw hats and white gloves. You can't be looking like orphans from the city, it just ain't proper. We don't want to embarrass his Lordship. But Janet, Rita cries. We were going to see the estate today with Boysey and Frobisher. He promised. And that you will my child. But church comes first. You have to be close to God on Sundays in order to enjoy his bounty the rest of the week. A few words from the good book never hurt anyone, she proclaims. Now run along and get ready. Boysey will be here in a minute. She cries out after us, and make sure you wash behind your ears. We don't want any potatoes growing back there. I'll get your breakfast going while you dress. The master wants you out front at ten o'clock. But I don't want to go to church, I whine. I never went in London except when I was christened. I want to go with Frobisher. Bess answers, you'll go with Frobisher after lunch. We'll have a nice cold lunch when you get back from church. We don't cook or play on the Lord's Day. Now run along, I don't want to hear any more. No church indeed, she mumbles. What are they, all heathens back in London? Rita and I reluctantly head back to our room, our joy for the day slowly diminishing. What is a heathen, Rita? Are we heathens? We must be, she answers. Cook says all Londoners are. Is it a good thing to be, I ask? If Cook says we are it must be good, she says. It is nice to be something different isn't it? I nod my head vigorously, it certainly is, and just think, you can only be a heathen if you come from London. I am really sorry that cook and the rest of the staff can't be heathens. Rita helps me get changed. I get to wear my lilac frock that Nana bought me before she died. We look at one another and laugh. Mum always said, laugh before noon and you will be crying before night. We parade in front of the big mirror in the wardrobe. We've never worn our straw hats before. Rita's is a little bit big and nearly covers her eyes. She puts it on backwards and the ribbons around the crown trail down on her face. She makes a funny face. We laugh so hard, it feels good and for a little while I feel very close to my sister. We pick up our white gloves and I pick up Heather. She has to go to church too because she is a heathen as well as I. We run back to the kitchen. Well don't you look handsome, my lovelies. Janet and Gladys nod in agreement with cook. Like little angels, Janet says. I don't feel like an angel. I feel like a suet pudding with a hat on it. We hear the back door bang and Boysey comes in all dressed in his Sunday best. He has on a grey jacket with matching short knee trousers with long grey knee socks and black lace up shoes. His unruly, curly hair has been plastered down with water to accommodate his grey peaked hat. It is just sort of perched on top and he has a scowl on his face. You look very nice young man, says Bess. Now let's have our breakfast. We children take our hats off and sit very quietly, eating. The only sound you hear is us chewing on our toast and marmalade. Cook says that children should be seen and not heard on Sundays because it is a day of rest and that means that our tongues should rest too. I am glad I am a heathen. I don't think I like Sundays in the country. We finish our breakfast and are told that we are to go up the stone staircase into the main house and to wait in the big hallway for the Squire and his wife and to not speak or touch anything. Ambrose glares at us. You are not taking that scruffy doll to church. Yes I am, I declare, defiantly. He shakes his head in disgust and tells us to follow him. We nervously climb the stairs. I have to hold onto the banister and do one stair at a time as they are very steep. I have a fear of falling down stairs. Eventually, at the top, we enter the grand hallway. Ambrose says for us to stay there and not move a muscle or speak a single word. I thought we were supposed to meet them outside I say to Rita. Well obviously they have changed the plans. Ambrose leaves us there for what seems an eternity. The silence is only broken by the loud ticking of the old grandfather clock. Suddenly we are startled and nearly jump out of our skin. The silence being broken by a loud whirring sound and then an ever so loud bonging as the clock strikes ten. Boysey starts to snigger. He always does when he gets nervous. I bite my lip till it hurts trying not to giggle but it is contagious. Rita takes her hanky from her pocket and stuffs it in her mouth. Her eyes are bulging as she tries to stifle her laughter. We hear footsteps approaching and promptly try to regain our composure which is very hard to do when you see Ambrose. He looks at us sullenly which only makes us want to chortle even harder. The master will be here any second, he grumbles and under his breath says, if I was him I'd send you packing back to London, you little hooligans. As Ambrose turns away, I poke my tongue out at him. It seems that he only says these nasty things when he thinks the Squire can't hear him. The master and Lady Margaret descend the stairs toward us. Lady Margaret is so beautiful. She has the most beautiful blue straw hat that I have ever seen. Good morning, children.

Her voice is melodious and soft. I am in awe of her. Is everything well with you? We hope you are happy and are getting along well and that Ambrose and the staff are taking good care of you. We three look at Ambrose, smile at him sweetly and nod, yes. Well come along then says the Squire. Let's not keep the Vicar waiting. Ambrose holds open the big heavy door to the outside. We follow the Squire and her Ladyship out. Boysey is the last through the door and I see him poke his tongue out at Ambrose as he passes by and then smile angelically as he joins us. Once outside, to our excitement and surprise, is a pony and trap. Are we really going to ride in that to church, we ask excitedly, praying earnestly that we are? Absolutely, says the Squire. I am thinking to myself, this day is really looking up. Petrol is so hard to come by now with the war on we use every other means we can and Rollie is one of them. He lifts me up to the horse to let me stroke its forehead. You are beautiful, I whisper. He has a white star emblazoned on his chest. I stroke him and he nuzzles my fingers. At first I am frightened that he will bite me but the Squire assures me that he is very gentle and won't bite. When we return from church, Lady Margaret says, you can feed him an apple. Do you promise, I say. Absolutely, she says. I can't wait. Rita and Boysey pet the white star on his chest. We are in awe. We have never touched a real horse. We used to see the milkman's horse in London but the milkman would never let us touch him. Ambrose helps us all into the trap. The Squire gently flicks the reins and Rollie clip clops up the long driveway, through the tall wrought iron gates and out onto the county lanes leading to the church. I will remember this moment forever. Upon arrival at the very old country stone church we alight from the trap and the Squire and his wife walk with us toward the heavy wooden church door, which is open, and into which many villagers dressed in their Sunday best are moving toward the Sanctuary. There are many village children going in as well. Everyone is acknowledging the Squire and Lady Margaret. The Vicar with his white robes and collar comes up to greet us. Welcome, welcome, good to see you. We see some of the children from London going in and we wave to them. I wonder if they were fortunate enough to come in a pony and trap. The Vicar welcomes the Squire and his wife very cordially and we are introduced. What a sad thing it is that these young children have to be torn from their mother's and father's arms he says. He takes our hands, one by one, into his and asks who we are. We are heathens from London, I say proudly.

THE GROUNDS OF TREWLANY

The pony and trap pull back into the long winding driveway of Trewlawny House and up to the impressive front door. Ambrose is at the door waiting for the Squire and Lady Margaret. He announces that Sunday lunch is waiting in the dining room. The Squire asks Ambrose to get Frobisher and tell him that as soon as the children have eaten their lunch he can take them on a tour of the estate. In chorus we all thank him and Lady Margaret. We are so excited. Ambrose briskly directs us hurriedly downstairs to the kitchen where cook has lunch waiting for us. Janet and Gladys are scurrying around with large silver trays of food readying them for upstairs. Salads and cold meats is all you'll get today says cook. Why is that I ask boldly? My goodness me, cook clucks her tongue. Where were you children raised, in the devil's kitchen? We don't cook any vitals after breakfast on Sundays. As I told you young n's it is the Lord's Day and a day of rest. Anyone who cooks on a Sunday is a heathen. There. I knew it all along. It is just like I told the Vicar, heathens. Mum definitely must have been raised in the Devil's kitchen. She cooks a big Sunday dinner every Sunday. Besides, she always says it is as hot as hell in this kitchen. We pull up our chairs to the table. Janet lifts me onto mine with a big stuffed cushion underneath me so that I can reach the table. We are all so anxious to see what is to eat. Each meal is an adventure after having so little for so long. Mum and Dad always deprived themselves of their rations so that we could eat and stay healthy. I just wish that I could send some of this wonderful food home. Hopefully they are getting more to eat now that we are gone. A silly thought comes into my head. Maybe that is the reason they really sent us away. They were so hungry that they couldn't keep us anymore. I would rather be hungry and be home with them than be here and eat all of this food. I will ask Rita to write them a letter tonight and tell them how I feel. Cook puts the plates on the table. There is salad with beetroot and salad cream drizzled over it and a big crusty bread roll with the most beautiful pink ham overflowing off the bun and it is all for me. Rita, Boysey and I look at each other in wonderment at so much food. I save part of my roll and ask Janet and Gladys if I can take it with me this afternoon to give to Rollie. They find me a brown paper bag and add an apple and a carrot to the roll. I am so excited with my prize. I can't wait to get out to Rollie to surprise him. Bess says, you have to share it with your brother and sister so that they can feed him too. She pops in another carrot and apple. I just want to hug Bess. She is so kind to us even though we are heathens. It is an afternoon filled with adventure and excitement. Even Rita and Boysey don't tease me for once. They are having too good a time to bother me. Frobisher lets us take turns riding up front with him. We all feel equally important. At one point he lets each one of us hold the reins, his big brown rough hands comfortingly covering ours, as he gently guides Rollie on our adventure. They remind me of my Daddy's hands. The warmth of when you put your hand in his and the comforting knowledge that he loves you very much. The feeling of being wanted and that he would protect us from whatever might happen in this crazy war. I don't understand why I can't hold his hand anymore and explore his fingers one by one and marvel at the size of his hand compared to mine. His hands are rough and calloused and I would kiss each callous to make it better. They are beautiful hands that soothe you on the forehead when you awake from a bad dream to lull you back to sleep. They are hands that guide you across the street safely.

They pick you up when you fall and scrape your knees and pat you on the back until you stopped crying. They are hands that work ten hours a day in freezing temperatures or in the pouring rain to feed us and to house us with never a complaint. He loves us. Frobisher's hands give me comfort even with my unending question as to why we are here and not with Mummy and Daddy at home.

The estate is like a great park. We pass fields with sheep and stop to watch them graze. They are so woolly and sweet with their misty green eyes. The mothers are very protective of their young. The only sheep I have ever known was on the Sunday dinner table with mint sauce and roast potatoes. How could we eat these beautiful creatures? I don't want to think about that. We see cows all huddled together in one field drinking out of an old dented tin tub. Some of them turn to stare at us as if to say, what are you doing here? Then they wander away to graze on the grass. I have never seen much green grass in London. You have to go to the park to be able to play in the grass and even then Mummy said there were signs saying, stay off or you will be fined five pounds for playing in the grass. So then why would you have grass? Sometimes I would see grownups sitting on the grass kissing and holding hands. Kissing in the grass isn't playing. I am so confused but I will worry about that later. We stop by a stream. Frobisher reins in Rollie and we all get out and walk over an old stone bridge. Rita and Boysey lean over but Frobisher has to pick me up so I can see. There we watch as the water slowly meanders downstream over the many rocks and you can see many tiddlers swimming around. Boysey shouts, there is a brown speckled fish. Oh my, it really is. I wriggle out of Frobisher's grasp. We are all jumping up and down with such excitement. Boysey's face is one big grin and he giggles and jumps. It is so good to see him happy. I like it and I jump all the more. I am so glad to see him happy. He has been so sad. Frobisher says, I will take you fishing one afternoon Boysey if you would like to go. Boysey is absolutely gob smacked and he will never let Frobisher forget his promise. Can we go to, Rita and I echo in chorus? Frobisher says; well, will you think you will be wanting to put a live worm on a hook? Rita and I look at one another and say, Ooh, no thank you. So Boysey is safe from having us put our oar in on his and Frobisher's promised outing. We are safely seated back in the trap, all of us arguing as to whose turn it is to sit up front. We head towards a large stone building. We descend from the trap and Frobisher tethers Rollie to a rail out in front. Rita and Boysey feed Rollie his bag lunch. I am too afraid to feed him. Frobisher tells us to follow him closely. We do and I can smell the tweedy scent of his jacket mixed with the smell of his pipe which when he isn't smoking he keeps in his breast pocket. I look down and see his leather gaiters wrapped around his lower legs and tan riding britches. His feet are encased in brown shoe boots. He certainly dresses very differently from Daddy who wears blue overalls over his trousers, a white shirt and a tie. He doesn't have gaiters. He wears bicycle clips to keep his overall legs from catching in his bike chain and wears black leather lace up shoes. He rides his bike to work every day. Sometimes he will have to go miles and miles away and would carry his tools in a stiff old army haversack over his shoulders. It must be very heavy. There is always a pencil behind one ear and a half smoked woodbine fag over the other to be enjoyed later. That completed his ensemble. I treasure that memory. We follow Frobisher through two big doors that are wide open. We can smell the sweet smell of horse manure, fresh hay and damp straw. On either side of the cobblestone floors are wooden stalls, each with its own door the top half of which is open. Frobisher lifts me up to one of the stall doors and there is the most beautiful horse that I have ever seen. It is chestnut in colour. Frobisher

131

calls to it by clicking his tongue and it turns from its iron trough maw that is full of hay, looks at us and slowly walks toward us. The horse stops at the door and puts its head forward as if to be petted. Frobisher reaches out and pets its forelock. I pull back afraid. It is very large, much larger than Rollie. Frobisher reaches into his tweed jacket pocket and brings out a handful of sugar cubes. He puts his open hand out to the horse's mouth. The horse nuzzles its mouth into his hand making soft snorting noises and pawing one of its hoofs upon the straw covered ground. I see its big lips go back as if to smile revealing the largest yellow teeth I have ever seen. I am so sure that it is about to bite Frobisher that I cry out. No, no, don't bite him. Please don't bite him. He laughs. It won't bite me my Lovey, it loves the sugar. He is so right. The horse takes the sugar from his open hand without a scratch leaving a wet warm palm. Now you try he says. Rita and Boysey are anxious to feed him. We will try. Let us. We are not afraid they chorus. Frobisher gives them each several lumps of sugar. They stretch out their hands. Boysey, rather timidly, withdrawing his hand slightly. Rita is bold when proffered the promised cubes. Hold your hand out flat warns Frobisher. I envy her courage. She does as she is told and the horse gently takes the sugar from her. She shivers with excitement and looks proud. She has no fear. Boysey looks like he is going to wet his britches as he holds out his shaking hand. Frobisher takes in the situation, reaches out and holds his hand to steady him and give him courage. Boysey takes a deep breath and tries again. This time they connect. The horse takes his reward and Boysey stands there glowing with pleasure even though shaking in his shoes. Now it is my turn. I am so scared but I know that I have to try but I just know that the horse is going to bite my hand off and Mummy would grumble about how awful this was. I put my arms tightly around Frobisher's neck and hold on for dear life. My brother and sister start jeering and laughing. Baby, Baby Bunting, Daddy has gone a Hunting. Right now I hate them. They are so mean. Frobisher whispers in my ear, Come on me little lady, let's show em how it's done. I will help you. He gently pulls my one arm from his neck and puts the sugar in my palm which I clutch tightly. Now my wee one, open up your hand as flat as can be. I timidly do as he says because I trust him. He holds his big brown hand under mine and guides it gently toward the horse. I can't even breathe and my heart is pounding in my chest in anticipation of what is about to happen. I close my eyes tightly so as not to see and I suddenly feel hot breath on my hand and the gentlest tickling on my palm. I slowly open my eyes and see and feel a big pink tongue warmly licking any remaining taste of sugar from my hand. I laugh. It didn't bite me. It didn't bite me. Emboldened, I take my hand out of Frobisher's and stroke the horse's forelock. It is silky to the touch, warm and alive. I have never seen such a beautiful horse. It is truly a wonderful afternoon. Frobisher lets us all take turns petting the horse. He tells us that she is a mare and that her name is Duchess. We all wish we could have a horse like Duchess. Frobisher calls out to one of the stable boys who are mucking out one of the stalls. His name is Freddie. He has ginger hair, the colour of carrots. His face is sprinkled with freckles. He smiles widely at us showing the gap between his strong square teeth. Take Duchess outside to the exercise area and saddle her. Freddie leads her out by her bridal. We follow excitely as she clip clops along the stone flagged passageway to the outside and the bright sunshine. We watch, absolutely fascinated as Freddie saddles her up. Our eyes are wide with excitement at what was to happen next and at this moment it is way beyond our comprehension. Frobisher beckons for Boysey to come over to the horse and without a word lifts him up and puts him in the saddle, adjusts the stirrups and puts his feet into them. He puts the reins in his hands. Rita and I stand there in complete shock and awe. Frobisher then takes the lead and starts to walk slowly beside Duchess leading her around the cobblestone courtyard. Oh, my. Boysey has a cheeky grin on his face and sits the horse well. After his turn around the yard Frobisher lifts Boysey off, his young legs are trembling with excitement and I am sure with a little fear too. It is Rita's turn. She is eager and ready to be helped up into the saddle. She takes to it like she had been born into the saddle. I am proud and envious of her at the same time. Envious of her courage to sit up so high in the saddle and also fearful that she could fall off and she wouldn't be with me anymore. Her turn being over it is my time to ride. I am lifted up into the saddle. I cling to Frobisher tightly. I won't let go. I clasp him so tightly around his neck he can hardly breathe. I can't do it. Please put me down. I am so afraid I will fall off. Stupidly, I start to cry. I beg and implore to be put down. Frobisher doesn't insist and gently lifts me down to the ground. I am very embarrassed at having put up such a fuss and cling to Rita as if never to let go. It is all right my little one. You and Duchess will get to be friends and we'll try again. Thank you, Frobisher. I am so grateful to him for being so understanding.

It has been such a wonderful day, so much excitement and new adventures. We don't want it to end but all good things do come to an end. In bed that night Rita and I talk about the day and what fun it was. We look forward to tomorrow and to whatever time we will spend here. If we can't be back in London with our family, this is a good place to be. We hug goodnight and leave each other to our own thoughts of home.

WE ARE HAPPY HERE

The days at the Trewlawny estate pass peacefully. Rita and Boysey go off to the local village school. I wish I could go too so that I could learn to read and wouldn't have to ask Rita to read to me before bed every night. Frobisher drives them in every morning and picks them up in the afternoons. I wait at the main gates with Bingo the old sheep dog that belongs to Ben the gardener who shot my rabbit. Frobisher toots the old horn when they come home as they reach the gates and Bingo and I help Frobisher open the big gates and ride the rest of the way up to the house. My sister and brother are glad to go to school. They get to see all of their school chums. Rita is overjoyed to be back with Betty. They are so close, about as close as sisters. She always says that she wishes that Betty was her sister. That hurts. Sometimes Betty will ride home from school with them and stay at the house and have tea with us in the big kitchen. Cook always has fresh bread and butter, homemade strawberry jam, wonderful tea cakes and on occasion a lovely Swiss roll. My absolute favourite is the chocolate one filled with cream. Betty says she doesn't get that at her billet and that her caregivers don't believe in spoiling her. Day old brown bread and butter is sufficient. They believe that if you give more, more and more will be expected and children need to learn that they can't have everything they want. I am glad I don't live with them. If I can't be home with Mum and Dad then this is the best place to be. I miss Mummy and Daddy so much, every day I try to envision their faces and to lock them into my memory but they keep fading away. I try so hard to hold on to them. I feel guilty when I can't. I know

135

Rita and Boysey miss them too. Boysey is sometimes very quiet and seems sad. I don't see him smile very much anymore even though Frobisher and Bess do all they can to make him happy down at the Lodge house. He is so homesick and nothing can replace home. Rita seems to enjoy her partial freedom from Mum and Dad's parental guidance. She and Betty confide in one another and share many secrets. I wish they would tell me some of them. Only Heather knows my secrets and she won't tell. The days and weeks pass slowly and idyllically. I spend a lot of time with Ben the gardener who I forgave after he gave me a rabbit in a hutch to take care of. He has given me a small plot of earth and I have planted some seeds. I run out every day to see if anything has sprung up overnight. I water and weed it diligently. Sometimes I am not sure what are weeds and what are the lettuce and green beans. I watch it somewhat impatiently. Grow, grow, I say. Ben says, patience is a virtue when gardening. When it is raining I wear my Mac and Wellingtons and plod around in the mud. I reach down and squeeze the mud in my hands and watch it squish out of my fingers and then I run to find big puddles in the driveway to jump in with both feet. I love to watch the water fly up around me in a big splash. Bingo loves to jump into the puddles with me. On sunny days, I help Janet and Gladys with the laundry. I hand them the pegs while they hang the sheets and pillowcases on the lines in the back garden. I love to watch them billow in the breeze as small clouds scud across the blue sky. They look like ghost ships going across a vast ocean of blue. When everything is dry I help them fold and put them in the laundry baskets. I bury my face in the sheets and smell the wonderful sweetness of fresh air and sun. Later, Janet and Gladys will be ironing them with the big black flatirons heated on top of the Rayburn. They spit on theflatirons to see if they sizzle which tells them they are hot enough to iron with. On other sunny days, Heather and I spend time in the big sand pit. She sits and watches while I make castles with my bucket and spade. I get water from the old hand pump in the garden which Ben helps me to get as the pump handle is too stiff for me to work. He lifts me up and I help him pull the pump handle up and down. It is such fun to see the water gushing out into the bucket. I make moats around the castle and fill them with water and then Bingo jumps in on all fours and with his back legs flying digs up all of the castle and moat. He thinks it is great fun. I laugh at him and he licks my face till it is all wet and slobbery. We roll around on the grass, me laughing and he barking. He is Heathers and my best friend. I tell him and Heather all of my secrets, fears and joy. They both look at me and say nothing but I know they understand. Today, it is after lunch and Heather and I are lying in the grass looking at the sky, languidly listening to the bees as they buzz back and forth in the honeysuckle bushes. I am making pictures out of the clouds. Sometimes I can see mountains and giants and once I know I saw an angel. It was so peaceful but what I and nobody else could see were the storm clouds slowly gathering on the far horizon. We have been here now for six weeks. It is Thursday evening. We are seated around the large kitchen table. Rita and Boysey are playing a game of Ludo. Boysey says that Rita is cheating and she retaliates by throwing the dice cup at him. Boysey starts to grumble and says he will never play with her again. I am methodically cutting out paper dolls from a book and pasting them on a sheet of red cardboard that Bess has given me. They are a bit crooked and there is more paste on me and the cardboard than the dolls. Rita and Boysey make fun of them but they are mine and I have done them. I will have Frobisher put them in the post tomorrow to Mum. I know she will like them. Amid all the mayhem we hear Bess coming down the stairs. We think she is coming down to reprimand us for all the commotion going on. She sounds out of breath. Those stairs will be the death of me she says as she comes into the kitchen. She goes over to the big stone sink and draws some water into the big old white enamel tea kettle. I think a nice cup of tea is what we all need right now she says. Settle our nerves. She puts the kettle on the hob and busies herself getting out the tea things. She seems nervous and preoccupied. Something is wrong and besides we never have a cup of tea at this time of evening. We always have our hot cocoa before we go to bed, never tea. After the tea is made Bess tells us that she had been called upstairs a little while ago because the Squire and his wife needed to talk to her and now it is her place to tell us what she was told. She relates that the Squire received a visitor today from the local authorities. A billeting officer came to inform him that we, the Harvey children, are not supposed to be in Plynt. That owing to a big paper snafu in London the Heber Road evacuees should have been sent to Polperro and that another London area school reportedly should have been sent to Plynt and that this very serious mishap would have to be rectified immediately. We will have to be transferred with all haste to our original appointed billets. Cook says, Lady Margaret and the Squire told the billeting officer that they thought that this would be detrimental to us children to be moved and uprooted again and that they would like permission from the government for us to stay with them. They were then told that the order to move us was resolute and it was to be done by Saturday at noon. We are to assemble at the local school with the other Heber Road evacuees where buses will be waiting to take us on the three hour journey to Polperro. There is a very heavy silence in the kitchen with just the ticking of the mantel clock which resonates through the now semi-darkness of the kitchen. I feel that everyone can hear my heart beating so fast. I can hear it. I think maybe it is going to break. Bess breaks the pervading silence. I am so very sorry my wee ones. I would do anything I can to keep you but it is completely out of my hands or anybody else's. It is a terrible thing, this war, with the breaking up of families and all of the senseless killings of thousands of innocent people. Where will it all end? The three of us sit there in stunned utter bewilderment. Can Heather go with me I ask, my voice breaking? I just can't bear the thought of leaving. If it was leaving to go home it would be everything that I had prayed for and God was finally listening to me but to be sent to another village far away is unbearable. Of course she can go with you my little one. She needs you to take care of her. I pick Heather up from the kitchen table and hold her close. Don't cry Heather, I will take care of you, always. I will never send you away. Tears well up in Rita's eyes and she lays her curly head down on her arms and sobs gently, her small shoulders heaving. I don't want to go she says. I want to stay here where we are safe, with you, Janet and Gladys. I can't bear it. I can't take care of everyone. I need my mother. If she was here she would know what to do. Please, please, don't send us away. I feel so utterly desolate. I look at Boysey's face which is white and pinched. His mouth is set in a tight pale line as he clenches his teeth in an effort not to cry. He has been happy here. Homesick yes, but he really looks up to Frobisher who has been such a good friend to him. Bess pushes her chair back from the table. Come to Bess my lovelies. Rita and I climb down from our chairs and sobbingly run over to Bess. She takes us in her loving arms and hugs us to her warm opulent chest with her white starched apron bib rubbing our cheeks. I don't want to leave the comfort of her arms, ever. Boysey lingers behind. The back door bangs shut and Frobisher enters the kitchen, his boots squeaking on Cook's freshly washed floor. Boysey runs to him and throws his arms around the top of Frobisher's legs. Don't send me away, he begs. Frobisher bends down and picks him up into his arms. Boysey buries his head into Frobisher's tweed jacket and finally, the tears come.

WE DON'T WANT TO GO

We have grown to love it here. We feel wanted and cared for. It is like being on a wonderful country holiday except one vital thing is missing, Mum and Dad. Now the holiday is over and I think it is time to go home but we aren't going home and Mum and Dad are not coming to get us and to take us back. The fact is that we are on the move again. It is now a whole new game. Maybe they really are sending us home and they are just not telling us yet, so it is going to be a very big surprise, but in my heart I don't believe that this is what is really happening. I ask Rita, can we go home now? Please. I so want to go home. No, we can't she answers crossly. Not yet. But Why, I ask? Because Mummy can't take care of us anymore and she had to give us away. But why would she do that? I start to cry. She does want us. She wouldn't give us away. Oh for goodness sakes stop your snivelling or I will go bury Heather in your silly old garden and you will never see her again either. She doesn't mean that. She is just confused at the situation that we are in. I clutch Heather to my chest. Nobody will ever take her from me again. She is the only one in the world who understands how I feel and my confusion. Mummy didn't give us away, I cry. She would never do that. Daddy wouldn't let her and I hate you for saying that. I hate you so much. Well, just maybe, Rita responds, there isn't a house there anymore for us to go back to. But why would our house not be there, I persist and ask, who would have taken it away? Where would they have taken it to? At a loss for words, she answers, they wouldn't take it anywhere you silly, and that in all probability a big German bomb fell on it and knocked it down and broke it. No, No, it is not true, I scream at her. You are cruel and hateful. It is still there, I know it. I just know that it is still there. I ask, please God, don't let a German bomb fall on our house. I will be so good I promise. I will say please, and thank you, that I forget to do so often and I won't lean on my elbows while at the table and I will never ever fight or poke my tongue out at Rita or Boysey ever, ever again if you will just please let our house still be there because God, if our house is knocked down by a big German bomb Mummy and Daddy might be in it and they would die and go away to Heaven like my beautiful Nana did. Nana used to say, Sheila if you are a good girl and always do as you are told and be seen and not heard you will go to Heaven someday. All good people go to Heaven. Mum and Dad are good people. They will go to Heaven but I don't want them to be good. I want them to stay here. This whole thing is so very confusing and it gets so very tiresome trying to be so good. I hope God understands because I don't. Rita doesn't mean to be cross with me and as usual she is right, we are not going home. We have to leave. We are going to miss our adopted family desperately. Janet and Gladys have taken us into their hearts and they lovingly call us their little Cockney orphans. They speak to us in their soft West Country dialect which we always try to imitate and they end up giggling at our sorry attempts. Is it even possible that we might miss Ambrose and his contempt for us? He might even miss having us to order about and pick on all the time. Most of all we will miss Bess and Frobisher. I love sitting in the big kitchen with Bess. That is her domain and she rules it with an iron hand and what she says below stairs is law. She has a heart and a laugh so big they match her wide girth and when we are wrought with home sickness she encloses us in her opulent arms as she sits in her big chair by the fireside. It is always a warm and happy place to be. I know that she understands my deep hollow loneliness. She somehow makes my world a little more right. We are called her poor wee bairns. Bess is always trying to fatten us up and much to our delight, at meal times Bess will give us extra food and there is always lots of white crusty farm bread with real Cornish creamery butter that comes from the cows on the estate and homemade strawberry jam spread lavishly on top. Bess makes the jam. I can see the glass jars lined up on the table waiting to be filled with the sweet red hot liquid from the big copper pan that is bubbling on the stove, filled with strawberries picked from the gardens which I proudly lay some claim to. I can't remember ever having anything like it and now probably won't again for a long time to come. Never before have we experienced such luxury. I vow that when I grow up I will buy all of the crusty white fresh baked loaves and eat only that forever. Bess has been our comfort and haven in this wretched war. Frobisher is such a friend. More like a favourite uncle. Boysey, his biggest fan, idolizes him. He taught us little tykes a lot about the countryside. He took us on many nature walks and educated us on flowers, trees and all the farm animals. He even showed us how to milk cows which was an amazing, educating experience. As city kids we believed milk came in bottles from the United Dairy but he taught us differently. He would let us hold the warm udders. We would pull and pull but nothing would happen and the cows would turn their heads with their large brown eyes looking at us questioningly. When Frobisher gently covered the teats with his big freckled hands and squeezed and pulled we heard a gently swishing of warm steamy milk frothing into the bucket. He let each one of us experience this miracle and we each got to drink a tin mug of the most wonderful fresh sweet milk. I will carry the memories of this wonderful man with me to wherever we go next. We thank you Frobisher, for teaching us so much.

We will miss everyone but especially the Squire and Lady Margaret for rescuing three lonely kids and the giving and sharing of their home with us. We were all a little afraid of them at first as they were so posh and upstairs but we know that they must have cared to take in three London working class children with nothing to their names but their battered suitcases and their gas masks. We thank them so much and know that they will all be in Heaven some day because as Nana said, all good people go to Heaven. Maybe not Ambrose but then maybe Ambrose doesn't know that you have to be good to go to Heaven.

WE SAY GOODBYE

Rita and I sit on the big feather bed that we have shared for the last six weeks. The bed holds many secrets that it will never tell. They include the nights that I cried openly away from my family, so terribly homesick. My sister would try to comfort me by telling stories of home and Mummy and Daddy. She would sing my baby song that Mum always sang to me before going to bed. Lula, Lula, Bye, Bye was the song. If and when I become a mother I will sing that song to my children. I would fall asleep, my face tear stained, tightly clutching my doll Heather. Then I would wake up in the cold darkness of the morning and hear my sister crying into her pillow, trying to muffle the sounds, so that I would not hear her and be worried that she was afraid too. I honoured her wishes because we were always told that you must be brave and never cry. To cry is to be weak. I would whisper, it is all right Rita, I love you. She wouldn't answer but I know that she heard me. Later in the morning Janet and Gladys come into our room and take down our old warn suitcases from the top of the old mahogany wardrobe with the large mirror on the door. From the bed I can see the reflections of their faces in it. They look sad. The mirror has seen happier days. This mirror is where I saw myself in full length for the first time. I pirouetted around in my pale lilac Sunday school dress and put on my straw hat and gloves. It was like looking at my twin. I talked to her but she never answered. I felt so rich and beautiful. Rita told me that I was vain and to stop looking in the mirror. I poked my tongue out at her and then laughed to see it reflected in the mirror. I am sure that Janet and Gladys are thinking that they will probably never see us again and are wondering what is to become of us in the months to come but they don't speak or voice their thoughts. We are to leave early tomorrow morning. They start to pack our clothes and check to make sure everything is labelled. There are no toys to pack as we weren't allowed to bring any with us from London, just a few books and of course, Heather. Of the few things allowed on the government list, I would be allowed to bring Heather and Rita brought several books by Enid Blyton, her favourites and my favourite book that she would read to me at night was Milly, Mollie, Mandy. I would look at the pictures and wish desperately that I had short straight black hair with a fringe like Milly's instead of my very blonde long curly hair that always tangled and hurt so bad when Rita would drag the hair brush through it, pulling it, and then smacking me on the head with the brush when I snivelled and complained. Our clothes for the trip tomorrow are laid out. We even get clean underwear for the excursion. It really is a big event. Gladys says, you should always wear clean underwear when you go on a trip in case you get in an accident. Our big ugly name tags are pinned back onto our coats and our gas masks are placed on top of the suitcases. We really are going. There is no turning back. The packing is done. Janet says that it is time for our bath. We can't send you away dirty. Whatever would they think? Whatever would who think I wonder? It is our last evening here. Bess is preparing a very special grand tea for us and Boysey is coming up from the Lodge house to eat with us. Frobisher is helping him pack and they will come as soon as they are done. Ambrose has the evening off and has gone to the pictures in the village. I am sure, to get away from us. This will be the last time we will all sit together in the kitchen seated at the big scrub table. It is such a lovely cozy kitchen. I feel safe and warm here. Cook lets us pick what we want to eat for tea this last cold rainy night. A storm has sprung up outside. You can hear the heavy rain as it lashes up against the sides of the old stone house. I look out of the windows and see the heavily leaden sky laden with rain. Darkness is drawing in. I look to the tree lined driveway and watch and listen to the wind as it howls and blows through the Chestnut and Poplar trees. Their branches like arms outstretched and pleading in the moaning wind. Falling leaves rollicking and prancing across the manicured lawns even the ever circling seagulls have left to find shelter from the storm. It looks so cold and lonely out there. Janet comes over and draws the heavy dark blue curtains and shuts out the storm and the ever growing darkness. We hear the back door bang and feel a blast of cold air into the room. Boysey and Frobisher are here. I am so glad. I turn toward the warmth of the kitchen and the flickering fire in the hearth and catch it's reflections on the old Welsh cupboard with its cups, saucers and dinner plates shining in its glow. The oil lamps are lit. It is all right. We are safe and warm. Cook starts to dish up the tea. She takes the china plates from the warming oven in the Rayburn and fills them with our upmost favourites. Our eyes are round and filled with expectancy. Big golden brown pork sausages glistening from the sizzling fat in the big cast iron frying pan, lovely fried red tomatoes, big golden chips, fresh baked bread, butter and jam. Cups filled with hot tea from the big old brown tea pot with lots of sugar and milk; there is no rationing here, at least not tonight. I must say I do have some feelings of guilt stuffing my face with so much good food when Mum and Dad are doing without. I can hear her saying, Sheila your eyes are bigger than your belly. She was right of course. Never the less I made a hearty effort to do justice to a meal that I would not soon forget. Boysey as usual, picks at his food and shovels it around the plate. He always is a picky eater. He used to drive Mum mad at home. He would be made to sit at the table till he finished no matter how long it took. Sometimes he would sit for hours and often as not he would still be sitting there at the next meal. I would wait till Mum wasn't nearby and offer to eat it for him if it was something I really liked but she caught on fast to that little game and I was made to sit there with him till he ate it. However, tonight, Cook is in a very benevolent mood as this is our last evening at Trewlawny. She lets him be excused from the table without any reprimands. I know that Boysey is dreading leaving Frobisher and that is why he isn't interested in his food. We all help with the washing up with much idle chatter going on amidst the clatter of the washing of the dishes. None of us want to mention tomorrow and try not to think of it. With the washing up done, Bess tells Janet to turn on the wireless. Janet is humming to herself. I recognize it right away and join in with her on the White cliffs of Dover. I choke up on it because it is so sad but also filled with hope for the days and years to come. As the song goes, and Johnny will go to sleep in his own little room again. Will we ever sleep in our own little rooms again? Right now, I don't think so. The wireless comes alive with music. It is that man again, the Tommy Handley show. We all sit around the wireless. Rita and Boysey sit cross legged on the floor and the grownups in the arm chairs. I curl up on Bess's wide comfortable lap. It is the Itmar Show with Tommy Handly and Mrs. Mop. T.T.F.N. and Can I do you now Sir? Her famous lines are legend in England and keep Londoners and the rest of the country laughing through the dark war years. I don't understand all the jokes and fun but I laugh when everyone else does. I just want to be grown up and to let them think that I understand it all. Cook is laughing so hard that tears are rolling down her fat, rosy cheeks and Janet and Gladys are giggling as they sit at the kitchen table knitting socks on four needles while listening to the show. The socks are being made for the British troops overseas. They and other women all over the country are contributing to the war effort, knitting mittens and socks. They patiently try to teach me but I am all fingers and thumbs and drop stitches. If the troops have to wait for me to learn to knit then there are going to be a lot of cold hands and feet overseas. Rita of course is a very good knitter. Mum taught her while we were in Sussex. She and Mum used to unravel old jumpers and rewind the yarn into balls as new wool is a rare commodity during this war.

 The Itmar show is over and we hear the ever familiar Pips and the Chimes of Big Ben and know the BBC is ready to broadcast the seven o'clock news. Everyone suddenly becomes very quiet with all ears and eyes turned toward the wireless. This is the BBC Home Service and here is the news. Last night eight hundred people perished in the beginning of the Blitz as bombs rained down on London and Coventry. Five hundred or more were severely injured. Hundreds of homes and docks were destroyed today. Prime Minister Winston Churchill and his wife Clementine toured the East end of London surveying the bomb damage and offering hope and consolation to Londoners who are digging out from the rubble of the destruction. Cook shakes her head in sheer disbelief. Those bloody Germans, she says. I would like to give them some of their own medicine. I just can't believe that anyone can be that wicked. There, there my lovelies, don't you worry because you're safe here. We won't let nobody hurt you. I cover my ears. I don't want to hear anymore. Mummy and Daddy, are they dead? We are all stunned. Maybe it just doesn't matter anymore, besides we will be gone tomorrow. Who is going to take care of us then? I don't understand why the Germans want to kill us. What did we do to make them so angry at us? Don't they have little girls and boys over there too? Do they also have to go far away from their Mummies and Daddies and do they cry themselves to sleep because they want to go home? Are they afraid like I am that their parents will die when the big bombs drop and that they might never see them again? I wish so hard that I could understand it all. I try not to think of our parents dying last night when the German bombs fell on London. I think I would know in my heart if they were not alive and my heart tells me that they must be okay.

The big clock strikes eight and brings us back to reality. Cook says it is time you were all in bed. You have a long trip tomorrow. Frobisher helps Boysey up and helps him on with his Mack and Wellies. He hoists him up on his back for a wet piggy back ride down to the Lodge. We all say goodnight. Bess, Janet and Gladys go over to Boysey and he reaches down and gives them a hug goodbye. They ruffle his hair and tell him to be here at eight in the morning. I can't look at him for fear I will cry and then he will too. I know he doesn't want to leave. He is gone. The kitchen is quiet. The cocoa is made and we drink it slowly trying to make it last so that we don't have to leave the warmth of the fire. This will be the last time we will all sit here together. We hug Bess goodnight. She holds on to us for longer than usual. Bess says don't you worry me lovelies, your Ma and Da will be all right. I just know it. I will put in a special prayer for them tonight to keep them both safe. Janet and Gladys light the oil lamps, take our hands and walk with us to our room. They help us get into our night clothes and pull back the covers. Gladys warms the bed with the copper bed warmer pan filled with hot coals from the fire grate in Bess's kitchen. Rita and I kneel by the bed to say our prayers. I close my eyes tightly and pray that when I open them I will be home on Upland Road and that there is no war and that Heather and I are sleeping in our own little bed with the cozy blue eiderdown. That Mummy is tucking me in and then will reach over and kiss me on the forehead. The voice I know so well will say, night, night my child, sleep tight, see you in the morning. I am afraid to open my eyes because I don't want to lose her. She is going now, night, night Mummy. Don't go. I struggle to hold on to her. I love you and miss you so much. I climb into the big bed with Rita. Heather is in my arms. Janet and Gladys tuck us in and say how much they are going to miss us. We are going to miss them as well. More than we know. Gladys pulls back the curtains and they take the oil lamps and leave, whispering their good nights. Rita and I lay there. We cannot sleep. We are both afraid of tomorrow but we don't speak. Words cannot convey how we feel. I look to the window and see that the rain has abated and the moon is scudding across the black sky. The old tree outside is swaying in the wind. I am not afraid of it anymore. Heather and I snuggle down into the covers. Tomorrow is a whole new day, a new start for the three of us. Rita reaches for my hand. We hold onto one another tightly. Please God, let tomorrow be good.

REFLECTIONS:

More than sixty thousand people died between 1940 and 1944 and fifty one thousand were seriously injured.

MY SADDEST DAY

The morning dawns, the sun is coming up and it is windy. The night passed way too quickly. It is seven AM. We are getting washed and dressed for our journey. Rita is very quiet and withdrawn as she finishes washing and I am being, as my Father would say, obstreperous. I don't want to brush my teeth and refuse to do it, throwing my tooth brush into the open chamber pot, which had not been emptied yet, with a resounding plop. That gets her attention extremely fast. She grabs me by the shoulders. You little wretch, she shrieks, shaking me so hard that I can hear my teeth rattle. She drags me over to the chamber pot and screams, get it out now. I fight pushing up against her as she yanks my left arm behind my back forcing me down onto my knees. Put your hand in there and get it out. I wail in pain but she won't release me. She screams again, pick it up, pick it up. Gingerly I reach in, curl my little wet fingers around the wet brush and start to remove it. I want to retch. Now brush your teeth with it. Her voice is seething with anger. I won't, I won't, I bellow and at that very moment Gladys barges through the bedroom door. What in God's heaven is going on in here? She separates us, with each at arm's length. Rita tells her angrily and breathlessly what just happened. Gladys clucks her tongue. Sheila, Sheila what a bad little girl you are this morning. You know bad little girls don't go to Heaven. There is that unequivocal phrase again. I believe it is one that just adults are privileged to quote. The way I am going I am never going to get into Heaven. Gladys cleans the tooth brush and disinfects it with Dettol and Rita wins. I brush my teeth under the watchful eyes of Gladys.

Finally all of our ablutions are completed and order is restored. Well, somewhat. Our nerves are raw and close to eruptive. In the kitchen we attempt to eat a cold breakfast. Neither of us, it seems, has an appetite. Everything I try to eat gets stuck in my throat. Rita and I push back from the table and leave the food, glaring at one another. Cook is chattering away trying to appear happy. She tells us she has prepared three lunches for us to take on the bus which she hopes will sustain us until we reach our journeys end. Rita packs them carefully in her rucksack. There is not much conversation this morning. Everybody is alone with their own thoughts. Poor Rita, why do I make it so bad for her? She won't even look at me. When anyone speaks it is as if in whispers. It is as though if they speak aloud their true thoughts will be revealed. Ambrose is his usual grumpy self, muttering under his breath as he takes our suitcases up the narrow stairs. We are to assemble above stairs in the grand hallway to bid our farewells to the Squire and Lady Margaret. Cook helps us on with our coats. Our big labels are pinned onto the lapels. I can't believe that this is really happening. We won't be sleeping here tonight. Where will we be resting our heads, I wonder? We put our gas masks over our arms and across our chest. This is it. It is time. I hate this. I hate saying goodbye. I can still see Mummy running by the train trying to keep up with the moving locomotive as it gathered speed. All of us kids reaching out of the windows with hands outstretched hearing the mournful sound of the train's steam whistle. No. Goodbyes are sad. I will always have a loathing for them. Gladys and Doris say their goodbyes and hold us tightly to them, not wanting to let us go. Their cheeks are wet with tears but I can't cry anymore. I am angry with them for letting us go. They make us promise to write and tell me to behave, why not Rita? They remain below stairs. Bess climbs the stairs in front of us. The stairway darkens with her bulk. I will miss her so much. We wait in the hallway. Ambrose is outside putting our cases into the truck. Frobisher's shadow crosses the doorway. Boysey is with him, ready and dressed in his school clothes. His school cap with the Heber Road emblem is on his bowed head shielding the pain in his eyes. We hear footsteps descending on the grand staircase. The Squire and his wife are coming down to say their farewells. Lady Margaret is so beautiful. Her dark blonde hair bounces when she moves on the stairs. I just want to touch her. She looks so very, very upstairs in her dark green cashmere jumper with a simple strand of pearls encircling her neck. Her tweedy skirt brushes against her silk clad legs. I so want to look and be just like her when I grow up. She and the Squire come across the foyer toward us, their feet echoing on the marble floors. So this is how it ends. Goodbye. Goodbye, always goodbye. I hate it. I can't say it and I won't. The Squire looks at us sadly. Children we want you to know that we did all that we could in order for all of you to be able to continue to stay with us until the war is over and until you could go home. But, as you know, our pleas were denied and sadly we have to let you go. The Squire looks tired and drawn as he talks to us. I really would like to reach out to make him feel better and tell him that we understand the problem and not to feel sad but we don't understand any of it. We were never asked how we felt or what we would like to happen or where we would like to live. We are just three of many, many children being shuffled around the English countryside. We don't have a face. We are just numbers on sheets of paper somewhere in a musty, stuffy old office in London. The Squire and Lady Margaret proffer their hands to us. We solemnly shake them. I have never shaken hands before but it must be an adult thing to do. The Squire tells us to be good, travel safe and that he will keep us in his prayers. Lady Margaret holds our hands in both of hers as she speaks to us. I don't want her to ever let me go. I hold on for dear life. Maybe if I hadn't

153

thrown my toothbrush in the chamber pot this morning this wouldn't be happening. It is all my fault, I know it is. I am sorry. I am sorry, but nobody can hear me. Only I can. Their ears are deaf. Frobisher motions for us to follow him outside. Come children, it is time to go. Goodbye, children. Take good care of Heather, Sheila. Don't lose her. Stay safe. These are the last words we hear from the Squire and Lady Margaret. Bess follows us outside. We turn and wave to our now former caregivers. Bess gathers the three of us to her. Boysey is crying softly into Bess's white apron. He doesn't have a hanky. He wipes his nose on the sleeve of his jacket and quickly turns away, embarrassed by his own tear stained face. Frobisher helps him into the farm truck. I say; I'll miss you Bess. Please, please don't cry. I can't stand it. My heart will break. I will not feel the warmth of her ample arms and her lap before I go to bed. I can't look at her. It hurts too much. I hear her snuffling as Frobisher takes me from her. He picks me up and puts me in the back seat. Rita hugs Bess, one last time and climbs into the front seat. Her face is white and pinched. She says nothing. Frobisher gets behind the wheel. He is to take us to Plynt where we will board the buses with the other evacuees to take us to our next billet. Ambrose closes the back tailgate, turns and walks back to the big house without a word. At the last moment, he turns and waves goodbye. We wave back. We have given him a run for his money. He has had to put up with a lot of pranks, poor Ambrose. As we pull away from the house the wheels crunching on the gravel in the driveway we turn and look at Bess, one more time. All three of us knowing this will be the very last time we will ever see her. She waves and wipes her eyes on the corner of her apron. It is done. As the truck moves forward she is gradually lost from our sight. I can't bear it. My chest feels tight. My throat is all choked up. Boysey and I sit like stone in the back seat. As we pull through the gates of the estate the gardener and other household help, including our beloved Janet and Gladys are assembled and all are waving frantically and calling, goodbye and telling us to take care of ourselves. Bingo is running alongside us and is called back. Rita, Boysey and I lean out of the windows and wave back, calling out our farewells that are lost in the wind as the truck gathers speed. Soon they are distant figures and now except for the drone of the motor the truck is deathly quiet. All alone with our unspoken thoughts and fears and I never said goodbye and I will never see them again.

Frobisher drives us to the school in Plynt where all of the evacuees are assembled to be relocated. There is quite a crowd of children and adults already waiting for the coaches that are to take us to our new billets. Frobisher parks the old farm truck. We don't want to get out. We don't want to leave him. He gets our luggage out and adds it to the ever growing pile of assorted, battered suitcases waiting to go on the awaited buses. We slowly alight from the truck. Rita and Boysey run over to say hello to their school friends. Rita and Betty Jones are joyous to see one another. I stay apart from the ever growing tide of arriving children. It is just Heather and I. I am so glad to have her. I tell her, it is okay Heather. No more train rides, no more falling onto the tracks, just you and I. It is now time for Frobisher to leave. The coaches are arriving. Familiar figures emerge from the growing crowd. It is Mr Martin and the rest of the teachers. It is comforting to see them again. It is like seeing someone from home. We treasure any memories of home. Whistles are blowing to get our attention so that we can be given instructions. It is a world of constantly being told what to do. Frobisher gathers Rita, I and Boysey to him. It is time to say goodbye, children. I will never forget you, be brave and this will all be over someday. All of you will be going home. I know that he must be worried about what will really happen to us. Will we ever go home? He hugs and holds each one of us close. This is so hard. I don't ever want to let him go. Don't go, please don't go, I cry. He turns and walks away, back to the farm truck. We stand there forlornly, alone in the crowd, holding on to one another, rooted to the spot. We desperately want to run after him. Come back, please, please come back. Don't leave us here. But, we know he can't, he has to go. We watch him reach the truck. He pauses as if undecided about something. We wait for him to turn around and say goodbye. He doesn't and the truck pulls away. He is gone. He loves us. I know. He didn't want us to see his pain. Boysey is bereft. The whistles are blowing again. Everyone is being assembled into lines. Luggage is being loaded onto the green coaches. We slowly join onto the end of our line where happily Rita again finds Betty Jones. Again, I am very envious of Betty. I wish I was her. Then Rita would like me too. Rita tries hard to be loving and understanding of me but it is hard for her because she is scared about what is going on all around us and of not understanding any of it. She feels very responsible for me and Boysey. What a role to be thrust on one so young. So many times she is brusque with me and I cry. I love her so. She wasn't this way at home. She loved me there but that was then and this is now, a very different world. She is so afraid to show her love and true feelings because if she does let her guard down she will not have the strength to carry this huge responsibility that has been thrust upon her shoulders.

The teachers are going through the lines checking to see if we have our identity labels pinned to our coats and to be sure that we have our gas masks before we board the coaches going to where? It is like going on a mystery tour when you are on holiday. Evacuees and their host families are saying their goodbyes. I am sure that a majority of host families are glad to be seeing the back of us and really have their lives returned to some normalcy. Who can blame them? I am sure that will all be short lived as other evacuees will be assigned here. I envy those greatly that will get to go to Trewlawny. How could Bess love them more than us? There are many tears and sodden wet hankies. Many children have become close to their adoptive families but it is time to go. We climb aboard and find our seats, everyone scrambling for a window seat. It is so noisy, everyone seems to be in the aisles screeching, laughing and crying. Maybe this is all a bad dream and I will wake up. Our teachers, Miss Gwenn and Miss Thompson try to restore order and tell everyone to sit down in their seats. Of course all of us want to get to a window. Noses and hands are pressed up against steamy closed windows with all trying to say their last goodbyes. The four coaches are moving, two hundred children finally on our way. I am glad and relieved that this morning is over. Goodbyes are so sad. I never can say goodbye without becoming emotional. The coaches are winding their way through narrow country lanes with hedgerows on either side of the road and many wild blackberry bushes. I wish we could stop to pick some. Rita tells me that they are so good, juicy and sweet. Now and again there is a break in the hedgerows and the green rolling fields go on forever. Old grey stone farm houses dot the landscape. Sheep and cows are in the fields. The calves are with their mothers, nursing. What do they know of war? Ignorance is bliss. We pass through a small village with charming thatched cottages and an old stone church and cemetery. We slowly pass a local pub with its swinging creaking sign, The King's Head. Villagers are out front sitting on wooden benches having a pint with lunch and wave at us as we drive by while wondering what four coaches packed with children are doing passing through their village. Just outside the village the coach slows down and comes to a stop. We are yelling, are we there yet? There is an excited scramble into the aisles. We are told to sit down and be quiet. We look out ahead of us and see a farmer and a young boy herding about twenty five cows from the field across the lane to the barn farmyard to be milked. The cows stay close to one another and slowly move across to the other side. The farmer prods them with a stick to keep them moving; all of them mooing, all waiting to be milked and soon the warm milk will be swishing into the buckets. We are ready to be on the move again. The bus is noisy. The teachers are trying to keep order but it seems that no one is paying attention. Some mean boys are teasing the girls. One hooligan reaches over my seat and pulls my hair very hard and pokes his tongue out at me. Why is he picking on me? Rita tells him to leave me alone and to pick on someone his own size. He moves on to pick on somebody else. I can hear some children crying in their seats. They are confused and homesick. The teachers try to comfort as many as they can. Some have motion sickness and are throwing up in the aisles. This is all so impossible. The noise grows louder. Boys are always so very noisy and dirty. Voices get louder. Fighting ensues in the back of the coach. Punches are thrown and noses are bloodied. Tempers are frayed. A little boy in the seat in front of us is being sick all over the floor and himself. The stink of the warm vomit rises and permeates the already fetid air of the closed coach. The windows are all sealed shut and taped in case of German bomb attacks. Boysey is sitting next to the sick child and gets a dollop of the vomit on his short trousers and bare knees. He turns and looks at us, his face white and stiff with anger and shame. Everything with my brother has always had to be perfect. There is not a neater child that you could ever know. Miss Thompson comes rushing over and tries to clean the both of them up. There is no water   on the bus so she pulls out her handkerchief, spits on it, and wipes the little boys face. Boysey sits there paralyzed, afraid to move, with a lapful of someone else's breakfast. Luckily Miss Thompson finds a towel in her knapsack and uses it to clean the two of them up but it can't get rid of the offending odour. Children are now crying out to use the lavatories. There are none on the coach. We are told that we will have to wait till we get to the next town. Some can't hold it. One little girl with her legs tightly crossed, wets her knickers in the aisle. She starts crying. She is so humiliated. A warm puddle slowly spreads and travels down the coach floor. I have to go so badly as well and if I don't I will soon wet my knickers and I will also be ashamed. When will this nightmare end? The coach starts to slow down and stops by the side of the road and we are allowed to use toilets only there weren't any so it is a squat in the grass for the girls and for the boys the trees get a good watering. Shoes and socks were splashed but at this point who really cares? Hungrily we eat our packed lunches, our last memories of Trewlawny and Bess are fading. They seem so far away now. Miles and miles away, never to be reached and yet it was just this morning when they sadly said their goodbyes. The teachers are blowing their whistles for us to get back onto the coaches. We are on the road again. Miss Gwenn stands up and announces that we will be arriving at our final destination in about thirty minutes. We are so excited to hear this but with some trepidation as we do not know what to expect when we arrive. The countryside is becoming flatter. There are a few cottages and farms. The only other traffic we see on the one lane roads is a horse and cart or occasionally a tractor going to another field. When this happens we have to pull way over and stop to let them pass. It is now late afternoon and the sun is getting low in the sky. Suddenly a ribbon of brilliant blue sparkling in the late afternoon sun appears off the side of the road way down below us. It is the ocean. It goes on for miles and suddenly as if falling off the earth the coaches begin a steep descent on one of the steepest tree lined hills that I have ever encountered in my young life. Everyone is scrambling to get a look out of the windows, to get a glimpse of the ocean through the trees. As we travel downward green hills rise to our left, obscuring our view of the ocean. Sheep are grazing, oblivious to us in a world of their own, untouched. Air raids and bombs will never reach this shire but the war for the people below is about to become a reality with our imminent arrival. All four coaches wind slowly down the steep curving hill. The late afternoon sun is now hidden from view. The road begins to bear to the left. On the right a rushing stream is rushing over rocks and racing down toward the village in front of us. As we reach the bottom of the hill the coach begins to slow even more. To our right is an old mill house with a gigantic wheel on the outside. It is being turned by the water from the stream racing over its wooden spokes and continuing on down the hill. None of us have ever seen anything like it before. We are watching the force of the water push the wheel around. It fascinates us. The coaches wind their way on into the village. We see whitewashed stone cottages with slate roofs, mullioned windows and small fenced gardens that front the stream. Many villagers and their children are standing out in front of a school hall watching us arrive with a quiet curiosity. Some of the village children shyly wave. The adults do not. Their faces are sombre and reserved. We are all clambering to the dirty windows. Our faces squashed against them. All of us are trying to get a glimpse of where we are to live till the war is over. The coaches are stopping because the roads in the village are too narrow to go any further. Later, we are to find out that no vehicles are allowed to drive into the village. Off to the left of the coaches is a one story brick building with dark green iron railings surrounding it. Tall windows look out sombrely onto the narrow road going down into the village. We have arrived. Villagers are gathering outside, waiting to see this sad, dejected, dirty and dishevelled group of children and teachers about to alight from the green coaches. We can hear them asking, who are they and where did they come from? Unfounded gossip has preceded us and has travelled like wildfire. It is said that we are Cockneys from a faraway city that they have heard of in school, namely London, but that few if any have ever visited there and that our speech in unintelligible. It is said that we are very dirty, probably diseased and with lice. They certainly don't want us here invading their quiet way of life in this centuries old village of Polperro. Their way of life is about to change in many ways and not for the better. Our teachers, with their belongings get off first and stand in front of their respective coaches. We begin to assemble in the aisles in readiness to get off. I feel so very scared as to what is waiting for us. Surely it can't be any worse than the last time waiting to be picked by a host family. I think about my Mum and know that she must be wondering where we are and if we are all right? Little does she know that there were a hundred or so people looking us over like cattle and deciding our lives for months to come? I grab for Rita's hand. I turn to look to see where Boysey is. He is further back in the line. I try to beckon him to come up with us but he doesn't see me as everyone is pushing and shoving, all anxious to get off. I hold onto Heather tightly. I tell her not to worry because whoever takes me will have to take her too. We slowly move forward. I hold so tightly onto Rita, not wanting to fall on the stairs of the coach. My stomach is sick. It hurts. My head is throbbing and I want to go home and this certainly is not home. We line up two abreast. Betty is right behind us with another girl called Joan. Boysey is toward the back. Rita calls out to him to get up here with us or we will be separated when the villagers get to pick which children they will begrudgingly take home. Maybe not all of them feel that way. We could be lucky. Still, since the government allocation is ten and sixpence per child that will mean more food on the table for some of them. Not necessarily though for the evacuees. In some families, not all, the evacuees will be fed as well as the host families and will have to sit and watch the household enjoy the more plentiful desired food, while their fare is a lot less. This will give cause for stealing food. War is a terrible thing for everybody. We start to walk, slowly, following the other lines of children. Our luggage is unloaded off of the coach and taken inside the school. What a sorry sight we look, dirty faces and hands, socks hanging around our ankles, runny noses on some, sad faces, unkempt hair and scruffy looking clothes rumpled from the long ride. We hear village children ask; why are they here? They pull on their mother's skirts. Don't they have a home? Why do they have to live with us? What do they know of war, bombing and death? Looking as we do who would want us? We cross the street to the village school with the green railings. The villagers follow us with much curiosity.

TEARS AND LAUGHTER END
THE SADDEST DAY

Dusk has deepened and lengthened the shadows. My shadow on the pavement makes me look tall and skinny. It is not me at all. Soon there will be no shadows as it darkens. Tempers are short as we are herded like sheep into yet another school hall. They are beginning to all look alike. A large empty room, a stage with droopy curtains at one end, wide planked floors, dreary oil enamelled walls that are peeling and bubbling and scratched worn wooden benches piled and pushed to the sides to make room for us to be viewed and chosen. There are no cakes, sandwiches and hot cocoa to make us feel welcome this time as in Plynt. Just a gloomy damp chill in the large room and unknown faces gazing at us. Mr Martin tells us to line up and for brothers and sisters to stay together in hopes that they won't be separated. It is the same routine as before. We are getting to know the rules. We all know them far too well. Betty stands with us. She is an only child and she is hoping that she can stay with us. I really hope that she can't so that I can have Rita to myself. Mr Martin announces that a doctor and a nurse wish to give us a quick look over to see if any of us need any form of medical attention before being assigned to our host families. In other words, are we carrying any communicable diseases? The doctor appears quite jovial, smiling and chuckling as he greets us. He has a very ruddy face with big jowls, a whiter than snow moustache and beard and the bluest twinkling eyes. He is very rotund in his tweeds. He obviously takes great pleasure in food. A faint smell of gin exudes from

163

his person. Gin is my paternal grandmother's favourite choice of drink and I don't think it is medicinal. He introduces himself to us as Dr Brown and acquaints us with his nurse Miss Wellstone. My instincts tell me she doesn't like children. Her mouth is set in a grim line and she is as skinny as he is fat. She is wearing a navy blue serge dress with a silver watch pin pinned to her pocket. Her dress nearly comes to her ankles which are encased in black wool stockings with black lace up shoes. She smells of musty moth balls. A navy beret is pulled down over her iron grey hair which is pulled back into a greasy bun. I instantly don't like her. I am also afraid of her. What will she do to me? I feel so small. They start to move along the lines. We are in the third line. What is going on up there? We are all straining our necks to see. It is strangely quiet in here except for the sound of occasional gagging and shuffling of feet as some children are told to move over to the side of the room. The doctor and the nurse finally reach our line. I hate doctors. They do bad things to hurt you. Betty is first in line, then Rita me and Boysey. I peer around Rita's legs to see what they are doing to Betty but the bulk of Dr Brown in in the way. Betty seems to have survived as they move on to Rita. She is told to open her mouth wide. A wooden tongue depressor is poked into her mouth and she is told to say ah. She sputters but does as she is told. He then holds his finger up and tells her to follow it with her eyes. He also looks in her ears. She is then told to bend her head down. She obeys. He takes a comb from the nurse and starts to part her thick short curly hair and look at the roots. I wonder what he is looking for. He nods to the nurse and she scribbles vigorously on her clipboard. All of our names must be on that clipboard. He moves on to me. I don't feel at all well. My tooth is starting to ache again and we don't have any salt to bung in it. My belly is making strange noises. I know that everyone in the hall can hear it. I look frantically around. Where can I run to? I see a wall of faces. The villagers look stone facedly onto this scene. Surely some of them must feel compassion for us. The doctor looms above me. He bends forward and tells me to open my mouth. My mouth is small and it doesn't open very wide. Wider he booms, wider. I try. He sticks the same tongue depressor that he has used on all the others into my mouth. I start to gag. I can't breathe. Say ah, say ah he says. I want to bite down on his invading pork sausage like fingers. I hear beside me, my brother, saying; say ah Sheila. You can do it he pleads with me. I wretch and utter a small strange sound. The doctor finally withdraws the wet stick from my mouth and says to me. It looks like we have a nasty tooth in there. It will have to be pulled out before you can go to school. Note that nurse, please. No, no. Mum says no. It is not to be done until I get back to London. The thoughts are racing through my head but no sound is coming out because if I talk he may put his fingers back in my mouth. He waves his fat index finger back and forth before my eyes. I hate his fingers. He pulls my ears as he peers into them and jokingly says; any potatoes in there I wonder? I am not amused. Rita takes my hair ribbons off so that he can look through my hair. If there are fleas in it I hope that they jump out and bite him. He pulls painfully through my long hair tangled from the trip. I hear him tell the nurse, cut. What does that mean? I didn't hear him say that when he looked at Rita's hair. Or, maybe, I just wasn't paying attention. He then checks Boysey out and moves on down the line. It seems to take forever. I want to sit down. My legs are so tired. I want to go to sleep and make this all go away. Finally the doctor and nurse are through examining us and both move to the front to confer with our teacher Mr Martin who shakes his head vigorously over something that the doctor tells him. Mr Martin tells us that we are to be called out to the front in groups of six at a time. He says that when your name is called, please move forward. What are they going to do now I wonder? I feel like we are in the London Zoo with all of the villagers looking at us, gossiping amongst themselves and pointing fingers at us as if asking; which one do you want? Their voices get louder. Oh, I think I'll take that one over there. It looks clean. Well, I can't take more than one. I have enough mouths to feed without taking in London Cockneys at any price. I look toward them. I am not worth very much really. I see some sadness and compassion for us in a few of the faces. Maybe they are thinking that we could be their children put in this distressing situation that is playing out in front of them. All of the evacuees must also feel the vulnerability I feel at this point in time, none of us knowing what the future has in store for us. We children are moving out in groups of six. We are told to leave our coats and gas masks on the chairs. As names are called they follow the nurse into a room where the door is closed after them. They do not reappear. The doctor has left the room. Rita is called. She is the last of the six in that group. She pries my fingers loose from her. I grab for her skirt and hold on for dear life. No, no you can't go without me. Take me with you please. Please don't leave me here. I'll be good. I am so terrified she might not come back. Boysey grabs me around the waist and pulls me from her. He tries to soothe me. It is all right Sheila, shush, don't cry. People are watching. Mum would be very cross if she knew that you were making a scene. It is going to be all right. I let go of Rita and stand there trembling, clutching tightly to my brothers hand. I tearfully watch Rita leave with Betty and the nurse with her black clipboard. I hate her for taking my sister away. That is all I can feel at this moment in time. Hate and anger for what she is doing. The door closes behind them. It seems like an awfully long time before the next six are called. We are called for we know not what. We move forward with trepidation. Are we going into a room with a big open pit in it that we are all going to fall into, be covered up and gotten rid of? In my way of thinking this would be the answer to the villager's problems. As my Mum always tells me, my vivid imagination is working overtime. Slowly, full of misgiving, we follow the ramrod figure of Miss Wellstone to the closed door. There is an interruption in the back of the hall. We can't see what is happening as it is coming from behind the towns people. We six dawdle along so that we can see who it is that we are hearing. Soft crying, sniffling of noses and muffled voices issue forth. I recognize the utterances. They are back. Wherever they went they came back. That means they are all right and that Rita is with them. No open pit to fall in. Everything is okay. I feel much braver and happier. I will now march in there with my head held high. But, why were some of the smaller children crying? I am just happy that they are back and I will see them again. We evacuees have become a family, a very broken family, but a family none the less. The nurse turns to us. Get moving children, we don't have all day, come along, come along, let's go. We enter an old classroom with tall unopened windows. There is a peculiar smell that I don't recognize assailing my nostrils. We are told to sit at wooden desks with inkwells. The desks are worn, stained with ink and etched with past scholars' names and dates. I run my fingers over the desktop feeling the grooves of the names. How many children have sat here and spent their young years learning to read, write and do sums? Some gleaning all they can, others gazing out of the windows, daydreaming and wishing to be outside and done with school. I break away from my flight of fantasy. This is reality. We sit quietly trying to anticipate what is to happen next. What can go awry? I wish Mum was here. Unexpectedly, a door opens in the back of the classroom. Oh, no. It is old doctor Brown again, garbed in a white coat like my doctor back home wears. Why is he back here and what does this all mean? We soon find out. He is joined by Miss Wellstone and two apron clad women from the village. They are all assembled on the teacher's platform. The late sun is casting shadows on a long table behind them. There are two high stools in front of the ladies. The doctor moves off the platform to the side of the room to another table covered in a long cloth. Nurse Wellstone calls out the names of two children. Not me yet. I don't know what is worse. To go first and have it over with or to be last and hope that it won't happen. I look at Boysey at the next desk. He bravely grins at me. So it can't be all that serious. Emily Baker and Brian Twaites shuffle unwillingly up to the front. They are helped up onto the stools. We watch, anxiously waiting our turns. The two aproned ladies drape towels around their necks; they turn to the table and turn around armed with their combs and scissors. Emily starts to cry. She is told to be quiet and not be such a baby. Her hair ribbons are removed. They take bunches of her long red curly hair and start to cut with the sheers. I am sure that I will not forget the sound of the blade as it crunches and cuts through her thick tresses. Her beautiful hair falls to the floor. Her chin is trembling, trying to hold back the tears. I scrunch my eyes tightly so as not to cry but the tears roll down my cheeks. I hate them. How can they do this to her? The boys call out for them to stop it. We are told to hush by Miss Wellstone. She explains to us that we all probably have head lice and possibly scabies and they are fearful that we could contaminate all the locals so sadly therefore these steps have to be carried out. Emily's hair is now gone. It is short and uneven. She looks sadly at the pile of her red hair on the floor, surrounding her stool. She now looks like an orphan waif. She emits a big choking sob that is heard around the hushed intimidated classroom. Her shoulders heave. She cries out; Mummy, make them stop. A bottle with a small brush is produced and her roots are painted with Gentian Violet. She is told to get down and go to the other side of the room. She slowly gets off of the stool. Her body seems to be paralyzed. I can't look. Brian is next. His hair is short except for the long forelock on his forehead. He tries to smile as they shear and clip all of that off close to the scalp. They paint him purple too and a dribble of the grape colour runs down his forehead. He wipes it off with the back of his hand which he then uses to wipe the snot off of his nose and the Gentian Violet is now smeared over his top lip and nose. He looks so embarrassed. I look away. I want to cry for him. He is the school bully but whatever; nobody should be treated like that. Brian retreats like a dog with his tail between his legs to the other side of the room to join Emily. He reaches out for her hand to comfort her. This is a change for him. I wonder how long it will last. Why did Mum let us come here? Mum has always said that my hair is my crowning glory and now they are going to take that away. I see myself as short and stubby with an ever so round face and a turned up nose which gets very red when it is cold and when I am crying. Mum always calls it a retroussé nose but Mums always try to make you feel good about yourself. I am beautiful in my parents eyes but I am about to lose my hair and I will be ugly. Now nobody will pick me. I now know why I heard the crying when the other children came back into the hall. My reverie is abruptly broken by Miss Wellstone's nasally clipped tones. Sheila Harvey, that's me, Angela Thurgood come up to the platform right away please we are in a hurry. We have other children waiting so come along right now. Furthermore we don't want any more cry-babies today. I can't move. My legs are trembling. I want Rita but she can't come. Did she cry? I look desperately over at Boysey. He just stares straight ahead with his fingers clenched tightly around the edges of his chair. They are so white and bloodless. Please help me, but my cries are not heard. They are just echoing around inside my head. I feel a jerk on my arm as I am pulled up out of my seat. Nasty Miss Wellstone has taken matters into her own hands. No, I won't go; I don't want my hair cut. Don't do it. I am angry now and crying at the same time. My Mum will be really angry. She won't let you do it. No. No. I stubbornly stand my ground. She drags me onto the platform and puts me onto the chair. The other ladies hold onto me tightly with my arms to my sides as I struggle to get free, Heather falls to the floor. I see Boysey looking away. I know that he is saying, please Sheila be good, please. My cheeks are red and wet with anger and crying. My nose is all stopped up. All I can do is sob intermittently. Angela seems so composed and has accepted what is about to happen. I can't fight anymore. I give in but I have lost something so precious to me, my independence. I wince as they take my ribbons off. I glance over at Angela. She manages a sad smile. She is so very placid. How can she be so quiet? I hear the first cut of the shears. Angela's dark brown braids are cut off. It looks strange to see them laying on the floor with the plaid ribbons still on them. They have no life anymore. They used to bounce on her shoulders when she played. Those same plaid ribbons that had been tied onto them just this morning when her hair was braided. Now they are gone. Five years to grow and in the time it takes to count to five they are gone. They are now applying the Gentian Violet. I look at her horrified. Her individuality is gone. All of us, including me, are beginning to look alike. At least everybody in the village will know that we are evacuees. We are now very distinguishable. I just give in to losing my hair. I can't fight them anymore. They are going to prevail anyhow. I close my eyes tightly as the nurse approaches with the shears. I feel her bony fingers grab a thick clump of my hair. I hear the scissors straining to cut through my thick curls. I sense something soft falling past my shoulders and when it is repeated I whisper, please no more. I feel a shiver across my head as purple disinfectant is applied. It is cold. I shudder. Oh the humiliation. My eyes open, I look to the floor, long pale blonde curly hair lays lifeless in a heap. It is all gone and underneath it all a patch of dark green velvet.

It is Heather, buried in my hair, poor Heather. I look over at my brother. I want to see the look in his eyes but he turns his face away from me. Will I ever have the courage again to look into a mirror? Angela and I are told to join the other children on the other side of the room. Sadly, I reach down and recover Heather from her hairy grave. I look at my ribbons and touch my curls but they are dead to me. I turn and join the others. We stand huddled together, our heads down, not wanting to watch the embarrassment and pain of the remaining few, especially my brother. I cannot stand to see him hurt. I cover my ears in case he cries out but I know he won't. He will remain pale and stoic. It is over. Boysey and the others join us. Strangely I feel joy. It is funny how you can still feel joy after this but still the feeling comes over you. Joy that it is over and that you have made it through and that we are all still here. The back door is opened. We are to be reunited with the rest of our school. I don't want anyone to see me. I want to run and hide under a desk to hide my repulsiveness but there is no hiding. I wonder if Heather still loves me. I can't wait to tell her of my sorrow tonight when we are in bed. We have shared so much today. We will cry together. We are all reassembled in the hall of the school. The overhead bare light bulbs give off a garish light to the scene below them. There is a heavy buzz of conversation, some laughter and some weeping as some brothers, sisters and friends are reunited. They hug, trying to get strength from one another. Most boys' huddle together trying to act tough to cover up their real true feelings, ridiculing one another on their looks, pointing fingers and a lot of name calling ensues. Egghead, queball, purple dome, bladder bonce and so on, and so on. A lot of nervous giggling follows. The girls have not as yet been able to find the humour in this traumatic event. We gather together for much needed comfort. Our teachers muster around us and offer reassurance. Your hair will grow back fast, you will see. Their

171

hair has not been shorn from their heads and they don't smell like disinfectant. I must suppose from this that grownups don't get head lice but then they are not Cockney kids. The funny thing is, Cockneys live in the east end of London and I have never been there but I was born within the sound of Bow Bells and any child who is born within the church bells is a true Cockney. Strangely, none of whom the villagers were calling Cockneys from the Heber road school are. I am now desperately looking for my sister and Betty. Boysey is dragging me by the hand. I am trying to keep up with him but my whole being is tired and exhausted. I just want to find Rita and go to sleep. What if they don't recognize me or I them? I hear Rita calling my name. All I can see are legs, lower bodies, dirty knees and baggy socks in the crowd all trying to find and unite with family and friends. Boysey pushes through the melee with me in tow, hanging on for dear life. We move in the direction of her voice. Sheila, Boysey, over here, I am here. I have never been so glad to see her. I look up at her. Don't laugh. Please don't laugh, I plead. Oh Sheila, bless your heart she says. My eyes see her face and her now short, short purple streaked curls. Her hazel eyes look enormous in her pale face. A purple streak runs down her nose. Had she looked into a mirror yet and if she looks like that what do I look like? Poor Betty has a look of pain on her face but suddenly, all looking at one another, we all start to giggle. We look so ridiculous. We laugh so hard. I can see in Rita's eyes, through the laughter, despair, compassion and unfounded guilt. She tells me, I failed you as a big sister to protect you, she being only the tender age of eleven. To cover up the awkward moment she bends down and brusquely pulls me towards her. She takes her grubby hanky out of her knickers pocket, spits on it and tries to wipe away the purple disinfectant from my face. She rubs hard as if to rub away the sadness of this day. A whistle is blown loudly, the shrillness of it stilling the clamour in the hall. All is silent except for the intermittent sobs, sniffling and nervous giggling as we come to terms with our new looks. We are told to form into lines. Betty stands with Rita, Boysey and I. What now, but deep down we really know what is next? Maybe we will be fortunate like last time and another Squire Trewlawny with his Lady will come and rescue us. I feel right now that Bess, Janet and Gladys are thousands of miles away and jealously think that some other little boys and girls are feeling their love and warmth and are being lovingly tucked into bed. I feel so alone. I hold Heather tighter to my chest. What a day she has gone through, the poor little thing. She smells of disinfectant and also has a purple stain down her little green velvet dress but I still love her no matter what or whatever she looks like. Here come the shoppers. Which of us look like the least of trouble? The way we look I don't know who could want us. What a forlorn bunch. Children are being singled out. Several villagers seem interested in us but they won't take all four of us or even three. We will have to be separated. We are gawked at, told to turn all the way around. I want to scream at them to please leave us alone. We are so very tired. Won't somebody please take us home to our new billet? A trim lady approaches us. She looks quite nice and friendly. She introduces herself as Mrs Allen. Her eyes twinkle behind pebble glasses. She has a round apple cheeked face devoid of any makeup. Come to think of it I haven't seen lipstick on any of the village ladies. Painted lips are the Devil's work. Mrs Allen's short brown hair is parted on the side and scurfed up with a hairclip. She looks down at us. I look at her white summer sandal feet encased in Lyle stockings and follow upward to her pink flowered print dress with a white cardigan around her shoulders held together at the neck with a silver chain. She has a big white handbag with a gold fastener over her left arm. She seems more sophisticated than the other women of the village. You can hear the Cornish dialect as she asks our names and how many we are. Rita answers, there are four of us. There is no way I can take all four of you. I don't have the room or the patience for more than two so who will it be and I definitely don't want a boy? They are way too noisy for my liking. Poor Boysey looks on hopefully. He can't help it that God made him a noisy boy. I am glad that God made me a girl. At least I have a chance to be picked by Mrs Allen, whether that is good or bad. I know Rita would love for Betty and her to be together but duty prevails and Rita says it will be she and I. Betty looks forlorn at this announcement but she knows that there is no other way. Mrs Allen intervenes and tells us that her next door neighbours who could not be here this afternoon, the Goodwin sisters, will take Betty in but unfortunately not Boysey so Betty can come along with us. Rita is happy for that. Go get your belongings and follow me, says Mrs Allen. I think that she is as nervous as we are. No, no, Rita says. We cannot leave until our brother has been chosen. Mrs Allen's lips purse into a hard line but before she can utter another word Mr Martin our head master comes down the line with a very bony middle aged woman at his side. Her face looks like old parchment, weather beaten with many wrinkles. She looks very tired. Her grey hair is covered in a black scarf tied in a knot under her chin, a black baggy dress covers her wraith like body which is then covered over by a green wrap around apron that is stained with what looks like grease and who knows what else. Her leg coverings are wrinkled around her ankles and she is wearing what look like wooden clogs that are covered in fish scales on her feet. Oive got room for just one boy child she says, coughing into a grimy hanky. Her voice is raspy, she sounds like she has a bad cold. Her eyes are watery. She has a sad yet vulnerable hard look. I wonder if she has ever laughed or at the very least smiled. She walks up the line looking at all the boys that are left in the school hall. Children with no sibling have already been chosen and are on their way to their new billets with their host families so there are not a lot for her to choose from. She looks curiously at each one and has them turn around. Most of the bravado that the school boys exhibited earlier has gone. Heads are down, tiredness and hunger has set in and they have resigned themselves to this. She gets to Boysey and has him turn around like the others. I watch her take his chin in her work worn hand, her fingernails are broken and dirt rimmed. She raises his head and looks him straight in the eyes. Are you strong boy, she asks, willing to work hard? He has no choice but to nod his head yes. Her clutch on his chin will not allow him to answer any way but positively. She releases her firm hold on him, turns to Mr Martin and says; I'll take this one, pointing at Boysey. Boysey doesn't have a choice who he wants to go with. Mr Martin calls over one of the other teachers, Mr Horn, to get Boysey's belongings from the pile of cases by the school door. Rita's, Betty's and my luggage is also located. We are all ready to go. We have to hurry up and say our goodbyes. Rita and Betty will see him in school on Monday. I won't as I will be going to the village infant school. I hope and pray that I get to see him soon. I miss him already. My heart feels so heavy. Why can't we be a family? Boysey is just eight years old. He is just a little boy trying to wear big shoes. He looks vulnerable as he puts his gas mask over his shoulder and struggles with his heavy case. We say goodbye and try to smile but it is hard to hold back the tears. Bye, bye Boysey, be good, Rita says. Bye, Boysey, I echo. I will miss you so much. I turn away from him. I don't want him to see how sad I am. Ta, ta, he says and turns to walk away, dragging his case and following his guardian Mrs Gillis. He stops at the open school door and turns around, standing tall and brave. Please don't call me Boysey. I am not a child. Remember what Dad said; call me Len. Tonight, I am all grown up. The school door bangs shut behind him. Boysey is gone, really gone. Sadly, I whisper, Ta, ta Len.

REFLECTIONS:

When I think back on Cornwall I know that at that time we didn't appreciate its beauty as I do now whenever I revisit Polperro. The pain that I felt upon arriving there has since disappeared with the years and I love to revisit whenever I can. It is truly a beautiful part of England with warm and loving people.

ANOTHER NEW BEGINNING

We pick up our cases and gas masks. I hope that we don't have to carry them too far because my case, turned on its end, is as big as I am. I half drag and carry it. It is scuffed and worn on the corners from so much moving. It is made of cardboard and painted brown. Mum and Dad bought three of them for us kids. It was such a big expense for them, especially with work so hard to come by for Dad. Dad said; with the war going on nobody is fixing up their houses. Work for a paper hanger is hard to come by. What use is new wallpaper and paint when it could all so easily go down into a heap of rubble overnight?

It is going to be such a relief to me not to have to drag my case and gas mask around anymore and God willing not to have to wear these big identity labels tied to my coat with string. Our teachers make sure we have all of our belongings and tell Mrs Allen to make sure that we will be in school on Monday. Mrs Allen informs our teachers that her odd job man, Oliver, will pick up ours and Bettys suitcases later and deliver them by cart as Betty's family is right next to hers. I want to keep Heather with me but she tells me to put her in my case. Our teachers tell us to be good and to obey Mrs Allen. We nod and wave goodbye to them. They have been the one constant for us, almost like family, since we left London. It seems we cling to any authority figure that has warmth in his or her voice. The three of us follow Mrs Allen out of the school. We hurry to keep up, following her like ducks in a row with me at the rear. The narrow cobblestone street doesn't make it any the easier to stay close. We walk in silence. I just want to sit on the cobblestone street and never move again but that is not possible. We walk past the village shops. The closed signs are up in the doorways. It must be past five o'clock. We glance in the bakery windows. The shelves are all empty of any tempting cakes and cream buns. I peer in the bow windows of the butcher shop. Its marble shelves are scrubbed spotless. The only thing remaining is a large brown and white platter with a couple of sprigs of parsley that just this morning probably held a lovely joint roast. I peer harder and see the butchers straw boater and blue and white striped apron hanging on a meat hook. The only butchers I have seen in my short life have been noticeably stout with very rosy cheeked faces. I think they must save all of the best cuts of meat for themselves. I don't imagine that during this war there will be many porky butchers in London. I mean, after all, one lamb chop each once a week was luxury for us and you don't get fat on that. I continue gawking in the window and in a wink I realize someone is staring back at me. Who is it? It can't be. But it is. It is me. Oh, my. I reach up to touch my head. It really did happen. I finger through the short hair. I am ashamed. It used to be that grownups would say to my Mum; your Sheila is so pretty with all that lovely blonde hair. Now people will laugh at me. I know they will. I am so ugly and I feel so very lonely. I am abruptly shaken out of my sad reverie. Mrs Allen is calling me to stop dawdling and keep up with the others. It is getting late and it is nearly time for tea. Come along child. Food, oh I wonder if there will be cakes with tea. Tea without cake is very boring. I wish my short sturdy little legs were as long and skinny as Rita and Bettys. Then I could keep up with them and we could get to tea faster. I do go a little faster, thinking of tea and cakes. We pass the other shops. There aren't very many. Not like the bustling crowded High Street where we live in London. We pass the green grocers, the dairy with its big brass creamer in the window and my favourite, of course, the sweet shop. Oh what delights await in there. I wonder if Mrs Allen will give us pocket money. My Dad gave us sixpence a week every Sunday which we eagerly lined up for. Dad would take us to the sweet shop and we would select from the big tall sweet jars on the shelves. Humbugs, toffees, liquorice all sorts, pear drops, I would look up to the counter and point at which jar I wanted. My mouth watered in anticipation of the flavours that were about to delight me. My sixpence clutched tightly in my fist, I would contemplate the jars and point to what I wanted. Two ounces liquorice all sorts, two ounces Humbugs and two ounces of toffees. Mrs Channing, the shop keeper, would reach for the big jars, unscrewing the black lids and pouring the sweets onto the scale until it wavered on two ounces and then pouring them off of the scale shovel into the white paper bags, three whole bags of tantalizing delight. My whole body would shudder and my chin would quiver with expectation but that was then in my world of being nurtured, loved and feeling wanted. Now my world is one of uncertainty, fear and alienation. We walk on. The cobblestones are so hard to walk on. I go over on my ankle and wince but nobody pays attention. I am sure that Mrs Allen has other things on her mind than to worry about the strange little whining wretch trailing behind her. I grit my teeth and start to limp. But maybe I am misjudging her. Across the street from us are cottages situated along a stream, each one has a different coloured front door with a brass knocker and brass letterboxes. Some villagers are out on their whitened front door steps. I am sure they are gossiping over the momentous events of the day after living their otherwise quiet lives. They look and point at us as we go by. Their voices carry as if by intention. They say; there go some more of those Cockney evacuees from London. They have had very few outsiders in their village, ever. The war has changed all of that. One of the villagers asks another; I wonder just how long we are going to have to put up with foreigners in our village? How can they not know that we don't want to be here either? We feel as intrusive as a sore toe. We pass by the village chapel which will become our home on Sundays. We turn right onto a lane. It can't be much farther now, surely. Mrs Allen lets us stop and rest for a while. What a relief it is. Quaint two story cottages dot either side of the cobblestone lane. There is a narrow old low stone bridge. We can hear the sound of rushing water. Rita and Betty run over and lean way over the side of the bridge. They call out, Sheila come, come quick. I can't run. My ankle is hurting from twisting it but I have got to see what is going on. I can't be outdone by Betty. I hobble over and join them. Maybe they will feel sorry for me. I am very good at putting it on. I want them to feel sorry for me. I guess it is really a cry for attention, but it is not working too well. Rita lifts me up to see over the side of the bridge and there below us, to all of our delight, is a narrow stream, crystal clear, dancing and racing over stones and rocks. The late evening sun glinting off the water like diamonds as it races toward the harbour and eventually finds its way out to sea. We giggle with pleasure at the sight, the pain forgotten for the first time in this seemingly never ending day. It is the first time today that we have been able to feel any emotion other than loneliness and humiliation. Seagulls are screeching and circling, landing and nesting amongst the crowded, blackened chimney pots atop the stone cottages that grace either side of the stream. Some of the dwellings are unlike anything we have ever seen. They are perched on wooden poles that are buried deep below the swollen waters that constantly wash around them. Rita puts me back down onto the cobblestone street and asks Mrs Allen why are some of these cottages standing on stilts? She explains that when very high tides occur and severe winter storms move in the water rises rapidly as it flows from over swollen streams above and in from the sea and that the dwellings would be submerged by the torrent of water if they were not built up high. I sit on the ground and think what fun it would be to live in a house on stilts and lay on the floor of the lower level listening to the sounds of water rushing below, feeling safe that it could not touch you or take you away to sea. It is time to move on again, our brief rest is over and we must be on our way. Mrs Allen says; it is just a short walk now, we are almost there. We are always almost there. Why do adults always tell you that? It is like it has a double meaning. It is like when you ask your parents if you can have some sweets when you go shopping with them on the High Street on a Saturday afternoon and the answer is always," we'll see". We'll see what? That is what I want to know. I just do not understand grownups at all. We leave the bridge and turn right onto another narrow village lane. There are small stone row cottages huddled together on either side. There are no front gardens. All of the front doors open onto the street. The only sounds that I can hear now are the seagulls circling overhead and settling down among the sooty chimney pots for the oncoming night. People are all indoors having their tea. I wonder if we will get tea when we get where we are going. She said we would. The road steadily climbs, steepens and widens. My legs ache so badly. The cottages now have gardens in front of them and are detached. We catch our breath as the lane widens up before us and it seems to go on forever. I think that we will walk many miles up and down Llandaviddy Lane during our stay in Cornwall as the school is in the village. The hill to the right of us sheers and drops off clear down to the village below. We can see the school, the church and the shops. We are up really high. The few cottages on that side seem to be perched on a cliff ready to tumble down onto the village far beneath us. We continue on. I am getting winded and I am struggling to keep up. Please God, let it not be much farther. The answer to my prayer has come. We are here announces

181

Mrs Allen. She stops in front of a two story yellow snowcem house with windows on either side of a dark green front door. There are also two windows upstairs. She opens a large green iron gate on the walk leading up to tiled stairs with railings on either side to the house which makes it seem like it is nestled in the hillside. I have never in my life seen a yellow house before let alone a green front door with a brass knocker and a brass letter box. This house is so very different from the smoke caked red brick houses with hundreds of black chimneys belching smoke into the air in London. This is Park House where you will be staying Mrs Allen tells us. There is a swinging painted sign over the front door proclaiming that truly this is Park House. Our new adopted home. Mrs Allen tells us to wait on the walk for her while she takes Betty over next door to the Goodwins where Betty will be living. Right next door, jolly good luck if you ask me.? It is a blue house called Gull Cottage. Mrs Allen tells Rita to say her goodbyes. She tells us we will be seeing Betty in church tomorrow. I am sure by that time we will have lots and lots to talk about. I do hope that Betty likes her new billet. She was lucky as were we last time. I wish I had a friend like Betty. Rita is lucky for that. I worry about my brother. Who does he have? At least I have Rita even though she has a go at me all the time and wishes that I would get lost. But it is certainly better than being on your own and I have the satisfaction of making her life more miserable. Well, not all the time because deep down inside I really do love her and admire her. How I wish she really loved me and would show it. Just a touch, a hug would mean so much. I ache for her acceptance. I am sure that she doesn't realize how much I need her love. She has pain and is hurting too. Mrs Allen returns after leaving Betty at Gull cottage. She motions us to follow her up the steps. I count them as I go. Ten so far, they are steep and my legs have trouble traversing them one at a time. On both sides of the stairs there are sloping flower beds, very neatly kept. Crazy paving winds around them. Rose bushes run along both sides of the garden all the way down to the road. Beautiful colours of yellow, white and red and a fragrance of sweet pea drifts across to us on the early evening breeze. Below the flower beds on the right is the strangest tree I have ever seen. It looks like something you might see in a jungle picture. We pause on our climb to look at it. Look Rita, look at the tree. It looks like a jungle tree. It is she says. It is a monkey tree. Oh, my goodness. Do they have monkeys here too, I ask, expecting at any moment to see one clambering up the trunk of the tree? She looks at me and shakes her head in disbelief at my stupidity. Don't be silly she says, of course not. But how am I to know? We have reached the house and are taking another path that leads us up beside the house. We follow her and she tells us that the front door is only to be used by invited visiting relatives or close friends. We are to use the back door which is also used by workmen and delivery boys. At the back of the house the steps continue up the steep hillside to the top of a cliff. There is a vegetable garden on one side and flowerbeds on the other. I don't see any place for us to play. I guess young children were not in Mrs Allen's plans. Or, maybe it is like what my Mum says; children are to be seen and not heard. We are at the back door. Mrs Allen turns the door handle and lets us in. We follow her into the house. I reach for Rita's hand. I feel quite nervous. We are in a big bright yellow kitchen. A large wood fired Agar cooker on one wall with shelves above it filled with copper saucepans. On the opposite wall is a white kitchen dresser. Its shelves are filled with white china dinner ware. In the centre of the kitchen is a wooden table and chairs. On the back wall a large old clock is tick tocking away the minutes. Children this is where you will eat your meals and spend your free time when you are not in school or chapel. Now come with me and I will show you the rest of the house. We nervously follow her into a passageway. There is a closed white painted door with a black knob halfway down the hallway. She opens that door. This is the drawing room she says. You will never use this room unless you are invited to with the exceptions of Christmas day or Easter. We pass reverently into the room through a dark brown velvet curtain which is hanging inside the door in order to prevent cold drafts, in the winter, from coming up the passageway and into the room from the front door. The room feels cold and austere. It is furnished with a dark blue velvet upholstered couch edged with heavy gold fringe, its arms and back covered with antimacassars. Two matching flowered overstuffed chairs face an open painted and tiled fireplace with a black leaded grate. A brass fire guard stands in front and this is surrounded by a brass fender. This is all so posh. We are afraid to speak. It is like being in a library or a museum. Small round dark wood tables covered with framed photographs, all of old people who must be dead by now, are in front of the couch and beside the chairs. She picks up one of the photographs and shows it to us. This is my husband, a naval captain who is out at sea. Because he is away I am allowing you to stay at our home. China knickknacks collected over the years are everywhere. There are so many things to dust or be broken. On one wall, there is a dark wood Welch cupboard. It has a big silver tray and a painted bone china tea service. The china cups hang from hooks and fancy painted plates and tureens line the shelves. It is all very overwhelming. Mrs Allen tells us that these dishes are rarely used except for high days and holidays and for us to never touch them. Two very ornate floor lamps with silk tasselled shades are on either side of the couch under the lace curtained window which looks out from the front of the house onto the garden. Across from the couch on the other wall is a small chapel organ with all the pull stops and big foot pedals. A fancy carved mahogany music stand holds hymn books. There is a round swivel stool that has been polished to a high gleam; I am sure by numerous bottoms sitting on it over the years. A dark blue and red, worn, Indian carpet covers the old wide planked hardwood floors in the room. Dark Victorian wallpaper covers the walls. Afraid to move, we stand in the middle of the room fearing that even our breathing might break something. Our house in London seems very bare in comparison with Mrs Allen's. She informs us that we are never to enter this room uninvited and that any invitation must come from her. She needn't fret about that, we don't need to be told twice. She turns to leave and beckons us to follow her back through the curtained door which she closes quietly behind us. We are now in the pink and white flowered passage which leads to the leaded window paned front door. There is a door mat in front of it where hopefully the letters from home will fall when slipped through the letterbox. I can't read yet but Rita will read them to me when they come. I know that they will come but how will they know where we are? I whisper to Rita; you have to post the postcard that they gave us with our new address on it as soon as possible. She nods in agreement. Mrs Allen tells us to follow her and she will show us the rooms that we are to be allowed in. We begin to ascend a white railed staircase just in side of the front door. She tells us that she would like us to call her Auntie Phyllis. I don't want to call her that. She is not my auntie. I will just try not to call her anything. At the top of the stairs she shows us the bathroom. It is all green with an old copper hot water gas geyser which will fill the bathtub and we look like we are in dire need of a bath right now. She tells us that we will bathe once a week and on a Saturday night so we will take a bath tonight. The reason being for Saturday night is that we have to be very clean and tidy for chapel on Sundays. She tells us that everything must be kept immaculately clean like we have never used it. Next door to the bathroom is a small room with a separate loo with a long hanging chain to pull to flush. It smells strongly of disinfectant. The walls are painted shiny green enamel. High up is a small window that is open. It is cold in here. The window, we are told, is to be left open at all times, in all weather, bad or good, cold or hot. Auntie Phyllis says now I will now show you where you girls will sleep. Sleep, it sounds surreal. We need sleep desperately and to finally be on our own to talk about where we are and how scared we are. There are two bedrooms at the back of the house off of the landing. Mr and Mrs Allen's room of which she tells us not to go into on any account and the other bedroom which she tells us is her son, Edward's room. He is away like his father serving his country. She mentions to us that if he was home she would not have been able to take us in, but then added, everybody has to do their part you know and we are her contribution to the war effort. Our room is in the front of the house off of the upper landing. It is quite large with low gabled windows in the eves looking out over the hillside to the village far below. It is sparsely furnished with two narrow single beds, each topped with feather eiderdowns. The feathered eiderdowns remind me of home. She shows us covered chamber pots under each bed and tells us we are responsible for emptying them each morning into the outside loo. We are not to use the upstairs lavatory during the night after we go to bed because of too much noise from the cistern flushing. Across the room from the beds is a large mirror fronted wardrobe for our suitcases and our hanging clothes. There is a chest of drawers with a small wood framed mirror, a white and brown washbowl and a jug for water for our morning ablutions. My maid Mary, a local village girl who comes in the mornings to do housework, will leave you a large enamel white jug of hot water outside your bedroom door every morning for you to wash with. White towels are hanging on a wooden standing towel rack by the washbowl alongside a white china soap dish with a bar of soap.

Please do not come down to breakfast until you are washed, teeth cleaned, beds made and dressed. And by her tone I know that she means it. The old wood floors look cold with just a little frayed rug between the beds. She continues, the room is to be used only to sleep in. No reading, laying or playing on the beds other than if you are sick or it is bedtime. I hope that my doll Heather is allowed to sit on the bed. I can't wait to get her out of the suitcase. She doesn't like being in the dark. She is scared of the dark like I am. We hear a door closing downstairs. Mrs Allen says that will be Oliver bringing your suitcases in. She calls down to him to wipe his feet and bring them upstairs. I am so excited. Heather is here. Oliver does as he is bidden and Mrs Allen gives him some money as he touches his cap and says thanks missus. He tries not to look at us but we know that he wants to so that he can tell his family that he saw some of the Cockney evacuees from London. He turns to leave, clomping off back down the stairs. Mrs Allen tells us to unpack quickly and come down stairs. I am going down to put the kettle on and get tea, she says but first she removes our identity labels from our coats. You won't need these for a while. I will hang your coats and gas masks on the hall tree downstairs. She finally leaves. We are on our own. Rita unpacks our school clothes and underwear. Not too much to be done really. We fold our Sunday dresses carefully for tomorrow and put our straw hats and gloves in the bottom of the wardrobe. Our nightgowns are placed under our pillows on the bed and I carefully take Heather out and place her on my pillow. She is so happy. I can see a smile on her face. I give her a kiss. Rita hangs our dressing gowns on the back of the bedroom door and puts our slippers by our beds. The squire's wife Margaret bought the dressing gowns for us just before we left. Finished, we go out on the landing to look for the bathroom. We wash our hands and faces very quietly being careful not to splash or make a mess. We whisper when we talk. Are we to use the indoor loo or the outdoor loo? I have already forgotten what the rules for it are so we both decide that we either hold it or use the outdoor loo because pulling on the hanging chain handle up here would give it away. Mrs Allen calls to us, tea is ready. We go down. She is toasting large fat slices of bread on a long pronged fork by the fire. A steaming cheese concoction from an iron saucepan on the Agar stove is put on top of the bread which she tells us is called Welsh rarebit. We sit down at the table. She pours milk from a blue and white china pitcher into large china mugs. The Welsh rarebit is hot and very delicious but we are so tired that our appetites have disappeared. But we struggle on as Mrs Allen tells us it is a sin to leave food on your plate when other people in England and the rest of the world are going hungry. We are finally excused from the table and are told to follow Mrs Allen upstairs to the bathroom. She lights the gas copper geyser which she says must never be touched by us. We hear a loud whoosh as she lights it. She starts to run water into the big claw foot bathtub. A big rubber stopper is put in the drain. Water comes steaming out of the geyser spout. She adds a couple of pieces of glass like soda lumps to the water to soften it, just like Mum does at home. When about an inch of hot water is in the cold tap on the tub is turned on to cool the water and add the other remaining half inch. Mrs Allen tells us to get on with it, me taking my bath first. She tells Rita to tend to me and to call when we are done and she will then run the bath for Rita. My sister tells me to get undressed and get in. She goes to get my nightie, dressing gown and slippers. The bathtub is quite high and takes some time for me to get in. Finally in, I sit down and it is like sitting in a big puddle. Rita gets the flannel and soap and does the best she can. She gets soap in my eyes when she scrubs my face with the flannel to get off the purple disinfectant and of course, I cry because it hurts and stings. She gets cross with me. Oh how I wish that

Gladys and Janet were here. I miss them so much. We had lots of water and no soap in the eyes and they would cuddle me when I got out of the bath by wrapping me in a big white, warm fluffy towel. But that is not happening tonight. My sister helps me out of the bath and hands me a stiff small towel to dry myself with. I do so as quickly as I can. It is so very chilly in here. Rita closes the window over the bath but it is still cold. I am shivering and have goose bumps. She helps me on with my nightie. She jokingly calls me chubby face as my neck pops up from the opening in my nightie. She says it must be all of that good butter and cream at Squire Trelawney's. I look down at my short little legs and feet. They do look a little chubbier than they used to. We have both gained some much needed weight from staying at the Squire's and Lady Margaret's. We didn't just gain weight. We gained their love when we thought that there was none after we left London. Rita tells me to jump into bed and say my prayers. How good it feels to be in bed. She tucks Heather and me in. No hair to brush tonight. There isn't that much to brush. There is a low lit oil lamp in our bedroom. She leaves it on and says that she will be back after her bath. I hear her calling out to Mrs Allen. I do hope she hurries back. After all she is all I have and it must be so hard for her to love me when I am such a handful at times. I close my eyes tightly and try to see Mummy and Daddy's faces but I can't remember what my parents look like. I try and try. I can smell my mother's scent and see her beautiful hands that used to tuck me in. I can hear my father's laugh and see his thick curly hair but I can't see their faces. I try so hard to conjure them up in my mind but they won't come. As I begin to drift off I wonder how my brother is doing tonight. Is he lying in his bed thinking of us and home and missing Mum and Dad? He would never tell us but I am sure that he is. I miss Len. I feel my eyes getting heavy and I know that I am going to sleep. In my dreams my Mum and Dad come to me but there are no faces. I am screaming, Mummy, Mummy, Daddy. I know that they are there in my dreams but there faces won't come. Will I ever be able to remember them again? I so desperately want to feel the warmth that came with the special magical smiles on the faces of my parents that told me that I was loved without words ever having to be spoken.

I wake. It is morning. My sister and I never got to talk last night. I look over at Rita's bed and see her short, short curly hair sticking out from under the covers. I am so glad that she is still with me. I hear a soft knock on our bedroom door. Good Morning. It is Mary. Your hot water be outside your door. You have an hour till breakfast to be washed and dressed for church. With that I hear her going back down the stairs. Rita rolls over and groans. It is another day, another place and another new experience. Are we ready for it? If we don't get up we will never know and besides it is Sunday. What can go wrong?

SUNDAY, A DAY OF REST AND HOW!

We wash and clean our teeth. The sun is warm and streaming in the windows under the eaves. It feels so good. We put on our Sunday dresses and our best shoes, clean socks and underwear. We put our dirty disinfectant soiled clothes in the laundry basket. I don't care if I never see them again. I want to forget about yesterday but how can you ever forget? When brushing your hair you are reminded about what happened. I look for the first time in the three way mirror on the dressing table. It looks like it was cut with blunt sheers. I hate it so much. I look ugly. How could anyone in the village ever want us? Rita comes over to me and put her arms around me. I can see her face in the mirror. Not to worry Sheila, it will grow back fast. Rita's looks kind of pretty with all of her curls, like Shirley Temple. All of my curls are gone and my hair just sticks out all over the place. Well I guess I have to think of the benefits. No more Rita tugging and pulling on it when she is brushing all of the tangles out. Every morning I used to grizzle, moan and fidget the whole time. I hated it. I am quite sure that Rita also is delighted with this event. We make funny faces in the mirror and start giggling. Rita tickles me. It feels good to laugh but it doesn't last long. Mary is knocking on the door again, only much louder now, to be heard over our frivolity. Mrs Allen wants you downstairs and dressed immediately. We will be right there we chorus back. Rita hands me my straw hat and gloves. Here put your hat on it will cover your hair. I pull it down on my head. It is now too big with no hair. It rests on

191

my ears and nearly covers my eyes. I cross my eyes and put my tongue out and we start laughing again as we go down the stairs. Maybe it won't be so bad here at Park house after all. We go down the stairs and into the kitchen where the table is set for breakfast. Umm, could it be bacon, eggs and fried bread but I don't smell any of those smells wafting up? We are told to sit down and I am told to take my church meeting hat off. Mrs Allen says we don't wear hats in the house; we only cover our heads in the house of the Lord. Shredded wheat is poured into our bowls and cold milk is poured onto it. Mary is toasting bread in the Agar fire. We are told to bow our heads while Mrs Allen says Grace. We don't say Grace at home. I suppose that is why we are as Bess always said, heathens. It goes on for what seems like an awfully long time. She finally finishes and tells us to eat with no talking at the table, ever. Oh, no. This is torture for me. I am such a chatterbox and always getting into trouble for it. It is so quiet in the kitchen, just the clinking of spoons against the sides of our bowls. It is torture. I know that the others can hear me crunching on my shredded wheat. It is echoing in my head. I try to do it more quietly. If it had hot milk on it like at Trewlawny Lodge and home you wouldn't be able to hear it because then it goes all mushy. I look at Rita and she looks at me. We don't have to talk. Our eyes say all there is to say. Mrs Allen doesn't see our looks. Her eyes are down with her thick pebble glasses on. I believe that she is either reading the bible or a prayer book. I bet she doesn't miss anything with those glasses. Rita and I hurry up and ask if we can be excused. She looks up and looks over at our plates and tells us yes. Please go up and make your beds and bring your chamber pots down, if used and empty them into the outside lavatory. Do not run. Please walk quietly and never ever run in the house. We quietly go up the stairs, returning to our room. We make our beds. I hug Heather tightly and put her back on my pillow. She can't go to church. Rita helps me with my bed.

We talk softly in whispers about the rules that Mrs Allen has. Did you use your chamber pot she asks? I hesitatingly say yes, not wanting to tell her. Why does she have to ask? Oh, Sheila, can't you go all night like I do? Really, you have to try. I can't. I have tried. I get so nervous I have to go real bad. Well you are going to have to try harder, she says because I am not taking it down for you. You are going to have to do it yourself and maybe that will teach you to have more control and to not guzzle milk or tea before bed. I don't want to have to take it down but I know that I have to. I reach down under the bed and slowly pull out the China rose studded Poe being very careful not to spill. Can I just put it into the upstairs lav up here and flush it? No, Sheila. Mrs Allen said no using the upstairs lav during the day. You know the rules. Blow the rules. I hate rules. At five years old there should be no rules. I bend and pick up the pot very carefully. It is heavy. Maybe my sister is right. Maybe I will learn control. I seriously wonder. I start making the slow treacherous journey down the stairs. Rita comes down behind me. She is smart. She doesn't want to get her Sunday best besmirched. I feel utterly humiliated and absurd at the same time as I climb very carefully, one at a time, down the stairs in my lavender silk dress with cap sleeves, my white straw Sunday hat with lavender ribbons and white short gloves clutching a Poe closely to my chest. How ridiculous this must look. I dare not spill a drop and I will never use it again, ever, I vow for the rest of my life. I want to cry but I just bite my lip, my lower lip. I am finally down the stairs and I now only have to walk through the kitchen and out the back door to the outside lav. Mary is at the sink.
She turns and looks. Mrs Allen opens the back door for me. She looks disapprovingly at me. I feel her looking at my hat. I know I shouldn't wear it in the house but I couldn't carry it in my hand. My face is a bright fiery red. I feel the colour creeping up from my neck. I vow I will never ever use this

chamber pot ever again. I will hold it until my eyes cross. This has to be the most embarrassing event in my short life, so far. I had thought yesterday was. I am beginning to realize in the past two days that evacuation is now very ugly and demoralizing. We are waiting for Mrs Allen to leave for church. I am excited. We will soon get out of the house and get to see Len (not Boysey anymore). I can't wait to talk to him. I hope he is okay. He looked so sad when we parted yesterday. There is a knock on the back door. Mrs Allen opens it. It is Betty, all dressed for church. Rita and I crowd to the door. The sisters aren't with her. Apparently they don't go to church so they must be heathens too. Hurrah, something I understand. Needless to say Rita is so happy and we are all talking at once. She asks if she can take Betty upstairs to show her our room but Mrs Allen doesn't go along with that request at all. Today is Sunday, a day of prayer and rest and besides she says; I do not allow children to play in the house. We are told to sit quietly and wait until Mrs Allen is ready to leave. Rita and Betty can chatter on the walk down to the chapel in the village. I know that they are bursting at the seams. We sit around the table looking at one another with tightly sealed lips. I feel this nervous giggle beginning to rise from deep down in my belly but one long stern look from Mrs Allen quells it quickly. She announces that she is at fault for not telling us earlier the house rules for Sundays, the Lord's Day, but she will explain them to us now and will expect us to respect them explicitly. Number one; we do not play games of any kind. No other children in the house from Sunday morning until Monday AM. She looks at Betty seriously. Maybe we can go over to Betty's house. I hope that the rules over at her house are better than ours. We will be allowed to read sitting on chairs in the kitchen but that doesn't do me any good because I can't read. Number two; no talking unless absolutely necessary. Number three; there is no cooking on Sundays. The Sunday joint, roast beef is put into a baking tin on Saturday evening, having been bought the same day at the butchers. Vegetables are peeled and prepared also the night before to put around the joint. Yorkshire pudding is also prepared early and allowed to be beaten early Sunday morning. The baking tins are then carried down the hill on the way to chapel and taken to the local bakery and put in the big ovens with all of the other villager's joints. The owners name is put on the side of the tins so as to cause no mishaps such as someone getting somebody else's choice meat and you getting a bit of old mutton. You then, on emerging from chapel, pick up your dinner which is ready and take it back up the hill to be eaten forthwith. How strange is that? The washing up from Sunday is done on Mondays when Mary comes. Number four; you will attend chapel three times, morning service 10:00 AM, afternoon service 3:00 PM and evening service at 6:00 PM. My goodness, that is going to be a lot of hill climbing, three times down and three times up, and a lot of praying. Number five; no writing letters home on Sunday and when you do during the week they are not to be sealed until I have read them and I will post them if appropriate. As a side note, I will be writing to your parents every two weeks to tell them of your adjustment, health and of any difficulties that I am having with you and what appropriate punishment I will meet out. I think to myself, why is she so strict, but one good thing that is to come out of this, Mum and Dad will at last know where we are and can write to us. I think it must be terribly sad for them to not know where we are. It is like we just disappeared into nowhere. They must wonder if we are safe and if we are being treated kindly? I hear Mrs Allen's voice again. Rule number six; I wonder to myself, what are the rest of the days going to be like. Are there going to be weekday rules too? Rule no six; no wireless is to be played from Saturday night until Monday morning and with that being said, Mrs Allen in her white flowered dress puts on her

195

matching straw hat with the red cherries on it and white gloves. She looks quite posh. I constantly wonder if she can see us very clearly behind her pebble glasses. I have not seen her without them but I am betting she doesn't miss anything. Mary pulls on a navy beret over her brown bobbed hair. It sort of matches her shapeless long blue dress with black lace up shoes that complete her outfit. Not quite as posh as Mrs Allen. We are finally ready to go. The baking tins are all carefully covered in red and white checked tea towels and are picked up. I am so glad I don't have to carry any. After all I did my chore early on with the chamber pot. I guess that is one good thing about being small. We are off down the hill and it is such a wonderful morning, sun, blue skies with scudding clouds and a light breeze. It feels so good to be outside. I run down the steps and check to see if there are any monkeys in the monkey tree, no, not today. On my way down the path and out of the front gate I start to run down the hill to be ahead of the group but I am suddenly pulled back by my arm and told to walk like a little lady and not like a little city hooligan. Mrs Allen asks; what will the neighbours think. She holds on tightly to my hand and it hurts. Please, I must not have known that this was rule number seven. Other villagers are coming out of their cottages with their Sunday joints and Yorkshire puddings in hand. It makes for quite a scene. It is like a street parade. The women and girls wearing dresses, straw hats and gloves the men and boys wearing their ill-fitting suits, starched collars and polished boots are all parading to church. There are other evacuees from our group straggling behind their host families. We wave but dare not call out. I wonder if the same Sunday rules that we have apply to them. We are to find out, fear of God and superstitions are found everywhere in these Cornish villages, such a different culture to ours. We feel like we are worlds apart. Pleasantries are passed around. Glares, stares and tongues poked out at us from the local children. At the same time their Mums and Dads are looking curiously at us Londoners, as if to say; who are they? Is it really necessary for them to be here? I am sure they wish that we would go away. Are we worth ten shilling and sixpence a week to them? I doubt it. I believe some of them would pay ten shilling and sixpence to ship us back but as I learn later there are those who really enjoy helping, are loving to us and pleased to have evacuees in their homes. They are glad to do their bit to help in the war effort. I mean look how lucky we were in Plynt at Squire Trelawney's; we were welcomed with open loving arms. I feel very lonely for them right now. Whoever is with them now in our place are very fortunate. I wonder if the family thinks of us. The parade continues down the street toward the bakery for all of the dinners to be dropped off. It is a very busy place. We wait outside and gaze through the open door. I see my brother standing with an assembled group of classmates. I call to him, Len. He doesn't appear to hear me. I drop Rita's hand and run over to the group. I am so glad to see him. I have a big smile on my face. His back is to me and I tug on his blazer, Len, Len. He looks over his shoulder and down at me. A frown crosses his face. Hello Sheila, are you doing okay? Yes, I am but I miss you. Can't you come and live with us, please. He acts embarrassed to see me. It just isn't on to talk to a girl, especially your baby sister in front of your mates. He bends over as if to retie his shoe and says gruffly so as not to be overheard, I'll talk to you after church. Go on, go on now, Rita is waiting for you. I want so desperately to talk some more but he turns his back to me and turns to his mates and says something that I can't hear and they all start laughing. Unwillingly, I go back to Rita who is already yelling to me to get back over to her. Standing outside the bakery we can feel the heat on our faces from the big bread ovens. The villagers queue up in orderly fashion and are quickly helped by the bakers and are then on their way to chapel. Why are the bakers allowed to cook? Are they heathens? The bakery has got to be extra busy today from all the new additions to families. We wait with Mrs Allen until our Sunday dinner is left off. That being done we walk down a few doors to the chapel. People are congregating outside, talking and gossiping over the amazing events of the last two days. Nothing like this has ever happened before. Outsiders to their village are a rarity. Everyone turns to look as the evacuees begin to assemble. I am so happy that our teachers are here waiting for us. I see Ms Green and wave to her. It is so good to see them and hear our familiar London dialect. The Cornish dialect is so foreign to us. We have to listen very carefully to understand it at all. All of our teachers are billeted in rooms above the one and only century's old pub in the village, down in the harbour called the Blue Anchor. Umm, umm, pub grub. Why am I always thing of food? Food has become a very good friend, in fact, my only friend other than Heather. Mr Martin, our head teacher and the others tell all of the evacuees to stay outside and wait until all of us are present. Our teachers, whom I didn't know until evacuation, were to have been my teachers this autumn in London if the war had not come. Now they will be my teachers starting tomorrow. For the first time in my young life I will be joining the children of my age when I attend infant school on Monday. They must feel a great weight on their shoulders, being responsible for over one hundred children. Our teachers are all single so in many cases we are their only family now, whether they want to or not but they now have to be teachers and surrogate parents. Mrs Allen, with all of the other villagers goes on into the chapel. We evacuees are so excited to see one another again, like long lost families. The teachers call out to us to line up, two abreast, and ask us to follow them into the sanctuary and tell us that at no time is there to be any talking. There we are. What a group. The boys in their grey worsted knee shorts, grey knee socks, matching blazers with pale grey shirts and red and grey striped ties, their grey school caps with the Heber Road emblem on them perched atop their shorn heads. We girls did not have to wear uniforms on Sundays but come Monday we would all look the same. You would not be able to confuse us with the village children who do not wear school uniforms. Everyone knows who we are, evacuees, down from London. We are different. Some of us are short, some tall, thin ones, fat ones, others with spectacles, a few snotty nosed ones. What a group. We will have to stick together to survive. We are a band of evacuees. We line up as instructed. We five year old boys and girls are to be in front of the line and the older boys and girls to the rear. Of course, girls line up with girls and boys line up with boys. As usual, lots of pushing and giggling. A fat little boy tries to stand with me. I tell him to go away to be with the other boys. I hate boys, except for my brother. I am finally paired with another little girl. We look at one another, questioningly, she with her large dark eyes. I saw her on the bus to Polperro. She was one of the ones who were sick all over the floor. I can still smell the vomit. I reach out for her hand. She looks surprised but puts her warm hand in mine. It feels comforting. Our fingers clasp together. What is your name, I ask? Angela, Angela Poulter. Now I remember her because she was with me when our hair was cut off. She tells me she has a brother Brian back in the line and she wants to be with him but they won't let me. I know, I tell her, my brother Len is back there too and my older sister Rita who I tell her is mean and cross, well I guess not all the time, she always wants to be with her best friend Betty. She laughs. She suddenly looks happier. I wish I had a sister she says. No you don't I say, they are too bossy. What is your name she asks? Sheila, Sheila Harvey. We will be going to school tomorrow she says. Will you sit next to me? It will be my first school. I will I say. I am scared, are you? Yes, I am too. But at least we will have each other. She is right and today I have made my first girlfriend ever.

DOES GOD REALLY LOVE US?

The congregation is seated, still and hushed as we enter the outer sanctuary through double doors that lead into the main chapel. The villagers turn their heads to stare as we strangers from London start to join them. Stairway's on either side of the hallway lead up to a gallery overlooking the main floor. The older children are told to ascend each of the stairways in pairs and to be very quiet. A lot of the children in our group have never been to church in their young lives except maybe once to be christened and they don't have a clue how to act. Some are whacked on the head with a ruler wielded by the teachers who are going up with them, all in order to let them know what silence means. Soon all you can hear is the shuffling and clumping of leather shoes as they go up the steps. Len waves as he and the others leave and I see my sister with Betty. One teacher remains downstairs, Miss Cartwright. She is quite pretty and young compared to some of the others who look old and cross and completely fed up with the whole evacuee situation. The five year olds are to remain downstairs but I want to go up the stairs with the others. Why is it I have to miss out on so much just because I am young? Rita and Len get to do everything. The London evacuees are upstairs. The village people and their children are downstairs. I am sure that they will live to regret putting the older evacuees up in the gallery. We infant evacuees sit in the pews allocated us in the main sanctuary. I doubt whether the chapel has ever been this full in all of its years. We children walk two abreast down the centre aisle with Miss Cartwright leading the way. Many inquisitive eyes are boring into the back of our heads. I myself feel as if I have a knot hole in mine. My new friend Angela and I hold on tightly to one another. I am feeling self-conscious. I know that I must be walking strangely. I am so nervous. The silence in the chapel is deafening. It feels like the rest of the congregation are snickering behind our backs. The empty wooden front pews look like they are miles away. I can't wait to sit down and just disappear into the woodwork. I don't look to the right or to the left, just straight ahead. I wonder if the rest of the children feel like me. I am sure they do. The deafening silence is suddenly broken. A little girl behind me, about my age, starts to cry. I want to go home; I don't want to be here she sobs. It seems to echo through the church hall. She tries to pull away from her partner, fat Derek, who holds onto her and tries to quieten her. My stomach is starting to hurt. Miss Cartwright, our Sunday school teacher, goes back to get her and brings her up front with us. Doesn't that child know that crying isn't allowed? Her mother must not have told her. The child, Mary, continues to snivel. We reach the four long pews on the right side of the church reserved for us. I have an aisle seat. I look down the long row. Miss Cartwright has given Mary something out of her handbag to try to distract her from her sadness and thankfully a hankie to stifle the snivels. It seems to be working. I silently ask, please, please don't cry anymore. It makes me sad and mad. I grit my teeth tightly together. I mustn't cry. It is forbidden. The word of the day is, be brave. In gritting my teeth so hard I accidently bite the edge of my tongue. I can taste the warm, red, salty blood. I swallow it. It takes my mind off of my sadness and I can now concentrate on my stupidity for biting my tongue. I dare to turn my head to look up to the gallery. The junior and senior kids are being ever so quiet but are making funny faces, thumbing noses and poking out tongues. Luckily for them the gallery is behind the parishioners below and they are not seen.

The elders of the church will definitely need to rethink this one. I am sure that the congregation is aware of what is happening behind them and the situation will definitely be brought up at the next village weekly meeting. All is quiet now. A side door suddenly opens on the left side of the raised podium. A choir of men dressed in black, emerges and moves to the empty pews on the stage. They are followed by the vicar. He looks quite friendly. A lot like Fred the butcher, in Dulwich. I certainly hope he doesn't use the same language as Fred. I would always get wide eyed listening to him as I waited with my mother in the queue to get served. He always joked and chatted up all the ladies and if you played the game with him you got the better cuts of meat and more so if you had a pretty turn of the ankle. Fred was a flirt, with his ruddy complexion, white hair, bushy eyebrows and a handlebar moustache that was waxed on the ends. You felt like you wanted to reach up and touch it, but I never did. He wore a straw boater and a dark blue and white striped apron that covered his wide girth. He would wipe his cutting knives on it. But what fascinated me the most were his huge red hands. They looked cold and wet, a bit like dead red fish.

The vicar introduces himself to his new church members. His handlebar moustache seems to droop at the ends. Maybe he doesn't know about the wax that Fred used. He tells us his name is the Reverend Smith and he welcomes us evacuees into the warmth of his bosom and tells us he hopes that we will be able to go back home to reunite with our families soon. His black cassock covers his ample body. His blue eyes twinkle as he blesses his flock. He tells us to look for Hymn 109 in our hymnal, O God our help in ages past. We are to join in the last verse. The men's choir starts to sing accompanied on an old organ similar to the one that is in Mrs Allen's parlour, only much bigger. A lady elder in her straw hat and white gloves

202

starts to play. There is a rude noise as she pumps air into the organ. There are giggles from the gallery and stern looks from the organist and vicar. The music suddenly fills the sanctuary and the choir's voices are raised to the heavens. It is a beauteous sound. The whole congregation is hushed. Even little Mary stops snivelling and listens. It is worth going to meetings just to hear the men's choir. The service continues. Hymns are sung. Prayers are said. Collection plates are passed. The Vicar preaches and asks forgiveness for our putrid souls in a loud tenor voice that carries to the rafters. He prays to God for our safe return to London and an end to this wicked, wicked war. There are a lot of Amens to that on either side of the aisle. We do have a voice after all. We children catch on fast calling out Amens all over the place, warranted or not but the loudest Amens come from the gallery. It has probably been the noisiest service in the church's history (Those rotten evacuees). We are finally sent home being told to be back for afternoon and evening services. We evacuees exit into the bright sunlight and gather outside the church. A wonderful savoury aroma assails our nostrils. We all feel like the Bisto kids sniffing into the wind. It is of course the dinners baking in the big ovens at the bakery. Mr Martin, our head master, rounds us all up to give us instructions for tomorrow, our first day of school. I am so excited about going to school. He tells us where to go, the times of classes and what to bring. No need to bring or carry your gas masks. Everyone shouts, Hip, Hip Hurray. I hate those things. He continues, the school nurse will be in the school to administer cod liver oil and un-reconstituted orange juice. A table spoon of each will be administered to each pupil every day to keep us healthy as our diets had been lacking in London. He tells us, billeting officers will be available every fortnight to help us if we are having a billet problem and that they will try to relocate us if that is the case but I am thinking to myself that a lot of us are not going to know if we have a problem until we have been here for a week or two and will they listen to us if we do or will they just consider it childish complaints. Also the villagers have the choice of getting rid of us if they don't think we are adjusting to their lifestyle or that we are unmanageable and they then may request more manageable children. We are playing a wait and see game. Mrs Allen calls out to us in the crowd and tells us to make sure that we are back at Park house by two PM sharp for dinner. We children are all excited. We are allowed one whole hour to be ourselves. Mr Martin tells us that they are going to take us down to see the harbour and to look around a bit. There is much chatter, excitement and laughter as we feel free for the first time in days. We follow the crowd. Angela and I stay together. Rita and Betty come back to walk with us but they don't really pay much attention to us. They are busy with their own plans. I do ask my sister if I and Angela can go up into the gallery at this afternoon's meeting. You are much too young she says. Only the older children are allowed. She is always so bossy. I will ask my brother when we catch up to him. I ask Betty if she likes her billet. She says it is very nice and that the two sisters are very kind. They make big fishing nets in their front parlour for the Polperro fishermen. Betty asks my sister if she can come over and live with her at the sister's house because that would be so much fun. Rita says that she would give anything to be able to but she can't because she did promise my mother that she would stay with me and not be separated. Ending with, my sister is such a little nuisance. She always says that I am. I am used to it. She always knows the right thing to say but I can't think about that now. We are off to the harbour. We skip, run and walk down the cobblestone street. We are free. Life is good. The seagulls are screeching over our heads. It gets remarkably louder as we turn to the right and the harbour spreads out before us like a giant half circle with a big grey granite breakwater that

204

protects the harbour and village from the choppy, grey, cold Atlantic waters. On the left side of the harbour a small winding cobblestone road rises up with little stone whitewashed cottages looking over the road into the harbour. Len tells me this is where he is staying, in one of the fishermen's cottages with the Gillises whose livelihood is fishing which is the mainstay of Polperro. On the far side of the harbour are the fish sheds where all of the freshly caught fish are brought to be processed for the fish shops and for sale to villagers and hotels. A busy place but it is empty and quiet today as it is a day of rest but the smell is strong and extremely fishy. Big empty fish baskets line the quay. The noise of the gulls fills the air as they look for any remaining morsels of fish. There are many fishing boats rocking at anchor, as the tide is in, just waiting for the tide and first light of morning to go back out again. We walk around to the fish sheds and up a steep path to the cliffs. We are standing on the lower part of the cliff and looking out toward the open ocean. What an incredible sight. Way below there is a beach with tidal pools. We can't wait to get rid of our shoes and socks. There is a mad rush for the stone steps cut out of the cliff side down to the beach. It is very steep and I don't like heights. We hear a shrill whistle being blown three times. We know what that means, full stop, but nobody listens. Some of the older kids are already halfway down the steps to the beach below, calling up to the rest of us to come on, hands reaching up to help the less brave. I am so afraid that I am going to fall down these steep stairs with so many children pushing and shoving. Angela and I sit on the stairs and go down one at a time. That way it feels safer. We get stepped on a lot of times as they step over and around us but our complaints don't bother them. They just keep on going. All we can see is a sea of moving legs which suddenly come to a stop as the whistle blows even louder. We look up to see our teachers standing on the top of the cliff face. Mr

Martin is standing on a bench so that we can all see him, blowing his whistle loudly. He then yells to us to get back up, right now. There are many groans of disappointment and a lot of grumbling. A lot of the boys have already reached the beach and are waving back up to us and hooting and hollering and jumping up and down. We all wave and beckon them to come back up. Kids are scrambling back up the cliff. The older kids are getting very brave and not using the steps, just climbing the rocks. There are patches of gorse and wild flowers in the crevices that they can grab hold of to help them. Some of them climbing on all fours, they look like gambling mountain goats. Angela and I, scared as we are, go back up the way we went down, on our bottoms, one stair at a time. Our nickers must be quite grey by now and we only get to change them once a week. Everyone is voicing their disappointment that we can't go down on the beach and play in the tidal pools. In a way, I am glad, because I am very frightened of that cliff. I was afraid that I was going to fall. I would never tell that to anyone because they would then call me scaredy cat. I won't even tell Angela, my new best friend. When everyone is assembled back on top of the cliff we dust ourselves off and there are many among us with scraped knees. Mr Martin announces, we can only go to the beach as a group and never alone. It will only be allowed after school during the weekdays and on Saturdays if our caregivers allow. We will be taken on nature walks two or three times a week or more as classroom space will not always be available, with an exception. There it is, always an exception. The infants will not get to go as it is too dangerous and their balance is not as good. I hate that. That means that I will have to stay behind while Len and Rita go and have all the fun. Oh, how I wish, that I was old like them. We are then told to go back to our billets to have lunch and get clean for afternoon chapel. We do look quite dishevelled with boys knee socks hanging around their ankles, their Sunday shirts hanging out, scraped knees and hands, girls Sunday straw hats askew and a few of them missing having been blown over the cliff. As we go back down the steep lane we see a quay outside the harbour with fishing boats tied up to it, with the ever present seagulls circling and screeching overhead. The water is always high enough there for the boats to go out and fish any time of the day and if storms are forecast the boats are moved back into the safety of the inner harbour. We have learned a lot today. I didn't even know what a harbour was yesterday, or looked like, let alone a Cornish fishing boat flying a black and gold Cornish flag. I had always believed that there was only one flag that meant anything, the Union Jack. It was like being worlds away from home. Back home, our grey brick row houses , street after street of them, all looking the same, very few trees except in the parks, very few open spaces, many grey rainy days lashing the houses, making them appear even darker and greyer, people lining up for food at the green grocers, butchers and bakers and dairy and having to leave empty handed and disappointed when things ran out and you were turned away, the smell of the trains, crowded buses, wet umbrellas and damp steamy clothes as you stood packed in the aisles of the bus. I can still smell it and to me it is very comforting. So being in Cornwall is so very different from what we are used to. It is beautiful here, open and clean, cliffs, beaches, cottages, the ocean, no crowds, no air raids, no running to crowded smelly shelters, much more food but they don't have the one thing we miss the most and that we all crave and are hungry for, our families, mums, dads, grandparents, aunts and uncles. We are lonely. Be our homes ever so humble there is never any place like your own home. Will the homesickness ever go away?

<u>Note:</u>

Cornish men's choirs are an important part of Cornish life and to this day continue as they travel all over the world to entertain and compete. Their recordings are always very popular and in demand.

AN EVENTFUL SUNDAY AFTERNOON

Sunday dinner is served. The no talking rule at the table is observed. The only sound is the clicking of the cutlery against the plates. It always kills me not to talk. I can't eat my greens, I hate them. The only thing worse is liver. Mrs Allen excuses Rita from the table and I am told to sit there by myself till I eat them. The grease from the gravy and the batter pudding has congealed onto the cold greens. Two hours later, the greens are still not eaten but it is time to return to chapel for the afternoon Sunday school. Even chapel is better than greens. Mrs Allen finally excuses me from the table but tells me they will be there when we get back and I will have to eat them for my tea while she and Rita will have bread and butter, cakes and jam. She hates me, I know it. I don't even get my afters, tinned peaches and evaporated milk. I had to watch Rita and Mrs Allen eat theirs. My mouth is watering. Why am I so stubborn? My greens sit on my plate. It is so disgusting. How could my sister like greens? But she is probably the smart one; she got the peaches and cream. We meet Betty and walk down to the village. Mrs Allen stays home to take her Sunday afternoon nap. At Sunday school we are split into groups with Sunday school teachers from the village. They tell us stories from the bible and show us pictures of Jesus. I enjoy it a lot especially the story the story of Joseph and his coat of many colours. There is only one problem, seven year old Derek Evans. Why did I get stuck in Sunday school with him? He is pimply faced, fat and his knee socks are always hanging around his ankles but worst of all he picks boogers out of his nose and eats them in front of me. He teases me with them and asks me if I want one. He holds one out on his finger when no one is looking and says, if you don't eat one I will hit you. He says they are salty and tasty like crisps. I hate him. Angela tells me he is teasing me because he likes me. I now hate all boys, especially Derek. He is a disgusting little boy. I choose to ignore him. We are given little scripture cards by our teachers, with a different scripture on each card and told to learn it for next Sunday at which time we will be asked to read them out loud. But, I can't read yet. Don't they know that? Then we are told that those who can't read are to have their older sister or brother or adopted family member to read them to us, no excuse accepted. Angela and I look at one another with tortured looks. We are finally released into the bright afternoon sunshine. Our own London teachers do not attend Sunday school but they will have to be at evening chapel. Why shouldn't they be punished too? I mean why should we have all the fun? Angela asks me to walk with her to her billet in the village but Rita says no because we need to talk to Len to see if he is all right. Mum said we have to watch out for one another. Angela and I say goodbye. She runs off to catch up with her brother. They are both billeted together. We find Len in the noisy and pushing crowd outside the chapel. I am so glad to see him but he looks sad. I miss him. Rita asks him how he likes where he is billeted. He is living in a fisherman's cottage overlooking the harbour. He says that Mrs Gillis is nice enough, always scrubbing floors and gutting fish, and she hasn't much time for him and that even though it is summer the cottage is very cold inside and that the thick walls are always wet and damp. He says that his clothes always feel wet and cold. He has a narrow bed in a tiny room he shares with one of the grownup sons, David. He says he is afraid of Mr Gillis and that Mr Gillis and David came home last night after the Blue Anchor Pub closed and were cursing and yelling in the small dark kitchen. Len says he huddled under the bed clothes very frightened. He heard David stumbling into bed smelling very boozy, reminds me of my paternal grandmother. He doesn't want to go back there. He is afraid David might miss his own bed and land on him. Rita tells him not to worry, we will walk back with him to the cottage before we go back to Park place and that he should wait and see if things get better. Maybe it is just a one-time thing, but if it isn't we will talk to Mr Martin about getting him moved, if that is at all possible. My sister, brother, Betty and I walk through the village and up the winding Coombe lane curving and overlooking the other side of the harbour. The small whitewashed Coomb cottages look down onto the beautiful harbour sparkling below in the late afternoon sunshine, so serene on this beautiful Sunday afternoon. What could ever be wrong here? As we walk up the empty street lace curtains on front windows, occasionally and discreetly twitch aside and quickly flick back. We are being observed. We are being observed by curious eyes. We come to a stone whitewashed cottage called Seagull cottage, aptly named for the seagulls perched on the sooty chimney top. This is where Len is staying. There is a small front garden with a low stone wall surrounding it and a peeling wooden ramshackle gate that is hanging open on one hinge. A large skinny black cat is stretched out on the front step soaking up the afternoon sun. He raises his head and looks at us lazily. A few struggling geraniums are trying to grow in the sandy earth. Two grubby lace curtained windows front the house, one on either side of the blue painted front door with a big black door knocker and letter box. Rita, Betty and I sit on the low wall looking down into the harbour. The sun feels good on our pale faces and our whiter than white legs. Len stands there uncomfortably. He doesn't want to go knock on the door. I feel that he is afraid of what is behind it. Why can't he go around to the back of the house like we do at Mrs Allen's? So who is going to knock on the front door? I am certainly not going to do it. My excuse is that I can't reach it and I am too young and Betty isn't family so it is all down to Rita. She does come in handy, being the eldest. For once I don't mind being the youngest. She asks Len why he can't use the back door. Mrs Gillis doesn't want anyone coming in un-announced unless it is her sons or her husband. Poor Len, I know he must miss Frobisher and the gate house and the warmth of Bess's kitchen. I do too but that is in the past. No more to be. Polperro is so very beautiful but also a little scary. Will we ever belong? I don't think so. Betty, Len and I huddle at the gate as Rita walks up the short path to the front door. She walks slowly turning once to look at us. We bravely motion her on from our safe haven. The three of us crouch down so no one can see us. I am so nervous and afraid that someone might jump out of the door at me. I bet Rita's knees are knocking. She gets to the front door and reaches up to bang with the knocker. At that precise moment the door swings inward. Rita falls to the ground halfway in and halfway out of the entrance. A very surprised Mrs Gillis stands looking down at her. Well you'd better get up and come in child the proper way like normal folks do. Rita pulls herself up. Her face is red with embarrassment. She beckons to us hiding by the gate to come up to the front door and join her. We want to run but our feet are frozen to the ground. Betty shoves Len and I forward. She stays behind the gate. Mrs Gillis calls to us, well get in here all of you, don't waste any more of my time. We go into the dark passageway. Would we ever come back out? There is a smell of fish cooking. Not frying like fish and chips but boiling. Len hates fish. She ushers us into a small parlour. Grimy lace curtains cover the windows not letting much light in. A small shaft of sunlight shows the dust upon the wooden chairs and table. Two worn overstuffed chairs face a small coal black fireplace. There had been a fire in it but it is cold now and the old ashes haven't been cleaned out. The walls look like they had been painted yellow donkey's years ago. The smoke and soot from the oil lamps and fires over the years have darkened it to a sticky brownish colour. A single fly paper hangs from the bare bulb ceiling light with many dead flies stuck to it. A newly doomed one is still struggling to get free. Its transparent wings struggle to flutter but its legs are glued strongly to the paper. The will to survive is strong, even in a black fly. We don't sit down, we are not invited to. Mrs Gillis's thin long face twitches either with anger or with nervousness with us being there. I need to go to the lavatory but I am afraid to ask if I can use it. The silence is broken in the room by Rita. We just came to walk our brother home and see where he lives. We hope you don't mind. Our Mum and Dad will want to know how he is when I write to them. Mrs Gillis retorts; now that you have seen it you can leave. I am sure that your guardian will be wondering where you are and what has your brother been telling you she asks? Rita blurts out, oh he hasn't said anything. Poor Len stands there head down, looking miserable. My heart breaks for him. Len asks Mrs Gillis if he can show us his room. I suppose so if you must but do it quickly and be gone. I don't think she means to be so cross. I think she has never had anyone be nice to her. I smile at her but it is not returned. Len takes us back out to the dinghy passage way through to the scullery where the smell of boiled fish overcomes you. There is a scrubbed wooden table and four mismatched chairs, an oil lamp and an old small gas stove with bubbling pots atop, some crockery on an old cupboard and a stone sink with a single pump spigot complete the kitchen. A window looks out onto the back garden of the house. Len tells me the lavatory is outside but I am too scared to go. I will just fidget and wait. Len's room is off the kitchen at the back of the house. From his window you can see the

213

craggy cliff beyond the garden out back. It blacks out the sun from coming into the room. Len is right; it is cold in this house. His room is cold and damp. I shiver either from the cold or from having to widdle. There are just two hard looking narrow beds in the room. A row of old nails driven into the wall hold Len's clothes all hung one atop the other. As we look around the room there is water dribbling down the back wall. Rita looks out the small curtain less window. It is coming down from the Cliffside in a steady stream. It is so damp and the air smells musty. Len's small striped pyjamas are folded on his pillow. His bed is neatly made as usual but not the other one. It was climbed out of this morning and will be climbed back into as it is. The sheets are a dinghy grey, all rumpled from weeks of use. The smell of dirty clothes and stale beer pervade the small room. My brother has always been an overly neat person, not at all like me who leaves stuff all over the place; he gets angry when things are untidy. There is no bathroom in the cottage so Len has to wash in the kitchen and pump cold water into the sink. He will get to take a bath once a week in an old tin tub that is bought in from the garden, just like at home. Len wants us to stay but we can't as Mrs Gillis is standing there waiting for us to leave and we have to return to our own billets. She tells us we can come to tea next Sunday if we wish. I don't think that I want to have tea here, besides it doesn't look like they have enough to feed themselves. Rita says that Len can come to tea with us if Mrs Allen says it is all right. We reluctantly say goodbye to Len, telling him we will see him in church this evening for the bloomin third time.

MY FIRST DAY OF SCHOOL

It is Monday morning and I am all excited. I get to go to school for the first time in my life. Rita and I rush through getting washed and our teeth brushed. She also helps me make my bed and get into my school uniform which is a dark green drill slip, white blouse and a green and white tie. I can't tie mine but Rita is good at it. She says it is best to leave it knotted when you take it off and that is a lot easier than tying it every day. I will probably never learn to tie it so I will do the same. I am wearing white ankle socks and black leather lace up shoes. Rita hands me my new satchel that Mum and Dad sent with the rest of our uniforms. I feel so grown up. The finishing touch is my school beret with the badge on front. Rita says, be careful how you act now because everyone will know who you are, an evacuee so what you do can be reported to the head master. She doesn't have to comb or brush my hair because there isn't much left to comb. She has tidied it up with a pair of Mrs Allen's scissors. It is so short. That makes her happy and me too. None of the usual screaming matches. I am ravenously hungry and can't wait to get downstairs and have breakfast. I didn't get tea last evening as I didn't eat those wretched greens. I had to sit on a chair and watch them have fresh bread and butter, strawberry jam and tea and cake. I was so envious. My leftover cold greasy greens were served up on a clean white plate at my place at the table. Again I stubbornly refused to eat them. Rita tried to cajole me into being a good girl for everyone's sake but everyone else doesn't have to eat those wretched greens so I went to bed hungry. I now hate Sundays and I think I always will. Rita is being very nice to me this morning. She even takes the chamber pot down. I think maybe she had to go during the night too and feels a little bit guilty but she would never admit to it. Rita goes ahead of me downstairs. I stay in the bedroom and look in the mirror at myself. I look all grown up at five. I put my dark green blazer on. I look so posh. I wish Mum and Dad could see me. If I look hard enough into the mirror I can imagine them standing behind me in the looking glass, smiling at me. I wave to them. Don't go away. Please stay. I even promise them that I will eat my greens next Sunday to have them stay. I scrunch my eyes hard trying not to cry. When I open them they are both gone. Mrs Allen is calling to me from downstairs. Hurry up Sheila, you will be late for school I hug and kiss Heather and tell her I will tell her all about my first day when I get back. I put her on the pillow. She looks sad. I wish I could put her in my satchel and take her with me. After all I only have two pencils, a ruler and a rubber. There would be plenty of room for her but that would be against the rules. No toys in class. I don't want to get into trouble on the first day. Breakfast is eaten and Mrs Allen hustles us along. I am certain she can't wait to get us out of the house. She is barking orders at Mary. Mary gives us a wink. She understands how things are. She has fixed us each a sandwich for our lunches, which are tucked into our satchels. Mrs Allen reminds Rita to meet me on the corner by the chapel after school and to walk me home. I know that Rita thinks I am a nuisance. Again I am messing with her and Betty's fun but as I am in the infant school I will be getting out earlier than Rita and I will have to wait for her. I hope desperately that she won't forget me. I don't want to have to walk up that long lane by myself. I have never walked alone before. Mum, Dad and Nanny have always been around for me. Only the infants, five through seven, have to go to the village school with the village children. There is no room for the older students there. They will go to the chapel for special classes for evacuees only. As infants we will be in our own evacuee classes

216

with our own teachers but we will get to mingle with the village children on the playground. Rita and I wait outside the house for Betty. She comes running over to Park house. She seems very happy. She tells us she likes her new guardians, the two spinster sisters. She says they are a little weird and eccentric but are very kind and understanding to her, lucky her. Rita and Betty walk with me down the winding lane to the village. They are so busy chattering grown up talk I don't think they know that I am here. We have to wait at the corner until all of the girls and boys are assembled. My teacher, Miss Ship, arrives. She is young and very pretty. I think I love her. She makes us line up two by two in a long line. Of course Angela and I line up together. We are so happy to see each other and both of us are thinking how posh we look in our new uniforms. Miss Ship tells us to follow her. I wave goodbye to Rita and Betty. I am five, all grown up and off to school. Miss Ship calls us to a halt in front of the dark green cast iron gates of the school. I look up to the windows of the school and it brings back the fresh memories of several days ago. I don't think any of us really want to go back in there. We wonder what is waiting for us behind those tall dark windows. Miss Ship gets our attention telling us she wants no talking and to stay in line while we enter the school and to remember that we are guests here and to act as guests, well-mannered and quiet. We enter the gates. We are doomed. I am always very melodramatic but I am scared. Angela and I hang on tightly to one another's hands. We enter the stark looking main hallway that is all too familiar to us. We are met and welcomed by the headmaster of the school, Mr Trevan. He gives us a tour and shows us where our cloakrooms are. He then takes us out the back door to show us where the most important things to us are, the playground and lavatories. A craggy cliff face overshadows the playground. It is very quiet right now but soon will be filled with shouting, fighting, playing children. There are the usual swings and slide and a long one story building with small high windows that houses the boys and girls loos. I was to be educated, what goes on, in the schools toilets, even at five years of age. That is where all sexual orientation goes on. Bullying is rampant and friendships are forged or broken. Bad dirty words are learned and daringly said to loud nervous laughter. I am to find out all too soon that for a new copper penny or some hard boiled sweets you may even be coerced into showing the boys your knickers or that some real common older girls may even take a larger bribe to pull out their elastic waist bands on their navy knickers and to give a quick look to the boys. Boys are so curious about what is down there. I have no idea what they think is down there, money? Lavatories are to be the only place to get away from teachers prying eyes and ears.

Black clouds are gathering over the cliff and it looks like rain. We march back inside and are shown our classroom for the next year. A year sounds like an eternity to me. Miss Ship assigns us our desks. They are old and worn and names have been carved in them over the many years. The inkwells are chipped. This is my first initiation to a school room. It looks dull and dusty and unexciting. There are tall windows that let in light and you can see the sky. A platform is in front of the class along with a desk for our teacher. Also on the platform is a large blackboard on an easel with a dusty, chalky rubber eraser set on the ledge of the easel frame. On the other side of the room is a big black fireplace that has a black metal fire guard around it waiting for the long chilly, rainy days of winter. It smells musty and old in here. Miss Ship takes a long wooden pole with a metal hook on it, pulls down and opens the windows. Some are painted shut but a few slowly squeak open. This is where I will be spending my days during the week. This is where I will learn to read, write and do sums.

This is also where I will learn about discrimination, segregation, ignorance, pain, friendship, love, jealousy and the complete difference between boys and girls. Miss Ship passes out textbooks. We are to copy onto our paper our letters. We are told to be conservative with our paper as we will have to use the same piece for our sums as paper is rationed. Within five minutes everyone is laboriously bent over their books, some biting on their pencils, but all doing our best to do our letters. It is very quiet except for a few yawns and occasional coughs. It seems like an eternity before we will be able to go outside and play. We study our ABCs. My paper doesn't look very neat and there is the never ending tick tock of the big clock on the wall. I don't know my numbers yet and I can't tell time but it feels like we have been here for hours and then suddenly the silence is shattered by the loud clanging of a hand bell outside the classroom door. Miss Ship tells us to stop and lay down our pencils. We line up ready to go for a twenty minute playtime. We are all so excited to go out and we are all talking at once. Angela and I pair up. She sits behind me in class. We both wish that we could sit together. We have a lot to chat about but for now it is off to the loos and play. We hurry. Twenty minutes goes very fast. There are queues outside the girl's toilets. All of the girls from my class join on the end. All the village girls, some my age and some older, are in front of us. We are the only evacuee class at their school. The village elders must have thought that the older evacuees and village children would squabble and fight so they didn't put them together thinking that the younger children would get along. We are looked at strangely. There is no doubting who we are. We stick out in our school uniforms and cropped hair. The village children get to wear whatever they have and most of them have long hair and some of them look unwashed. Some of the village girls come up behind us. They are bigger than us. The village girls in front tell us to move to the back of the line again and to let their friends through. We do. We are the outsiders. We will have to wait until the local children are all done. We daren't say anything. One older, pimply faced girl, calls us dirty cockneys and tells us that we all have fleas and that anyone who comes from Lonnon is dirty and smelly. I bet you all have smelly knickers, she says and the rest of her friends join in, smelly knickers, smelly knickers. All evacuees have smelly knickers. No wonder your parents don't want you. We don't want you either so go back to London. I clench my fists. I want to punch their silly fat faces but I can't because there are way too many of them. When finally we get into the lavatories, Angela and I share one together. We are too scared to go in separately. All of our class tries to stay together in a group. When we are through we walk over to the swings and slide to see what is going on but there isn't going to be a chance for any of us getting to play on them. Some of the boy evacuees tell us they had trouble on their side of the loos also. A lot of name calling and pushing and shoving but they kept their silence. When you are five years old and are the new kids it is safer to shut your mouth than to get a thick ear. Besides there are so many more of them than us and this is their school. They block the swings when one becomes free. Some of us walk over to use it but are pushed aside and again called dirty cockneys. They tell us these are their swings and this is their school. None of you belong here so stay off. Fat Derek who is in our class tells them they have to share. Oh, he is brave. An older boy pushes him hard. Derek falls to the ground. The other boy starts pummelling him. We all scream at them to stop. A shrill whistle is heard and a teacher from the village school who is on playground duty runs over on her short stocky legs encased in wool stockings blowing loudly on her whistle, pushing to get through the crowd of children surrounding the melee. We are all screaming for the bullies to stop. Poor Derek, he really is getting the worst of it. He is

220

pinned underneath a boy while his legs are trying to kick off his attacker and he is crying. The teacher finally makes her way through the crowd and manages to pull the older village boy off of Derek. She helps him to his feet. He looks bad. His bottom lip is swollen and bleeding. The pocket is torn and hanging off of his new school blazer and it is dirty. His knees are scraped and grazed from the gravelled playground. There is blood on his white shirt and the knot of his tie is pulled around to the side of his neck. He wipes his eyes with tightly clenched fists angrily trying to hold back the tears. The bully looks none the worse for wear except he is breathing hard and his beefy face is red and sweaty. His piggy eyes are glaring angrily at Derek. He is ready to go again. The teacher asks who started the fight. The village kids shout us down and of course the blame goes on us, the evacuees. The teacher gives up on her investigation and escorts both of them unwillingly off the playground and into the school. Another whistle sounds and we are told to line up and march back into the school to our classrooms, quietly and with no talking. So this is what school is all about. I just want to go back to London and home. In the afternoon it is announced that the evacuees will take their playtime, lunch and home time dismissal at a different time of day so as not to have confrontations in school and after school. Of course Derek recovers but I bet he will never open his mouth to the village kids again. I know I won't.

The school day for us is over. Our class is released early to avoid any more fights but we know this won't be the end of the fighting. Miss Ship is going to a meeting and is unavailable to walk us down the lane. She tells us to stay together two abreast until we reach the chapel on the corner where our older brothers, sisters or guardians will meet us to take us home. We wait on the corner in the warm afternoon sun. It is a little after three. I know that because I heard the chapel bell ring three times. Rita and Betty don't get out of school until half past three and I am not allowed to walk up the hill alone. I don't understand why I can't. It is about a one and a half mile uphill walk to Park house. I guess that is what happens when you are just five years old. Slowly the children are starting to leave. One by one they are being picked up by older siblings or guardians. Oh how I wish I was ten. Then I could go to the chapel school with all the older children and I wouldn't have to stand here waiting for my sister. As I stand waiting I wonder if Rita will get the chance to talk to Mr Martin about poor Len. If this war hadn't happened we wouldn't have had to be here and Mum would have known what to do about Len. Angela is the last one left waiting with me. I am so lucky to have her for my friend. Her brother from the senior school shows up. He gruffly tells Angela to come on. See you tomorrow she says. I tell her ta, ta. I don't want her to go. I am now left on my own. The street is quiet now. People have gone inside for their tea. A slight breeze has sprung up, rustling the leaves in the tree where I am standing. I watch as the trees fallen leaves dance across the empty street. My sister should have been here by now. I hear the chapel bell strike four times. I can only count up to five. I wonder where she is. I am hungry and have to widdle real bad. Maybe if I just sit on the ground and pull my knees tight up to my chest it will help stop the urge to go. I sit down and prop myself up at the roots of the tree throwing my new satchel on the ground. I pull my knees up and cover them with my drill slip. I squeeze my legs tightly together but it isn't stopping me from having to go. The pressure is getting worse. I put my legs out straight and cross them tightly. Oh, please, please don't let me wet my knickers. I have never done so before but I am scared that I will and this would be the worst thing in my life and this predicament is all Hitler's fault. The time seems to go by so slowly. I am trying to think of anything that will take my mind off of this awful situation. I think of what Mummy and Daddy would be doing right now, probably having their tea though if the bombs are falling they could be in the shelter. Do they miss us and talk about us? Was it hard for them to give us away or have they forgotten all about us? I start to cry softly. I don't believe that they really wanted us to go. Mummy said it would be best for us to be safe. The tears start to come down my face. Oh, this is terrible. I really hate myself for crying and feeling sorry about myself. Mum would say to stop that crying or I will give you something to cry about my girl. I clench my teeth tightly. I just can't wait any longer. I have to go. I try to get up to leave for Park house by myself but it is too late. I feel a sudden warm wetness. This cannot be. I am ashamed and humiliated. I have wet my knickers and my drill slip. I watch in shame and fear as the wetness spreads at the sandy base of the tree, trickling down and soaking into the sand. My socks and shoes are feeling damp. I can't move but I can't be found here. People will laugh at me and call me names. I scramble to my feet. I am miserably uncomfortable and tremble with shame for what I have done. I will start walking back to Park house and try to get up the stairs without Mrs Allen seeing me. There will be no forgiveness for this from her. She will look at me with condemnation and probably give me away to someone else if anyone else will have me and really, who could blame her. It is starting to get cool as evening begins to settle in. When I hear voices, Sheila, Sheila where are you going. Wait for me. You were told to wait for me. It is my sister and Betty Jones. Why didn't you come for me I ask? We are sorry that we are late. We went down to the harbour after school with some mates and just forgot the time. They look at one another with that private smile that they always share. Are you all right, Rita asks? I am fine, I lie. I just can't tell her in front of Betty. They would just snicker and make fun. Well come on then. Mrs Allen is going to be very cross that we are late for tea. I want to say being late for tea is the last thing she will be angry about; besides this is not my fault. If they had been on time none of this would have happened. I am just a nuisance to them both. I know that they wish that they could lose me so that they could have more fun. Rita is really too young to take on such a responsibility but war changes everything. Betty and Rita walk on ahead of me. Good job too. Walking up the hill is miserably slow, wet and cold. Do I smell? That would give it away. If I stay back they won't smell me. Rita says; Sheila quit dawdling and catch up with us. I just have to tell her what happened but I can't bare the shame of Betty knowing as well. I can't bear to think about it. But what is the difference, Rita will tell her anyway. They share everything. But I have to tell her before we reach the house. I need my sister's help. Mrs Allen mustn't find out or she could give both of us away. In my young life up to now this is one of the worst of things that have happened to me other than having to leave Mum and Dad. Mrs Allen is trying to do her bit for the war but wetting your knickers is not part of the war effort. I call to Rita to wait for me. I have something to tell you, I say. Can't it wait till we get home she says? It can't. Something terrible has happened so please; please don't be angry with me. I didn't mean to do it. They stop and turn. What have you done now Rita asks? Did something happen at school? No, nothing happened in school. I blurt it out. I wet my knickers while I was waiting for you. I promise I couldn't help it. I tried not to. I promise you. I plead, please don't tell Mrs Allen. She will give us away to someone else. I don't want to be given away again. Betty and Rita stand there looking askance at me. Please don't make fun of me I beg. Betty tries to keep a straight face. She bites her bottom lip and then she can't hold it in any longer and she bursts into laughter. Sheila wee weed her knickers she calls out. Rita elbows Betty in the ribs and tells her to stop it and leave me alone. She is just a little kid. She couldn't help it. There, there don't cry Sheila. We

224

will go in the back way and clean you up in the gardeners shed before we go in. Oh my, you do pong a bit. They hold their noses in the air and both laugh. I have to begin to see the funny side of it. Rita says, not to worry Sheila, I won't tell on you and I promise we won't be given away. Rita says goodbye to Betty. I won't talk to Betty. She thinks it is a big joke. Bye, bye stinky knickers she whispers. I poke my tongue out at her. Rita drags me by the hand through the back gate and tells me to crouch down by the hedge and crawl along so Mrs Allen won't see us. We are heading for the shed. This is so exciting like something out of some adventure book. The shed door creaks as she reaches up to open it. We crawl in on the dirty floor. It is filled with old broken deck chairs, flower pots, watering cans, garden tools and a push lawn mower. There are two small windows on either side of the door but nobody can see in as the windows are dirty and cob webby. We are safe from prying eyes for the present. Rita rinses out my navy knickers and socks in a partially full watering can. I stand there bare bottomed, sockless and ashamed. How are we going to dry them I ask plaintively. We can't hang them out on the line. No, she says, we will hang them out of the window of our bedroom when we go to bed but if Mrs Allen sees us going up the stairs she will ask me where my socks are. Well, tell her you took them off after school because you had a stone in your shoe and you lost them. That is better than saying that you wet your knickers. She will be cross about you losing them but the alternative would be worse. With my socks and knickers in my satchel we creep around to the front door, bending down by the front windows in case Mrs Allen is looking out. But no curtains twitch so we are in luck. Rita opens the forbidden front door cautiously. We listen and hear the wireless playing in the kitchen. So far we are in luck. We then do a quick bunk up the carpeted stairway avoiding the one creaky stair. Please God, don't let Mrs Allen come out into the hallway and catch us. At last we are safely in our bedroom with the door closed. Our cheeks are flushed with the excitement of the deceit. Rita gets me clean socks and knickers. We change out of our uniforms into our day clothes. We will hang out the evidence later at bed time. We go down the stairs just as Mrs Allen comes into the hallway from the kitchen. She chastises us severely for being late. Next time you are late you will go to bed without your tea. Now please wash your hands, have your tea and then go right to bed. That was hard but it could have been worse. Rita reaches for the long pump handle and pumps water into the sink to wash her hands. I can't reach so Rita hoists me up in front of her, but I still can't reach the water. Put that child down Mrs Allen admonishes and wash your own hands. I will take care of her. She pulls a kitchen chair over to the sink and yanks me up on it by one arm. She pumps some more water and says, wash girl, wash. But again I can't reach the water. She grabs a scrubbing brush and rubs lifebouy soap on it and brusquely takes my chubby little hand and scrubs it vigorously and then scrubs the other hand. It hurts badly. The brush is so hard. This is what we call washing your hands, she says. You will always remember this I hope. I will and I want to cry but I won't. I fight back the tears. I will never let her see me cry. I look at my small red hands. She rinses them off and gives me a rough kitchen towel to dry them. She then pulls me off the chair with the other arm and tells me to sit at the table. Rita is quiet and looks down at her plate. We eat in silence. Tea is finally over and we are excused from the table and told to wash in the upstairs bathroom and get ready for bed. It is daylight outside and the sun is still shining and we have to go to bed. But we dare not complain. Mrs Allen reminds us to say our prayers and ask God for his forgiveness and wishes us goodnight. We reluctantly go upstairs and get ready for bed. Rita attempts to sponge off my drill slip with a wet flannel. I tell her my hands are sore and that they hurt. I know she says.

She takes each one in her hands and kisses them just like Mum used to do whenever I was hurt. She says, there, there, all better. She really can be so kind. I love her but she doesn't know it because I don't tell her. We hang out my knickers and socks on the open window handles and lay my drill slip over the window ledge. Rita says pray it won't rain. We get into our night clothes and get into bed. We forget to kneel by the bed and say our prayers to ask for forgiveness. So Rita says, let's just say our prayers in bed. But I don't ask God to forgive me for wetting myself. Rita says, goodnight Sheila and please be a good girl tomorrow and then gruffly says she is sorry that she was late today. I lay there, my first day of school, I will never forget it.

THE DREAM

I have trouble going to sleep and I lay wondering, what if I never stop wetting my knickers? Maybe it is a bad disease that I have and if it is will I have to go to the doctor? I do so hate going to the doctor's. They give you bad tasting medicine and poke and prod you. I think that it may have to be very bad tasting medicine for wetting your knickers. I can feel myself finally drifting off to sleep. I hope I dream good dreams. I am running, running, running on the platform at the train station in London, trying to catch up to someone. I can't see who it is. They are running away from me. They turn to look to see who is following them. I realize that it is my Mum and Dad. It is me, I cry out. Help. Wait for me. They don't hear me and they don't turn around again. Please wait, I cry. I am here. See me? I am here. I promise I won't wet myself anymore. Come back, come back. Please come back. Look Mummy, I am going into the ladies lavatories. Please wait. I won't do it again ever, I promise. I run down the line pushing all the doors open, looking for an empty loo. I find one waiting for me, a big huge white porcelain bowl, the biggest that I have ever seen. It is big enough for a giant. I pull up my nightie and hoist myself up onto the seat, my chubby little legs hanging over the bowl and I hold desperately tight onto the sides of the seat so I don't fall in. I am so relieved. I am safe now. No more accidents. I feel a comforting release. The bowl flushes with a loud gurgling sound. With a feeling of accomplishment my chubby hands release from the rim of the seat but not fast enough, the bowl flushes with a rushing swirling force of water which I suddenly fall into and I am being pulled downwards. I try desperately to claw my way out. I scream and scream but the screams are silent. I claw at the swirling water. Help, I am choking, but nobody hears me. I am swept down and down, water swirling everywhere, around and around. I pass people that I know, Nanny, Mummy and Daddy, Rita and Len, the cat meat lady, Uncle Eric, Auntie Madge and George the cat. I reach out and cry frantically to them to help me. Save me, save me, I cry but they don't see or hear me. They just turn away. I pass Mrs Allen shaking her finger at me. Oh, no she is angry at me again. I am pulled further and further into the vortex. I keep screaming but nobody cares or hears me. I finally hit bottom with a loud thud. Someone is shaking me to see if I am all right. Wake up Sheila, wake up. Rita is shaking me, hard. I open my eyes and Rita is leaning over me, Sheila, are you awake. You were screaming in your sleep. Are you all right? Shush, you will have Mrs Allen in here in a minute and then we will really be in for it. What on earth were you dreaming about? I suddenly realize that it was all a bad dream. It wasn't real. There was no oversized lavatory. There was no Mum and Dad or the cat meat lady. But there is one part of the awful dream that is real, I had used the loo but it wasn't the loo in my dream world. It was my own little bed. The sudden realization of what I have done overwhelms me. I am so full of shame. I am cold and wet. How could I possibly have done this? The dream was so real. I had been good. I had used the lavatory. What have I done? Rita, help me. I am so scared. I have wet again. I thought I was on the loo. Mrs Allen will find out and she will get rid of us. I am so sorry. I start to sob. Oh my gosh Sheila, what have you done? This is terrible. This is terrible. If Mum knew she would kill you. You are such a nuisance. Get up and take that wet nightie off. Put your dressing gown on and sit on my bed. My feet are so cold on the bare floor, so I climb up onto her bed gratefully. I am so very ashamed at what I have done. I want to die. I have never wet my bed before. When my Mum finds out she will be so vexed and disappointed in me. Rita pulls the soiled bottom sheet off the bed. What are we going to do with it she asks? She looks all around the room. Nothing for it she says but to try to hang it out of the window. So in the early morning darkness we try to drape the sheet out of the window. We then realize that the other garments are still out there from this afternoon. Rita reaches for them and drapes them over the chair both of us hoping that they will be dry enough for me to wear in the morning. Between us we finally get the sheet outside and draped on the sloping roof below the casement windows. Sheila, all I ask of you is please use the Poe. You can't keep doing this. You never did this at home or at Trewlawny. Whatever is the matter with you? I don't want to do it, I tell her. I don't know what is wrong with me. You do know that Mrs Allen is going to kill you if she finds out about this. On hearing this I know, right then, that my life is over. It has to be. This is too, too much to bear. I know that there is no way that Mrs Allen won't eventually find out. Even the black and white ticking mattress is wet. You will have to sleep on the mat on the floor because I don't want to share my bed with you in case you wet again. I don't blame her. I wouldn't want that either. She puts a blanket on top of me, hands Heather to me and gives me my pillow. I don't sleep. I am afraid to in case the dream re-occurs and I am also very worried of what Mrs Allen will say. At this moment I am such a miserable little girl. I must have finally dozed off because when I stir myself it is because of the early morning sun streaming into the room. I am stiff all over from sleeping on the floor. Oh my goodness, the dream was real.

I AM A CONVICTED BED WETTER

The clock on the wall chimes seven o'clock. Mary will be up with the hot water any minute and I know that hot water is what I am going to be in at any moment. I climb onto Rita's bed and shake her. Wake up Rita, Mary will be up any moment. Please help me. She grumbles, leave me alone. She is always grumpy in the mornings but this morning she is more so because of the situation that I have created. She struggles out of bed and goes to the open window. Get over here Sheila and help me pull the sheet in. We pull the sheet in through the open window and onto the floor. It is cold and still wet. Now what are we going to do? Rita picks it up quickly and bungs it back out through the open window. There is nothing else that we can do. My clothes on the chair are still damp but I will have to wear them at least my drill slip as I only have one. Oh, misery. Rita says I will probably smell as my drill slip warms up through the day. There is the knock on the door. It is Mary with our hot water. Rita opens the door. Oh, thank you Mary. I will take it. Are you sure dear, it is heavy? I can take it in for you. No thank you Mary, I am fine. Rita leans on the closed door. Whew, that was close, but we are safe for now. She puts the water on the wash stand. When we go down stairs we'll tell them that we have already made our beds and tidied up. That way they won't go into our room and Sheila pray that the sheet and bed will dry while we are in school. But I ask what if she looks up and sees the sheet hanging out of the window when she goes shopping in the village? We are living dangerously.

My day passes ever so slowly. I am worried that the kids will smell me and know that I wet myself. In my class I watch a lazy fly buzzing in the tall window of the classroom. He can't get out. He is just like me. He is going to die. I don't want to go home this afternoon to Park house. I feel sick and anxious. Will Mrs Allen or Mary see the sheet or have they gone into our room? I am stirred out of my thought by Angela poking her ruler into my side. Psst, Sheila, Miss Ship is talking to you. I hear Miss Ship's voice, are you dozing off because I am so boring? Maybe you would like to stand in the corner with your hands on your head for a full half hour. Maybe that will wake you up. The place to sleep is in your bed at night and not here in my class. Little does she know why I didn't sleep last night? All of the kids in the class have turned around in their seats to stare and snigger. One rotten little boy pokes his tongue out at me. Now Sheila, please pay attention with the rest of the class. My face is red. I don't think I am in love with her anymore.

On the playground at lunch Angela and I sit on the ground in a sunny corner to eat our sandwiches. My drill slip feels almost dry. I hope Angela can't smell it. If she can will she not like me anymore? Should I tell her my most embarrassing secret? I don't think so. Angela says she has a secret and that I am the only one she is going to tell and swears me to keep it to the death. Angela tells me that she has decided to run away and go back to London. She hates it here so much and is so homesick. She starts to cry and tells me; I miss my Mum and my Nan so much that I cry myself to sleep every night that I am away from them. I tell her that wish I could go with her but I can't. My sister would give me a clout around the ear hole if I even mentioned it. Angela says you are so lucky having a big sister. I hate to admit it but I suppose that she is right even though my sister is mean and picks on me. She does watch out for me. Angela, please don't go. I won't have a friend to play and talk with if you run away. I will be sad and it could be very dangerous. An old tramp might get you on the way home and then you would never see your Mum and Nan ever again. She looks at me and a big smile creases her face. You are so silly she says. Whoever told you about tramps? My brother, he told me that they are dirty, never wash, their clothes are all raggedy and their shoes have big holes in them. Their hair is long, tangled and greasy. They never wash, they have scraggly beards with bits of food in them and they steal your food. I am breathless from my brother's vivid description of a tramp. Angela's eyes grow round. Never, she says, then I am not going. You have made me realize how scary it would be. I think we all have to go through this painful loneliness together. Someday we will all go home again. I am so glad she shared her secret with me but I will never tell Angela my ugly secret. After school Angela and I walk back up into the village. Rita is there waiting for me. I am so happy. She will be with me if Mrs Allen has discovered the sheet and bed. I say good bye to Angela. I am so very glad that she is not running away. Rita and I hurry up the hill. Oh, please, please don't let her have found the sheet. As we make the turn up to Park house there is no need to wonder any more. It is gone. The sheet is gone. It is not hanging from the window any more. My heart plummets to my socks. What will Mrs Allen do to me? I am so very afraid. Rita says, don't worry, I will stay with you as we go into the house. Don't be frightened. We go around to the back of the house and there is my bed sheet hanging on the clothes line, flapping in the breeze like a flag of surrender. The back door is closed. Never did a door look so big and ominous to me, just like it is hiding something behind it. Doom. Rita turns the brass door knob and the door swings open. It is very quiet in the house. Not a sound. Maybe she is gone. We step over the threshold with me using Rita as a shield. We stand there in the quiet holding our breath. You could have heard a pin drop. I wonder what is to come next. The quiet is suddenly shattered by a tight strained voice, Mrs Allen's. Rita and Sheila please come into the parlour. I believe we have several things to discuss. It has to be something bad as the parlour is usually off limits. We shuffle nervously into the room. I am standing behind Rita. We are dreading the anger that we know is to come. Mrs Allen is sitting on a straight back chair that she has placed in the centre of the room, facing the door. There is no avoiding her. Her hands are neatly folded in her lap. She looks like she is calm and in complete control except for her thin lips that are pursed in a quiet, angry line give her away. I am drawn to looking at her lips. They look like the twitching mouth of a bunny rabbit. She tells us to stand in front of her and to hold our heads up. I don't like to talk to the top of your heads, she says so we reluctantly raise our heads. She speaks to us with a tone of disgust in her voice. When I took you both in to my house and I might say, against my better judgement, I was trying to do my part for the war. I gave you the rules of the house which it seems both of you have chosen to ignore. Lying is a sin to God which both of you have chosen to commit. I hang my head in shame. I didn't lie to her. Look at me you deceitful child. I know that she is talking to me. Slowly I look at her, biting my bottom lip to stop the tears from flowing. Rita doesn't speak. I know that she is afraid of Mrs Allen. Did you both think that you could deceive me? Wetting the bed is disgusting but to lie and deceive is against God's will and abhorrent to me. Speak, she says, looking at me. What do you have to say for yourself child? I tell her that I am very ashamed and sorry for what happened. It was a bad accident and we were afraid to tell you because we knew that you would be very cross with us and that I would be punished. Sheila couldn't help it Mrs Allen. She has never done anything like it ever before and she is not a deceitful child. Honestly she isn't. That is quite enough out of your disobedient mouth Mrs Allen tells my sister. Did you children not ever think about what the other villagers must have thought or would have thought if they had seen the sheet hanging out of my window? I believe

234

such behaviour may be accepted in London and from your mother but not here. Do you hear me? We both nod sadly. I dislike her so. She continues, I wonder if she will ever stop. I have written today to your mother, I believe it will catch the evening post, about your habit of wetting the bed. It isn't a habit. It just started, I tell her. Don't interrupt me. I would never have taken you in if I had known that this nasty habit existed and I will not tolerate it while you are living in this house. Oh crummy. My Mum is going to be so angry. She is still talking. This afternoon I instructed Mary to install a rubber sheet on your bed and it will not be removed until you have learned to control yourself. You will also never have any liquids after three in the afternoon and that also means no tea with your tea. No liquids of any kind until breakfast. And for the next week you will both go to your room after you get home from school. No reading, no listening to the wireless, no playing with Heather. I think to myself, oh, no, not Heather. She has been removed from your room and will be kept from you till you have learnt your lesson. I want you to both sit in your room and contemplate your sins and pray to God for his forgiveness and I will also pray that he does forgive you. And with that she tells us to leave and go to our room. I will call you when tea is ready she says. She can't do this to me. Heather is my only comfort, who I laugh with and cry with. She knows all of my secrets. I can't be without her. She is in my heart. When we get to our room I don't see Heather and we sit dejectedly on our beds. Why do you do these things Sheila? I have to get punished for what you do. I am sorry, I am really sorry. I didn't want to do it. I didn't mean to, it was an accident. I pull down the blanket on my bed and Heather is gone, really gone. How could Mrs Allen have done this to me? In place of the usual sheet is the cold rubber sheet with no top sheet over it. I hate my young life. I should have encouraged Angela to run away. I now feel I would have gone with her. I am going to be

235

so desolate without having Heather to hold onto. She is my life and my lifeline. At the moment she is the only one who understands me. But what is worrying me the most right now is what my Mum will say when she gets the letter. She is going to be so cross and very disappointed in me. I can take her being cross with me but her being disappointed in me is more than I can bear.

LETTERS FROM HOME

The days are passing slowly. I try to stay awake at night for fear of a wet bed and the consequences of that. The rubber sheet is cold and clammy. It squeaks when I move and sticks to my skin. I know I will wet again someday and I am scared just thinking about it.

It seems like an eternity until a reply from Mum arrives in the post. On Monday, Rita and I see two letters on the front doormat. We usually get excited when we see Mum's hand writing because we know it is news from home. Rita gingerly picks them up and puts them on the hall table. One is addressed to Mrs Allen and the other one to Rita and me. We are not allowed to open any post even if it is addressed to us. Mrs Allen always has to read it first. She even makes us show her our letters to home now, so that as she tells us we can't tell tales about our life here. In a letter that Rita wrote two weeks ago she told Mum and Dad how unhappy we are here and that we want to come home. Mrs Allen opened it before she posted it and told Rita she was a very wicked girl for writing such lies. Our punishment was to stay in our room for a whole Saturday, no games, no reading. We had to just sit there and contemplate our sins. At supper there is a stony silence. Mrs Allen's rule of not talking at the table is observed with no slipups from me. You will meet me in the parlour after you have cleared the table she announces. She seems very aggravated. We timidly enter the parlour. Mrs Allen is seated in the antimacassar backed chair with the two letters in her lap. She motions us to the upright Victorian couch across from her. Rita helps me up onto it. I look around to see if Heather is anywhere in sight but she is not. I would like to call out to her to let her know that I am here but I can't risk getting into any more trouble than I am already in. I know that Heather has got to be so sad and unhappy without me. Mrs Allen picks up one of the letters. This one she announces is from your mother to me. She opens the envelope with a slim knife. I had never seen anyone open a letter that way before and in my silly imagination I thought maybe she could hurt us with the knife for punishment. But, then, as I say my imagination always runs wild. We watch her take the letter out of the envelope and unfold it. I recognize Mums blue note paper and in my mind I can see her handwriting. I love her handwriting. It always makes me think of home and that makes me miss her all the more. Daring not to make a sound or a movement we watch as she reads the letter. It seems to take so long. I wish she would read it out loud. Oh, dear, she has a sour look on her face. That is not good. Well, she utters in indignation and puts the letter down. What does that mean I wonder? Your Mother she says obviously has no understanding of the situation here. Oh gosh, what did my Mum say? I just want her to tell us. She picks up the other letter that is addressed to us. Will she read it out loud? Rita grabs my hand. We hold on tight, holding our breath, daring not to breathe. I think I'll burst. Your mother says that you Sheila never had this problem at home and that she doesn't understand what is going on here to cause this. Oh how can Mrs Allen not understand why this wetting has become a problem? She looks at me accusingly and asks; just what is causing this problem, Sheila? Is it your disobedience and inability to understand and your complete disregard for rules and manners. I truly believe that you do it to upset me and for my undivided attention. The attention you will get and there will also be punishment. I shall communicate with your mother and tell her the real reason for this problem. You and your parents obviously are quite oblivious to what we have to go through here with the evacuee situation while they sit back there in London with no obligations. I look up at Rita. Her face is white. She gets that way when she is very cross. Her hand is squeezing mine so tightly that it hurts. I know that she wants to rip into Mrs Allen and tell her that she has absolutely no idea what my parents and other people are going through in war torn London and many other cities, about the bombs and the killing and maiming of innocent people but Rita dares not because to say anything would be suicide. To be fair, Mrs Allen and the other villagers have no comprehension of bombs dropping every day and night, men women and children being killed and homes being destroyed. In Mummies last letter to us, before we got here, she told us of the night sky being so lit up from the fires you would believe that the city could not survive and that so many innocent lives were being taken. Mrs Allen looks at us. What do you have to say to this she asks? We shake our heads in unison. Speak up, she says. We utter very softly, nothing. Take your letter she says, I have heard enough for one night from your mother. We get off the couch. Does she mean it, that we can have the letter? Rita goes to take it from her hand. Mrs Allen thrusts it at her. And please, she says, do not write any more lies to your parents. Leave me now and go to your room. I do not wish to see you again till morning. We do not need to be told twice. In bed, Rita reads the letter using her torch. We daren't turn on the light to see. I nearly pee the bed with excitement. Hurry up Rita, read to me please. Okay, Mum says she is so sorry that you Sheila are having this wetting problem. She knows there must be a good reason for it and says please try to be good Sheila, do try. When this war is over, which shouldn't be too long now, we will come and get all three of you and bring you home. We will all be together soon. Please believe that. We have not given you away as I know, especially you Sheila, think that we have.

We miss you and love you very much. Are you both saying your prayers? I hope so. Georgie the cat misses you. He looks for you everywhere, under the beds and in the wardrobes. He looks at me very soulfully as if to say, what have you done with them, where are they? He will be so happy to see the three of you. And, Sheila how is Heather. I hope that you are taking good care of her. Hug her for me. Rita, I know that you are being a good sister in taking care of the younger ones. Thank you for that. You won't believe it Rita but Sylvester the parrot still calls out to you, run Rita run can't catch me. We all miss you; Uncle Ivan, Uncle Eric and Auntie Madge all send their love. Uncle Ivan may come down to see you. He will be home on leave from Africa in a month. Daddy is on duty tonight with the Home Guard trying to shoot old Gerry out of the sky. He looks very smart in his uniform. You would be proud of him. I am knitting you some jumpers for the winter. George is sitting on my lap and playing with the wool. He is very helpful you know. God Bless my darlings. Write Mummy and Daddy very soon. It is hard for Rita to read. Her voice keeps breaking. She turns the torch off and says; time to go to sleep, Sheila. I hear her crying into her pillow. I turn over toward her bed. Can I come in with you just for tonight, I ask. I am so sad and I miss Heather I sob. All right come on then but don't you dare wet my bed. I jump into bed with her and we snuggle up together. You had better not tell anyone about this she says or you are horse meat. I am glad that Mum didn't give us away, I whisper me too, and she says; now go to sleep.

BIRTHDAYS AND TOOTH ACHES

I wasn't able to celebrate my fifth birthday in April, before we were evacuated, so today the sixteenth of May we will celebrate it. I am now five. I feel very grownup. There will be no birthday party as my celebration day has come on a Sunday and we are not allowed to play and have fun on Sundays. So, I spend the day in chapel, morning, afternoon and evening but there are cards from London and a parcel which Mrs Allen allows me to have on the Saturday. Mummy and Daddy have sent me a beautiful pleated plaid skirt and the most beautiful pale blue jumper that she has knitted. She says in her card that she has chosen the colour to match my eyes. Mrs Allen says that I can wear it to church if I behave. I put it on upstairs and then go down to show Rita and Mrs Allen. I feel so beautiful. I am even sure that Mrs Allen will like it but it is not to be. You will not go out of this house wearing it like that, she declares, as I enter the kitchen. I have tucked the jumper down in the waist band of my skirt. I think it looks very posh, like the Squires wife, but Mrs Allen tells me the jumper has to be on the outside so that just a little bit of the pleats of the skirt show. She pulls the jumper out and I tuck it back in. She pulls it out and the battle begins. A battle of wills, that is. After all it is my birthday and I will wear it as I want. Mrs Allen's patience is wearing very thin and our voices escalate. I am crying with rage at her insistence. After all it is my birthday present. Rita steps in front of me. Oh, Sheila, please don't be so obstinate. Do as you are told for once and pull the jumper out. No, I won't, I scream. How does your mother handle such a child, Mrs Allen asks? Rita replies, she doesn't do this at home. She wouldn't get away with it. Mrs Allen throws her hands up. I cannot handle this precocious child. She then hurries out of the room to get away from me. This is a victory for me. I tuck the jumper back in the skirt. I have to try to be very good after this episode. I struggle to be good all day. I want to win Mrs Allen's favour. It works. When we come home from church Mrs Allen wishes me a happy birthday and tell me to run upstairs, that someone is waiting for me. I run as fast as I can taking two stairs at a time and into our room and there is Heather sitting on my bed as if nothing had happened. Mrs Allen does have a soft spot in her heart after all and I am so grateful. I can't express the joy and relief that I feel. I hug Heather hold her to my chest so that she can hear my heart and vow to her that we will never be parted again. I will be as good as gold for Mrs Allen. Heather and I have so much to share. She knows my deepest darkest secrets. We talk for hours that night. It is so comforting. I am so happy and now I don't hate Mrs Allen anymore. I will try to get along with her.

As the days go by the bed wetting episodes are getting fewer, especially when Rita lets me sleep with her. I wonder why this is good. I wake up on Monday in the early morning hours with a throbbing toothache. I wake my sister to tell her. It hurts so bad that I can't help crying. These are not my usual crocodile tears. These are real. Rita goes down stairs to get some salt to put in the tooth. It is supposed to stop the pain but it doesn't. My back tooth started to ache in London but we didn't have time to go back to the dentist before evacuation. Mum had thought as had many others that we would be back home in a few weeks. We will get it fixed then she had told me. It is now six months later. Mrs Allen asks why I am crying at breakfast and not eating. Rita tells her that I have a bad tooth ache. Mrs

Allen thinks it is another one of my games to get out of school. She doesn't buy it. She makes me go to school any way. At school I keep my head on my desk. The pain is so intense. My teacher Miss Ship is so very nice and tries to make me feel better. The pain eases some and as luck would have it Miss Ship tells me a traveling dentist will be coming around the schools for evacuees who have toothaches. He will be at our school on Thursday and they will take care of me then. Polperro is too small to have its own dentist and Loo is the closest town where there is a regular dentist and that is about an hours bus ride away. At school I am given a card by the head teacher to take home to tell Mrs Allen of the upcoming visit. It tells her that she can have the choice of taking me into Loo to the regular dentist. She chooses the school dentist for Thursday morning. She tells me she is too busy to take me into Loo with all of her church meetings. I am so frightened and have many misgivings. I hope I don't bite the dentist's finger by accident as I did in London. Rita tells me it won't hurt and maybe they can fix it for you. On Wednesday morning when I get up after a sleepless night, Rita looks at me and says, what on earth has happened to your face? I run to the wardrobe mirror and look. I look like a squirrel with his cheeks filled with nuts for the winter. I can't believe how swollen and funny looking I am. I gingerly put my fingers on my cheeks. They look like they might burst. It hurts so much to touch the left side where the bad tooth is. Rita laughs nervously. Oh my, she says you look like the fat girl of Peckham. Oh please don't say that. If I stay like this forever, everyone will stare and laugh at me. My sister can be so mean, sometimes.

Mrs Allen lets me stay home from school for today. I wonder, is there a heart hidden deep within? I know that she doesn't like us to stay home. She would rather have us out of the house all day. She gets us out even on Saturdays. She sends us to the

beach and cliffs with our sandwiches and junket and tells us
not to come back until supper time. We don't mind that. Most
of the other evacuees are sent there too on Saturdays and it is
good to see all of them, to be together and talk about home.
Mrs Allen gives me some cold wet rags to hold to my face to
help the swelling and makes me take an Aspro and go back to
bed. I am miserable, lonely and in pain. I have Heather to talk
to but she doesn't answer back sometimes. I can't wait for the
day to be over and for Rita to come home.

I spend another night with throbbing and extreme pain and
much crying while waiting for the morning to come and when
it does it is very grey and rainy. I am really frightened not
knowing for certain what is going to happen today. I tuck
Heather in my satchel. She understands and will help me
through this day. Mrs Allen stands her ground. I have to go to
school today and see the school dentist. There is to be no
waiting until the abscessed tooth recedes. Rita helps me get
ready. She wraps her brown furry scarf around my face so that
the cold air and rain do not aggravate it. We leave the house
huddled under an umbrella as we splash through the puddles
in our wellies. The cold driving rain tries to push up back up
the hill. Betty comes running down behind us. Wait for me she
cries, her voice getting lost to the wind and rain. She catches
up to us. Sheila, are you really going to the dentist today? Rita
and I nod. She says, I can't believe it, let me see your face. I
have never seen an abscess before. Rita pulls my scarf down to
show her. Whoa, she says. That is the fattest face that I have
ever seen. Thanks for letting me see it. I try to smile at her but
I can't. I pull on Rita's sleeve, please let's go. We are getting so
wet standing here and I am so cold. I just want to get it over
with. Betty helps adjust my scarf. She says it looks so very
painful and I am so very sorry for you. I think she really means
it. Maybe she isn't so bad after all. I mean Rita likes her so she

can't be all that bad. They walk with me to my school. Rita says I will pick you up on my way home. Please don't cry Sheila, it will be all right I promise. Betty puts her arm around my shoulder to comfort me. I don't want them to go. I just want to hold onto them. They reluctantly leave and I walk into the school with everyone else crowding into the hallway which is full of evacuees and local kids. Everyone is talking and pushing into the cloakrooms to hang up their wet coats and macs. I can smell the wet wool and old plimsolls. I change in to my plimsolls and hang up my mac and scarf. I feel like everyone is staring at my fat face and snickering. I am sure that they wouldn't laugh if they knew the misery that I am in. I hang my head down and hope that nobody will notice. Angela comes in and hangs up her wet clothes next to mine. She looks at me. Oh, goodness, you look like you are in a lot of pain. When do you see the dentist? I don't know. It is getting hard to speak now. I tell her that I am really scared and I believe that it is going to hurt really badly. She says I would be scared as well. We hold hands and walk to our classroom. All of my classmates are looking at my face and wondering what has happened. Maybe they feel sorry for me. Miss Ship calls attendance. Some children are absent today. Maybe they are escaping the dentist. After attendance Miss Ship asks us all to pay attention as she will be calling out the names of all those children scheduled to see the dentist. Please pay attention when I call your name. I just know everyone can hear my knees knocking. When my name is called I walk to the front, still clutching my satchel. Please don't look at me. I want to run away. There are ten kids in all whose names are called. We are each handed a postcard stamped in bright green, the word "extraction". I don't know what that word means and maybe I don't want to know. Miss Ship announces, Mr Martin is here to take you to another classroom where you will wait for the dentist. We ten stay close together for comfort as we go out of the classroom. The rest of the kids are sighing in relief that they are not in our group. Be good, children, Miss Ship calls out to us as we leave. Right now I just want someone to hold my hand and let me know that it will be all right but it doesn't happen. We walk into an empty classroom and are seated at a row of desks. Everyone here has toothaches. There are to be no fillings, just extractions. Mr Martin, out head master, explains to us that the traveling dentist is a nice man and just wants to help, and please children do try to be good when you are called to go in. It will be all over before you know it. I wish that I was Mr Martin and could stay here safe. I want to get Heather out of my satchel to hold her and take her with me. I reach inside my satchel for her but Mr Martin tells me that she will have to stay here and that I can have her when I get back. Although I need her I reluctantly return her to my satchel. Mr Martin asks us who will volunteer to go in first. A little girl at the end of the row starts weeping. I don't want to go, I want my mummy, I want to go home. Mr Martin tries to comfort her. All of a sudden, I don't know where it is coming from or why but I stand up on my stocky legs and say, I will go first. What on earth have I done? But it is me and it is now too late to take it back. Why am I always so headstrong? It surely can't be that bad but now I am confused. I ask myself, Oh Mum where are you, why aren't you here? Why did you let this happen to me? Why did you send me away? I am so angry with you. You could have stopped this and should have. Little do I realize how stupid these thoughts are but I don't understand why. I know everything has answers. I hear Mr Martin say, good girl, Sheila and feel him pat me on my shoulder. He tells me to follow him. I trot behind him reluctantly. I feel so small and so pathetically alone. What kind of world is this I wonder? We walk down the long corridor, painted an ugly bright green. The enamel paint is peeling. I drag my fingernail across a really loose part and I watch it peel away in a big piece. It feels good to do that. It is like you can peel away the bad to find the good. The corridor seems longer than it ever has. I can hear the hum of voices behind closed classroom doors as the children are doing their lessons. I have been dawdling and now must hurry to catch up with Mr Martin. He finally stops at the staff room for teachers where I will get to be the first pupil to see inside this room. It is usually off limits to all children. He opens the door. I can feel my fear and the chill of the air in the room. A very tall lady in a white uniform is working at a table set up by a lone high backed wooden chair with wide arms. I take it all in. Here is our first child says Mr Martin. This is Sheila. She is just five and I understand has a badly abscessed back tooth. I know that she is going to be a very good child, right Sheila? I quietly nod in response although not knowing quite what I am nodding about. The lady in the white uniform turns to look at us, she looks scary to me. It is her hair. I have never seen hair like it. It is so big and really frizzy and there are so many different colours. As my Mum would have said, it looks like a birch broom in a fit. There is black, brown, grey and red. The colours are amazing. I hear her say; we will take good care of her and we will bring her back to the classroom when we are done. Mr Martin winks at me as he leaves. He has a kind face. I want to go with him but my feet feel like they are nailed to the floor, they won't move and I think that I am going to be sick. Well hello Sheila, my name is Miss Jean. I will be helping the dentist to do your extraction. She closes the door. I am really on my own now and there is no escape. I look around me. There is a scrubbed table by the chair with all kinds of instruments on it. I recognize at least one, pliers. Daddy has pliers that he uses at the house to pull things out of the wall or woodwork. There are other gleaming instruments of which I know not but they look painful and dangerous. Come Sheila, climb up into the chair. Please hurry, there are others waiting. The dentist is a very busy man. I feel like I am going to be sick all over my shoes and socks. I can't move. She takes my arm and literally propels me to the chair. She then puts a small white towel around my neck and fastens it in back and tells me to sit back and relax. Is she joking? A middle aged portly man with big spectacles and a stiff white jacket comes through the door and then closes it. I don't know these people and I am feeling very nervous but I must not cry. I promised myself that I wouldn't. If I cry then the others waiting to see the dentist will hear me and be afraid. I will try to be strong. I wonder if my Mum knows where I am right now. Sheila, Dr Biggs and I are going to have to restrain you in the chair so that you don't try to reach out with your arms or kick with your legs. But why would I do that? Oh, please I beg, just don't tie me in the chair. Dr Biggs says I am sorry Sheila but it is necessary as we have no Novocaine for you. What is Novocaine I wonder? Well at least I don't have to have it. So that must be good. They strap my forearms and wrists to the chair with black straps. They are tight. I can't move. Oh God please help me. I am now panicking. I try to keep my knees tightly closed together so that they can't strap them to the chair. Now Sheila come along and cooperate with us. The sooner you do the sooner it will be over. Nurse Jean tries to pry my knees apart. She is hurting me. I have to give way and they tie my legs below the knee and ankles with the straps. I am frightened and now embarrassed. I know my drill slip is all pulled up because of the scuffle and I would give anything for them not to see my knickers. I know that my face must be red from my struggling and my embarrassment. I feel exposed and utterly defenceless. Dr Biggs says there is just one more thing and then we can get this over with. We are going to have to insert a dental bit into your mouth in order to keep it open and so that you won't bite us. It won't hurt at all. I promise. Open up real wide, please. He doesn't know how right he is. I would probably bite him if I could. He leans over me chatting away to Nurse Jean. I can feel his warm smelly breath on my cheeks and it is vaguely familiar and then I remember where I have smelled that before. It was my grandmother, when she used to tipple the bottle. I believe that Dr Biggs has been drinking out of the same bottle. He screws the bit onto my front teeth, top and bottom. I can't talk. This is the worst nightmare in my life. I hate the pressure of the bit. It makes my jaw hurt. I am now completely at their mercy. I try to tell them to take it out but the sounds come out so garbled. Don't do this please, please, I beg you, stop. But they ignore me. They can't understand me. I am all alone screaming into my head. The dentist is looking into my mouth and starts to probe at my bad tooth with a dental pick. I try to scream. It hurts. Oh God how it hurts. I can scream. I can scream. Not very loudly but I can do it. But I mustn't do it, I mustn't. I must stop or the other evacuees will be frightened. But now in my pain, I don't care if they hear me. Oh Mum, why did you let this happen to me? Nurse Jean with her hair of many colours slips something into the Dr of Pain's hand. I can't see what it is. In my panic my eyes are darting everywhere to look and see what he is going to do. Oh God, I feel something grabbing onto my tooth. Oh the pain, the throbbing. It is intolerable. I hear crunching of the bone. I am screaming in my head. The screaming won't stop. I am swirling into blackness, a vortex that goes faster and faster. I am crashing. Sheila, Sheila it is over, it is out. Tears of pain are streaming down my cheeks. It is over. It is finally over. They remove the bit. My jaw is stiff. I don't think I will ever be able to close my mouth. My chest is heaving with the sobbing. I have to take deep breaths in order to breathe. They pack cotton wool into the now big hole in my gum. They change it several times. It is soaked in puss and blood. It smells bad. They pack it one more time and leave it. The straps are being undone and I am free at last. They help me out of the chair. My legs are shaky and wobbly. I feel like I am going to fall over.

Mr Martin has just arrived to take me back to the classroom. He hands me my scarf, the soft brown velvet one that my sister gave me for today. The doctor says to wear it to keep the cold air out of the wound for several days. The doctor says you might want to give her an Aspro for the pain. Mr Martin gives me his handkerchief to wipe my eyes and blow my nose. My nose is all bubbly. He doesn't want the other children that are waiting for the dentist to see that I have been crying. Mr Martin says that if I like he will take me home to rest, but I tell him that I can't because Mrs Allen isn't home. I can taste blood in my mouth. It is running down my throat and it tastes warm and salty. It makes me cough. I don't feel well at all. This has to be the worst day of my young life and I have had many but I have survived them and I will continue to survive come what may. I am a survivor.

SUMMER HOLIDAYS

It is celebration time. This is the last day of school. The school
year is coming to an end. We are getting out for summer
holidays, three glorious weeks of no teachers, uniforms or
school dinners. Everyone is happy and smiling including our
teachers. We are celebrating today in the playground. The
swings are full. Spinning tops and skipping ropes are being put
to good use. Even the local kids are joining in our glee. There
is not even one fight. Across the playground someone has
started a Conga line and everyone is running to join in. Angela
and I run joyously to catch on to the end. We weave around
the playground laughing and singing. We go all the way
around those awful smelly lavatories, around to the front of
the school and back into the playground, screeching at the top
of our lungs. All of our troubles seem so far away at this point.
There is nothing like a good Conga line to make your spirits
rise. We all collapse onto the playground, laughing so hard
that we are fit to burst. There is only one thing in the world
that could make it perfect and that would be for all of us
evacuees to go back to London. Rita and Betty come to pick me
up from school to go back to our billets. They tell me that they
have had lots of fun celebrating with their classmates at the
church school. Lucky ducks. They even got to have fairy cakes
with icing, jelly and blancmange, how utterly unfair. The three
of us scream, we are free, free, free, for the summer. Poor Mrs
Allen she has so much to look forward to, three whole weeks.
That's twenty one days and equals five hundred and four hours
of us. Whoopee. The big question is which of us will survive
the ordeal? The next morning there is so much excitement at
the house. We have received a letter from Mummy with great

news. Our Uncle Ivan is home on leave in London and will come down to visit us. He will be arriving in two days and will spend three or four days with us. Yippee. I adore him and I think that he is so handsome. I can't wait to see him. I know that he will be absolutely smashing in his Captain's uniform. All of the other kids will be so envious. I am so proud of him. Mum says he will be staying at the Blue Anchor Pub overlooking the harbour. Oh, please, please be in your uniform when you get here. The next two days are the longest in history. I am sure that Mrs Allen will be glad to get us out from under foot for a few days. She has already told us that she doesn't want us around the house while we are on our holiday from school. She tells us she will pack our lunches and we should leave after breakfast and not return until tea time and to not under any circumstances cause any trouble while we are gone.

Finally, today is the day. Rita and I can't wait to get out of the house. We hastily pack our lunches into our haversacks. We are to meet Len at the bottom of Llandaviddy and then walk up to Crumplehorn to the bus stop. The village bus will bring Uncle Ivan here from the train station. We don't know what time he will be here but we are not taking any chances on missing him. There is only one bus every two hours but we don't care how long we have to wait because he is family, someone from home, someone who loves us. We walk slowly up to Crumplehorn because Len says his arms and legs hurt him and that he can't sleep at night because of the pain. He really doesn't look good. His face is pale and pinched and he has puffy blue circles under his eyes. Rita says we will have to have a talk about this and see if we can get him in to see the village doctor. We finally reach the bus stop and the three of us sit on the wooden bench and watch the big water wheel going around and around, the water sluicing through it and cascading downstream to the village. No bus yet. We watch, our eyes glued to the road. The only thing that goes past us is a horse and cart loaded with milk cans just brought in from one of the farms. The farmer doffs his cap to us. We wave back and then we see it, the green and white coach making its way slowly down the winding wooded road. We are ecstatic, hopping up and down, going from one leg to the other. Len looks excited. He even has some colour in his cheeks. He needs someone from home desperately, someone to talk to. The coach pulls up to the stop with its brakes screeching it to a halt. I watch the exit while Rita and Len run up the sides of the coach peering into the dusty windows to see if they can see him. Two village ladies get off carrying shopping baskets with a couple of stroppy children in tow. Oh, please be on it, Uncle Ivan. The coach driver leans out of the window and asks are you meeting someone? Rita and Len run back to the front of the bus and in chorus we say, our uncle. He is on leave and he is coming to see us. The driver turns around in his seat and calls out. Is there an uncle on board who is home on leave? There are three excited children waiting for you. There is a pause. Then we hear; must be me they are looking for. I would know that voice anywhere. We screech with excitement, it is him, it is him and he is here. We scream with joy. He alights down the steps, arms open wide and he seems to scoop all three of us up at once. Oh, blimey, I am shaking from the excitement. If I died tomorrow I would be happy and he is not wearing civvies. He has his uniform on. Thank you God, thank you. The other evacuees will be so jealous. The driver hands down Uncle Ivan's bag and tells us goodbye and all have a jolly good time. We will, we answer. Just past the bus stop there is a horse and wagon and for three pence the driver will take you down into the village. We climb aboard, all talking at once. What messages did Mum and Dad have for us? Did you bring presents from home and how is George the cat? I keep looking up at him and I touch him. I brush my hand across his sleeve. I am so afraid that this could be a dream and that I will wake up and he won't be here. No worry, this is very real. The horse and wagon stop at the end of the road by the village shops. No four wheeled vehicle is allowed to go through the narrow cobblestone streets so we will walk to the Blue Anchor where he will be staying. How proud we are to be walking alongside our Uncle in his officer's cap and uniform. He is so handsome with that black hair and dark eyes. He looks so much like Mummy. The villagers turn to stare. I think I see awe in their faces. This is a big event in this quiet little fishing village. We run into some of our school mates returning from Chapel pool. They stand and gawk. They have got to be wishing that they had someone from home visiting. Outside the Blue Anchor fishermen drinking their beer stop their chatter and just look as he walks inside. We kids have to wait outside because children under twenty one are not allowed. Uncle Ivan goes and checks in. He is lucky; he has a room that overlooks the harbour. He waves to us from his upstairs room and within a few minutes he comes through the pub door with a tray that has a tall beer for him and lemonade and crisps for us. Oh what a lovely life this is. We sit on the harbour wall munching happily away on our crisps. He tells us of home and gives each of us a letter from Mummy and Daddy. This is the most treasured gift of all to us and only to be read when we are alone in our billets. Len looks happy for the first time in ages. I am glad. It hurts Rita and me when he is so sad. I wonder what is really going on in his young life. Uncle Ivan has presents from home for us. He goes and gets them from his room. I can't wait. He tells us not to open them till we get back to our billets. The parcels are wrapped in brown paper and tied with string. Our names are written on the outside. I recognize Daddy's handwriting. It is painful to see it as this is my only connection with him. Before you know it is time for tea. We have to leave because Mrs Allen will be very vexed if we are late. Uncle Ivan will come tomorrow morning to meet Mrs Allen and to take us children out for the day. We have to say goodbye. He bends down, picks me up and gives me the biggest hug ever. I don't want him to put me down. I feel his warmth. It is so comforting. Rita gets her big hug and she is smiling from ear to ear. Len is embarrassed and hangs back. He bites his bottom lip and tries not to cry. Uncle Ivan says it is okay to cry Len. I understand. Come here my little Boysey. Len finally does. I know he feels better for that hug. We all do. Rita and I run all the way back to Park House so that we can open our parcels but that won't be till after tea. In our room, after tea, we just look at the parcels and feel them. The brown paper bulges where the string cuts into it. This is home. I can't wait any longer. I tear into mine, literally tearing the paper between the string. My sister as usual takes the more rational approach. She works at the knots in the string and slowly unties it. She rolls up the string to be saved for later as string is hard to come by and every little bit has to be saved for later. I wish I could be more patient like her but now my paper is all torn and my string is all knotted but I have reached my objective. There are sweets, a Mars bar, Smarties and Humbugs all bought with Mum and Dad's hard earned sweet rations. Mummy has made clothes for Heather, all very smart and beautiful. I am so happy as her one and only outfit was looking very tatty. I can't wait to try them all on her. I know that she will love them and that she will look so posh and for me there is a sun suit and shorts for the summer holidays. Whoops. There went all of their clothing coupons. Thanks Mum and Dad. Rita also gets sweets and clothes and a new swimming cossie. I can't wait. I am already trying my new stuff on and also stuffing my face with sweets. Rita carefully folds her brown wrapping paper. Mine is torn in pieces, no saving that. We are both so lucky to have a Mum and Dad who care.

Unfortunately a lot of evacuees don't get letters from home, let alone parcels. Rita reads our letters out loud and we go to sleep happy anticipating tomorrow. I don't think there will be any wet bed tonight. I feel surrounded by my families love.

Around ten the next morning my Uncle arrives at Park House to meet Mrs Allen. All goes quite well. She is very impressed by the Captain's uniform and his charm let alone his being so handsome. After breakfast we go to pick up Len. At the house I think Mrs Gillis is afraid of my Uncle's official presence. I myself wish he could scare Mr Gillis and his bully son. Len looks so happy today. He tells us he has opened his parcel and has been enjoying his sweets, the tin soldiers and the Biggles books. Len loves Biggles. Mum and Dad certainly knew what he needed. All of us are excited because Uncle Ivan is taking us fishing. We leave to go down to the quay. There my Uncle rents a fishing boat and some hand lines. He has also bought a lunch basket. We all get into the boat excitedly. He rows us out into Polperro harbour. It is a beautiful day. Polperro never looked as beautiful to me as it does right now. My loneliness never let me see its beauty before but with my Uncle here I see it in a different light. Out in the bay my Uncle drops the anchor over the side. We have never fished before so he helps us bait our hooks. I look away. I can't bear to see the worm wriggling in despair on the end of a hook. After all, as I see it, you have to kill the worm to kill the fish. Where is the justice in that? But I drop my line into the water with everyone else and sit and wait and wait. It is cool out here. The sun is shining brightly but a light breeze ripples the water and makes it chilly. I pull my old woolly coat together tightly over my summer frock. I am becoming bored and impatient. I can't stand to just sit and be quiet but my Uncle says if you talk you will disturb the fish and they won't bite. If I can't talk I am never going fishing again. I keep pulling in my line even though there is no pull on it and it is always empty. Fishing is for boring people. Then Len suddenly cries out excitedly, I have something on my hook. He is straining to bring it in. My Uncle helps him roll up the line to bring the fish into the boat. It lands with a big plop and flops around trying to get free and back into the water. My brother is a plodder and never gives up and because of that he has caught his first fish. The look of pride and the bright smile on his face is so warming to me. I am glad that it is he that landed the one and only fish of this day. We take a break for lunch and un-wrap our delicious Cornish pasties made fresh at the bakery just this morning. They smell scrumptious and taste delicious. But then the seagulls get a whiff of them on the breeze and start screeching and swooping around the boat. We begrudgingly throw them some crumbs but they won't leave us alone. They have also smelled out that there is a fish on-board. It is getting late so we decide it is time to return to the quay. The seagulls follow our boat all the way back squawking with the anticipation of fish for dinner, but not this time. No one is getting Len's fish but him although he is not having it for his tea tonight because he hates fish.

The tranquil times with my Uncle pass far too quickly. We spend the last remaining days swimming at Chapel, walking the beaches, playing in the tidal pools and going to the pictures in Looe. I don't want this time to end. I want him to stay forever but I know that he can't. He has to return to the front. All the eligible girls in the village will miss that handsome, dashing young officer who tenderly flirts with them in the tea shop and on the village streets. The girls return the favour with giggles, coy looks and the usual feminine wiles but this is short lived as a war is waiting. I think they will always remember him and he them. It is a sweet respite for what is awaiting us all. I will never forget him for the happiness that he brings into our lives at this time of our utmost need. Thank you my beautiful Uncle. You make us all feel better.

My Uncle is gone and the lazy days of summer are upon us. Why do we call them the lazy days when all they do is go at breakneck speed? Our summer holidays will be over before we know it and we will have to go back to school. During this summer we evacuees have become a village unto ourselves. Wherever you see a large group of raggedy children of all ages you know that is us, the evacuees. We scale the cliffs with the sea lying below us and the older children helping us younger ones. No one is left behind. Every morning we are told not to come home until tea time. It seems our host families are enjoying their summer as well. After we leave our billets we meet at Chapel. The seniors decide the day and put it to a vote. Today it is a long hike along the cliff tops to Talland Bay, picking blackberries and eating them along the way. At other times we have walked the beaches and rocks to the caves. The pirate caves. They are dark and scary with water dripping from the ceilings and eerily quiet. The seniors try to scare us young ones into crying by making blood curdling screams that echo into the vastness. I shake in my boots but never let on. Angela and I hang onto one another for dear life. It is very scary but so very exciting at the same time. The boys say the screams are from the ghosts of pirates past who used these same caves for their smuggling. The Cornish coast is a known smugglers hideout. Many tales are told in the Cornish pubs including tales of seeing mermaids and sea monsters. Just once, only once we were cut off by the tides and couldn't go back the way we came along the beach. I thought that we were all going to die. In fact I knew that we were going to die. We kids were all crying and screaming bloody murder as the water started to creep into the caves. The senior kids tried to calm us down. There was a way out and back to the village with the only problem being that it was up the face of the cliff to the path and then back into Polperro, easy for the big kids but what about us little nippers? We hastily evacuated from the caves, sloshing through the cold wet oncoming tide. Our sandals and socks were soaked and we were all shivering as the heat of the afternoon was leaving the caves. Once outside we all huddled together, glad for the warmth of the afternoon sun. Us younger ones were still scared and snivelling into our sleeves. Brian, our senior head boy split us up into three groups, seniors, juniors and infants. He gave instructions that the seniors would start the climb then help pull up the little ones. Then the juniors would follow up catching, if need be, and helping whoever they could. Sounded like a plan to me. Betty, Rita, Len and Angela's brother came and told us not to be scared because we would all make it and be home in time for tea. I hoped so because I was starving. The seniors started up the rocks trying to get foot holds in the clay and grabbing onto the gorse in the crevices to pull themselves up. Angela and I got behind the bigger girls and boys. The juniors gave us a boost from below. They grabbed onto our bottoms and pushed us up. Some of us were able to grab onto the gorse and some onto the helping hand of the seniors. There were about forty of us trying to scale the cliff to the coastal path and the safety of that path home. Angela and I found that the cliff was not as steep as it looked from the sea floor. It wasn't quite as bad as we thought it would be. There were plenty of footholds and roots to hold onto and many willing hands above us. But of course there were the whiners and the snivelers and not just from the infant class but I was not one of those. My knees were grazed and dirty and my hands were scratched and bleeding but Angela and I were not going to cry. Some of the evacuees scrambled up the cliffs like mountain goats and finally we had all made it. A little bit the worse for wear, dirty, dishevelled and with numerous cuts and scrapes we gave three cheers in recognition of our achievement. It was achieved with a lot of endeavour and encouragement and luckily with no serious injuries. Angela and I then made a pact to never go back to the smuggler's caves ever again.

There are lots of ripe blackberries on our trip today so our faces are stained black and we are all laughing at one another. We are having so much fun as a group and it is such a beautiful day to be young and free.

The last days of summer are idyllic. They are spent climbing up and down the slate steps cut into Chapel cliff leading down to Chapel pool. A natural saltwater pool formed by the crashing of the incoming tidal waves of the Atlantic Ocean. We swim and wade screaming with joy and laughter at being free in this all too brief summer. In the tidal pools we fish for tiddlers and examine a multitude of sea life all to be returned to their homes at the end of the day, emptied from the jam jars we have begged for from out host families. We head for home tired and hungry when the sun is going down. We are at this time a happy band of evacuees, homesick, yes, belonging, no, but happy in our summer of innocence.

ANOTHER VISITOR FROM HOME

It is a Monday. Two weeks before school is to start. It is cold today and there is a stiffening breeze. This morning we are having porridge for breakfast. It is supposed to stick to your ribs and keep you warm. It is so stodgy. I hate it and for me there is never enough sugar on it. Mary says; don't you girls leave before Mrs Allen talks to you. Mary fixes our lunches to go into our haversacks for the day, same lunch every day, cheese sandwiches with pickle and junket for afters and there is always a thermos of hot tea but unbeknownst to Mrs Allen Mary puts extra sugar in our tea and always gives us a wink as it is a secret just between the three of us. I love having secrets especially the ones kept from Mrs Allen. Rita and I walk out into the hallway to get our coats as Mrs Allen pops her head out from the parlour and tells us to come in straight away. It must be serious as we only get to go in there on Sunday evenings or special events like death or prayers. Upon our entering she says I will be brief with you girls. I have today received a letter from your parents. Oh, no what now. I haven't wet the bed lately. She continues, your mother is coming down to visit with you girls and your brother. We stand there with our mouths open, stunned. We are absolutely gob smacked. I can't breathe. I think I have forgotten how to breathe. I cough and come to. Rita and I look at one another and start to cry and laugh at the same time. We jump up and down with joy. Mrs Allen gives us a stern look for our exuberance because you just don't jump up and down in her parlour. Can it be true that she is really coming? There are so many questions. Will she be taking us home with her? Will she stay? How long will she be here? When is she coming? We can't wait to tell Len. Can she stay with us, please, please? We are going home. I know it. I can feel it in my bones, we are finally going home. Home is Mummy and Daddy, Aunts and Uncles. Our own beds, George the cat, treasured books and toys but Mrs Allen brings us back to reality quickly. Don't get over excited girls. I don't have any answers to all of your questions yet. You must wait until your mother arrives and I understand she is to be here by this Wednesday, depending on how the trains are running. In war there are train schedules but often they don't run on time. Many of the trains are filled with troops being transported. Trains are stopped because of air raids sometimes for hours. They are run off into sidings to wait for troop transports to pass. You have to fight for a seat with hundreds of people. It could now be a two to three day journey which in peace time would only take six hours. She will arrive at Liskeard and then she will have a bus ride to Looe if she is lucky enough to get on it. She will then take another village bus to Polperro which runs every two hours. She just has to be here by Wednesday. Mrs Allen excuses us. Rita and I literally run out of the house screeching at the top of our voices. She is coming, she is coming, she is really coming. Oh my God she is really coming. We hug each other tightly. Betty is waiting outside for us. She can't understand what our excitement is all about because Rita and I are both talking at once. Betty, our Mum is coming to see us. Betty's face looks sad. I wish mine was coming she says. Are you going back to London with her? Oh, we are sure that we will we chorus. Rita gets quiet all of a sudden. I know that she doesn't want to leave Betty here all by herself. They are such close friends. I am sorry, she says. I bet your Mum will be here soon to take you home as well. Betty nods bravely, holding back the tears. Oh, this is not going to be a good day.

The grey skies are threatening rain and Betty's sadness is adding to the day. But Rita's and my joy is overflowing. We try to hide it but it is difficult. We walk down to Chapel pool and meet Len and the other evacuees. No one is swimming today just spinning stones and fishing for tiddlers and sitting on the rocks all hunched up trying to stay warm. The wind is pushing in a light rain and it is chilly. Len has already heard the good news from Mrs Gillis. Mum has written her also. The relief on Len's face is a joy to see. I don't think he has really been happy since our uncle left. He is actually smiling in that impish way of his. He hasn't been having too good a time at his billet. He won't talk to us about it but we know that something is not right. He has been sullen, fighting with other kids, having trouble in school and he doesn't look good. His face is pale and he will sometimes stutter. He never did that before. He really needs Mum and for her to take us home. The three of us sit on the rocks and plan and plan how we will get ready for her arrival, what we will wear and who she will stay with, us or Len. Much to our disappointment we hear later that she will be staying at the Blue Anchor Pub. Neither Mrs Allen nor Mrs Gillis will take her in. After finding this out I cry myself to sleep and wet the bed for the first time in a long while and somehow I don't care at all what my punishment will be because I know that I am going to be going home.

Tuesday is a long day of painful waiting. The weather is also mournful with rain and wind. So we have to stay in and sit in our bedrooms and read on the hard upright chairs. We are not allowed on the beds during the day unless we are ill and on doctors' orders. Only Heather gets to lie on the bed. I told her that Mum is coming and she tells me that she is glad to be going home and that she doesn't like it when Mrs Allen hides her from me when I have been bad. She puts her in the most uncomfortable places like drawers or high cupboards. I wonder while I read, will my Mum really be here tomorrow? Please, God, let it be true. I don't think that I will sleep tonight just willing tomorrow to come.

Wednesday morning we are awake at five AM. The rain has stopped and the sun is starting to come up. Mary hasn't even brought our hot water to wash with yet so Rita and I sit in bed hugging our knees to our chests, just bubbling over with excitement. Should we pack now? We decide that this is a good time so Rita pushes a chair over to the wardrobe and stands on it to reach the suitcases on top. Best to be ready she says. She manages the first one and hands it to me. It is big and I fall backwards on my bum. We laugh and then catch ourselves. We can't wake Mrs Allen up or we will be in hot water. We finally have the suitcases spread on the floor but then decide that we had better wait till tonight to pack them or until Mum tells us what day we will be leaving to go back to London. The time seems to be dragging by so slowly. We finally get washed, dressed and go down to have breakfast. Mrs Allen tells us to go to the beach today. She says that we have no idea what time your Mum will be here but I will send her down to the beach if she arrives here before supper. She doesn't want us hanging around the house all day again like yesterday.

Most of the evacuees are on the beach today, happy to be out after being cooped up, forcibly, by the rain yesterday. Today there is lots of laughter, teasing, playing and screams of joy just to be outside. Where the evacuees are there is always noise. I think we like to be heard to prove to ourselves that we do count. Some of us take time out to eat our sandwiches. Len is sitting with the boys. He looks scruffy. His knee socks are concertinaed around his ankles, his grey short trousers are stained and his shoes are so scuffed. He needs a haircut. He has a wild look. He looks like he never gets a bath. Well, Mum will see to that when we get back to London. Len used to look like he came out of a band box, always so perfect about himself. I wonder what has caused him and a lot of other evacuees to be this way. I guess all of us have changed. The afternoon seems like it will never end. The sun is really warm and we swim in Chapel and lie on the warm rocks. I am not allowed to go in Chapel pool unless Rita or Len are with me as it is way too deep and I don't swim yet. Angela and I play in the tidal pools most of the day because the grown up kids get grumpy when they have to take care of us to see that we don't drown. It spoils their fun. I have tried all day to not think about Mum coming and then out of nowhere I see my brother come running towards us at the tidal pool, jumping from rock to rock, screaming, Sheila, Sheila Rita Mum is here. No. I look around and the only two adults I see are two teachers sun bathing on the rocks. I hear my brother crying out, Mum, Mum but I don't see her. Where is she? Len grabs my arm. Look up Sheila, look up and he points to the top of Chapel cliffs. I see a lady waving frantically and calling out our names. She is here. She is really here. The three of us are waving back and jumping up and down. Rita hastily packs up our knapsacks, grabbing my hand she drags me over to the steps that go up the cliff face to the top. I am so excited. I am breathing hard as we scramble up the stairs fast as we can. At the top of the cliff we see a lady coming towards us. It is our Mum. I think I surely remember what she looks like; after all it has only been months since we have seen her and who else could it be but her? Len runs to her and is gathered up in her arms. It is her otherwise he wouldn't be doing that so I run towards her. I don't want to be left out. I need her to love me. After being apart I am so starved for her love. I was torn from her and my Dad by evacuation but I didn't understand. I need to know now from her that I am loved be I good or bad. I have to believe and trust in her once again. Her arms are open wide. I run into them, sobbing, Mum, Mum. She gathers me into her arms and holds me close to her. I feel a happiness that she is here and a sadness that she has been gone so long unlike any I have ever known in my young life. I look deep into her eyes as she looks deep into mine as if to see into my soul. I see her infinite love for me. She puts me down and holds my face in her hands kisses me on my forehead and says; I love you my child. I don't ever want to let her go but I have to share her with my sister. Len is hugging and holding onto Mum around her waist. He is afraid that if he lets go she will be gone. Rita is standing back watching our reunion. She looks forlorn and lost. My Mum calls to her; Rita, come to me but she doesn't. You are not my Mum. I don't know you. My Mum wouldn't have sent us away. She speaks this without any emotion. Scalding tears are running down her cheeks. Why did you do it? I will never understand why you abandoned us. Oh my darling girl. I had no choice. Your father and I wanted you children to live so there was no other choice but to send you away. I hope that you will come to realize that someday. She goes over to Rita and pulls her in close to her. There, there it is all right, I am here now. Soon it will be better I promise. I see my sister's shoulders heave with a deep sobbing of despair and some relief as she puts her arms around my Mum. That's my girl my Mum says, cry it out. We four stand there on the top of the cliff holding one another close with renewed hope of being a family again and wanting this moment to last a lifetime. The seagulls are circling and crying out above our heads wondering what all the fuss is about and as if to say, what a to-do.

It is Thursday morning and I again wake up early. Was it a dream last night? No, it was not. I don't hear anyone else stirring in the house. I rest in the peace and quiet thinking over the wonderful time we had last night with Mum. I close my eyes and I can see her. She is so beautiful and so petite, with beautiful dark brown eyes that see deep inside your soul.

Her short dark brown hair curls naturally around her face. Her smile captures my heart and always will. She is my Mum and her name is Ruby. We had supper with her at the Blue Anchor and I, as a special treat, got to have a Tizer to drink. It was all bubbly and got up my nose. It was absolutely lovely. She told us all about home, George the cat and Polly the parrot and all the antics that they have been up to since we have been gone. We laughed and giggled from deep down in our bellies. It felt so good. She also gave us messages from Daddy, Aunts and Uncles and told us how everyone missed us but that no one ever could miss us as much as she does. We talked of happy things and not about the problems in our lives, the war back home, evacuation, the loneliness we feel and the alienation. It was never discussed. Nobody wanted to shatter this moment of joy so we pretended that it just didn't exist.

Today Mummy is coming to pick us up at our billet. She said that she would go get Len first and talk to Mrs Gillis then come and get us and talk with Mrs Allen. I know in my bones that she is going to tell Mrs Allen that we are leaving and going back to London. I have to think that Mrs Allen will be happy. I turn to look at Rita, she is still sleeping. I will have to wake her up so that we can get packed and ready to go. Heather and I talked about it a lot last night, in bed. I told her all about Mum arriving and that she had better be ready to go on a long train ride and that maybe we'd be sleeping in our own beds soon. Rita finally wakes up and we dress and go down to breakfast. Rita and I tell Mary that we are going home tomorrow and that we are going up to pack as soon as we have finished breakfast. Who told you that you are going home she asks? The wireless says that there is heavy bombing in London. I would think that it might be very dangerous for you girls to go home. I don't think that your Mum will allow it. I glare at Mary. I just know that she has got to be lying to us. She just wants to punish us

267

by keeping us here but that doesn't make sense. Mary has always been very nice to us. Rita says, we'll go up and pack anyway just to be ready. We run up the stairs chatting happily to one another. I love these happy moments with my sister. Rita packs our few things. It doesn't take long. We are so excited. Within half an hour we are all done and sitting on top of our suitcases waiting for Mum. The time seems to drag by. We watch out the upstairs windows to see if Mum and Len are coming up the hill from the harbour. We don't see them and time seems to drag. Finally, we see the two of them come into view. It will take them a few minutes to get up to the house as it is such a steep hill. Rita and I tear down the stairs, through the hallway, out the front door, down the walkway and out the front gate to the road. We scream out to Mum and Len, we're here, we're here. Mrs Allen comes out to the gate and watches us run partway down the hill to meet Mum and our brother. We fling ourselves at Mum and get big hugs. I look up at her. How could I have ever forgotten her? I love her so much and I love those beautiful hands that hold me, the hands that used to hold my face and kiss me good night and tuck me into bed every night. I will always have these visions tucked away in my memory. On her right hand her ring finger was severely injured when she was a child and turned septic and is quite misshapen. She tries to hide it but I think it is the most beautiful finger in the world. Back in London I used to hold it and kiss it before I turned over to go to sleep.

The three of us walk back up the hill. I try to hold Len's hand but he shakes me off. He thinks it is way too girly. I chatter idly all the way back up to the house. I have always been such a chatterbox. My teacher says that if I paid as much attention to my school work as I do to chattering I would be on the gold star list. It hasn't happened yet but I guess there is always hope. We reach the gate and Mrs Allen greets my Mum with a handshake and invites us into the house. I can see that they are eying one another up and down. I bet Mrs Allen is wondering what kind of woman my Mum is that she would let her children go and live with strangers and my Mum is wondering what kind of person Mrs Allen is since she is bringing up her daughters at this point in their young lives. Mrs Allen ushers our Mum into the parlour. I am sure that my Mum doesn't realize what a privilege this is. Mum tells the three of us to go play out in the garden until she calls us in. She needs to talk to Mrs Allen alone. Outside the three of us sit cross legged on the grass under the monkey tree. Rita says, I bet Mum must be telling her that we are going back home with her. We speak in hushed but excited tones and I am trembling with excitement at the prospect of leaving. I am sure that Mrs Allen won't be disappointed at the thought of losing us. She'll have her house back to herself and not be inconvenienced by having to be responsible for children. It seems to take forever for Mum to come out to us. Rita asks Len if Mum said anything to him after she talked to Mrs Gillis. He shakes his head, no. I think he needs to go home more than Rita and I do. He is so alone at the Gillis's. I wish that he now would tell us why he is so sad but I know that he will change when we get home. Len asks us if we would like to see his pet spider. Oh yes, please I say. He pulls out a matchbox from his trouser pocket. Will it bite I ask? No, don't be afraid, he is very tame. We gather close. He pushes open the box and there it is, a small brown spider sitting on the bottom of the box. It doesn't move. Why isn't it moving, Rita asks? Can I touch it? Len nods his head yes. Rita pokes at it with a small twig but it doesn't move. Is it dead, I ask? Len says, no it is just sleeping and with that he quickly closes the match box and puts it back in his pocket. He seems very protective of the spider. I wish I had a pet spider too but then I always want what everyone else has. We look up to see Mum standing in the doorway of the house.

She beckons us to come in. This is it. It is all happening now. Smiling, we run over to her. Are you taking us back home with you Mum? She tells us to go on into the front parlour and sit down. I am so excited that I am jumping from one foot to the other. Rita pulls me down next to her and Len on the settee. Our Mum sits across from us in the big upholstered arm chair. She looks like she is lost in it. Mrs Allen is nowhere in sight. Maybe she is sad that we are leaving and has gone to have a good cry. I really don't believe that but you never know. Mum says, my children I want you to listen to me very carefully. I made the journey down here to see you because I needed to know in my mind that you were well and unhurt. I had to see for myself because a lot of rumours abound back home regarding evacuees and now I see that you are well. I know that this isn't the perfect situation for any one of you but I do know that you are safe and that the bombs can't reach you down here. What is she saying? No, this can't be. Does she mean that we are not going home? She continues, as much as I want to take you home with me, I can't. Too many people are dying in London and I don't want to be responsible for you getting hurt or dying in the raids. I could never live with that. It would kill me and your Father to lose you. War is a terrible thing, separation of families, hunger and all of the dying. We are not going home. She is leaving us here. We run across the room to her and kneel by her feet. Oh please, please Mum, don't leave us here. We don't mind dying. We just want to be with you and Daddy. We will be so good. You won't even know that we are there. I am sorry my children but this is the way that it has to be. It has to be the lesser of the two evils. I want you to live. Why did she come? I think I hate her. I want her to go now. My brother looks drained of all emotion. Why won't he tell her that he has a lot of verbal abuse and trouble at the Gillis's but he doesn't utter a word? Maybe it is better this way. What does it matter? It won't change the facts. Rita has tears streaming down her cheeks. She cries almost silently. I am very, very cross. I will never forgive her for not taking us home. Mum tries to comfort us with hugs but we are too numb at the moment to accept her love. She says that she has some other news for Rita and me and needs our understanding and to be very grown up to accept what she has to tell us. Where does all of this end? What she divulges to Rita and I is disheartening and demoralizing on top of our not being able to go home. I feel the hugest lump in my throat. Where can I run to? There is no way out. Mrs Allen talked with my mother and told her that she cannot take care of us anymore. Her husband is coming home on leave from the Navy and we will have to leave. So, as I see it, we can't go home because it is too dangerous and we could die and Mrs Allen cannot care for us anymore. Does anyone want us, no? Mrs Allen wasn't as warm and giving as the Squire and his wife at Trewlawny. We felt their love. We have learned to live with Mrs Allen's rules and quirky ways even if the love isn't there. Still, she took us in when we had no other place to go and she has done her best for us. Be brave my children, are my Mum's parting words before she leaves to return to London. Well, I am so tired of being brave and being told not to cry and to keep a stiff upper lip. I just know that I feel deserted, angry and self-conscious. I now hate the village children that get to live with their Mums and Dads. I am feeling like I have a big E for evacuee on my forehead and that all of the villagers point at it and say, oh that's one of them. I know that many of us evacuees feel that way. I am definitely not alone in this.

A DECISION IS MADE

My Mum is gone and school is to start in less than two weeks.
Where will Rita and I go? Mrs Allen met with the billeting
officers twice this week and we are called into the parlour one
evening. It must be important because all of the big decisions
are made in the parlour. Rita and I stand ramrod straight,
afraid to sit and afraid to touch. Mrs Allen or Auntie Phyllis as
she always wanted us to call her which Rita does but I won't
because she is not my Aunt, tells us that she and the billeting
officers are frantically searching for someone to take us in.
They want us to be settled before school starts. My wish is that
someone will take pity and take three of us in. Len needs to be
with us but we are told that Len will stay at the Gillis's. Maybe
they need the ten shilling and six pence that they get per child,
per week for clothing, housing and feeding as a Government
allocation. The word is that a farm about three miles out of the
village, way out on Llandaviddy Lane may be able to take Rita
and I in but the billeting officers are concerned that we would
have to walk the three miles to school and walk the three miles
back. It is all downhill going to the school and all uphill going
back. It would be a very lonely walk. There are no houses once
past Mrs Allen's and the sisters' house where Betty lives, just
fields, copses, trees and one other farm. The billeting officer
tells Mrs Allen that they should know for sure if we can go
there by the end of the week. The Rosses who own the farm
will talk about taking us in and we will have an answer on
Friday, but first they want to see us before they consider Rita
and me living with them out at the farm. We are to meet them
on Friday afternoon and we will be informed if they want us

272

after our meeting. Myself, I think it is going to be just another cattle sale. Mrs Allen tells us to go up to bed and make sure that our suitcases are still packed in readiness for us to hopefully leave on Sunday evening for the farm. My heart truly aches. I cry into my pillow tonight. I tell Heather that we are moving and how I hurt. Rita doesn't talk to me. She is so sad. I know how much she will miss living next door to Betty and I know that she worries how we will adjust to a new family and how they will treat us. Will they like us? Will we like them? I know that I will never let myself get close to any adult again. You can't trust or believe them. Even my Mum who I thought was going to take us home but didn't.

Friday afternoon arrives way too soon. The farmer and his wife will be here early this afternoon. When they do arrive we are told to wait in the kitchen while the billeting officers and Mrs Allen talk with them. What is Mrs Allen going to tell them? If she tells them that I wet the bed we are sunk. Before they arrived Mrs Allen informed us to only speak when spoken to and to not under any circumstances ask questions. The time seems to drag in the silent kitchen except for the ticking of the wall clock that seems to get louder by the minute. Rita and I don't talk. What can we say to one another? I am just glad that we will be together wherever we may go. Even though we fight and argue, she is my sister and I need her so much even though I know that I am no solace to her. I have Heather to talk to and she has become so real to me. She can't speak but she talks to me in my head. I wish I could share her with Rita but I can't. Heather would never talk to me again and I couldn't bear that. How would I exist? Finally, we hear Mrs Allen calling out to us. She ends our painful silence. We are told to go into the parlour. This is it, I know it, our fate has been decided by adults and government. I don't want to ever remember walking in there. It will be easier that way. My sister and I are told to stand in front of the organ so that they can get a good look at us. Mrs Allen hustles us along. Hurry up children; they have to get back to their farm. After all it is war time and they have to feed a hungry nation. Hold your heads up girls so that Mr and Mrs Ross can see your faces. I don't want to look at these new people's faces but I do as I am told. Mrs Ross asks if we are good children and do we love God. We nod slowly, yes. Speak up girls, cat got your tongue? Mrs Ross is a very thin wiry lady with grey hair that is pulled in a very tight bun. She looks like her face has been stretched. Her clothes are dusty, dowdy and dark. Mr Ross sits next to her. He is also quite thin with a very long face. He is wearing a cloth cap on his head and there are black tufts of hair peeking out from underneath the cap and behind his ears. He wears leather leggings on his legs with a walking stick between his knees that he drums nervously on the floor. He doesn't seem to pay us much mind, just seems anxious to get on with the business and be gone from this place and not to be kept here with two homeless children. We will take the bairns, he says in a deep gruff voice. They will have their chores to do and as long as they do their work they'll be housed and fed. We haven't lost a child yet to hard work. Mother and I will send the pony and trap down for them on Sunday after chapel. Have them and their luggage ready. With that they are gone. The billeting officers relax. Silent relief floods Mrs Allen's face and I think I even see a fleeting smile. I believe she is really relieved that we have a place to go and she won't have to worry about us. She has taken us in when no one else would and she has her naval officer husband to consider. I wish I could meet him. We have two days before we have to go to the farm. We spend the rest of the Friday with our brother and some of the evacuees. He puts on a good face but he knows in his heart that he won't see us as much as he now does. He will have to walk three and a half miles to visit us. Rita will see him in school and I will only get to see him on Sundays after chapel. I feel sick and lonely. Angela, my best friend, is also sad that I am going. We won't be able to spend time after school together as we do now. I worry that she will find a new best friend and that I will lose her.

It is Saturday already. It has come way too quickly. Mary helps us pack up the last few things. She hugs us close and tells us that she will miss us. I believe that she really will miss us. She always tries to make things better for us with Mrs Allen. We hear Betty calling us from outside. Mary says we can go now and see her and spend the day with the rest of our friends, our last day. We pick up our haversacks and dash out. The three of us are going down to the harbour and meet our band of evacuees and decide what to do for the last day of our school holidays. As usual all the big kids get to make that decision and we younger ones will all follow. Our leader is a thirteen year old, blonde haired boy, named Brian. Brian has his cronies and everyone looks up to them or maybe it is because we are scared to death of them. My brother is too young to be a crony. He is also a little afraid of them. Brian feels very powerful over us little kids. We hang on to his every word. I think it is his way of being in control and maybe handling his pain of separation in this war. Today's plan is to walk along the top of the cliffs to Talon Bay and swim in the bay. In some ways it is a scary walk. Some of the older kids walk close to the edge of the cliffs and tease us, embarrass us and dare us younger ones into doing it. It is a long, long way down onto the jagged rocks below with the sea crashing over the shore and onto the rocks. I don't care if they call me names like scaredy, scaredy custard. Angela and I don't want any part of it. We are scared. Brian and his cronies dare all of us to look over the edge and cheers us on if we will do it. They chant, closer, closer, closer. Some of the kids are snivelling with fear. It is a stupid game. Some of us run on ahead to get away from it. We want to get to Talon, swim and have our sandwiches. It is a long climb down to the beach, steep and rocky. The path winds down and down. Us little ones scoot down on our backsides. We hear a yell behind us. The cronies are showing off and jumping from rock to rock to get down to the beach. Brian is at the front. They are yelling like Tarzan and beating their chests. They think that they are so good. Us young ones move aside for them and we watch the leaping game. Then all of a sudden there is a cessation of the pounding of chests and yelling. Brian misses a rock and loses his balance. The other boys are frozen on their rocks and afraid to move. Brian tumbles and tumbles, frantically trying to grab on to some gorse or rocks to stop his fall. He is screaming with pain and fear. None of us can move. His body comes to rest on the sand below. That helps softens his landing. All of us are now screaming, Brian, Brian and running to his aid the best that we can. The older boys scramble down to him. We all mass around him. He doesn't move. Someone gets lemonade from their thermos and throws it on his face. He starts groaning and tries to move. The boys try to help him get to his feet. He screams in pain. He can't put any weight on his left ankle. They sit him on one of the rocks. Blood is pouring down his face, onto his shirt and he is crying pitifully. How the mighty have fallen. I have never seen so much blood in my life. John, one of his cronies turns Brian's head to see where he is bleeding from. Oh, gross, his left ear is hanging on a piece of loose skin. Everyone is gagging, retching and turning away. John picks up the ear and holds it to Brian's head. Get help he screams. We see a fishing boat pulled up on the beach. That is our only hope, but where are the fishermen. We all start screaming Help, Help. Even the seagulls are screaming overhead. Our cries for help are finally heard. Two fishermen that were on the rocks come running down the beach and rush up to us and Brian. John is still holding onto

Brian's' ear. Brian appears to be in intolerable pain. His ankle has swollen up like a soccer ball. He has cuts and grazes over his legs and arms. He is a mess. He is not giving any orders now. The two fishermen pick him up very carefully and ask Johnny to walk beside them holding onto his ear. All of them head for the boat with us all in tow. They will take him to Polperro for there is no way he can walk back and there is no way for a car or pony and trap to get out here to get him. Unfortunately there is no regular village doctor in Polperro. The visiting doctor only comes twice a week and not on a Saturday. They will have to get him into Looe where there is a cottage hospital. Only John can go with them to hold the detached ear to the side of his head. The rest of us will have to walk back. No one wants to continue on to Talon to swim or eat our sandwiches. We are all so quiet and numb with shock. It is decided that we will go back to the village straight away. I think it is the quietest that all of us have ever been since our arrival in Cornwall. On the journey back no one plays dare on the cliffs, or even speaks. We stay together, a sad lot, on our very last day of summer. I feel that there is to be a big change on the horizon.

ROSKILLY FARM

It is Sunday evening already. The pony and trap is to arrive promptly at five o'clock. For us it has been a very eventful weekend. We heard in chapel this morning that Brian will recover completely except for his pride. Some say that they tried to sew his ear back on. I can't imagine the pain of having a doctor try to sew your ear to your head with a needle and thread. It makes me cringe to think about it but I am glad to hear that he is all right. My sister and I are waiting outside under the monkey tree with our suitcases and gas masks. I am so glad that I haven't had to use mine because if you don't die from the lethal gas you will die from the suffocation of the mask. Mrs Allen comes out to say goodbye and to wish us luck. She gives each of us a perfunctory hug. I want her to hold onto me and I want to scream that I don't want to go. I would even beg, please don't make me and ask if I could go back up to our room and go to bed where at least I know who I am. I would promise her that I would not be bad anymore and that I would do anything that she says and I would never, ever wet the bed again. In my heart I believe that it is my fault that we are being sent away again. Of course, I don't say anything. I just choke on the thoughts. Mary gives each of us a bag of sweets. I will miss her very much. She helped make life bearable for Rita, Heather and I. I will never forget you Mary. Farmer Ross arrives and climbs down off the trap and puts our luggage on the back. He helps Rita up onto the wooden seat. I am too short to climb up that high step. He has to lift me up onto the seat. I look at his dark stubbly face and into his dark brown glittery eyes. I can't see any humour in them. He has the bushiest eyebrows. Some of the grey hairs are so long that they curl into his eyes. I think that they make him look grumpy. My face brushes against his tweed jacket and I smell pipe tobacco and it reminds me of the grounds keeper at Trewlawny. I wonder if he will be as nice. He doesn't speak. He just puts me between Rita and himself so that I don't fall out. He doffs his cap to Mrs Allen, picks up the reins, flicks them and makes that clicking sound with his tongue. The dark brown mare moves forward. We sadly wave goodbye and watch them recede into the distance. The last thing I can see of Park House is the monkey tree. When I first came to Park House I really believed that there were live monkeys in the monkey tree and after all it was called a monkey tree. I believed that they were in hiding and wouldn't come out if they could see me. So I would hide around the corner of the house and watch for them but they never came. There must have been monkeys. But then I am just a child and I also believe in fairies. The ride up to the farm is slow. It is a very long steep ride. The horse takes her time and chooses her path carefully. Mr Ross is very patient with her. Not a word is spoken. Just the sound of her clip clopping. The road starts to smooth out. There are fields and woods on either side of the country road. We see some pigs rooting in some turnips in a muddy pen alongside the road. Cows are grazing in the pastures and many sheep dot the grassy hillsides. But I am now wondering how I can walk this far to school every day and back. Farmer Ross breaks my reverie. We are almost there he says. You'll get some tea soon as we get in. Mother will have it ready. That's encouraging. Food always makes me feel better and I am always hungry. Rita always tells me that I am a greedy guts. He points out the farm house with a wave of his arm. It looks so very bleak. It sits there all by itself. It is built of grey Cornish stone. There are two stories, two smoky looking chimney pots and the slowly setting sun glints off the windows. The black slate roof looks weathered from winter storms and cold, very cold. I hate cold. I see barns in the outer area of the farm and farmland on either side of the country road. The pony and trap are slowing down. We turn into a tree lined driveway and enter a big stone flagged courtyard where we finally stop. There are chickens and roosters walking around pecking at grain on the ground. They pay us no mind. It will be fun to chase them tomorrow if I get the chance. We can hear a loud chorus of mooing coming from one of the barns at the perimeter of the courtyard. Farmer Ross says that the cows are ready for milking and always express their desire to be milked. Rita and I are used to these sounds. They bring back loving memories of Trewlawny. Three men with leather leggings and soft caps come out of the back door of the house and head for the milking cow sheds. They give us a quick wave of welcome. The mooing will soon subside. Mrs Ross comes out of the back door to greet us. You are late she says in an annoyed voice. Sorry my dear but we had to get the suitcases loaded and the children were slow with their good byes. She retorts that we will have to learn the rules here because this is a working farm and not a school playground. Rita and I don't say a word. As Mum would say, it is better to be seen and not heard. She motions for us to come into the house. Farmer Ross helps us down from the trap then leads the horse and trap off into one of the barns. Our feet feel like we have lead in our shoes as we cross the threshold and into the next chapter of our lives.

The kitchen is very big. Long stone counters, a huge stone sink with a pump that has a long handle to pump water into the sink. Tall kitchen cupboards go all the way up to the ceiling. The floors are dark grey flagstone. An immense well-scrubbed wooden table is in the centre of the large kitchen and I count on all ten fingers, ten kitchen chairs. I think a lot of people must live here. A huge dresser also reaches to the ceiling. Its shelves are filled with plates, bowls, cups, saucers, jugs and tureens. On one wall of the kitchen there is a gigantic Rayburn stove. A large pile of chopped firewood sits beside it. I don't feel even a slight warmth coming out of it and it feels cold in here and gloomy. Mrs Ross tells us to sit down and have our tea. She says that everyone else has had there tea and are out doing there chores around the farm. White china cups, saucers and plates are set at one end of the table. A plate of scones, bread and thick farmhouse butter are put in front of us. She pours our tea from the most massive Brown Betty teapot. Twenty people could have a cup out of that. There is milk in the big pitcher and sugar in a biscuit tin. I am hungry but we are exhausted and even missing Mrs Allen at this point. Can you believe that? We are really scared of our new environment. We struggle through a few mouthfuls of food. I feel like I have a mouth full of cotton wool. Mrs Ross goes to the back door where the top opens and she leans on the bottom half and screams loudly, bring them chickens up here now, I have work to do and two more mouths to feed. There is a big commotion going on in the courtyard with much squawking, dogs barking and men laughing. I have got to see what is happening out in the courtyard. I ask to be excused from the table as loud as I can so that Mrs Ross can hear me. Rita says; come on, this sounds like fun. We don't wait for Mrs Ross to answer us. She can't hear us anyway. We push up in front of Mrs Ross. She opens up the bottom half of the door. You may as well see where your dinner comes from. You have been coddled too long down there in the village. We pay no mind to her and burst through the unlatched door and are stopped dead in our tracks, just like we have brakes on our shoes, abruptly and I mean abruptly. A chicken is running around the courtyard like a drunken sailor, crazily, with no direction in mind. He makes no sound. The chicken has no head. Blood is pulsating up from its neck, dripping onto its brown feathers. The dogs are chasing it and the men are cheering. Get it Bo, get it. Bo does. Feathers are flying as he brings her to the ground. She flops once and then is still. The men call Bo off. He comes back to them and wags his tail as if proud that he has pleased them. They throw the chicken's bloody head with open eyes to him, which is his reward, and he munches on it contentedly. The other chickens are frantic and running hither and thither in the courtyard waiting for the murderer's bloody axe. My legs are shaking with fear. I look at Rita. Her face is white and sweaty. Her hands are clenched. She is promptly sick and vomits over the stone steps. The farm hands start to laugh and chide us. Get used to it girlies, this is where your dinner comes from. We are going to let you do it next time. I scream at them. I hate you. I hate you. You killed it. I hope you die. They all laugh. Mrs Ross hustles us inside. You had to see it sometime girls. I am sorry that it was on your first day but you wanted out there. Didn't you ever wonder how the chicken got on your plate? You'll get used to it. Never! Never! I hate her too. Tears spring to my eyes. I don't want her to see so I brush them away with my clenched knuckles. I will never forgive her. She takes Rita's arm and pulls her to the stone sink to clean her up. Rita can't even talk. Mrs Ross pumps water in to the big sink and attempts to wash the sick off of Rita's face and frock with a rough flannel. Rita flinches and tries to pull away but Mrs Ross isn't having it. She is a strong woman with muscular arms. Good for strangling chickens. Rita still reeks of sick. I want to show you the house and where you will be sleeping, Mrs Ross tells us. She lights a taper and holds it to the wick on the oil lamp that is sitting on the dresser. It flames up. It is getting dark outside and now the courtyard seems eerily quiet. Rita and I huddle together for comfort. We follow the farmer's wife up the dark passageway, our shoes clicking on the stone floors, both of us fearing what might come next. She opens a big dark wooden door on her right and ushers us in to a dimly lit room. She tells us that this is the main living room. It feels huge and lonely. The evening shadows cast an eerie vision of swaying trees upon the walls. There are many trees outside the large window and along the driveway. Heavy wool curtains can be pulled to shut out the light or burning lights inside which could guide Gerry on to London, poor old London. Mrs Ross briskly pulls the curtains across to shut out the light. A huge open fireplace takes up the whole wall at the end of the room. The smoke has blackened the stone surrounding the hearth from years of wood and coal fires. Nothing burns there tonight. There are two well used, overstuffed couches. They look saggy. I wonder how many generations have sat on them and farted. I want to giggle so badly, thinking about it. These thoughts have become a hilarious sport since being evacuated. Before evacuation I hadn't paid them much mind. My parents had told us that it was very rude to laugh when someone passed wind. I remember when my grandmother would start to sing very loudly the song, On the Road to Mandalay, we all knew she was about to blow off and we would run for cover. But now, I mean after all, when a whole group of children from all walks of life, ages five through twelve, are thrown together it becomes a great source of amusement. In chapel on Sundays the boys sit up in the gallery imitating farts while the vicar is giving his passionate sermon on how evil the world is. The rest of us down below are snickering into our handkerchiefs, trying not to laugh out loud. Rita and I used to hear pious Mrs Allen letting one go in her chair when she fell asleep after supper. Some were quite sonorous. Rita and I imitated the sound with our tongues between our lips and blowing. We would fall about laughing while stuffing our hands in our mouths so she wouldn't hear us and wake up. It was our greatest form of entertainment before bed time. It makes me laugh and feel good just thinking about it right now. I am sure that Mrs Ross must be thinking about why I am smiling right now. If only she knew. Two arm chairs sit on either side of the fireplace with sheepskins and ottomans for your feet. Dark wood tables with big oil lamps and hard chairs are at the other end of the room. Never ending bookshelves cover the walls. So many old books that you could spend years with those books and never finish. There are no carpets in the room just the cold stone floors. Mrs Ross breaks the silence. We have church services here on Sunday evenings. Six PM sharp and everyone on the farm must attend, no excuses. I wonder, do the axe murderers repent and pray for forgiveness? Rita and I look at one another. We realize that this means no more trips to the village chapel, no more seeing our friends and fellow evacuees, no more getting into trouble for our practical jokes, whispering under our breath while the Vicar is speaking and where the organist glares at us when we sing off key on purpose. There will be no more imitation farts where everyone will look to their neighbour thinking, was it you or was it you. Oh those poor village people. It was hilarious and worth going to chapel for. Rita and I are glum thinking about it but we dare not say anything. If we thought life was difficult and lonely back in the village we haven't seen anything yet. But the saddest part is that we won't get to see our brother. Mrs Ross closes the big dark door of the living room uttering a moral point. You are not allowed in the big room until after supper and never before six PM. The only exceptions are Sunday services, Christmas and special holidays. She opens another door off of the dark passageway. A steep dark stairway reaches before us. To me it seems very spooky. I hold on tight to Rita. Mrs Ross leads the way up with the oil lamp which casts scary shadows on the walls. I am paralyzed. My legs won't move. Who or what is going to jump out at us? Rita yanks me up. I know that I will never be able to climb these stairs every night to go to bed. We do make it to the landing without being attacked. There are five closed doors, three on one side of the landing and two on the other. She leads us to the last doorway on the right and opens it inwards. It creaks at the hinges. Mrs Ross informs us that this is our bedroom and tells us, you will make your bed immediately upon arising in the mornings. Hot water jugs will be outside your door at six thirty for your personal hygiene. All I can think of at this moment is what is my personal hygiene? Where is it? I didn't even know that I had one. I yank on Rita's hand and try to ask her where it is but she shushes me to be quiet. I am sure that she will tell me later but I certainly didn't know that I would have to wash it. Mrs Ross continues with the rules of do's and don'ts. Don't use the bathroom for your personal business till the farm hands have gone down to breakfast. The bathroom is usually vacant around six AM. If your personal business has to be taken care of before that then there is a chamber pot under the bed. That's another problem for me, personal business in the chamber pot? What is that all about? Sometimes I don't understand grownups. My sister and I look around the bedroom to see where we will be spending our evenings and nights. There is a large marble washstand with the usual jug and bowl to wash with, a soap dish, a tooth brush holder and two thin scrubby looking towels and flannels that hang on a towel horse, a wooden towel horse. The rules continue. You will empty your dirty wash water into the lavatory and pull the chain. You will have a bath once a week on a Friday afternoon and only then. Hair is to be washed every two weeks. There are so many rules. I hope Rita is taking this down. I know that I will never remember it all. I look around the room which is to be our only sanctuary. We have a double bed with a big eiderdown. The floors are wood with two sparse rugs on either side of the bed. There is a big chest of drawers with an oil lamp on top and an old wooden ladder back chair. The biggest, tallest dark wooden wardrobe that I have ever seen dominates the room. This is where you will hang your clothes and I never want to see them on the floor or on the bed. Mrs Ross opens the door. Of course I imagine that something frightening and ugly will jump out of it. Nothing does. It is dark inside the wardrobe and will be awfully hard for me to reach into it. I will have to stand on the chair to put my clothes away or to get them out. There are empty coat hangers hanging on a wooden rod. They look sinister in the darkness and in my imaginative mind, ready to attack. This is not going to be my favourite place. Mrs Ross walks over to the two tall windows that look down onto the front garden below. I go over and look out. The trees are bending in the wind and making weird rustling sounds and the light is leaving fast. Night is setting in. She pulls the curtains roughly across the windows. We hear a noise on the staircase. Mr Ross, the farmer, comes bundling into the room with our suitcases. Here you go lasses, unpack and get ready for bed. Mother will bring you up some mugs of hot milk. In the morning I will tell you what your farm duties are both before school and after school. Good night to the both of you now. With that he is out of the door and gone, leaving us with Mrs Ross. She tells us to follow her and leads us into a large bathroom. A bare light bulb overhead casts a garish light on the cold white ceramic stone floor. There is a huge high lavatory with a long chain and a china handle to pull. From my vantage point, I will have to stand on the closed seat to pull it. There is a big china sink with a small chipped mirror above it and a claw foot bathtub with two taps that sits in the middle of the room. She tells us that there is only cold water in the taps and for hot water some water will have to be heated on the Rayburn stove in the scullery kitchen and be carried up the stairs in large white enamelled jugs on bath day. We are told that our bath days will be on Fridays and on that day we will even get clean knickers, vests, socks and nighties. That being said, she concludes our tour telling us to never open the other doors on the landing. They are the bedrooms for her and Mr Ross and the farmhands. I don't want to hear about any more rules. I don't want to think about anything. I am so tired and cold. For once I will even go to bed without being told to but first I have to rescue Heather from my suitcase. Poor Heather, she will be so happy to be out of the suitcase. After rescuing her and giving her a hug I put my nightie on and get ready to go to sleep in this new place. I am so afraid and lonely. I am glad that Rita and I are sharing a bed. I have her to hold onto. Before we go to sleep I ask her to look under the bed. I am so afraid of the Boogeymen. They come out at night you know and steal little girls away. Rita asks God to bless me, Mummy, Daddy and Len. She says that we will talk in the morning. Please God. Don't let me wet the bed in this strange house.

OUR NEXT DAY AT ROSKILLY

It is Monday morning and is to be our first full day at Roskilly. I was hoping to wake up from this nightmare, but no, it is real. We are at Roskilly Farm. There is a loud knocking on our bedroom door. Mrs Ross is calling out to us. Time to get up! Don't make me tell you twice or there will be punishment. We struggle to wipe the sleep from our eyes. It is still dark out. Oh, how I hate to get out of our warm bed and put my feet down onto the cold linoleum floor. Our bed is so high off of the floor that I have to lay on my stomach and swing my legs over the side and keep inching down until I feel the frigid linoleum beneath my feet. I tuck Heather back into bed so that she can stay warm. Rita is grumpy this morning. We both are. She says that I woke her up last night when I had to use the chamber pot. I tell her, what do you expect? It was so dark and I couldn't feel the floor under my feet. It seemed that it took ages to reach the floor and then I couldn't find the pot so I had to crawl under the bed and feel around until my hands found that cold china pot. I then told her that I had to drag that heavy pot till it was clear of the bed, pull up my nightie and sit on it and that it was so cold and how can anyone wee in a china pot and not make a sound? I would like to see you do it, I said. I bet her that she can't. She never has to get up during the night. I wish that I didn't have to but it is better than wetting the bed. Rita goes outside the door to bring in the hot water jugs from the landing. We wash ourselves and brush our teeth and finish dressing. Rita looks at our rule list to see if we can use the bathroom yet, for as Mrs Ross says, our personal business and yes it is our turn to use the lavatory. We put the china lid on the pot and between us carefully carry it into the bathroom and then very carefully empty it into the loo. Our private business accomplished, we then empty our grey wash water and we leave the bathroom to climb, very carefully, down the dark narrow stairs and at the bottom open the door into the large kitchen to see Mrs Ross standing at the Rayburn stirring a pot. Sit yourselves down children. All of the farm hands have already eaten and have left for work. She ladles us out some very grey looking lumpy porridge into two bowls. She continues, I want you both to come straight home from school every day as there are many farm duties for the two of you to do before supper every evening and I will expect you to do them every day except for Sundays, so no playing in the village after school with your evacuee friends. Is that clear? Rita is visibly upset. I can see it in her eyes. But what about my friends, she complains. I always hang around with them after school. You will not do that anymore. This is a working farm and that is the end of it. I don't want to hear any more of your grumbling and if either of you doesn't come home directly from school you will be punished. Oh, there is that word punishment again. This is not good. Why, oh why did Mrs Allen's husband have to come home from the Navy? We cover our porridge with sugar and milk. It gags you. It is so thick with the skim on top. It probably has been cooking since five o'clock this morning. Maybe the first servings were edible. We get some of it down. Mrs Ross sets two large brown boiled eggs in egg cups in front of us. I don't think I have ever seen such large eggs. They are all speckled. She put large slices of bread on a toasting fork and toasts them in front of the open fire in the Rayburn. She scrapes off the burned parts and puts butter on them. It seems that there is plenty of fresh butter and eggs here on the farm. We mustn't complain. They don't have this back in London. I am anticipating this lovely brown egg. Mrs Rowe peels off the top of the still warm shell and puts salt and pepper on it for me. My mouth is watering in anticipation. I put the spoon into the egg, scooping up a spoonful. It is yummy. On my second helping my spoon goes deeper into the deep rich yellow yolk. I bring it up to my mouth and then freeze my spoon in mid-air. I scream out loud in shock. There is bright red blood streaked through that bright yellow. I am absolutely traumatized. I scream and start to cry out; there is blood in my egg, bright red blood in my egg. Mrs Ross asks, good heavens child what is the matter with you? There is blood in my egg, I sob. She comes over to look. Stop snivelling and eat it she says sternly. It was just a chick trying to grow in the egg that didn't make it. I killed the chick, I killed it, I cry. Rita pushes her egg away. What a commotion. You didn't kill it she says. It couldn't have lived. It wasn't ever formed. Rita implores me to stop crying. Please Sheila, stop. I eventually stop sobbing and tell Rita, through my tears, that I will never eat an egg again. It is now getting late and we must leave for school. If we are late there will be consequences. There are always consequences for everything. We both go out through the courtyard. The farm dogs start to chase us out to the road, barking and growling. They are not friendly at all. The sheep dog, Bo, tries to round us up like sheep and the collie tries to nip at our backsides. They think it is a game. One of the farmhands calls to them and they turn back at the farm gate. I am sure they will be waiting for us when we return. I guess that they will get used to us. I certainly hope so.

The walk to school is long. Three whole miles but at least it is all downhill going to school. I don't even want to think about coming home as that will be all uphill. Farmlands are all along on either side of the narrow country road with hedgerows on either side protecting them. We stop and watch some hogs in a large pen rutting around in the very wet mud. They love it. We pick some of the last blackberries of the summer in the bushes along the way. I am so hungry and that is all because I didn't eat my breakfast. I eat the blackberries. Rita is disgusted. She says that my teeth are black and that my fingers and mouth are stained. She pulls out her hanky from her knickers, spits on it and tries to wash the stain off of my face. She is so rough. Come on she says, we will have to hurry or we will be late for school. Rita says that Betty is going to meet us on the way down the hill to the village. I know that she can't wait to see and tell Betty how bad it is up on the farm. Betty is waiting outside her house. Rita and Betty fling themselves at one another as if it has been years since they have seen one another. I know I am just jealous. I walk ahead of them and leave them to their chat. I say goodbye to them at the church corner. I don't think that they even notice that I am gone. Rita calls out to me. I'll meet you at half past three. Don't be late. As if I am the one who is always late. It is good in a weird sort of way to be back in school. All of these people are my friends. We share a very common bond. We belong because we are different. The village children still give us the cold shoulder but they have given up on teasing us and calling us Dirty Cockneys. The scuffles are not as bad as they used to be. We keep to ourselves but then of course this is just our first day back at school. Miss Ship, my teacher, asks me how my new billet is. I tell her that I hate it and how I so badly want to go back to Mrs Allen. I am sorry Sheila, she says. Maybe it won't be for much longer. You just have to believe with all of your heart that you will be going home someday soon. Home, it seems like a million miles away in the land of make believe. The day passes uneventfully. It is so good to be with Angela again. I tell her that maybe she can come up to the farm to visit us. She tells me that she is very homesick and that it is her sixth birthday next Tuesday and that she wants to go home to be with her Mum, Dad, Nana, Granddad and all the rest of her family but she knows that it is not going to happen. We have heard on the wireless that the bombing is not as bad but it is still too dangerous to go home because of the threat of invasion. I hurt for her. I can't wait for school to get out today. Rita is there at the corner with Betty just like she said she would be. I am happy to see her. I don't want to make the long lonely walk by myself. I follow them up the hill to Betty's billet. I wait for Rita to say her goodbyes so that we can be on our way but that doesn't happen. She turns to me and kneels down in front of me so that she can look into my face. She takes my hands in hers and says, look Sheila, I want you to tell Mrs Ross that I am having my tea with Betty and that I will be home about six o'clock to do my work. She lied to me. I will have to walk that uphill road by myself. I knew that this would happen. I start to protest but what is the use. Off you go now she says. Go straight back to the farm. Don't stop anywhere. I ask, can't I have tea with you and Betty? I will behave. I won't spill my tea in the saucer and then slurp it. No, no, Rita says. We don't want Mrs Ross being cross with both of us. Now go. Betty looks at me, tilts her head and says quietly, sorry Sheila, maybe next time. Yes, like there will be a next time. I may be only six but I certainly know when I am not wanted. I watch them from the road as they go up the pathway to the house together, their heads in deep conversation. I feel so sad. I start up the hill; it is so steep and deserted. Everyone is home having tea but me. It is very warm for September. The afternoon sun is beating down on my head. I am hot and sweaty. I stop and pull off my dark blue beret and stuff it in my satchel. I push down my knee socks and tie my blazer around my waist. I am all ready for the trek up the hill. I push my satchel back onto my shoulder and start off again. I am so hungry. My cheese sandwich for lunch was a long time ago. The road is narrowing. The trees on either side of the road bend over to meet and form a green swaying, leafy arch. The sun penetrates through and dapples the leaves. It is much

cooler now. I have reached an arbour of trees. There is a
narrow stream running down hill on the right. I stop to look.
The water is so clear running over the stones. It goes way
down into the village and picks up the stream coursing out to
sea. It makes me so thirsty just to look at it. I kneel down in
the copse, bend over and cup my hands to catch the water. It is
so icy cold. My hands look so white. In the reflections of the
stream my face looks so round and fat. I lower my head to
drink. It is so cold and delicious. The best I have ever tasted.
All of a sudden I smell wood smoke. I wonder where it could
be coming from. I am suddenly feeling chilled from the cold
liquid and the shade of the trees. I feel unusually
uncomfortable and so alone. I raise my head up and realize the
uncomfortable feeling is coming from fear. At least I think this
is fear. I sense someone is very close to me. There are eyes,
human eyes, staring at me from the copse on the other side of
the stream. What should I do? Should I run, scream or ask
who they are? There is a rustling as two hands slowly part the
bushes. I hold my breath and I see a dirty, very dirty; old man
is sitting on the ground. I struggle to get to my feet, scared but
I am also very curious and I become rooted to the spot. The
dirty old man speaks; don't be afraid little lady. I am just
having my tea. Would you like to join me? I don't get many
guests. I somehow feel that this is wrong. I answer. Oh, no I
have to be home for my tea or they will come looking for me.
He offers out a filthy claw like gnarled hand to me in
friendship and for me to shake. The fingernails are long and
have black dirt under them. Don't be afraid he says I won't
hurt you. I live here in the copse. My name is Ben. I gingerly
offer my wet cold hand. Hello, Ben. I am called Sheila. Are you
a real tramp? I have heard all about them in stories but you are
the first one that I have ever got to meet in person. I think to
myself, whoa, Rita is not going to believe this story. Ben, do
you live and sleep outside all the time? Ben chuckles, yes I do

and I guess that is what people call me, a tramp. I suppose we are called that because we tramp all over the countryside looking for food and places to live. Like Gypsies, I ask? Not quite he says. They have caravans to sleep in. Me I don't like being indoors. Never have. He reaches out his hand to me, come I will show you my camp. Well this is an adventure that I will be able to tell everyone about. I feel no fear whatsoever. I trust him. He helps me cross the babbling stream. My shoes and socks get wet as I cross over. How will I explain this to Mrs Ross? Oh well, I will worry about that later? We walk together a few feet to a clearing and there is his camp. There is a small twig fire burning. That was what I smelled. There is a tripod with a blackened tea kettle hanging from it and steam is coming from its spout. If I am dreaming this I don't want to wake up, it is too much fun. There are old dirty looking blankets lying on the ground. My new friend Ben picks up two old, chipped tin mugs and pours a steaming dark brown liquid into the cups. He opens up an old biscuit tin and puts sugar into each of them. He then takes a cup of milk from a pail and pours some of it into our cups. He tells me, I go and milk a stray cow when the farmer isn't around in case you wonder where the milk comes from. He hands me my mug. I take a sip of the golden liquid. It is the best cup of tea that I have ever had, hot and sweet. Be you one of the evacuees that I have heard about, he asks? Yes I am, I answer. My sister and I live up at Roskilly farm. That is at least until we can go back to London. Gosh, I wonder what my mother would say if she knew where I was right now? He smiles gently. He has a kind but very dirty face. Long, long filthy dirty matted grey hair and a long beard. Some of his tea dribbles down into it. His boots, baggy pants and jacket are stiff with dirt. I look at him with wonder. Ben, do you like living outside all by yourself? Don't you get very lonely? No, he answers. I never have to be anywhere at any certain time, no one telling me what to do. I don't have to wash myself or my clothes and nobody ever tells me what time to go to bed, I steal eggs from the chickens, milk from the cows, fruit in the summer from the orchards, berries from the bushes and sometimes a loaf of bread that is set out to cool at farm house windows. Sometimes I steal tea and sugar from the grocery store. I set traps and catch rabbits. Life is good. You mean you don't even have to take a bath on Friday nights, I ask? I am in awe of that. Never, he says. I have so many questions for him, like did he ever have a Mum and Dad or Sisters and Brothers. The questions keep coming and the time races by. Finally he tells me I should be on my way home before they come looking for me. He says they wouldn't understand if they caught us together. Why I ask? Well never you mind, he says. I ask him, may I see you again? I am so utterly fascinated with him. I have got to see him again. I may be here for another day or two he says and then I have to move on. You may come but don't come with anyone else. They wouldn't understand. Can't I even tell my sister I ask? She wouldn't tell anyone. No, no one, he says, promise me. Very well, I shan't tell anyone. I absolutely promise. But I will tell my doll Heather. I tell her everything. You would like her. He nods his head and smiles. He walks me back to the stream, helps me across and then turns and disappears back into the bushes. This is absolutely the most smashing afternoon I have ever had. No one will ever believe it but I can't break my promise. Rita had tea with Betty but I had tea with Ben, my secret new friend.

On arriving back at the farm I am punished for being late for tea and for wet shoes and socks. Explain, explain Mrs Ross says and where is your sister? I can't mention Ben, I promised him. I tell Mrs Ross that it was hot and I took a paddle in the stream on the way home, hence wet socks and shoes and that Rita is having tea with Betty. Mrs Ross is furious with us both.

She says that while you are staying with us you will obey the rules and when you do not you will be punished and now you will go straight to your room, change your clothes and go straight to bed. One of Mrs Ross's oldest sons, Roger, who works the farm, comes in through the back door. He is so handsome, black curly hair and the darkest eyes. To me he looks like a film star. He winks at me and smiles as he goes to wash at the kitchen sink. I am thinking that I can't wait to get to school tomorrow to tell Angela about him and of course my new friend Ben. Maybe it won't be so bad here after all. Can I have my tea, I ask, I am so very hungry. How dare you ask for tea, you are being punished my girl. Run along upstairs. I will bring along some bread and milk when you get in bed. I hate bread with hot milk. It is like hot white school paste with sugar. I climb the dark stairs without an oil lamp as it isn't dark outside yet and there is just enough light on the stair to feel your way up. I make it as quick as I can. I am afraid of who might be waiting around the turn of the stair. Once I get into our bedroom I pull Heather out from the bed covers and tell her about my exciting day and how sorry I am that I can't take her to school with me as I would love for her to meet Ben. You would really like him, I say. He is disgustingly gloriously dirty and no one tells him to wash or go to bed. He just does what he jolly well likes. I undress and put my night gown on but before I can get into bed I have to hang up my clothes in that big dark wardrobe or I will be in trouble for being untidy. So I pull a chair over and climb up on it so that I can open the huge door. It squeaks as it opens. It is so very dark inside and so big. I still can't reach the rod to hang my clothes on and so carefully I step up on the bottom of the wardrobe. I reach into the darkness for a wooden hanger and I am suddenly frightened to death as a strident voice tells me to get down from there, immediately. From fright I fall onto the hard edge of the chair and then onto the floor. Nothing is hurt badly, just a few bumps and bruises and my pride. Don't you ever step on my furniture. What is wrong with you child? I can't reach it I cry out. Then for heaven sake leave them for your unruly sister to hang up. Never ever stand on my wardrobe again. Come with me. She grabs my arm and pulls me up off the floor and tells me to look inside the big ugly wardrobe. She thrusts my body forward into the wardrobe. Look closely child she says. I cry to her, it is so dark and scary in here, please let me out. She says, if you ever stand on that again the floor of the wardrobe will give away and you will be sucked in and fall forever and ever down, down, down all the way to Australia and you will never ever see your parents again. Do you hear me? Remember child Australia is a long, long way away and you would never get back. I can't bear the thought. She puts me down and lets me go. No way will I ever stand on that wardrobe again. I really believe that I will be sucked down never to see my sister or my family again. I feel like that would be the worst thing ever. Mrs Ross tells me to get into bed. I'll be back she says. I climb into my bed and pull the covers over my head to shut out all of the scary thoughts and the fear of never seeing my family again. What a day. I do so wish that Rita was here. I have to tell her about the wardrobe and what will happen if she stands on it. I don't have to wait too long. Rita comes in with two bowls of warm bread and milk, slop. Here is our supper she says and we are not allowed out of our room until the morning. Oh, crumbs and it is only six o'clock. The worst is we won't get to listen to the news from London on the wireless but the good part is that we won't have to do our tasks today. Mrs Ross is very cross with the both of us. Where on earth were you Sheila and why were you so late? I told you to go right home. What happened? I can't possibly tell her the truth. I made a promise to Ben and it is our secret. I would truly cut my tongue out before I would tell our secret so I tell her that I was paddling in the stream because it was so hot and picking some blackberries and that I lost track of time. Well because of you she says I can't have tea with Betty anymore and we have to go straight home every day. Thanks a lot, Sheila. Oh, no this is a real crisis. I won't be able to have time with my new friend Ben. It makes me sad to think about it. Should I tell Rita? I will make her promise with her life not to tell. I just don't want her to stay cross with me. If I tell her maybe she will be nice to me. I decide to tell her. Rita, I have something to tell you. The real reason why I was late home, but you must cross your heart and hope to die if you tell. She agrees and I believe her. I tell her excitedly and in loud whispers of my afternoon and that I want to take her to meet old Ben tomorrow. She has a look of complete shock on her face. Sheila, Mum has always told you never to talk to strangers. What on earth is wrong with you? If she ever finds out we will both be in for a jolly good hiding. She would be so angry. You must never see him again. Do you understand me? No, I don't understand. You just want to spoil it all because it didn't happen to you and that it is my secret. I also tell her about the wardrobe and that she must never stand on it or else she will disappear to Australia. Rita says: "Don't be so soppy Sheila, that can't happen". I retort, well, all I can say is I warned you to not stand on the wardrobe. We go to bed angry at one another but I know that she won't tell Mrs Ross. Out of curiosity the next afternoon we check on the way home to see if he is there but he is gone. All that remains of my friend are cold ashes from his campfire. I wonder what happened to him. You will always be my friend, Ben.

HARVEST TIME

September through October is the time to bring in the harvest, before the long winter months set in. The farm is at its busiest. Farmers from other local farms arrive to help in the fields. Even the Women's Land Army helps out. They help fill the jobs of the men on the farms who have been called up to fight this wretched war. Rita is so taken by their dark green and khaki uniforms that she wants to be one when she grows up. The Rosses will reciprocate everyone's help by going to their farms when their harvest is brought in. Many hands are needed on the land. In the kitchen the women are making dinners and suppers. Dinners are taken out to the workers at noon. Hot Cornish pasties tied up in red and white kerchiefs to keep them warm. Oh, the aroma. I want to eat them as soon as they come out of the oven. There is hard apple cider to drink from a large wooden staved barrel. It is so delicious to drink on a hot day like this but I am told it can be quite potent if drunk in large quantities. Wheat is threshed, hayricks are made, and hay is to be stored in the barns. Fields are to be ploughed to lay fallow for the winter. The farm house is to be scrubbed clean top to bottom for this special occasion. Farmer Ross's two nieces Joanie and Meggie come to stay at the farm for a few days to help out with the cleaning. Their ages are ten and eleven. Why can't anyone be my age? But, they are actually a lot of fun and we get into a lot of mischief but Rita and the two older ones blame me for everything when they get caught. They tell me that it is because I am just a little girl and won't get as bad a punishment as they would.

Today is Harvest Festival, an especially busy day. The stone floors in the kitchen and hallway have been scrubbed within an inch of their life. Newspapers have been put down to keep them clean until dry for tonight is the big family and friends supper to celebrate the successful bringing in of the harvest. Everything has to be the best. Best food, best dishes, best silverware, best clothes and children that are to be seen and not heard. Mrs Ross asks Rita, Joanie and Meggie to go into the big room and bring all the best white china into the kitchen for there will be twenty to thirty people tonight. The long kitchen table is to be set with provisions for all the farm hands and extra workers. The girls' job is to bring into the kitchen the stacks of dinner plates and they are heavy. I see Rita struggling under the load of her stack of plates. She is so skinny, not much of her. The biggest thing about her is her hair, thick and very curly. It has grown in beautifully since getting shorn when we arrived in the village. The girls are doing well. They are on their third trip back to the kitchen when Rita notices an article in the newspaper on the floor regarding the war. She crouches down to read it and Joanie who is close on her heels, runs into Rita. Rita falls forward and all of her dishes crash to the floor. Joanie lets go of hers and they all go sailing into the air and then fall with the most rendering crash onto the stone floors. White china pieces are flying everywhere. I want to scream but nothing comes out. There are two seconds of primal silence and then the screams of anger and the running of feet start. The girls look paralyzed with fear. They don't move. Meggie stands like stone with her dishes still clutched in her hands. My heart is pounding in my chest. If anyone is listening I am sure that they can hear it. This is bad, really bad. Rita and Joanie are jerked up by their arms to a standing position. Mrs Ross's face is bright red. I can see her mouth opening and closing like a fish gasping for air. I cover my ears so as not to hear the loud tirade. Rita and Joanie are crying miserably and apologizing profusely to no avail. The kitchen helpers come in and are shocked at the mess of broken china. They try to calm down the apoplectic Mrs Ross but she just won't have it. She drags the two girls through the open kitchen door and applies the carpet beater to their behinds. They cry and scream but to no avail. They get struck at least fifteen times each. The exhausted but still angry Mrs Ross then tells them to get out of her sight for the rest of the day. Their egos are severely bruised and their bottoms are red and smarting. Meggie and I escape from the kitchen as fast as we can before we are also found guilty and given a clout just for being there. We run out after the other girls and we know where they are bolting to, our place of sanctuary, the barn. They are lying in the hay on the floor. Their tear stained faces are now wreathed in laughter. The more they think about Mrs Ross's red face the more they laugh and soon we are all doubled over, lying in the hay laughing. It is infectious. Poor Mrs Ross, if only she knew. Not daring to go back to the farmhouse before supper we pass the rest of the day climbing the ladder into the hay loft and jumping onto all of the mounds of hay on the floor that is waiting to be pitchforked up into the loft for winter feed. We are squealing with joy and having a great old time when a large shadow crosses the barn door. Oh, no we have been too noisy and they have heard us all the way up at the house. The silence is all of a sudden deafening, you can hear a pin drop. Then we hear a deep throaty laugh and Roger pops his handsome head around the big barn door. Found you, he says laughing. I thought that you might be hungry. Here are some apples. The men are just about done picking in the orchards so I picked out the four larges, reddest, juiciest apples for you girls. I hear that you are all in trouble. It is better for you to not go back to the house until it is time to wash for supper. Hopefully Mother will have cooled off by then but I can't promise. We thank him and tell him that we are truly sorry that we caused such a commotion and upset the harvest festival. He tells us to make ourselves scarce and stay out of Mother's way and then leaves. We all flop back on the hay and the three older girls cry out in unison, Oh, Roger and giggle girlishly. I don't really understand it all but I guess I will eventually.

So harvest has come to a close with a crash. Dishes are borrowed from neighbouring farms and a good time is had by all. The four of us are sent to bed without our supper and not allowed to join in the evening festivities. It could be worse. We listen from the landing as the Cornish men's church choir sings to end the evening with the beautiful song "Going Home, I am going Home". Cornish men have such beautiful voices and their choirs sing at all special events. It is a fitting and emotional end to harvest time and yes I believe in my heart that as the song says I will eventually be going home.

WAR HAS NOT GONE AWAY

The war is now creeping towards us. As we listen to the wireless tonight, the BBC News announces that Plymouth and Devonport are being severely bombed again. The bombs light up the night time skies with fires from their deadly explosions. Germany is reaching out towards us. There are many deaths and much destruction. Bombing started in Plymouth in July of this year and has gotten steadily worse. You can now see Plymouth burning from the Cornish coastline. Late tonight all the evacuees are meeting at the chapel in Polperro with all of the villagers to go down to the rocks and cliffs to see for ourselves the red skies over Plymouth. Rita and I are being allowed to go. Roger takes us in the van to the village to join the others on the cliffs. When we arrive it seems that half of Polperro is camped out on the rocks. We are all watching the bright red glow and smoke in the night sky from the German bombs pounding Plymouth. It seems a lot closer than it actually is. It brings home to us the reality of war. We are inconsolable for the people of Plymouth who are dying and suffering tonight. Each of us is praying in our own way for their suffering to be eased and for this terrible carnage to stop. We are safe for now and I think that we all feel some guilt for that. They are not safe and their lives will be horrendously changed forever. This is war and as bad as it is we evacuees still want to go back to London because the draw of family is the most important thing to us. I know that tonight many of the evacuees, after seeing what is happening to Plymouth, are now even more afraid of what is happening in London and are so frightened of what could be happening to their families and homes but they still desperately want to be there with them, no matter what. Why, oh why is there war? I am just a child. I don't understand why. Why would grownups want to fight, maim, kill and destroy families, property and lives that cannot be replaced for generations to come? Tonight, here on the rocks, we aren't Cornish people or Londoners. There is no divide. We are now as one fighting for our freedom and our country, our beloved sceptred isle, England. We, in Polperro, are prepared for war. We have our own uniformed, tin hatted air raid warden named Willy. We nicknamed him Wee Willie Winkie who would run, huffing and puffing, up and down the village streets blowing on his silver whistle to alert everyone that there is a German raid on Plymouth and to warn us that there may be a chance that a left over Luftwaffe bomb could be dropped on the village on their way back to Germany. It hasn't happened but Willy is doing his bit for the war and we all feel much safer for that.

AUTUMN AND EARLY WINTER TASKS

The start of winter has come to the Cornish coast. We are
having rainy, blustery, cold days and nights. Oh, so cold. This
morning is no exception. I hate to get out of my warm bed and
put my feet onto the cold linoleum. My small body is
shuddering and shivering. I go to the window to see the nearly
bare tree limbs bowing and blowing in the cold North wind. It
blows and whistles around the house. It makes me feel like I
want to just jump back into bed. After all it took all night to
warm it up and now I have to get out of it. I stand here in my
knickers and liberty bodice and wash in water that is icy cold.
It has been sitting outside our bedroom door for an hour. The
soap won't suds up on my flannel because the water is so cold.
If it wasn't for the fact that Rita is watching me I would never
wash until summer. The farmhouse is always cold. There is no
heat except in the kitchen from the Rayburn. I can't wait to get
down there this morning. I am always first for breakfast.

No fire is built in the parlour fireplace until evening after
everyone has had their supper and then of course there is the
pecking order for seating. Farmer Ross and his wife are in the
armchairs in front of the fire, farm hands are next on two old
creaky couches and that also includes their handsome, dreamy
son Roger and then there are Rita and I. We are subjugated to
two hard back chairs in the freezing rear of the room which
does not start to warm up until it is time for us to go up the
dark stairway to bed. This evening, in the front room, the
wireless is on for the news from London. The bombing of

London and all the big cities continues. I hear the pips announcing the news and I cover my ears. I always try to cover my ears whenever I hear the pips. I just don't want to hear about the suffering and how the bombing of London continues. The longer it goes on I think that I might not see my Mum and Dad again. In her letters, Mum says that when the sirens go off announcing a raid, George the cat runs under the bed and won't come out till the all clear sounds. Tonight the news says that larger and more intense raids are hitting London and all the big cities. When will it ever end? After the news the evening hour around the fire continues. It consists of knitting, mending, darning socks, reading and cards for the men. Mrs Ross is teaching Rita to knit socks on four needles. It is part of the war effort, making socks, mittens and scarfs for the service men. I try to learn on just two needles to make a scarf but I fumble and drop stitches so there are holes in it. I get frustrated, give up and pull it off the needles. I hate knitting. So, I read my Rupert book over and over again until my hot water bottle is filled from a big kettle hanging over the fire and then wrapped in a large blanket as it is so hot and you could burn yourself so badly. It is used to heat up our cold frigid bed.

Bath night on Fridays is another miserable cold event. Our clean underwear is airing in the bathroom on the clothes horse. We only get to change our underwear once a week as clothes freeze on the clothes lines after being washed and take forever to dry. The frozen clothes are brought in from outside to the kitchen to be hung on racks close to the ceiling. You can lower the racks by a rope and hoist them back up again. The racks are always in full use during the winter. Therefore a daily change of clothes is just not possible. Hot water for our baths is brought up in jugs and dumped into the bathtub. A dash of cold water from the bathtub tap is mixed in for comfort. A handful of soda crystals are added to make the hard water softer. My sister, because she is older than I, insists that she gets to take her bath first. Why does she always have to go first? Then by the time I get into the tub the water is cold, grey and scummy. Mrs Ross adds one more jug of hot water to it but it is still only luke warm and still scummy. We have to wash our hair in the same water and rinse it from the cold water tap. It is all so very difficult, especially to try to comb your hair, very curly hair, when it is wet and cold. Such a tangled mess that it is always a screaming session with Rita dragging the comb through my very wet hair. It is sheer torture. Secretly, I think she enjoys it. When we are finished we empty the bath and rinse it for the next two people whoever they may be. For my sister and me our daily farm tasks are the worst in this cold. After breakfast and before school we have to draw water from the well in the courtyard for the chickens, pigs, rabbits, dogs and ducks. The water in the well is icy cold and sometimes will freeze in the buckets before we are able to get it into the barns. A freezing wind will freeze the water as we walk and we have to break the thin ice cover in order to pour it into the troughs. We get very bad chilblains on our fingers which are so painful. We wear mittens but they get wet and then stiff from the cold. We can't feel our toes in our rubber wellingtons. They are numb for hours. The chilblains on our feet are punishing. It reminds me of Sussex. We try to warm them up in front of the Rayburn before school which only makes them hurt more. Itching and pain are the norm for us. Our next chore is scattering the feed in the courtyard for the ducks and roosters plus putting the feed in the hen house and hoping that they won't peck us as they are protective of their nests. Next on our list is to swill the pigs. All of the potato and vegetable peelings, old apples and leftover tea leaves from the tea pot are put into the swill buckets. It is disgusting. There are three of them every morning. Rita and I can only manage with one swill bucket between us at a time. We struggle across the courtyard to the pig pens. We are not allowed into the pig pens as they will surround you and knock you over for the food so we chuck it over the low wall that surrounds their pens, to the troughs. Sometimes I try to lean over the wall and try to touch their snouts until I am yanked back by one of the farm hands. You want your hand eaten off to the elbow lass? It be dangerous to do that. I warn you. I just wanted to feel their wet pink snouts. They don't look dangerous I tell him. But I am telling you lass that those piggies don't know no difference between hands and swill. I tell you what. When they have their babies in the spring I will let you hold one. Oh, thank you, I say. I can't wait till spring. I think that I shall absolutely die waiting. Our last task before leaving for school is to collect eggs. When we first started to do it I was scared that the hens would bite me with their sharp beaks but the farmhand Max showed us how to gently put our hands under the warm feathered breast of each chicken and feel for the eggs. The warmth from their feathers and the nest makes you want to keep your hand there forever. To bring out an egg is like a miracle. Imagine a warm brown egg in your hand. I think it is amazing as long as I don't have to eat it. Some of the chickens leave their straw nests to feed making it easier for us to collect their three or more eggs. We fill our baskets and hurry back to the farmhouse glad to be done and to get warm before that long three mile walk to school, often in pouring rain. Even at school in our classroom it is bitterly cold. There is one large fireplace for heat in each classroom but due to rationing coal is scarce and has to be used for ships, factories, trains and such so therefore only a few knobs are allowed a day for the fireplaces. It looks like Mr Scrooges fireplace. You need to sit on top of it to feel any warmth. Only the kids in the front desks and the teacher feel any small bit of comfort. Our teacher rotates us throughout the day to the front row so we can all get some of the heat to warm us. We wear our mittens, pixie hats, balaclavas and coats in the classroom to keep out the penetrating cold. I wonder, will I ever feel warm and cozy again? In the early evening when we arrive home from school we are sent upstairs to change our clothes so that we can do our evening tasks. Before starting we are given a cup of tea and a scone. I love my cup of tea and when I was little my Dad called me a tea pot sucker. I was started on tea at about eighteen months of age, mostly milk with a spot of tea and sugar in a bottle with a teat. I have loved it ever since. Not from a bottle, of course. Rita and I hate evening chores. Our first job is to break up twigs. There is a huge stack of large dry twigs that have to be broken every evening to fire the fireplace in the parlour and the large Rayburn in the kitchen. The wood has to last until the next evening. Rita and I stand outside in the twilight breaking the large twigs apart and putting them in sizeable large buckets. Our chilblained hands are itching and cold and the twigs are cold and hard to break. I of course start snivelling while snapping them apart. A lot of good it does me. It is so cold. Rita tells me to stop snivelling as she is as cold as I am and to just get on with it. The stacks of twigs are beneath the outside kitchen windows which shed some light on our work. We are cold and our life is cold. We have to fill the buckets before we can go in to get warm and have our supper. After everyone has eaten we clear the table. Rita pumps water into the old stone sink. I always want to get on the pump and have a go but she never lets me. After adding a kettle of hot water from the Rayburn, we have to wash up all of the dirty supper ware. I have to pull over a kitchen chair to the draining board, stand on it to reach the high counter and dry the china ware and the pots and pans. My dishtowel gets sopping wet but we are only allowed one and after we are done we hang it in front of the Rayburn to dry for the morning dishes. We then take a large broom and sweep the floor. I run behind Rita with the dust pan waiting for her to sweep the dirt into the pan to be emptied into the outside dustbin. But better than that is Friday nights. That is treat night. We have to get down on our hands and knees with big scrub brushes, buckets of water and scrub the flagstone kitchen floor. The kitchen is so big it seems to take us forever. We have more water on the floors than in the bucket. After they are clean we then put old newspapers down onto the floors to be picked up the next morning. Mrs Ross pops in and out to inspect and to make sure that we aren't playing around. Luckily she doesn't see us run slide and skid across the wet floors. It makes work so much more fun. I think we are the only five and eleven year olds to have house maid knees in all of England. Weekends are spent helping to muck out cow sheds and chicken coops, sweeping the courtyards, beating carpets on the clothes lines and helping Mrs Ross in the large kitchen to prepare food for Saturday and Sunday. I love the smells of the apple tarts and currant cakes baking in the Rayburn. There is no cooking on Sundays because of church. It isn't allowed and also because of Sunday night meetings in the parlour. So everything is prepared the day before and warmed up on Sunday. We are lucky because there is no shortage of food on the farm. There is always breakfast, a packed lunch and a supper for us on the weekdays and three meals on Saturdays and Sundays. One of my all-time favourite times on the farm is when farmer Ross takes me out to the cow sheds at milking time. He lets me sit on the stool and squeeze the teats of one of the cows. The teats are so warm and pink. I love watching the warm milk splash into the pail. Squeeze and pull or pull and squeeze, I can't remember. The pails steam in the cold air and are emptied into the big steel milk cans which are later picked up by the big old blue lorry to be taken to the dairy. Roger tells me that in the spring he will take the cows out to the pasture after the morning milking and bring them back in the evening to be milked again. He tells me that if I am allowed I can go with him. He doesn't know that I have an incredible crush on him. I really think that he is a big brother or an uncle figure to me. Rita says that she has a crush on him too and that my crush doesn't count. She says that he winks at her so I screw my face up trying to wink at him. I am sure that he just thinks that I have a tic. Rita says that he likes her best. I hate her.

In November, wouldn't you know, I become ill with what Mrs Ross thinks is probably the mumps. I feel so ill that I have to stay in bed. Mrs Ross goes into the village to get the Doctor because I am so ill. He comes out to the farm several hours later and I am diagnosed with the mumps because of the big lumps under my ears. His prescription is to stay in bed, put a scarf around my neck to keep out the chill and stay warm. And also gives me some foul tasting medicine to be taken four times a day. I literally have to choke it down because it is so ghastly. The only good thing to come out of this is that I will not have to do farm tasks for a week. It is very painful for me to swallow so I can't eat. Poor Rita, she has to do my chores. But she is being very kind to me while I am ill. She reads to me when she gets home from school and brings up a mug of tea or some soup and sits with me before she has to go do our tasks. Other than that Heather is my only company. All I really want is my Mum. You always want your Mum when you don't feel well. She would have tucked me in, kissed my forehead and brought me a present. But that is not going to happen. Mrs Ross brings me up that awful medicine and a tray twice a day but no kisses or hugs but she does her best. She does take care of me and I thank her for that. Mrs Ross even lets Rita out of her tasks on Saturday afternoon to go see Betty Jones and spend some time in the village. I am happy for her but I hate her at the same time for leaving me. It proves to Rita and I that even Mrs Ross has a heart tucked away in there some place. I am not sure where it is but I am sure it is in there someplace. We don't see it often but it is there. When I am well enough to go outside Mrs Ross sends me to collect eggs. I know the chickens have missed me, even the two killer dogs Shep and Billie come running over barking and jumping up and down excited to see me but I am scared of them. I saw what they did to a chicken. I will never forget that. I retreat from them and make my way cautiously into the chicken coops and shut the gate. There are lots of eggs this morning. My favourite round brown hen purrs for me like a cat. She is pleased to see me and lets me know it. I pet her for a few minutes after I have collected all of the eggs into my basket. I wish I could have a cat to cuddle but Mrs Ross will not allow cats into the house. The only cats allowed on the farm are the ones in the barns who kill the rats and mice. I have chased them many times to pet them but they won't let you catch them. Even if I did Mrs Ross would kick them out of the house if I bought one in. I am wasting time thinking about what cannot be. I have to get the eggs back to the house. The basket is heavy. I start out across the courtyard to the house. Some of the roosters and hens are outside eating feed. The dogs are barking on the other side of the coops. I better hurry and get the eggs into the house, but I am too late. The dogs come from behind the coops chasing a little grey bunny. Poor thing, it is terrified and running for its life. I hate those dogs. I turn to shout at the dogs to stop but they knock me down in their path of haste. I scream loudly as the basket and eggs go flying, Oh Cor Lummy, now I really am in trouble. There are broken eggs everywhere, golden yolks, sticky membranes and egg shells lying in puddles. The dogs have stopped dead in their tracks. The bunny is forgotten. Its life is spared for another day. The dogs are hungrily lapping up the runny eggs. I try to get up on my sticky hands and my bleeding knees. I make a futile attempt to push the dogs away. Shep turns violently on me, growls and deeply lunges quick as lightning. My wrist is in his mouth. I scream hysterically and the farm help come running. Roger is yelling at the dogs. Shep lets go of my wrist and runs yelping to safety. He is afraid of Roger. But then comes back and resumes his morning meal of eggs, nonplussed, as if nothing has happened. Roger drags him off and ties up both of them. He picks me up and takes me over to the pump and water is poured over my bleeding wrist. I sob with the pain and the sight of my red blood pumping out of the wound. It frightens me. Max, one of the farm hands, puts pressure on my wrist and above it to ease the blood flow. What a commotion in the farmyard this morning. Besides the dogs yelping the chickens are screaming and running around wild. I am picked up and put in the old truck and taken in to the village doctor again. The only good part to this morning is that Roger is driving. But at this point it doesn't matter. I am in pain and Roger's attractiveness, for the moment, is dimmed. Mrs Ross has come with us and keeps telling me not to cry and to be more careful in the future. All those wasted eggs, she says, Tut, tut. You should have paid more attention to what was going on around you instead of day dreaming. I think to myself, oh well at least the little grey bunny got away and Roger is still my hero. Now let me see, six stitches should be good for at least two weeks of no tasks. But unfortunately it is on the left wrist and when you are right handed, according to Mrs Ross, there is a lot that can be done with one hand. Like homework and going to school.

REFLECTIONS:

It is September of 1940. On September 7th, according to reports and reliable information, there is a chance of imminent invasion of the British coastline. On September the 8th, around 4PM in the afternoon three hundred and forty eight heavy bombers with an escort of six hundred and seventeen German fighters, almost one thousand aircraft flew across the English Channel towards the Thames estuary. They headed for London. The first of the bombers dropped their bombs on the dock lands, isle of dogs, Woolwich, Silvertown and continued on to the Wapping and Bermondsey area. From there they continued on to the heart of London. Between five and six PM some three hundred and twenty German Bombers supported by six hundred German fighters hit London and the suburbs. This was only the first wave. The second wave arrived guided by the hundreds of fires started by the first wave of bombing. Those fires were encouraged by strong westerly winds. Westminster, Kensington and others were the next targets. Between eight and ten PM some two hundred and fifty bombers resumed the attacks which then continued until four thirty AM. Sunday morning there were sixty large, out of control fires and nearly one thousand lesser fires. Four hundred and thirty people were killed and sixteen hundred were seriously injured. During the second night a further four hundred people were killed and seven hundred and forty seven were seriously injured. The Blitz had started. There were fifty seven consecutive nights of raids. Thousands of tons of bombs rained down on the English capital from the eighth of September to November the second. In just twenty three nights of bombing five thousand seven hundred and fifty people died and over ten thousand were injured. Will we survive? Will it ever end? But unfortunately, figures are to rise dramatically as bombing is severe throughout 1941 and into 1942 but more on that as my story continues.

THEN COMES CHRISTMAS

It is December of 1940 and two weeks to Christmas. Rita, Len and I have only one wish for the Christmas holidays and that is to be able to go home and spend Christmas with our family. I was so sure that we would be home by now. Everyone says that it will be over soon and you will be home before you know it but we are not and it won't happen. The German Luftwaffe is seeing to that. Rita, Len and I as well as all the other evacuees are sad not to be going home. We ask Mrs Ross if Len can come up to the farm for Christmas dinner. The three of us desperately need to be together. She has agreed to Christmas day. She is going to let us walk into Polperro on Christmas morning to accompany Len back to the farm. I can't wait to show him all the things on the farm. Today we got a letter from Mum. She tries not to talk about the war too much but we know from the wireless that it is bad. Not just for us on the homeland but for all of Europe. People are dying and suffering. But when we get a letter from home we know that they are still alive. Mum says she is posting some parcels for us with Christmas presents and that we are not to open them till Christmas day. She knows how much I hate that. I want to open them right away. It is so punishing to look at packages for a week or more, wondering what is in them, touching and feeling to guess what is inside. It is sheer torture for me. But then today, after the great letter from Mum, something bad happened. Rita came down with the Mumps, right before Christmas. How could she? She is so miserable. She looks like a chipmunk with fat, fat cheeks. She has to be in bed for a week. She is quite a grumble weed when she feels very poorly.

315

I hope and pray that she will be able to go downstairs on Christmas day when we open our pressies. Meanwhile it is two weeks till Christmas and Mrs Ross's niece, Tilldy, who is twelve years old, has come to live with us for a few months. Her mother is very ill and is up in London at a hospital for cancer. I ask her about her Mum but she doesn't want to talk about it and starts to cry. But I do understand Tilldy because my beloved Nana died from cancer before we left London for Cornwall and I don't like to talk about it either because it makes me very sad. I miss you Nana so much. Tilldy is going to help us get ready for Christmas. I just know she and Rita are going to be best friends when Rita is feeling better. They are the same age. Mrs Ross tells us that she can use all of our help over the Christmas holidays except we will not be allowed to carry the chinaware after the last incident. The next two weeks, the farmhouse is alive and buzzing with activity. The plumpest chickens and geese are being slaughtered for Christmas dinner. Tilldy and I have to help pluck them. Their bodies are still warm. I feel that I am going to wretch and wretch. I wonder how anyone can eat them after seeing this butchering. Tilldy and the neighbouring women who are helping have done it many times before and it doesn't seem to bother them at all. I am told that it is all part of living on a farm. I look at those beautiful warm, white and brown feathers. You have to pull hard to get the quills to release. Oh God, I don't want to hurt them, even though they are dead, so dead. Their pale naked bodies give the appearance of being covered in goose bumps. They must be so cold. I feel like I am intruding on their privacy. I mean, nakedness is a very private thing. At least that is what my Mum always told me. But the worst is yet to come. They have to be drawn after plucking and that takes strong adult hands. The heads and necks are placed on the chopping block with their scrawny necks and boot button eyes staring at me seeming to be asking, why, why me.

Then one quick decisive chop with the big cleaver and there is a gaping hole where the neck and head used to be. They are tipped to let their life's blood drain out. They are then held with the left hand, the right hand is inserted into the gaping hole and their innards are drawn out, giblets and all. The giblets and liver will be saved for gravy. The heart and all other organs are chopped up for the pig swill, dogs and cats. The poultry is then hung by the feet to completely drain and then put in the cold room until Christmas Eve day when it is to be roasted in the oven. We make the Christmas puddings two weeks before Christmas and they are left to settle and age in the cold room. The cold room is a stone house outside with very thick walls that helps things stay cool. There are many shelves and racks for harvested apples that are kept there along with milk, jams, poultry, beef, bacon, sides of bacon and cheese. The making of the Christmas puddings is one of my favourite memories from London and is a special tradition. My Mum would put aside a special evening two weeks before Christmas when we were all home to make the dark fruity puddings. We all got to have a hand in it. Mum would mix everything together, the dried fruit, candied peel, suet, spices and beer or brandy. So many ingredients, too numerous to mention all, but the best part was at the end of Mum mixing it together. Each one of us got to stir the pudding, make a wish and as tradition would have it, stir in threepenny bits and sixpences. Being the youngest child, I would have to go last. But then, Mum would let us all lick the spoons and scrape the bowls with our fingers. It was so delicious. The puddings were then wrapped in cloth, tied and set in a cold place until Christmas day to then be boiled until done. The aroma was amazing. When done, a sprig of holly was placed on top. Brandy was poured over the pudding and lit. The flaming pudding was then brought to the table to the cheers, oohs and aahs of the family. Aunts, Uncles and cousins all guessed who would be the luckiest one to get the most money from the pudding without swallowing the coins or breaking a tooth on them. That was the prize. After the pudding the crackers were then pulled with anticipation of the prize and funny paper hats inside. We all sat at table with our silly paper hats on and then listened to the King's Christmas day speech to the nation. We didn't utter a word. It would have been traitorous to do so. The national anthem was then played while we all stood in loyalty and allegiance to our King and Country. After dinner the fun would begin. Mum would thump away on the piano and we would, family and all, gather around and sing songs and we would always have a good old "Knees up mother brown". I always loved to sing the part, "knees up Mother Brown your drawers are coming down", that made me laugh. Mum always said that I was wicked. But that was then and this is now. The traditions are relatively the same but this isn't home and home and family is what makes Christmas. Mum says in her letters that in London everything is rationed. They queue up for hours, many times in the pouring rain, cold and snow just to get one loaf of bread. Meat, eggs, and cheese are always very scarce and sugar is almost non-existent. She says there are long queues everywhere and many times when you get to the front counter they are completely sold out and you go home with nothing and try again the next day. How my Mum manages I don't know. It must be a nightmare. We get plenty of good food here on the farm. Christmas in London will be very sparse this year. I feel almost guilty and I wonder if it will be like that when we get to go home.

It is time for me to go upstairs and keep my sister company. She is still in bed with high fever and headaches. She is feeling very tender and swollen just under her ears. I can just about sympathise with her, having just gone through it but I am thinking that she has a more severe case of the mumps than I did. She doesn't look too good to me. She has a warm scarf around her neck to keep her mumps warm but it is so cold here upstairs. How can you ever get well? I ask her if she will help me make paper chains to hang from the ceilings downstairs and make some calendars for presents but she says that she is just too ill to help me. I tell her about Tilldy arriving to stay and about the cancer her mother has. I thought it would make her feel better by telling her about the killing of the fowl and the making of the puddings and how very sorry I am that she didn't get to lick the spoons. She just glares at me. Tilldy is going to come up and see you this afternoon and read to you if you want. If I read to Rita she gets cross because I read too slowly. She just groans and turns away from me.

It is now just a week away from Christmas. We have been released from school until after the New Year. Mrs Ross hates having me under her feet. She just gives me extra jobs to keep me out of her sight. I miss seeing my friends, especially Angela and my brother Len. At least Len will be here on Christmas day. Rita is slowly getting well. Tilldy goes up to see her often. That way she has company of her own age. Yesterday I caught them talking and giggling about handsome Roger. They told me to go away but of course I wouldn't. That is, not until they threw the bed pillows at me. I miss out on all their fun. I wonder how Betty will feel about Tilldy as she will be walking to school with us after Christmas. I can't wait to see what happens. Someone's nose is going to be put out of joint.

It is here. It is here, it is Christmas Eve day. It is cold and sunny. Rita is feeling well enough to be allowed downstairs this evening and for tomorrow. This morning I rushed through my ablutions, a cat's lick and a promise is more like it. Rita yells at me from her bed. You dirty little beggar. Do it properly. Rita is too fastidious about her toiletries. She never goes a day without washing all over. She calls it an FTA, (fanny, tits and armpits). I am not allowed to say those words but I love to think them even though I am not sure what tits are. I am so excited that it is Christmas Eve day. Downstairs I get fried egg, bacon and fried bread and a lovely cuppa. Ooh, I love fried bread dipped into the hot fat from the bacon and fried until it is golden brown, with a little Daddy's sauce. Yum, yum, it makes the heart beat a little faster. After breakfast I am happy to do my tasks because tonight Father Christmas will be coming and I shall wait up for him as long as I can. Mrs Ross says, the earlier we go to bed the sooner Father Christmas will come and that he will never come if we are not asleep. I know that she just wants us in bed and out of the way. There is much commotion and high activity in the kitchen today. Everything must be prepared, cooked because tomorrow is a holiday and no cooking, baking, house cleaning or playing is allowed. I must be daft; I thought that was just on Sundays. I just can't believe it is on Christmas day too. Well, we will have to make the best of it. It surely can't be that bad. The day is passing quickly. Tilldy helps me make the paper chains. We are putting them up with the help of the lovely Roger. He strings them across the ceilings with a few balloons hanging from the centre of the chains. It is so festive looking. It really is beginning to look like Christmas. The parcels from home have arrived. We can only look and not touch. Tonight there is to be a family dinner and Rita is feeling well enough to be up and join us. All of the farm workers are here with Mr and Mrs Ross's relatives, stiff old aunts and uncles and Mrs Ross's brother Tom who has fiery red hair and the bushiest of eyebrows. He looks like he is angry all of the time. When he speaks he barks. He asks Mrs Ross if these be the Lunduners he has heard about. We are introduced to him and he glares at us. Just you mind your betters or I will have to deal with you myself he says. Girls are nothing but trouble. Rita and I get out of his sight as soon as possible. I am certainly glad that he is not here all of the time.

Mrs Ross tells us that his bark is worse than his bite. Don't let him bother you. I don't believe her. I would wager that he does bite. Dinner is set up in the kitchen at the long wooden table. It is snug in here as the Rayburn is filled with wood for all of the cooking. It does feel Christmassy and warm. I wish that Len was here tonight. I can't wait to see him tomorrow. Rita has knitted him a long yellow scarf as a present from both of us. I helped her wind the wool skeins into balls so I did do my part and we made him a card. We made cards for the Rosses and their sons as well. Dinner is a noisy, festive affair. A big fat sizzling goose, golden brown chicken, stuffing, roast potatoes, Brussels sprouts, dark greens (yuk) and gravy. There is no way that I can eat that chicken or goose. I saw what happened to them and I will never forget it. There is one thing that I am waiting for, the Christmas pud which in due course arrives and is absolutely delicious with custard. But it is also a little sad, Mrs Ross didn't put money in hers because she says that that is pagan but I guess I prefer being pagan, whatever pagan is. I wonder if that is the same as being a heathen. I wonder if Rita or Tilldy know what pagan means. I'll have to ask them later when we go to bed. We spend the rest of the evening in the parlour with a lovely big fire in the grate, opening presents from the Rosses. Rita got a sewing box with spools of cotton, needles, scissors and a thimble. She loves to sew. Tilldy gets a comb, brush and mirror set. I wished I had that. It is so grown up but I am happy with what I get a skipping rope. It is a beautiful skipping rope with polished ball bearing wood handles. The handles are bright red. It is very beautiful. Rita will teach me to skip rope on Boxing Day as we are not allowed to play on Christmas day. We are very happy and grateful for our presents. We had made calendars for the Rosses. They seem to like them. We are not going to open our parcels from home till Len gets here tomorrow. I will be awake all night wondering what is in the parcels. After the opening of presents we are sent off to bed so that the grownups can talk. We say our thanks and good nights even to grumpy old Tom. He tells me not to be awaiting that old man, Father Christmas, cos he won't be a coming. Never does come he says. I think to myself, what does he know; he is too old for Father Christmas. I know that he will come. He will come, won't he Rita, I ask as we climb the dark scary stairway to bed. The oil lamp is casting shadows on the yellowed walls. Rita says, of course he will come as long as you go to sleep right away and do what you are told. Tilldy giggles behind us. Yes, do as you are told Sheila. Why does she do that I wonder whenever Father Christmas is mentioned? If she is not nice he won't come for her either. We say good night to Tilldy. She sleeps down the hall from us. Don't stay up Sheila she says and winks at Rita. They are both so silly at their age. Rita and I undress quickly as it is so cold up here. I put my pillow slip at the bottom of my bed for Father Christmas to put my present in and jump into our bed warmed by our hot water bottles and eiderdowns. I hold Heather close to me. I tell her, he is coming tonight and I whisper Happy Christmas to her. Rita and I say our prayers and ask God to forgive us for not kneeling on the cold, cold floor. We both giggle at that. We say goodnight to Mum and Dad and wish that they were here to tuck us in. Rita says, maybe we will be home this time next year. I pray that it is so. I ask my sister, are you going to look out the windows later tonight to watch for Father Christmas? Don't be soppy Sheila, go to sleep. I turn over to face the window and suddenly we hear the strains of a fiddle playing downstairs. We can hear everyone laughing and singing and the clump of their feet as they dance to the music. Such fun tonight but tomorrow will be so different. Len would have enjoyed being here tonight. I wonder if old Tom is dancing. Rita says she bets that it is old Tom playing the fiddle. Finally the warmth of my cozy cocoon lulls Heather and me to sleep. I am awakened later by the window creaking from the wind. It is still dark but a swath of moonlight crosses the bare floor. I don't want to get up but I must go to the window and see what is outside. My feet touch the freezing cold floor, oh so cold, I tiptoe to the window and look up to the night sky. I watch and watch, nothing. I strain and rub my eyes but it is still an empty dark sky. I can't stand here any longer. My teeth are chattering from the cold. I run back to my warm bed and snuggle down with Heather. It just must be true Heather that he won't come unless you are asleep. Good night sweet dolly, Happy Christmas.

I wake up. It is Christmas morning. My hot water bottle is cold and clammy and I can see my warm breath when I breathe over the bed clothes. Oh how I hate to get up. It is even too cold to wee in the chamber pot so I will hold it until I am allowed into the lavatory after all of the adults have used it. But I realize that it is not too cold to jump out of bed to see what is in my pillow case. I reach to the end of the bed to pull it towards me. How can that be? There is nothing there, completely empty. Oh, my, he forgot us. Maybe he couldn't find us. Maybe he left the presents at Mrs Allen's by mistake. Maybe, maybe, I shake Rita awake. Wake up; he didn't come, there is nothing. He doesn't know that we are here. If we were in London he would have come. He has never forgotten us before. Rita lays there looking askance at me. Stop it Sheila, enough, finish. But I don't. I know that I should have waited at the window so that he would know where we are. Rita is losing her patience. She crossly says; maybe the Gerry's shot him down. Now be quiet. I ask her how she could say such a wicked monstrous thing. Sheila, I want you to listen to me, Father Christmas knew that we wouldn't be in London so he posted all of the Christmas presents to Mummy and Daddy ahead of time because in war time it is very dangerous for him to get around and that is what is in the parcels downstairs that we received from home. So, that is what happened, there is a Father Christmas and he is so very smart. He knows where all of the good girls and boys are all over the world and where the naughty ones are also. My sister tells me that I will have to be patient this morning and that we cannot open the parcels until Len gets here. After we have breakfast we sit through morning prayers. The frivolity of Christmas Eve is gone. I fidget and fidget, anxious to be gone down the lane to meet Len. Finally, prayers are over, Amen and Amen. It is now time for me to go down the lane to meet Len. Rita can't go as she is not completely better and it is very cold out. She ties my pixie hat and helps me get my gloves and scarf on. I wish I had some warm boots to wear but I am far too excited to worry about cold legs and feet. I will try to run most of the way. Halfway down the lane at the far end of the lane I see Len trudging up the hill. I run screaming towards him. I fling myself at him. I am so glad that he is here. I hug him tightly but he stands stiff. He gets embarrassed by attention. No fear. Not me, I am very demonstrative and love to show lots of love which embarrasses my family on occasion. Not the typical British way. It is considered not proper and very bad manners to show your emotional feelings. Even if you feel it, you cannot show it. I can never understand that, stiff upper lip. Love is a beautiful thing. I feel good when I am told that I am loved. Excitedly I tell Len about the parcels that Father Christmas sent to Mum and Dad for them to post to us. I chatter gaily on about everything. I have always been a veritable chatter box. I look up at my brother. He looks frozen stiff in his short trousers and knee socks. His legs look blue but he does have on a warm navy reefer coat that Mum sent to him and a knitted balaclava on his head. His face looks pinched and thin and his eyes are dark and sad. I do so wish that he could move in with us at the farm. He says, I didn't get much sleep last night. The Blue Anchor Pub emptied early and there were a lot of drunks singing and whooping it up in the village streets and the noise woke me up. Mr Gillis and his sons were also pounding loudly on the front door to get in. Mrs Gillis let them in and they were loud and unruly messing up the house and screaming at her. They barged into where Len was in bed and made him get up and dance for them while they sung dirty ditties. He was so frightened and cried and they called him bubble bonce. Life can be hell sometimes. I dislike them but this is how they live their lives. Len and I walk slowly up to the farm. He says his legs are aching and it gets really bad sometimes. I ask him if he has written to Mum about it. He says that he has and that she will get him to a doctor or specialist when we get back to London to see what is wrong with him. Oh, how I pray that that is soon. Arriving back at the farm we run into Roger, my hero. He is feeding the ducks, chickens, cockerels and the dogs. My tasks but he is doing this for me so that I could walk with Len. Roger I ask, will you take Len and I into the barns and the hen house to see all the animals? Come on then my wee bairns, let's go. The barns feel warm and smell of hay and manure. It is sweet. Roger even lets Len put some hay and feed into the cows' feeding troughs. Len reaches out and touches the cows' warm wet noses. They are breathing warm moist air onto him and nuzzle his fingers. I know it reminds him of Trewlawny. I would love to take Len up into the hay loft so that we could jump in the hay but this is Christmas, a religious holiday, so no play today. We walk from the barns to the farmhouse so that Len can meet the Rosses. I hope they will be nice to him. I so want them to like him but they have always been very formal. No hugs or emotion. Maybe they are afraid to give it. They do tell him that he is most welcome to the farm. I take Len into the parlour. He can't wait to see Rita. They were always such good chums at home. They are closer in age than me. They hug one another closely. Tilldy pokes her head around the door and says hello to Len. Len nods at her but doesn't speak. He is always embarrassed around girls. I wonder if he has noticed how pretty Tilldy is with her dark blue eyes and short dark curly hair. Rita tells Tilldy to join us and sit for a while. I can't stand it anymore. Please, please let's open our presents now that Len is here. I am ready to go. I have waited long enough. A cheer goes up from the three of us. Okay, let's do it. Each present is individually wrapped in brown paper with our names on them. There are three each. I waste no time and tear mine apart. Pieces of paper are everywhere. As usual Rita carefully unties the string and winds it up neatly. Then she slowly and carefully unwraps her presents and refolds, painstakingly, the paper into a neat pile. How can she do that? I can barely stand to watch it. I got paints, painting books and books to read. My favourite is the new Rupert Bear book. And there is a beautiful turquoise dress that Mum knitted especially for me. I love it so much. I hold the dress to my face to see if I can smell my mother on it. I know that I can smell her hands that knitted it for me. I will put it on for Christmas lunch. There are also sweets for us, Cadbury's chocolates, liquorice all sorts and lemon drops. Tilldy didn't get any presents. I feel so sad for her. Her Mum is so ill in the hospital and obviously couldn't post the presents from Father Christmas to Tilldy. I will share my sweets with her and let her read my books and use my paints. Rita gets a lovely hand knitted cardigan, red as a letter box and other practical clothes plus a brush, mirror and comb set similar to the one Tilldy got last night from the Rosses. Rita tells me, don't you ever touch this or I will give you a clout. This is mine, not yours. She knows how I am. But I will use it when she is not looking. Len's face is happy. He gets a Fair Isle hand knitted vest, Biggles books and a fort with toy soldiers. And of course, the three of us get sweets. But the best of all the pressies is a letter that Rita reads to us out loud telling us how much Mum and Dad miss us and how they are hoping that we will be able to come home this coming spring if the bombing dies down. Oh, please, please God let that be the case. We can always be hopeful. I wish I could make Tilldy feel better. I see the tears in her eyes as Rita reads how much our parents love us. Compared to Tilldy we must not grumble at our lot. Christmas day is passing quickly. Mrs Ross puts out a nice cold lunch of roast chicken, cheeses, crusty farm bread, mince pies, clotted cream, leftover Christmas pudding and custard and there are even Christmas crackers on the table. We are so lucky. Following lunch the four of us take a walk around the farm and eventually end up in the forbidden hay loft. We can play there without getting caught and without being heard as all of the adults are back at the house napping and snoring, tired from their previous revelling on Christmas Eve and full with too much food. It is so much fun jumping in the hay and laughing. The four of us play hide and seek in the hay and end up chucking it all at one another. It is such a lovely Christmas having Len here with us. Finally we have to leave to go back up to the house for tea. We even have Christmas cake with tea. I do so hope my Mum and Dad are having a good Christmas. The time seems to fly and before we know it is it time for Len to go back to the Gillis's. I hate for him to go and wish he could stay and never go back, but he has to. Roger will take him into the village in the old blue truck. I want to just hug him and not let go but I don't as I do not want to upset him. Hugging just makes it worse for him. He bravely holds back his tears and says Ta Ta, thanks for everything, turns quickly and leaves. Goodbyes are always so painful. I feel a lump in my throat and I want to run after the old truck and grab onto Len and never let him go. I always feel like I am losing everything and everyone is leaving me. I never can say goodbye.

SPRING (WHEN ALL THINGS ARE NEW)

It is April 1941. Spring has arrived but you wouldn't know it. The weather is harsh, ice, snow and wind. A surprising late winter storm has dumped six inches of snow onto the countryside. Farmer Ross and the men are worried as to how long this weather will continue. The problem is that the cows are out to pasture and will be calving soon. Also lambing is about to begin. The cows will have to be herded back into the barns. The sheep usually stay out because of their thick wool coats but to have their lambs outside in such bad weather could be a matter of life or death for the new-borns. The men plan to go out very early, before sunrise, to check on them to see if any animals have been born overnight. It is impossible for them to bring all of the cows and sheep into the barns. There just isn't enough room. They will only be bringing in the ones that look like they are in trouble. Baled hay and feed will be taken out to the pastures to feed them. The ice will be chopped out of their drinking troughs for them to be able to get water. As it is a Saturday tomorrow Rita and I are given permission to see how many they bring into the barns and, if we are lucky, to even get to see a new baby lamb or calf. This is one of the most exciting times in my young life and besides on top of that I am having a birthday in two days. I am going to be the grand total of six years old. I feel so grown up. I wanted to be home for my birthday. I really believed that it could or would happen. I pleaded in my letters to Mummy and Daddy to let us come home. Rita and Len begged also but nothing is said in return letters. It feels to me like they don't care anymore and that they are just going to leave us here forever. How could they do that? Especially when Len is really sick and Rita and I need them so. But for now the excitement of the new spring births helps cover our mourning for home.

It is the day of my birthday. There are birthday cards from home and also from the Rosses. I get a five shilling postal order form my uncles and a five shilling one from Mum and Dad, a whole ten shillings. I am rich. What will I do with it? So many things come to mind. But, as usual, Rita has to spoil it and say be a good girl Sheila and open up a post office savings account. Is she barmy? I could buy all of the cream buns from the bakery. My friend Angela and I could stuff our mouths until we are sick. But as usual I am talked into a compromise, five shillings into the post office and five shillings to spend. I would like to buy a whip and top. Rita says that if I do she will teach me how to spin it. I can't wait. And the rest of the money I will spend on buns for Angela and I. Ain't life grand? But unbeknownst to me the best part of the birthday is yet to come. After arriving home from school on Monday and after Rita and my many tasks are done supper is served. Rita and I are told that the parlour is off limits to us tonight. Just before bedtime Mrs Ross tells us that Arthur (Farmer Ross) wants to talk to us before bed. Oh, crikey, we must be in big trouble to be summoned by Farmer Ross before bed. My sister says, maybe it is because they can't take care of us anymore and just like Miss Allen did they are going to give us away. Where are we to go if this is the case? I tell Rita, if that is so I think we should just run away back to London. I tell myself that I really don't care if they don't want us but that is hardly the truth. We wait outside the parlour door, hardly able to breathe. I am so scared. Rita knocks softly, both of us thinking that if they can't hear us they can't send us away. Come in, come in children.

Arthur doesn't sound cross. Maybe it is not what we think. We push open the parlour door and peer around. Mr Ross and his sons John and Roger are seated on the floor, up front, by the wood fire in the fireplace. On other nights, they are usually sitting sprawled out on the settee or the old worn arm chairs with their long legs stretched out in front of them. They motion us into the room. Come close girls, come close. We have something to show you. And then there it is. That sound I will never, ever forget, a piteous bleating. Oh, my God, it is real. It is a baby lamb. The sons move back from the warmth of the fire and there on the floor, wrapped in a warm blue blanket is a tiny lamb, mewling like a kitten. Rita and I kneel down to marvel at this little miracle of life. We can't speak either one of us, we are so overwhelmed but I find my tongue fast, words just tumbling out of my mouth. Can we keep him? Can I hold him? Can I feed him? Is he mine? John says; slow down lassie and explains to us that his mother died last night giving birth and that the lamb was left an orphan. He has to be bottle fed every few hours and that it will be our jobs after school and after our usual tasks to take care of him. Can we stay home from school? I will feed him and cuddle him. Please, please. The answer is no. It is not to be, we have to go to school. I chatter on, well then can we take him up to our room for the night? But Roger says that it is way too cold for him upstairs and that they will keep the fire going all night to keep him warm. Mrs Ross (Edna) comes into the parlour. She is carrying a baby bottle with a thick mixture of liquid in it. She says to me, Sheila, take the bottle and feed him. You and your sister will be his caregivers when you are home from school and have done your work and as it is your birthday you get to feed him first. I sit on the floor and hold out my arms. Roger carefully wraps the blanket around the lamb and places him into my arms. It is wildly incredible, the warmth of that little living body. I hold him close to cuddle him. I feel the warmth of him

330

and a small fast beating heart against my chest. This is truly a miracle. It really is spring after all. He bleats hungrily and opens that tiny pink mouth. I give him the bottle and his mouth closes around the rubber nipple. He starts to suck. He knows just what to do and the only sound in the room is a snuffling sucking sound of pure contentment. I suddenly feel very protective of him as a mother would of her child. Rita wants her turn and I am going to have to give him to her. I don't want to. I want to keep him forever but I want my sister to experience the love of this baby lamb like I just did. She is very gentle with him. As far as I know the only other baby that she has ever held in her arms was me. She, like me, doesn't want to give him back to Roger but Mrs Ross announces, time to go to bed. Right away and don't make me tell you twice. She doesn't have to. We don't want to suffer the consequences of the carpet beater on our legs or bottoms. We go up to bed but are too excited to sleep. We lay awake thinking of names for the baby lamb. I love times like this when my sister and I talk. I feel grown up and close to her but we like all older and younger sisters have a divide at our ages. Regardless of how we fight, her and me, we will always be there for one another. We always are but are not aware of it at this age and time. We decide, after much arguing, and Rita saying to me, have it your way, you always do. So we call him Roger and what a smasher he is.

It is the end of April. There is much sunshine through the day and at night time gentle rains. Everything is coming to life. The tree limbs are budding, crocuses and daffodils are poking their heads above the earth to face the sun. The calving and lambing is over. The lambs and calves are with their moms nursing in the pastures, their dads standing idly by munching away. Roger the lamb is growing by leaps and bounds. He now gambles around on his shaky legs crashing into furniture and sometimes falling flat on his tummy with his four legs splayed out in front of him and behind him. We are having so much fun with him and we giggle at his antics but Roger says that he is getting too mischievous to stay in the house. He likes to chew on the furniture and baa's all night for attention and for us to come and pet him plus as Roger says a few turds have been left on the arm chairs. Then Roger tells us it is time to give up our little lamb. Rita and I are heartbroken and we cry many tears but it has to be. Our ever handsome Roger explains to us that the lamb is an animal and needs to be with his own kind to grow up to be a healthy sheep. Roger lets us go with him to release our baby and introduce him to the rest of the flock. We follow Roger as he carries him out to the pasture. He puts him down with his own kind. Rita and I hold hands very tightly. It is so hard to say goodbye to him. I can't say it. I just can't, too many goodbyes in my life. Baby Roger isn't going to have it either. The rest of the flock just ignore him as he bounces around as if looking for his mother. He turns to look at us and runs back towards us. He feels confused. Roger says that we must leave now and never to come back to see him. He has to learn to be a sheep. I know how baby Roger feels. I have been in his shoes too many times. Love hurts. I believe our Roger is secretly filled with pride that we named the lamb after him and I can only hope that the lamb grows up to be as handsome as Roger and that all of the ewes will swoon over him as the girls do over our Roger.

SPRING, SUMMER AND AUTUMN

It is the first of May, 1941. Spring is such a busy time on the farm and our tasks are greatly increased. We spend hours weeding the vegetable gardens, scrubbing floors, swilling pigs, cleaning the outside lavies that the farm labourers use and shovelling out the ashes from the Rayburn and fireplace. Rita and I are not allowed into the village anymore to see or play with our friends and our friends are not allowed out to the farm. The only way we get to see them is at school. All I have beside my sister is my doll Heather. I tell Rita that I will gladly share her. She says that that is really kind but she declines. There seems to be no time set aside for us to play, read or write letters home but my sister says that we have to somehow let Mummy and Daddy know what is going on. We are working for our room and board. I try so hard to do all of the jobs but seem to always be in trouble for not doing them correctly and I am constantly punished. We feel like we are in the workhouse. It was never this bad when we first came here but we continue this way until about the end of August when we realize that we have to tell our parents about our plight. Tonight, while in bed, we take a torch to give us light to write home about what is going on here and that we don't like it and are very unhappy. We plead to go home even if we have to die. We cry ourselves to sleep because going home seems so unobtainable. Rita and I know it will be forever before we get a letter back from home but a week later the letter comes. We have to wait all day until we have finished our tasks and are in our bedroom to read it so that Mrs Ross won't know that we are writing home to complain about our situation here. Mum and Dad say that they are very concerned about us and say that they will write to Mrs Ross about our plight. Rita and I gasp and look at one another in sheer consternation. We are going to be in serious trouble. Mr and Mrs Ross will know that we have been complaining. Mummy and Daddy also say it is still too dangerous for us to come home but that she will convey her concerns about our treatment to the Rosses. There it is again, tell Mrs Ross. There is no turning back now. The cat is out of the bag.

Saturday dawns overcast and dreary. No one would know that it is our Summer Holiday. We dread going down to breakfast. Suppose Mrs Ross got her letter today. The postman comes in the afternoon. If our letter came yesterday Mrs Ross's must surely come today. My sister and I make plans to run to the barn when we see the postman on his bicycle coming up the lane. We have a busy morning with all of our tasks. Around five and twenty past twelve we get a cheese sandwich and a glass of milk. Mrs Ross says that we can get an apple out of the cold house for afters and that we should get outside and attend to our weeding of the vegetable beds and not to dawdle eating our apples. Luckily now we get to watch the lane for the postman as we work. I don't mind weeding the vegetable patch that much. I find lots of worms to play with in the dirt. This afternoon I pretend to eat one and she screams. Where is her sense of humour? I collect the worms in a small milk bottle that I found at Ben's old place and nobody knows that I keep them in our bedroom. I give them grass to eat but they won't stay in the bottle and they escape. Last week Rita found one in her shoe as she put her foot in it. She was livid at me. Her face went all purple and the poor worm was all squished and dead. All the worms are missing and I don't know where they all went to but I am sure that they will show up sometime. When I hear a few screams I will know that they have been found. Out of Mrs Ross's sight and the house we sit on the ground and eat our apples and contemplate what our punishment will be when the letter arrives. Around one thirty we see the postman coming up the lane. He gets off of his bicycle and disappears to the back door of the house. That is our signal to run to the barn. We are so scared thinking of what could happen to us. We sit together on the straw hugging our knees tightly to our chests. The straw pokes at our skin but we don't move, just waiting for someone to come looking for us. The silence is terrible. Maybe this is just a dream and we will wake up. It seems like hours go by but in reality it isn't and then we hear the supper bell ring. We reluctantly leave and go up to the house to eat. Rita says the letter must not have come or they would have come to look for us and that we are safe for another day. Cautiously we open the back door to the kitchen. The farm labourers, the Rosses and sons are at table eating already, talking loudly about the day and happy about tomorrow being a day of rest. We walk in to sit at our place at the table. The chatter stops and all heads are down. No one looks at us. Mrs Ross says angrily; don't take your places at table, no supper for you. I don't want ungrateful little wretches at my supper table. Go to your room. I'll deal with you later. The letter must have come. Mrs Ross is visibly very angry. Rita and I climb the stairs to our room. I hold onto my sister's hand tightly, afraid to let go. In our room Rita says; maybe she'll put us out of the house and I ask where would we go? We have many questions. We sit on our bed waiting for Mrs Ross, nearly paralyzed with fear. It is now getting dark and we have no oil lamp. It is scary. I hate the dark. I hold Heather close for comfort and start to cry. Rita covers her face with her hands and starts to cry too. I think this is the most unhappy we have been since being at Roskilly and yet the punishment has yet to come. We hear and recognize Mrs Ross's footsteps on the landing outside our door. As she enters our room her oil lamp casts eerie long shadows around the room. She sets the lamp onto the walnut dresser. She stands there and just looks at us. We feel very uncomfortable. She speaks. Now then I would like to know what I did to you girls to deserve this gross ungratefulness. We have taken you in, fed you and kept you out of the Blitz in London. We are the reason that you are both alive to this day and to my dismay this is how you have repaid us. By writing to your parents complaining that we over work you and that you don't want to stay here with us anymore. She goes on, well let me tell you young ladies, idle hands are the devils work and there will be no devils work in this house and you can both stop your snivelling right now. I am going to write your mother and father tonight to inform them that if they want you to be able to stay here they will have to accept my way of rearing their children and that means hard work. Hard work never hurt anyone. If that is not good enough for them they can come and get you. Both of you had better pray for forgiveness while you are in chapel tomorrow because you are going to need it. Now get to your beds and there will be no supper for you ungrateful children. With that she and the oil lamp are gone and we are plunged into darkness. We are utterly miserable as we climb into bed with dirty tear stained faces. I sob into my pillow. I am sorry Mum and Dad. I didn't mean to make Mrs Ross unhappy. Whatever will tomorrow bring, I wonder, for Rita and I.

A week has passed since that guilt ridden night. Almost no one talks to us. Roger winks at us when he thinks no one is looking, thank you Roger. Mrs Ross is very short and curt with us. We hardly see Mr Ross. He is always busy with the farm and he never has had much to do with us anyway. Our lives consist of doing our work, eating our supper and going to bed. Rita tells Betty about our problems at the farm. Betty is lucky;

she loves her billet and the two spinster sisters who take care of her. Of course she misses her family desperately and would love to go home but she is quite happy until that time arrives. There are many good host families in the village and some that are not that good for there are a lot of unhappy and desperately homesick children. On Wednesday we get a letter from Mummy. She says she is coming down to see us next week. She wants to talk to the Rosses and to see for herself how things are for all three of her children. In her letter Mum says that it seems that many letters from the evacuees have been written from all over the village to London pleading to come home and because of that many children have already left to go back to war torn London. She ends with that she will hopefully see us next week. Rita, Len and I are very anxious to see our mother and to see what she and Daddy have decided for us. She arrives on the following Wednesday. It took her twenty four hours to get here. Air raids, huge crowds, military and civilians leaving London caused much of the delay. She visits the Gillises on Thursday morning to check on my brother's situation. She is meeting us after school today. When we see her we all cry and hug one another. I am not ever going to let her go, never ever again. She stands back and looks at us. She shakes her head and says; Dear O Law, look at the three of you. What is wrong with us? We are used to how we look. We think we look fine but she is not used to this picture. We are scruffy, dirty, our clothes worn and thin and our heads have been nearly shorn again to prevent the lice that are rampant among the evacuees and village children. The villagers say we brought them with us from London like the plague. Len and Rita are as skinny as bean poles. I have a little more weight on me, especially in my face. Mum says; Dad and I should have never let this happen. Does this mean that we are going home? I dare not foster such a thought. She holds us all close again not wanting to let us go. I look up and see my brother's pale

337

strained face; tears of happiness stain all of our cheeks. Mummy is going to walk Rita and I back up to the farm to talk to the Rosses. She tells Len that she will see him when she gets back to the village this evening. He is reluctant to let her go again but he does. I feel ever so safe now that Mummy is here. She will protect us I know but everything is still uncertain as to what will evolve from this visit. We chat gaily all the way up to the farm. I skip on ahead and pick my Mum the last of the wild flowers from the hedge rows. A few dandelions too as they are the most beautiful yellow, the colour of buttercups. I love them and so does my Mum. We arrive at the farm. Mrs Ross is surprised to see our Mum with us. She knew that she was coming but didn't know that she was already in the village. My Mum tells Rita and me to give her and the Rosses some privacy so that they can talk. Mrs Ross tells us that we have our work to do. Just having your mother here is no excuse for you not to be working. It seems like they are behind closed parlour doors forever. From outside we sneak into the hallway every now and then to listen. We hear voices but cannot make out what they are saying. Finally, around six o'clock, suppertime, they emerge. Rita and I search their faces for a sign of what happened but their faces tell us nothing. The Rosses are silent. Mummy asks them if she can take us up to our bedroom to talk to us. They nod their heads in agreement. We show Mummy up the stairs to our room. My stomach has an awfully big knot in it. We are so anxious to get whatever information we can. In our room the three of us sit on the bed. Mum sits in the middle and holds our hands. These are the hands that would hold your face and kiss you on the forehead, the hands that cooled your forehead when you were sick, the hands that spanked when you were naughty and the hands that fed you and dressed you. These are the hands that hold our family together. To me they are the most beautiful hands in the world. She looks at each of us with a very serious face.

This isn't good. Are we going to be punished for writing the letter? Mum continues to look at us and then simply says; you are going home. I catch my breath. It is over. It is finally over. She continues, your father and I have agonized over sending you away but we wanted you to live and we are agonizing now about the decision that we have made to bring you back to London. But when I saw you today I knew, right then, that your father and I have made the right choice, to bring you back home. Whatever happens there will happen but at least we will all be together. You three children have been very brave and your Dad and I expect you to continue being strong and to not ever give up. We will never give up. We are going to be a family again. Mum says it won't be easy but I know that I can rely on you to do what is expected of you. I feel like I am floating on fairy wings. You are going home is the most beautiful sentence in the English language. The answer to our prayers and tears has arrived. Can we go home now, we ask while laughing, hugging and kissing her. No my children, not for another fortnight. Your father and I have to find a house to live in on the outskirts of London. Our flat in London was damaged from the bombing and we have been staying with your uncle Eric. We will be very busy getting ready for you to come home. We did manage to save some things from the bombing but some will have to be replaced. Your father will come down on the train to get you and bring you home. At this very moment he is looking for extra work to get the fare for the train to bring you back. I don't think I will ever come back down to earth. I will just float on my fairy wings revelling in the utmost joy in my young life. No cares or worries. I feel as light as a feather. My mother brings me back down to reality. She has to go back to London straight away. She will stop at the Gillises just long enough to give our brother the news. She kisses us goodbye and we watch her leave down the lane, waving until she is just a speck. Two weeks seems like a double lifetime of a hundred years. I worry that we won't go home. Mum and Dad could die in a raid before Daddy can get to us or the train could be bombed on the way out of Paddington station. I even get to the point of paying attention in chapel on Sunday and pray for Jesus to forgive me of my sins and to let my father get here safely to take us back home. He answers my prayers. In a little less than two weeks, Daddy arrives. It is a rainy, windy Tuesday afternoon. Angela and I are walking out of the school house, huddled under our umbrellas. She is so sad that I am going back to London. We are best friends. We had clasped our little pinkie fingers as a link to be best friends forever. I will never forget Angela. When we grow up maybe we can meet again. Goodbye Angela. Rita and Len come running up to us, splashing through the puddles. Sheila, Sheila, daddy is here. He has come to take us home. They grab my hand and pull me away from Angela. I strain to look back at her. She waves and then she is gone. Is this to be the last time that I will ever see her? My Dad picks me up in his arms. Hello sunshine he says. I cling to him and nuzzle the collar of his jacket with my nose. It is damp and I can smell his soap intermingled with the damp wool of the jacket. This is home. I whisper to him, I've missed you Daddy I love you. Please don't send us away ever again. Besides the tears there are the good memories and the sad times, one being our beautiful baby lamb and another our new friend Tilldy who returned to her father after her mother sadly passed away of cancer.

REFLECTIONS:

Although there were many wonderful and decent host families there were reportedly some children who were abused mentally, physically and even sexually so in retrospect we could have been a lot worse off and I will always be very grateful for that.

LONDON, HOME AT LAST,
September 1941

Twenty four hours later we are pulling into Paddington station. We are back to where it all started over a year ago. We have slept on buses, in train stations and railway sidings on the long, seemingly never ending journey home. The packed train heading for London was filled to capacity carrying troops, civilians and many evacuee children returning to London. We were halted many times due to warnings of air raids but have arrived safe and sound. I wish my Mum could be at the station to meet us. Daddy tells us that Mummy wanted to but money is scarce for them and they couldn't afford to buy her any bus or train fare so that she could come to meet us. They had to give up a lot in order to have the money for Daddy to come and get us but it was money well spent. Dad says; your Mum is at the house getting everything ready for the three of you kids. Oh how excited we three are. We are going to a house, a real house. No more living in other people's houses. Will it be a grand house like Trewlawny? It doesn't really matter what it is because Mum and Dad will be there and that makes it a home. Paddington Station is a teeming mass of people, everyone coming or going someplace. The British Red Cross are on the job greeting the arriving and departing troop trains. They give out free tea, sandwiches, cakes, cigarettes and warm words of encouragement. There are evacuees leaving and being hustled onto the departing trains, some crying and some laughing just like we did. Their parents are running alongside the moving trains like ours did calling out their goodbyes and last minute instructions just like when we left. I want to run after them to tell them to not go. Stay. But parents are only doing what they think is the best for their children and themselves. People are queuing up everywhere for everything, trains, tickets, food, newspapers and cigarettes. It is so loud from the noise of the trains pulling in and out of the station, the loudspeakers calling out the arrivals and departures and the banging of carriage doors. All the platforms are crowded with people jostling with luggage, porters whistles signalling, trains leaving and loved one hugging loved ones. But with all of this it is an exciting time even though we are at war. We are all united in our cause to attain victory, whatever it takes.

Out of the station we push our way through the crowds to the long queues at the bus stops. I am overwhelmed by the crowds and the noise. The buses, trams and Lorries are all belching smoke. There are row after row of red brick Row Houses with blackened chimney pots. This is not the countryside any more. We three are running behind Daddy, trying to keep up and to keep him in view. We are so afraid of losing him. We are not used to all this mass of people. We have forgotten how that is. We are getting buffeted by umbrellas, luggage and gas masks and yes, guess what, it is starting to rain. Good old London. Our macs are in our cases so Dad takes off his jacket and tries to keep it over our heads to keep us dry but by the time our bus arrives we are pretty well drenched. A number 68 double red double decker rumbles to a stop. People start pushing to get on as others struggle to get off. I cling tightly to Heather. I am so afraid that she could get knocked to the ground and lost again. It seems that everyone needs the number 68. The conductor is calling out; one at a time, one at a time, upstairs is full, standing room only downstairs, have your fares ready please. We finally, with our Dad's help, get on. He stores our

343

cases under the stairs. We have to stand in the aisle and hold onto the rails of the seats. All I can see is legs of all sizes and wet steamy trousers. I am shoved up against a big round lady who has brown woollen stockings. They give off a wet wool smell. I can also smell cigarette smoke mixed up with the wet wool. It seems that most people have a fag hanging out of their mouths. There is a lot of coughing and hacking. People look sad and tired, tired of war, death, rationing and the struggles of daily life. The conductor is trying to squeeze past the people in the aisle to collect his fares. He says; fares please. Dad pays him and the conductor clips our tickets and puts the money in his big leather bag. I look up at him. I am an evacuee and I am going home to a real house today. Well good for you my little love, we all need a place to call home and maybe, ducks, when this ruddy war is over we can all go home. Blimey, wouldn't that be ever so nice? The bus ride is long, stopping at all the bus stops to let people off and more people on but I don't mind that it is a long trip because my six year old head is full of all the exciting things that are happening to me today. The four of us finally get seats with me sitting on my Dad's lap. I just have to sleep. I have fought it for so long, not wishing to miss a moment of the day. But I am afraid that if I fall asleep I might wake up back in Cornwall and this could all have been nothing but a beautiful dream. The next thing I know, my Dad is shaking me awake. It is time to get off the bus Sheila, we are here and this is home. I am so glad that it wasn't a dream. Rita and Len climb down off of the bus. My Dad carries me down to the pavement. I wave to the conductor. He says; Bye ducks, welcome home. The four of us stand at the bus stop with our cases waiting for our Dad to show us the way to the house. It is all so strange to us. Rita, Len and I are feeling completely lost in this totally new environment. It is like a different world or another planet. It is a world that we will have to get used to and it is scary. At this very moment I am sure the three of us are thinking that maybe Cornwall and our host families were not as bad as we thought. We three are scared of all of the new changes in our lives but I am sure that we will adapt. We turn a corner off of the main road at the bus stop and straight away we begin to see some of the devastation that bombs and war have wrought. We heard about it on the wireless while we were away but we are not prepared for this. We are silent and walk along in shock. So much has happened to the London that we once knew. Dad says southeast London is not damaged as much as central London where we had been living before the war. Some of the houses on Albert road were razed to the ground and others look like they have been sliced in half with one half completely gone, demolished and in rubble while the other half is still standing. By looking we feel like we are invading the privacy of the people who once lived in these houses that are only half standing. Torn clothing is fluttering in the late afternoon breeze from an open cupboard in one of the upstairs bedrooms and an iron bedstead stands in the remaining half of the room that is open to the rain and the wind. There is an open stairway with railings still standing and you expect someone to come running down the stairs at any moment. There is pretty flowered wallpaper on the one standing side of a living room with pictures still hanging from their nails, curtains hanging in blown out windows and broken and buried furniture sticking up from the bricks and rubble. Who were the people who lived here and where are they now? Have they survived the raid or are they gone like many others? There are no rules to war. At one house some people are picking over the rubble trying to collect possessions. Dad says that they must be family helping out to get what they need and that the house like others will finally be posted as condemned. This sight we see too often. Dad says it is about a twenty minute walk to our new house and we see houses standing with little or no damage and others that are completely razed to the ground. No wonder my Mum and Dad had sent us away. Even at my age I can understand the difficult, heart wrenching decision that they had had to make, whether or not to bring us back home, while not knowing if the worst was over as my Mum explained to us or if there was more devastation to come. Maybe my sister understands now too and can forgive Mum and Dad. Daddy tells us that in the last fortnight the raids have been few and far between and that people are encouraged and feeling that maybe at last we are in the clear and can start picking up the pieces of our lives. We turn the corner off of Fernham Road. My Dad says; here we are, this is our street, number Two Pendleton is our new address. My legs feel all wobbly. I am so excited. Mummy is at Number Two, home. It is not a very long street and has two story Victorian row houses on either side with dark green railings around the front gardens with a railing between each row house and each with a beautiful green iron front gate. We are lucky because our street has no bomb damage. There are some boys and girls playing in the street, skipping rope, spinning tops and kicking a football around. They stop their games and stare as we approach. I am beginning to miss my friend in Cornwall, Angela, and I wonder if she misses me as well. I do so hope that she gets to go home soon. Our house is the first on the right hand side of us. There is an empty garden next to us with no house. Dad says it is used as a builder's yard to store ladders, paints, bricks and other building supplies. We cross the street to Number Two. Daddy opens the squeaky, green iron gate. We kids stop and look up at the house. No bomb damage or scarring, just sparkling bay windows down stairs with lace curtains and two equally as clean windows upstairs. That is my Mum, clean as a whistle. To the right of the house is a green wooden back gate which adjoins the builder's yard with an alley that leads to the back of the house. The three of us walk up a red tile pathway which leads us to a varnished front door with leaded stain glass windows. There is a black lion's head knocker and a black iron letter box. Below is a freshly whitened door step. This is our house. Our Mum is behind that front door. We are going to be a family. Dad lifts the knocker and knocks twice. We hear footsteps from the inside sounding like someone is coming down stairs. The lock is turned and we fly over the door step into her wide open arms, wide enough for all three of us. We are finally home. Everyone is talking at once, kissing, hugging and laughing. I can't think of ever in my short life when I have felt happier. We are so very lucky because as we had heard before we left Cornwall many evacuees had gone back home because of the lull in the bombing of London and many other cities only to find, tragically, that their parents had perished in the Blitz and their homes had been destroyed. Grandmothers, grandfathers, and other family members took them in. The children's pain was inconsolable. Thanks to God, our family is able to start picking up the pieces of our lives and start on the long road back. I wonder how long a road that will be. Mum and Dad take us on a tour of the house. We are already in a narrow dark passageway with just enough room for an old oak hall tree which is used for our coats, macs, umbrellas and our gas masks. Mum shows us a lift up seat for our boots, galoshes and wellingtons. There are two closed doors to our right and in front of us a dark steep narrow stairway. The carpet on the stairs is thin and worn. There are dark brass banisters and a wooden railing to hold onto while climbing the stairs. We all start to climb up. I hold on as tightly as I can to the railing. I do not like dark stairways. We come out onto a landing with three open doors to the bedrooms. We look around and see a door up in the ceiling. We ask, what is behind that closed door Daddy? He says it opens to the attic where old and unused articles are stored. The thought of a dark attic scares me. I mean, after all, who could live there in the dark and could they possibly escape and come down at night while I am sleeping. I am so glad that Rita and I will share a room so that together we can keep the Boogey man away. My imagination runs completely out of control, as usual. On the landing there is a lot of light and lovely sunshine coming in from the windows in the bedrooms. We get to look at Len's room first. There are two steps down into the room. It has a large window overlooking a long garden, our own garden, to play in, to sit on the grass in the shade of the apple and pear trees and to be able to smell the beautiful aroma of honeysuckle and lilac blooms. My parents have put a divan bed into his room with a beautiful blue eiderdown. It sits against the right wall. There is a walnut, marble top dresser near the window with an easel oval mirror. For me, I am so glad to see that there is no wardrobe for him to fall into. I couldn't stand it if he ever fell through to Australia. I believe with all my heart that Mrs Ross was right about wardrobes. I worry about these things. I shall tell my Mum and Dad about the dangers if they have a wardrobe in their bedroom. There is an alcove to the left of the bedroom door covered with a curtain that serves for his clothes and toys. There is even a leaded black Victorian fireplace. Len's old fort and soldiers are set up on the floor and more of his favourite toys and books are ready for him to unpack. A big lopsided grin appears on his travelled, dirty little face. I know at the moment that he is sublimely happy. I love his room. It is so bright and there is no water dripping down the walls and it is all his very own. He can even shut the door and let nobody in if he doesn't want to. Not so Rita and I. We have to share a room. I know that she would like to have it all to herself. I can't blame her. I can be very bratty and hateful. Our room is between Len's and Mum and Dad's. It has pink striped wallpaper that Dad has put up especially for Rita and I and a deep pink lampshade over the light bulb hanging from the ceiling. On the far wall there is another old black lead fireplace with a mantel with Victorian painted tile on the front of it. All the bedrooms have beautiful fireplaces. On the same wall there is a white painted, tall cupboard for our clothes and toys. No wardrobe in this room, saved again. An old dressing table sits against the back wall near the door and there it is, on the top of it, the most beautiful gift that I could ever imagine, a wind up gramophone. Oh, I can't wait to play it. There are three records, Gladys the Girl Guide, Richard Tauber singing Dearly Beloved and a Ted and Barbara Andrews. I am going to play these over and over until the needle is blunt or the records get broken. I hope the latter isn't true. I think this is one of the most wonderful surprises that I could ever have. That is until my Dad says; Look Sheila, this was Rita's but now it is for you and with that he pulls back a sheet from an object on the floor that is in the corner by the tall cupboard. I hear Rita take in a loud gasp and utter angrily, that is mine and she can't have it. I'll never let her. I see the most beautiful doll's house that I could ever imagine or have ever seen in my life. I don't recognize it at all but my sister does. According to Mum, Daddy had built it for Rita when she was about two and I wasn't even a cold back then. I sit on the floor to look at it. A door opens up the back. You can see all the rooms. To me it is an enchanted house. I can't believe that it is mine. It has an upstairs with three bedrooms, one is a nursery with a cot and a tiny baby tucked into it. A winding stair goes down to the kitchen, scullery and front room. It is well furnished with even a miniature piano. The bathroom has a bathtub and sink where even the taps work and the toilet flushes by pulling the chain. All the windows open outward. The front door has a bell to ring and a letter box. It is truly the most exquisite doll house and it is being given to me. I hug my Father's legs fiercely and thank him over and over again but my sister isn't going to give in without a fight. It is mine; I'll never let her play with it. She is such a brat. Mummy speaks up. Rita don't you think you are a bit old to play with a doll's house? You are going to be thirteen this year. Let your sister play with it. She will need you to show her how everything works as you know it so well and besides, my child, there is a wonderful surprise waiting out in the garden for you and your brother. Rita glares at me and says under her breath, while passing me, I hate you, you always get your own way. I poke my tongue out at her and say, I hate you too, ha, ha but not loud enough for my parents to hear. I learned while evacuated to give as good back as I get. There are two beds in our room. Mine is an iron bedstead and oh my goodness, there is my teddy sitting on my pink eiderdown. I haven't seen him in so long. I hug him tightly and cry. I get his chewed ears all wet. He doesn't mind. Poor Teddy, he doesn't have much hair. He is nearly bald from so much loving. He has been in the family since Rita was born. I have not put Heather down since we arrived at the house. She is part of me but I place her next to him on the bed. She is very tired from the long journey home. She is glad to snuggle up to teddy. They look so cozy and cuddly that I want to join them and tell them both that they are safe now but that will have to wait till bedtime. Rita's bed has a wooden headboard and a lovely soft white eiderdown. Folded on her pillow is a new pair of silky pink pyjamas because she is so grown up. She thanks Mum and tries to appear happy. I can tell that she is sad. I believe she is missing her friend Betty very much. I know how glad she is to be home but as her sister I can't replace the friendship that she has with Betty. Only Betty can. It is the same for me with Angela. These are friendships formed in such a time of need. Mum and Dad's room is next to ours. I love the thought of them being so close but it also means that Rita and I can't fight as loudly as we are used to doing. My parents' room overlooks the street. A double bed with a green watered silk embroidered cover stands facing the windows where a large three mirrored dressing table stands between them. Mum's hair brushes, face cream and powder are on a glass tray as I remember them from Dulwich. Oh, no, I look to the right and there it is a dreaded tall wardrobe. I won't go near it. I hide behind my Dad. I haven't yet told my parents where you can go if you stand on the ledge to get your clothes. I know that I will have to tell them or one day they can just suddenly disappear. They will just laugh at me and call me a silly little girl. Their room also has a tiled Victorian fireplace. There is no other way to heat our house so therefore every room has to have a fireplace. Unfortunately, during this war, there is never enough coal to fire every fireplace. It is severely rationed and there is such a limited supply. Only one fire is allowed to be lit per household and that for us in in the kitchen where Mum says we will be spending most of our time together. My Dad says sometimes there is no coal at all and we have to burn sticks to keep warm in the winter. It is now time for us to go down the stairs to see the rest of the house. The stairs scare me. I go down very cautiously. I am always afraid of falling. I have come back from evacuation with way too many worries for a six year old. In the passageway Mummy opens the door closest to the front door. This is the front room and is only to be used on Christmas Day and maybe birthdays. Mum tells us that this is the coldest room in the house and that on Saturdays she puts her roasting joint in there to stay cold until it is prepared for the traditional Sunday dinner. The best furniture is in here and it is not to be used except with care at Christmas. But there is one special piece of furniture in the front room. It is an old upright piano with brass candlestick holders on the front. Rita and I are told that we will be able to use it when we start piano lessons. My brother laughs. He hates piano and wants to play the trumpet. My mother plays piano by ear and sings most beautifully. My Dad is also a musician. Against the wall is the banjo that my father always plays. There is a three piece leather suite with leather antimacassars on the backs of the furniture and on the arms. It sits in front of the fireplace that has a fender with two small seats on either side that hold coal when there is any and that is where the joint sits on the cold tiles in front of the fireplace. Under the bay windows that look out onto the front garden there is a folded gate leg table with two chairs and on the opposite wall a side board completes the room. I feel like we are in a very hallowed place and not to whisper or to touch anything for fear of retribution just like when we were with Mrs Allen. The door is closed reverently as we leave the room. That is my Mum and Dad's best room and they are proud of it. The last door of the passageway opens onto the kitchen. It is a warm liveable room and this is where we are to spend many hours. It is to be where we will have family discussions, a place to play, where punishment is to be meted out and also to serve as Daddy's office. If walls could speak they will tell of hopes, dreams, happy times and sad times. That would be a story unto itself. There is a fireplace with a long wooden mantel upon which sits a beautiful wood and silver wedding clock that ticks away the minutes of our lives. It is placed in the middle and on either end are brass hammered tins. They hold all sorts of treasures. They will become favourites to go through on cold and rainy days. There is also a picture of my beautiful Nana placed lovingly beside the clock. Above the mantel is a large oval mirror. At one end of the mirror is a paper cut out of a galleon on a storm tossed sea. Daddy tells us that he has glued it on to cover a large crack in the mirror. Mum says to us; whenever you ask if you can have something that costs money I will say to you, "When you see that ship sail to the other side of the mirror that means that my ship has come home and you can have anything you want", but you know what, that ship doesn't move. There is a chair on either side of the fireplace. One is a dark orange wicker arm chair with overstuffed pillows. This is Mum's chair where she says she likes to sit, knit and listen to the wireless. Daddy's chair is a cushioned chair bed. On a small occasional table sits a wireless. It is our connection to a world at war. On the wireless you can hear the chiming of Big Ben and the pips to announce that this is the BBC Home Service. Mum and Dad enjoy the war time comedy shows, Itmar, Ben Lyons and BB Daniels and many others that keep us laughing and for us to be able to face another day. Mum loves the music of our time, Vera Lynn, Housewives Choice, Worker's Playtime and most of all Mum and Dad enjoy the Palm Court Orchestra on Sunday evenings. To me this is very boring. My all-time favourite is Children's Hour at five PM. On the other side of the kitchen there is a tall cupboard for food and a well-scrubbed kitchen table with five chairs that sits in the middle of the room. Mum has it already set for tea. The kitchen floor is covered in lino as are all rooms in the house. We do have a large oval mat in front of the fireplace and Mum says that this is going to be where I will sit reading Rupert Bear, Winnie the Pooh and many other children's stories. Daddy has built a wooden desk with drawers and fitted it under the kitchen window that looks out onto the back garden and there he is, good old George. He is a big grey tabby cat sitting on top of the desk looking out of the window. He turns and looks at us very non-plussed like we had just been up to the shops and hadn't been gone for over a year. That is George for you. Unfortunately Polly the parrot isn't with us anymore. Mum says that she became unwell and they found her dead in the bottom of the cage but I believe George ate her because he looks awfully plump. He'll never tell, that scoundrel. I do feel sorrow for Polly. We will miss her but I am glad to see old George, the old crack pot. I wonder whose bed he will be sleeping on tonight. Mum says that she is going to put the kettle on for tea. We follow her. We are not letting her out of our sight for anything. There are three steps down to the scullery. There isn't much to see but what there is, gleams with much love and attention. A grey and white gas cooker and oven stand on one wall. Mum fills the kettle from an old stone sink with just one cold water tap. There is no hot water. She lights the stove with a match and pops on the kettle. The kitchen window over the sink looks out onto the garden. A net curtain covers over the bottom half. To the right of the sink, on a wall, is a small cracked mirror and this is where we are to wash, clean our teeth and comb our hair and for Daddy to shave. There is no bathroom in the house. Mornings are going to be a very busy time in front of that sink and I could get lost in the crowd and never have to wash or clean my teeth. I mean, who will notice with the five of us. Like my Mum would ever let that happen. To the left of the sink is a chipped metal drain board and to the left of that is a copper for boiling clothes on wash days. It will be just like it was in Dulwich. I hated wash days, especially in winter. On the wall by the back door that goes to the garden stands a white, claw foot bathtub with no taps but two holes where the saps were supposed to be. Over one end of the bath is a wooden board which Mum uses as a counter to prepare food. The tea pot and tea cups with the tea caddy sit on top. Mum says that Friday nights will still be bath nights. That hasn't changed since we left over a year ago. Our usual ration of two to three inches of bath water with more warm water from the stove added as each of us get our bath. Who will get the scummy tide? Whoever is last, that's who. But there is a good part of Friday nights. It is our weekly change of underwear, socks and pyjamas and what I love most, in the winter, Mum will warm them around the fire and that is lovely. But after that comes the part that I hate, Friday night is also Cod Liver Oil night. The three of us line up and we are told to stick out our tongues and one piece of a dark brown, nasty tasting chocolate is placed in our mouth. We then suck on it until dissolved and have to show Mum our clean tongues. My mother says you need a good clear out once a week. It is good for you whether you need it or not. In our scullery is a secret dark place, the coal cellar. It is under the stairs. Mum opens the door to it to show us. There is no light. It is black and coal dust covers the walls and sloped ceiling. It is so dark in there that you can't see into the very depths of it. There are but just a few nobs of coal in there. Coal is very expensive to buy and so little of it available because of war time. I heard my Mum say to my Dad that some house wives were being extra nice to the coal man and in return they get an extra sack of coal to stay warm. We will never get that extra sack. I wish my Mum would be nicer to the coal man but my Mum says that she would rather that we be cold. I will watch from a safe distance when the coal man comes. I will never open that door. I am afraid of what lurks in the depths of that dark black hole. When we lived in Dulwich I was always frightened of the coal man. I used to hide behind my mother. He was so big. He had to be to carry those huge bags of coal on his shoulders. His face was covered in black coal dust and the whites of his eyes shone out from that soot covered face. He wore a sewn up sack on his head to keep his hair clean. He looked like a black devil giant. He would wink at me and laugh as I hid behind my mother's skirts while he unloaded the coal off of his shoulders onto the floor of the cellar. The noise was like rolling thunder as the huge chunks of black coal fell to the floor but with my imagination I knew that it was the raw roar of the devils in the cellar. Daddy takes us out to the garden. We go through the back door, Rita and Len pushing past us to see what presents Mum and Dad had bought them and there was their surprise, two bicycles, one a boys' and one a girls'. They weren't all new and shiny like our host family had in Sussex but they work. I wonder what Mum and Dad gave up to get them. Rita's has a basket in front and a bell on the handle bars. She won't let me ring it. I mean who doesn't want to ring a bike bell? Rita's is pretty old fashioned but she and Len are as happy as clowns. There is a shed outside that Daddy has built to keep all of his work tools in. He has even put in windows. He shows it to us proudly but tells us that it is strictly off limits for playing in. In fact he has a padlock on it and he is the only one that has the key. I think it is a way for him to get away from all of us for a while. I can't blame him. We are a bit overwhelming to him after our being away for a year. Outside of the shed is a big old shoe iron with lasts for different sizes of shoes. Dad will buy leather to cut and mend our shoes. There will be no money and few coupons to buy new ones. Across from the shed is the lavatory with a wooden dark green door. If you are tall enough you can see over the top or if short enough see under the bottom of the door. Inside is a high white lavatory with a black seat. A long chain with a handle is hanging down to flush with and there are the usual old potato sacks covering the cistern so it won't freeze in the winter. There is no light. Mum says that if you have to use it at night you will have to take a torch out with you, no fear of me going out there in the dark. On the wall there is a nail with cutup newspaper squares for toilet paper as toilet paper is so scarce during this war. Even when you can get it, it is so stiff, as nearly stiff as the newspaper. As there is only one lavvy and that being outside we all have Gerrys under our beds. Chamber pots or Poes are nicknamed Gerrys because they are shaped like German helmets only with a handle on them. Mum says there is a problem with the lavvy door. Be careful because George will always cry outside and try to squeeze his big bulk under it to get petted. The garden is long and narrow. A beautiful lilac tree is growing by the kitchen window. Mum says it will bloom in spring with double white lilacs and that on my birthday in April Dad will cut many bouquets for friends at my party. On the other side of the garden there is a big honeysuckle covered bush. Mum says it will be so fragrant in the spring. I love that I will get to watch the bees being so busy in the vines getting the nectar like I used to at

Trewlawny. Farther down the garden are two apple trees and a pear tree and at the far end, Daddy points out there is a greengage tree and a plum tree. Mum says, "It is time for tea". It is a lovely time. We are all together. We chatter about everything. Daddy tells us that this coming week workers are coming to our road to take all of the beautiful Victorian iron railings down and take them away to the factories for war munitions. We have no choice in the matter. It is a government mandate and this is war so whatever your country needs you give. After the railings are gone workers are to be delivering to all the houses, supplies to build Anderson Air Raid Shelters in the back gardens. Dad says he is going to do ours with all of our help. We are excited at the thought of helping him. Are there to be more bombs? Obviously or they wouldn't be putting in the shelters in our seemingly safe haven. Is there more war to come even in the southeast?

It has been an exciting but exhausting day but the best day of my life. I will never forget it. Our home is the most beautiful place in the whole world and we are together. We are so lucky when others are not. We are upstairs getting ready for bed. My brother, sister and I are running up and down the landing in our pyjamas and nighties chasing one another in and out of the bedrooms, flopping onto one another's beds, laughing and yelling with joy, seemingly without a care in this whole wide world. Mum and Dad come up the stairs to settle us down for the night. They go into my brother's room to kiss him good night and tuck him up. I lay in my bed cuddling Heather and Teddy close to me, tingling with excitement and anticipation of my turn. It has been way over a year since I have slept in our own house in my own little room that I share with my sister and it will be the first night in such a long time that I will feel my Mother's and Father's loving arms around me as they kiss me good night. Rita says; how can you be so happy? You forget that they gave us away. She still feels betrayed. They come into the room, all smiles. I forgive them for whatever it is that I am supposed to forgive them for. Rita feels that they did wrong. She says that when she grows up and has children, war or no war, she will never send them away, no matter what. At this point I don't know if she is right or wrong. Poor Rita, these separations have been extra hard on her. She has had to grow up fast. She will be thirteen in November. My Mum leans over me and takes my face in her hands, kisses me on the forehead and says night, night my child, my dear child. If there was ever anything to forgive her for it is all forgiven now because I love my Mother so much. She has seldom uttered the words to me that she loves me but to me when she says my child that is all I need. I know she means that she loves me. She pulls my beautiful blue eiderdown up over me and I snuggle down into my little bed feeling so cozy, warm and loved. Daddy tucks me up and kisses me, two quick kisses on the forehead. How could there ever be so much love in one little room? After kissing and tucking Rita up they leave and close the door behind them. We are home and whatever is to come we will face it together as a family.

THE NEIGHBORHOOD

After settling into our new home the next week is a very busy one. Mum registers us in school. Rita being the oldest is enrolled at the senior school for girls that is about a thirty five minute walk from the house. It is sad for her, not knowing anyone and having to make new friends, when her other classmates will have all been together for the full year. We three feel very alone and miss our evacuee friends. There was a common bond from being there for one another. They have been our substitute family and they are hard to let go. They have been our most important lifeline. Len is enrolled at the Manor School for Boys, just a ten minute walk from the house. He has been very shy since he has been home. I am put into the Manor School for Girls five through eleven. It is called infant school. As it is close to home I can go home for dinner at twelve noon. As Len and I are going to the same school Daddy tells Len to let me walk with him but Len tells me to follow on behind and not close so I follow him at a respectable distance. He doesn't want other boys to know that he is walking with his baby sister. The neighbourhood boys would taunt him mercilessly if they found out that I am his sister. It is so hard for him to mix, after all we are the new kids and they are the bosses of the street. My brother hates going to school. They sit and wait for him around the corner of our road. They trip him up, throw his school cap over the bushes and swing him around on his satchel. They are such bullies. As we are new to the neighbourhood they consider us weird. The name calling is very painful and cruel. I tell them that I will tell my Mum on them. They retort; tell her, tell her, kick her up the old coal cellar. They then look at us, make funny faces and say; some mothers do have em and they live. But it isn't just my brother who is bullied; I encounter it too from several girls that live on our street. They aren't nice at all. They are jealous of my blonde curly hair and make fun of me for it. They call me white nigger. We settle in to the best of our ability to our new life. We become aware of our new neighbours Mr and Mrs Hale who are middle aged and live next door. They are both very tall people. They have no children. She always wears carpet slippers and strange hats that she knits. The Whitakers are next to them, two unmarried spinsters. Then comes the Hanes family, he works on the railway and is quite rotund. His wife is pleasant and quiet. They have two children, Doreen and Derek. Doreen is in high school and Derek is in my class. He is six, the same age as I am. He teases me constantly in class. Mum says that boys do that when they like you. I wish that he didn't like me so much. The Biggs, the bain of our lives live at Number Thirty Four. They have moved here from the East end. Mum calls them common. They are loud and abrasive. There are four children in their family. Vera, the same age as Rita, Billy, the same age as Len, Betty, age six and Jean, age four. Next to them is Mrs Graves, a widow who is very old. She asks kids to run to the shops for her for a penny. We kids line up to help. A penny can buy sweets or a currant bun. Across from us on the other side of the road are the Barrington's. They are middle aged with no children. They are very nosy and always gossiping, forever peering out from behind their net curtains. We know that they are watching. Whenever one of us goes out of the house or plays on the street we can see the twitch of their curtains. Next to them are the Cheesmans. They are always in their slippers and she always wears a hairnet. They have grandchildren that live further up the road. The Coulters, there is Thomas, Len's age and a great mate of Billy Biggs, Michael who is seven and David who is three. The

McFarlands are four doors up from the Cheesmans. They are from Scotland and think themselves very posh so are quite uppity. They hardly ever talk to anyone and when they do they act like our betters. They have three children, Audrey who is twelve, Irene who is six and Tommy who is two. They all have flaming red hair. Only occasionally are they allowed to play on the street because they might catch something from the riff raff. For the next few years these neighbours could be the most influential in our young lives.

On Saturday morning the workmen come to take out the railings surrounding the houses. It is very noisy. We all crowd around to watch. Some of the neighbours come out to watch the excavation and just shake their heads in disbelief and sadness and then go back indoors because they can't bear to see the houses shorn of all their Victorian character which is so appealing. The houses look naked, lonely and scarred and all that is left are the ugly holes from where they have wrenched out the railing posts. We know that it is for a very good cause but it is also very sad and ugly. With all of the traditional railings gone, our neighbours, the Barringtons across the street, build a beautiful wooden garden gate and paint it green like the railings had been. They put the gate at the end of the pathway to their front door. No fence on either side, just a gate with a latch and every time when they leave they walk down their path, carefully open the latch, go out the gate and then turn around to look at the gate lovingly and then close and latch it. They could easily walk around it but oh, no that gate is there for a purpose. It stands there like a green wooden shrine to what was. It is such a laugh. Everyone on our road gets a good laugh from it but you know it is good to laugh and guess what; it is the only gate on our road.

On Monday of the next week large Lorries are all over our neighbourhood, pulling up in front of our houses and unloading the supplies needed to build the Anderson shelters. Our road looks like an old junkyard. The small front gardens are tramped down by the workmen leaving all of the corrugated steel and bags of cement. There is great excitement amongst the children. This is going to be fun for all of us. By the next weekend the Anderson shelters are being built. My Dad installs ours. It takes him two weekends to complete. We help him as best we can but my Dad thinks that we are more in the way than a help. At our age we are just out to have fun. A big square hole has to be dug by hand deep into the ground. It is then lined and floored with cement. To us kids it looks like a small swimming pool. We just keep asking for Dad to fill it with water so we can swim in it but that is not to be. The corrugated steel is then arched over from side to side to make a roof. It is then covered with piles and piles of dirt from the original excavation. Neighbours are planting flowers on them and they look quite pretty considering their purpose. At one end of the shelter is an entrance for coming and going. As the shelters are underground a small set of steps is built to descend down inside the shelter. Each shelter sleeps four people in bunk beds on either side. There are no mattresses just the two inch metal straps criss-crossing the wooden frames that make up the beds. In front of the opening a blast wall is built of concrete to catch the blast of bombs exploding outside. I wonder to myself, what bombs? We haven't had any bombs since we have been home. My Mum fixes up the inside the best she can to make it more liveable and comfortable. From the house she brings down old quilts and pillows for the bunks, a kerosene lamp so that we can see and read books instead of just sitting in the pitch black and of course a bucket for the call of nature. I wonder how many days and nights we will have to spend in this concrete grave. It is damp, dark and very cold inside. All sorts of insects and spiders could be seeking shelter in there. Water seeps up from the earth into the bottom of the shelter which always has at least two inches of sitting water on it. Dad uses his stirrup pump to pump it out every day but it always comes back. We complain but Mum says that someday that beautiful concrete grave could save our lives.

BLACK OUT AND BARRAGE BALLOONS

Our lives are now filled with blackouts at night. There are barrage balloons in the skies, air raid wardens doing drills, and shelters being built in the Southeast of London. We are the last to put in the shelters as the Southeast has not had as many deadly air raids as Central London. Are they trying to tell us something? Does the government know something that we don't? Blackouts mean that you have to have heavy black curtains to cover all windows and they are to be pulled every night from sunset to sunrise so that not a chink of light can show. Air raid wardens patrol the streets every night looking for any violation. If they can see any shape or form of light they will blow their whistles loudly and shout, turn that bloody light out. Of course they are right to do that. That is what Gerry is looking for, a point to target with their bombs. Barrage balloons, this is fun for the whole neighbourhood, especially us kids watching them being launched into the sky. They look like big silver inflated elephants, their ears flapping as they rise up into the sky. They are tied to lines attached to their stations below. They are to be our protection from fast, low flying enemy planes. This morning a cry went out, balloon coming down in the neighbourhood. Everyone ran to watch. This huge majestic gas elephant descending like a wounded beast onto the earth as it lost its gas. One man standing there said he thought it was because of a slow leak. It is making the weirdest sounds. It sounds like a giant blowing off as it descends. We children find this quite amusing. We follow the balloon to earth where it blankets the football field up the hill. This is a trophy. The balloons are made of nylon and there is so much of it in a balloon that it can cover a large area. You can make clothes out of nylon and everyone wants a piece of it. Families are running, bringing their scissors to cut out their share. You can make blouses and underwear among other things and as coupons for clothing are so frugal everyone fights for their share. It is almost a party atmosphere. Nobody pushes or shoves, everyone gets their bit of nylon and all of us kids dance and scream on the deflated balloon. It is incredibly great fun but then the home guard arrive and try to restore order. They say to stay away because it is government property and try to move everyone away but it is useless because no one is listening. The guards scribble something in their notebooks and hurriedly leave to come back later and pick up the few remaining pieces. I think the guard is afraid that they could start another World War if they deny us any of this fabric.

WAR BECOMES PERSONAL TO US

We have only been home from evacuation for three weeks when our lives change drastically. It is a lazy Saturday, a beautiful crisp sunny morning. My Mum and Dad are busy fixing breakfast, our usual ration of corn flakes or lumpy porridge and burnt toast. As we have no toaster my Mum puts bread on a fork over the open gas flame of the gas cooker and usually it becomes very black which we scrape off and then put our marge on it. By nine o'clock, Daddy is out the door to fix someone's plumbing and to board up broken windows from previous bomb damage. Work for my Dad is very scarce. People don't want to fix up their homes when there is still a chance they could be destroyed the next day. Dad always rides his bike to work. He carries a big heavy bag of tools over his shoulder. He has bicycle clips around his trousers at the ankles, a pencil behind one ear and a dog end behind the other. He will smoke that later as times are hard and Weights and Woodbines are hard to come by. My brother goes outside to do some weeding for my Mum on the shelter. My sister Rita is still sleeping. Mum tells me to go upstairs to get her up. Tell her to get up or she'll get no breakfast, my Mum says. I am always pleased to oblige a chance to get her into trouble. I run upstairs, open the bedroom door very quietly, so as not to disturb her. I wind up the gramophone as tightly as it will go and turn it up as loud as it will play. I put a record on the felt turntable and proceed to play Richard Talber's Dearly Beloved. He starts out singing very fast and in a falsetto tone and as the turntable slows down it becomes slower and slower and the voice deeper and deeper. Rita wakes and screams at me. Get out, get out, you little beast and then she throws her pillow at me. I duck, she misses me and hits Mum in the face as she comes up to see what all the fuss is about. So, there we are, a lovely quiet Saturday. Later in the afternoon the four of us catch the bus into Croydon so Mum can go to the shops and get her weekend shopping done. The buses are crowded. Croydon and the shops are very busy with queues and people everywhere. Our only respite is that if we behave we can have an ice cream cone from Woolworth's before going home, that is if the queue isn't too long and they haven't run out. People seem in a festive mood. It is a beautiful day and Gerry has been absent for a long while. Maybe the worst is over for all of us. After we get home from Croydon Mum starts to fix our tea. She is singing as she cooks. She is really happy this evening. She had lined up at the fish shop for thirty five minutes and had been able to get kippers and we are to have kippers and brown bread and marge for tea, a sumptuous feast. My Daddy comes in through the back door from work and smells the kippers cooking and smiles gently at Mum. He loves Mum and smoked kippers and most of all his big mug of tea. He loves his tea; he will never refuse a cup of it. It is like the nectar of the Gods to him, nothing can compare. After tea Daddy says that he is going down to the shelter to see if any water has come in from a couple of days ago when it rained. He says you never know when we might need it. You can never be too careful and we cannot get too complacent. We all tease him, telling him that nothing has happened since we have been home so why is he worried now. He just laughs and goes off into the garden. In the evening Mum sets about darning a pile of socks as there is never any money for new ones. After finishing in the garden Daddy works on his ledgers at his desk. We kids are listening to the wireless and reading books. Around eight o'clock Mum tells us to get our pyjamas on and she will go and make our cocoa. Our hot cocoa is dark cocoa powder and hot water with a highly rationed scant teaspoon of sugar if we are lucky. Mum says that before the war she used to make it with milk. We don't care as long as it is hot and sweet. Milk is rationed and is only used for cooking, tea and breakfast cereal and not for drinking. As I am only six I am given a government issue of an extra pint a day. This is given to me at school and has to be drunk there and not carried home and used for someone else. Also I get a free teaspoonful of cod liver oil and concentrated orange juice. That rounds out the Government Issue. At eight o'clock Mum promptly sends us off to bed telling us that she and my Dad will come to tuck us up in a few minutes. We are given the perfunctory kiss on the forehead. My father double kisses me and I know that it comes with all the love in the world. .He doesn't need to use words. I know my Dad adores all of us in his quiet unobtrusive way. We are all tucked up, kissed goodnight; I say my prayers under the eiderdown. I do not want my sister to hear as prayers are very private and I don't want her to hear what I ask God for. She says you can't ask God for things that you want for yourself because that is evil and selfish. But I do ask for something for me and I only ask for one thing so how can that be evil? I ask for a puppy. Yesterday I saw six puppies. My Dad had given me my sixpence for pocket money and of course I had promptly run up to Redig's Sweet Shop. The highlight of my young life is to pick out my sweets, two penny worth of humbugs and two penny worth of liquorice allsorts. I watched Mrs Redig measure the two ounces of each into the scale from the big glass sweet jars and pour them into little white paper bags. Sixpence and some sweet coupons buy total bliss. After I pick out my sweets, Mr Redig comes in to the shop counter from their living quarters behind the shop and in his arms is a mewling bundle of puppies. He has six of them in a blanket.

He comes around to the front of the counter and bends down so that I can touch them. Their eyes aren't even open. They are squirming and crying. I reach out and touch a tiny black one. His body is so warm and his tummy is so fat that I want to hold him and keep him forever but Mr Redig says that he has to take them back to their mother out back. But if I want one I can have one in six weeks when they will be old enough to leave their mother. I just have to have that little black puppy. He is mine. Mr Redig says that I have to ask my Mum and Dad first to see if they will let me have one. But how am I to ask Mum and Dad if I can have one? I will have to pray about that too. I must have fallen asleep praying for the puppy because I am awakened out of my sleep by a loud piercing sound that repeats over and over and also the low droning sound of many aircraft flying overhead. It is an air raid. Our first and the noises are frightening and deafening. My Mum and Dad come running into our room, get up, get up, put your dressing gowns and slippers on and get downstairs right away, run, run. My Dad goes to wake my brother as well. I am so frightened. It sounds like the world is coming to an end. There are explosions all around us. I pull Heather out from under my bed clothes. I cannot leave her behind. The noise is deafening. The house shakes with every explosion. I stand there stunned and frightened in the middle of our room. I am afraid that if I move I will die. Rita grabs my hand and pulls me out of the bedroom onto the landing, just in time as the ceiling over Rita's bed opens up with a loud ripping sound. There is debris flying everywhere. An incendiary bomb lands on her bed and explodes into fire with a burning white heat. Rita and I are screaming as we run for the stairway. What is happening to us? Len is stunned and stands quietly at the top of the stair. Mum turns and comes back up the stairs and takes Len's hand to guide us down. My Dad has gone outside to get a bucket with sand to put the fire out. He runs, flying past us up the stairs. Get them to the shelter he screams at my Mum. We follow her out of the house into the garden. The sky is lit up with searchlights and fires everywhere. Windows are lit up as the small incendiary bombs explode inside. You can hear people screaming as they run for their shelters. There are incendiary bombs all over the ground. The burning fires light the way for Gerry to drop his bombs. My mother screams, don't touch the bombs because they may still explode. We quickly make our way down to the shelter. All of us glancing up and seeing the German bombers letting their payloads go. We can see over our fence other neighbours running down to their shelters as their houses burn behind them. This is hell. My parents know this all too well. After reaching our shelter we all huddle together on one bunk. I ask Mum where is George? She says that he hides in the loo as he hates the sirens. Why hasn't Dad come down yet? Where is he? Is he all right? We listen to all of the bombs whistling down and the sounds of the large explosions as they find their marks. I hate that whistling sound. Many will die tonight. I cover my ears with my hands and sing as loudly as I can to block out the terror. Mum takes my hands away from my ears and tells me to hush as I am scaring my brother and sister. We hear the ack ack guns over the bombs trying to shoot the German planes down. Whether they are shooting any down or not doesn't matter to us. It is somewhat comforting to hear them, knowing that we are fighting back and not giving in. Mum lights the oil lamp and tries to calm and bed us down. At least we can now see one another. Our faces are white and scared but we don't cry. Mum says that to cry is not the British way. We must be brave and carry on. Mum wants us to lie down but out Dad is not here. We all look to Mum for reassurance. Not to worry my children, he will be back. She is so brave. She has lived through this so many times. Most raids, she tells us, usually end in an hour or two. We will hear the all clear and will go back to the house and go back to bed. About an hour later my Dad pokes his head into the doorway of the shelter. Everyone okay, he asks? Mum tells him that we are scared but fine. The children are being very brave. Daddy has an air raid warden's tin hat on his head. I have never seen him wear it before. It helps keep him safe. I have to leave you now he says; a lot of us are helping to put out the fires and to rescue people. We kids beg him not to go. Please Dad, stay with us, but he can't. I will come back later to check on you. He tells us that right now they need as many wardens on the street as possible. Mum asks if the fire is out in the girls' bedroom. He says yes but that there is a lot of damage. A new roof, ceiling and a new bed will be needed but that is a small price to pay. We are still alive. Thank God that Rita was out of the bed and with that being said our Dad leaves us. We are all worried about him being out there in the raid but we don't voice our worry to him. Mum tucks us into our bunks and tells us that we are safe here and to go to sleep. I hold Heather close and tell her not to worry. But how can you sleep with all that is going on outside. I feel trapped and helpless. I want to see what is happening. I feel like I have been buried alive and just want to get out and run, screaming up to the sky. Screaming, go away, we hate you, go back, go back. Will the raid ever be over? Will the ear splitting noises ever cease? Will there be any place for us to live when it is all over? How many people will die tonight? My brain is overloaded. I hope the puppies up the road are safe. I suppose now is as good a time as any to tell Mum about the puppy. Mum, Mum, I can't sleep because I have something that I have to tell you. Rita and Len perk up as I start to tell of my meeting with Mr Redig at the sweet shop and the puppies and how much they need a home and the fact that they are free. My mother looks at me very thoughtfully. Do you know Sheila that the Redigs are German? They came over here just before the war started and nobody knows if they can really be trusted.

They appear to be really nice but in wartime you never know. You do hear what is happening outside, don't you? The Germans are trying to kill as many of us as they can and to destroy our way of life. Len asks if the Germans could blow up our shelter. No, hush says Mum they can't see it because it looks just like a garden from the sky. That is the whole idea of being underground. It is relatively safe. But Len won't let up. They could accidently miss the house and hit us couldn't they? Anything is possible my son but let's not dwell on that and let's finish talking about the puppies. Mum knows that by talking of this we will forget what things are going on outside and our fear will be lessened. She tells us of all of the responsibilities that come with bringing up a puppy, more so during these hard times with food so scarce. But Mum, I insist, he won't eat much and I will share my rations with him. Mum smiles her little smile. She tells us to remember that George the cat will not take too kindly to someone intruding in his life or his territory. I think to myself, well at least George can't eat the puppy. Not like Polly. The puppy would be too big for his mouth. I giggle to myself at this thought. Mum is wavering, I can tell. Oh, Mum, you will love him. I tell her he is like a fat little butterball. He is so precious and I promise we will take good care of him, won't we? I look at Rita and Len for support. We will, they chorus, we want him too. Please, Mum. Please, I beg. He will become a new member of the family. She can't win this battle. Well, maybe we'll go look at him tomorrow, if and when tomorrow comes she says sadly. We all cheer and bounce up and down. We are getting a puppy, and for a few seconds we forget the violence outside. Mum, if we are getting a German dog will he understand English. Everyone laughs. Len says that we can call him Adolph. All right, Mum says, that is enough of your nonsense. But Len and Rita are falling about laughing. It is such a nice relief for all of us and that I guess is the British spirit in times of peril. We can't sleep. We can't wait until tomorrow comes. Rita, Len and I think of all the names that we want to call that little black puppy. It is just like when Rita and I were given the lamb to take care of on the farm and how sad we were to give him back to his family. This time we will get to keep him forever.

The longest night of our young lives, so far, wears on. Mum tucks us up once more. Come along children, you must try to get some sleep. Mummy, will you sing to us please? Please sing, "Lula Lula Bye Bye", like you used to when we were little. Very well children, close your eyes and I will. I am so sorry children that we brought you home to all of this. Daddy and I should have stood firm and waited till the war was over but we missed you as much as you missed us and in spite of it all it is lovely having you home. We are glad too Mum. Don't ever send us away again, however bad it gets, never, ever, ever. Mum starts to sing and her beautiful voice fills the shelter. How strange, all the bombs are falling outside, destroying and killing and here underground our mother is singing her beautiful lullaby to her children. I must have slept because I awaken to the sound of a high pitched droning. It doesn't stop. It is annoying. Maybe a blue bottle got trapped in the shelter and is buzzing around. I struggle to wake up properly. My mother is looking down at me and shaking me gently. Sheila, wake up, it is over. The raid is finally over. The all clear is going and all of us can go back to the house. I love the sound of the all clear. It means we have survived the raid to live another day.

THE SADNESS OF THE NEXT DAY

We poke our heads out of the door of the shelter. It is early Sunday morning and the sun shines it's warmth on our upturned faces. It feels good. The birds are singing. Everything seems to be just like it was yesterday morning. It is almost as if last night didn't happen and that today is just another sunny Sunday morning, but it is different, very different and last night did happen. Life will never be the same. We climb up the ladder out of the dankness of the shelter into the garden and breathe in some fresher air. Neighbours are drifting up their gardens in dressing gowns and slippers. Not much chatter as they look at the damage that surrounds us. I look at our house. Ta God, our house still stands.

Some windows are blown out and Mum had just washed them on Friday but it is standing even with the roof damage. Our next door neighbours the Bales have some blast damage but other neighbours are not lucky. One house is gone except for one wall standing and a staircase to nowhere and down the row other houses survived, others on the street behind ours were not so lucky. Houses are still smouldering, lots of smoke and the smell of ash and death. So this is what war is, destroying families, homes and lives. For my family, we begin to feel guilty that our house has survived the raid and we can go home. Other families are in shock as they discover that they don't have a home to go back to any more. I can hear some children sobbing and pain in the voices of adults as they call out to one another. It is all so futile. The sounds of the ringing

374

bells of the ambulances and the bells of the fire brigade along with the whistles of the air wardens break the stillness of the spring morning. A small van with a loud speaker is going through our neighbourhood making announcements telling us to not touch any parts of burned out buildings, to not start digging to recover any items that might have survived. We must wait till the ashes have cooled. Air raid wardens are stopping to ask everyone if they know of anyone who is missing and where they were last seen. The wardens are the only ones who are usually allowed to dig in the hot ashes to see if there are survivors.

My dad is back from helping other families during the night. He comes into the back garden. He looks so very tired and dirty. His face is all sooty and his clothes are covered in a fine grey dust. He gathers us up to him so relieved that we are safe and all my Mum can say is, oh crikey Harry I'll bet you could go a cup of tea. Oh ta Ruby you're right there. I think there are a lot of homeless people right now that could stand a good cuppa. You'd better get out the biggest kettle that you have because I think we are going to be needing it all day today. I'll do it straight away Harry. But before we can go back up to the house, air raid wardens come running blowing their whistles to get everyone's attention on the street. They tell us, listen everyone, over on Tamwood Road there are people trapped and buried alive. We need all the help we can get to dig them out and while you are about it tell your nippers to not pick up the small incendiary bombs. There are so many of them on the ground and a lot of them are still live and can explode in their hands. Do not touch them. Wait for the bomb squads to gather them up. Do not touch or you could die or be seriously injured. He continues, ladies and gentlemen we need to form groups to start the dig out. Many volunteers, my Mum and Dad included, are given tin helmets to provide protection from such as falling bricks and mortar. We plead with our Mum and Dad to take us with them. We don't want to be left at home. What if the enemy comes back? I don't know what to expect at the dig out but I do know that I want to wear a tin helmet. My parents do not want us to go. They cannot bear us to witness death and agony at our age as they have but they realize that we will see death and pain sooner or later. For my parents to pull bodies from beneath the rubble is more than they would choose to bear but they do what they have to and carry on. They do agree to let us go with them with our promises that we will stay off to the side and be respectful. There are many other kids at the bombed out site. We are all very quiet and mystified as the digging in the dust and deep rubble begins. Bodies are brought out on stretchers. The dead are covered in blankets. The injured either silent in disbelief or crying out in pain. Some of the injured are mangled beyond recognition and lost arms and other limbs becomes a familiar sight. Families are sobbing as they recognize a victim who is being pulled out either by facial recognition or in many cases by just a piece of clothing or a shoe. There are also cries of joy and relief as some find that their loved ones have survived. We have come back from the peace and serenity of Cornwall to face death and destruction.

Some fires burn for at least three days. Many children die from picking up incendiaries especially curious young boys who play the chicken game. How very sad. What a completely senseless waste of life.

REFLECTIONS:

On just that one night seven hundred and eight tons of explosives were dropped on London, fourteen hundred civilians were killed, five thousand homes were destroyed and twelve thousand were made homeless. In all, forty three thousand people lost their lives in the Blitz from September 1940 to May 1941 and millions of homes were damaged or destroyed. As it went on these figures grew till the end of the war when the death toll was over sixty thousand. What a senseless waste of humanity. Will we ever learn?

LIFE GOES ON

Unfortunately for us kids our schools have survived the big raid with lots of damage but not enough for them to close their doors. So on the Monday that is where we are sent off to. I don't mind too much because I am head over heels in love with my teacher, Miss Cliff. She is very beautiful and awfully kind. For instance, on your birthday you get a brand new shiny penny and a lemon drop from a big jar on her desk. I always watch while the birthday boy or girl dive their hand down into the big jar to retrieve their lemon drop and then the big red lid is screwed back onto the jar until the next birthday. Unfortunately, my birthday has passed but I can just taste the tart sweet lemon drop as I watch the boy or girl suck on their sweet and just wish so hard that is was my turn. I can taste every suck. My Miss Cliff wears very pretty clothes and she is very gentle except when she has to tweak Derek Hards ear for dipping my now grown pigtails into the ink well on his desk. When he isn't dipping them into the ink well he is swinging me around by them on the playground. He is the love of my young life. Today, many children are absent from school and there are many empty desks. Miss Cliff tells us that some of our friends will not return. I wonder if those children have died or maybe their parents have died. Will we ever see them again? I hope that if they have died they have gone to Heaven. Miss Cliff announces that we are to have an air raid drill today at playtime and that we are to follow her instructions carefully. At twelve thirty, whistles blow on the playground and we line up by classrooms and form lines two by two. During the drill, as we line up two by two, I meet Kathleen who is to be my air raid partner. She is a new girl in the class just like I am and just back from evacuation also. She is the same age as I but there the similarities end. She is slim and has a quiet darkness about her. Her hair is dark brown, long and straight and mine is blonde and curly. Her eyes are dark brown, soulful and large while mine are blue. Her skin is like ivory while mine is rosy and ruddy. She is tall for six with very long legs and I, well I have my great grandmother Lodge's round face which gives way to family jokes at home. I have short strong legs and as I can see it, a pudgy body and a mind of my own for self-preservation. Kathleen is quiet, a little sulky, but me, I am the chatterbox who will not let you get a word in edgewise, speak before thinking, am loud and full of unbound energy. I am rambunctious and totally un-tidy. I am named fidget-ass at home. I can never sit still and as a child I am supposed to be seen and not heard but that is not me. You always know when I am around. If something is broken at home it is usually me who breaks it or if something is missing in the house it is always Sheila who must have taken it. How I would love to be like Kathleen, quiet, gentle, patient, neat and orderly. What a strange pair we are but we become fast friends and for me it takes away the sting of being without Angela. We have an unusually common bond. We share secrets together and vow in the girls lavatories where all secrets are revealed that we will never be evacuated again or we will run away together. We talk about dying in the raids and if we do die, will we go to Heaven and what is Heaven like. Are there bombs dropping there? We worry whether we will see each other the next day in school after a raid. Weekends become the worst, with me wondering if her house has been bombed during the night time raids and worrying if I will ever see her again. If it is cloudy or rainy we don't worry because Gerry won't come over to visit us.

We go about two weeks without a raid and we feel quite complacent. I even try to sneak out of the house without the dreaded gas mask but my Mum is ever vigilant. Will gas masks be part of our lives forever? I haven't been in a gas attack although I am told that my grandfather was in a mustard gas attack during World War I and my Mum tells me that without a mask you can die a terrible death. In the middle part of June we start getting some day raids. The first one is during our school day. We have just come back from having dinner at noon. We are filing in from the playground to our classrooms. Miss Cliff tells us to be seated and then the air raid siren sounds, piercing the air over the sound of our chairs being pushed and scraped under our desks. We all have a look of surprise on our faces with all of us looking toward our teacher for assurance. We have practiced our drills twice a week so we know what to do. She tells us to be calm and to leave our desks by rows and march to the door as quickly and quietly as possible. Please walk, do not run and take your gas masks. Kathleen and I hold hands tightly. We know that it will take at least five to ten minutes before the bombers will arrive overhead. The teacher says that the sirens go off when the bombers are spotted coming over the English coastline. All of us feel like we want to run out into the hallways and run, run, run to the shelter but we have to follow the rules so that everyone, including all of our teachers will make it to the safety of the shelter. There are other classes from our school in the shelter as well with their teachers so it is quiet noisy with everyone talking at once. Miss Lill our head mistress blows her whistle and quiets us all down. There are long wooden forms lined up in rows and we are told to sit and take our gas masks out of our gas mask boxes, to place them over our faces and pull the straps down in the back of our heads. The elongated oval eye piece made of clear plastic, fogs over as we breathe into the black rubber mask that has a short green metal snout.

We all hate the gas masks. Sometimes you panic and feel that you can't breathe but we are not allowed to take them off. Some kids can't take it and rip them off, crying. The teachers worry because there could be a gas attack without warning. Our teachers tell us we cannot show fear because fear is contagious. Kathleen and I sit there and pray for the all clear to sound. I wish I had Heather with me. That would help. Our teachers try to take our minds off of our situation. We are told to recite our times tables out loud starting from two and going through twelve. What a sight and sound that is with all of us mumbling behind our masks. Even the teachers can't tell if we are doing it right. They are wearing gas masks as well. To an outsider it would look like a scene from a comedy show. Some children are on their two times table and some are already doing their four times. Other children are crying which just fogs up the masks even worse. Some kids are laughing and some of us concentrate on making rude noises through the rubber masks but in all it seems very funny to me. We pray for the all clear to sound and luckily the raid only lasts for an hour but that seems like an eternity. We are lucky that there were no bombs dropped today. Will we know more days like this one or maybe worse?

WHERE IS MY BACON

After school today my Mum is waiting for me at the school gate. She wants me to go shopping with her so I won't be alone at the house. We go down to the high street where the shops are. After queuing up for an hour at the bakers we manage to get some bread and we are then on to the grocers. Mr Evans promised my Mum some bacon for her coupons today. We haven't been able to have any for over two months so she is really excited that we are going to get some today. We are outside of Evanses when the air raid sirens start screaming. People start running for shelter with Mums who are pushing prams with babies going into the shop doorways for protection. There is no time to get to the shelters. Double decker buses stop and people get off to take cover. Gerry is over us quickly today. They were over the coast before the warning went out. The German planes come in low. Some are strafing the high street and others are dropping their deadly bombs. It seems like the whole High street is in a Hell of its own. Bright flames are licking out of the pane less windows of the shops. Choking smoke creeps into our lungs. My Mum flings me down into the gutter and lies on top of me to protect me. A mother will protect her children no matter what it takes. There is another loud explosion and the raid is over as quickly as it started. The all clear sounds. The lucky ones have survived. People start picking themselves up and dusting off. Others don't get up. They are either injured or dead. The ringing bells of the ambulances and fire brigade fill the air. I can hear them from under my mother. Everyone is trying to put out fires with the sand buckets and to help the many injured. I am calling out but no one can hear me. I call out to my Mum. My face is pushed down into the gutter. I am gasping for breath. I am scared for my Mum. She doesn't move. Then I hear people running and calling out. It is okay, we are here. Get her. Is she hurt? Is she alive? People pull my mother off of me. A warden is looking down into my now upturned face. Come on ducks let's help you up, upsidaisy now. He helps me to my feet. My two front teeth have bitten through my lip and I am bleeding and shaking but otherwise I am well and alive. I start calling for my mother. There are people around her on the pavement. I ask, is she ok? I believe my heart has stopped beating. Have the Germans killed her? I cannot live without her. I just got her back. And then they are sitting her up and talking to her. Can you speak luv, they keep asking. She is in shock the warden says. No wounds and I believe that she will be all right. I lean over to her. Mum, Mum it is me, Sheila. Please be all right and don't leave me again. My Mum looks at me and tears course down her cheeks. Relief comes over her face as she sees that I am all right. The warden yells for someone to bring a hot cuppa for my Mum with as much sugar as they can spare. Tea always takes care of everything, especially shock. It is what keeps England going. There is always a kettle to be put on somewhere, even among all of this bomb damage. Mum gratefully drinks down the hot tea given to her by some shop keeper whose gas cooker still works. I sit next to her, holding her hand. Please God let her be all right. She says she thinks she can stand now but she is a bit wobbly holding on to me and the air raid warden. But she is able to get to her feet. She thanks everyone for their help. She grabs me to her for strength. She hates all of the fuss. I think my Mum has also lost some of her hearing as she is speaking very loudly. Hopefully it will be just temporary. She picks up her shopping bag and says come on Sheila I have to get my bacon. She pushes open the shattered shop door of Mr Evans the grocer. His shop is in shambles. He is trying to sweep away some of the debris from the counters. He is a little dazed. Mrs Harvey he says, and raises a cynical eyebrow. Mr Evans says she emphatically and with such true belief, I have come for my bacon.

MY DOG BONZO

My Mum decides after the High Street raid that life is too short and unpredictable so we should go look at the puppy that we had talked about in the shelter. Ta Jesus, ta ever so, I thank you for this. The next day, after school, the three of us kids and my Mum walk up to Redig's Sweet Shop. Mr Redig is in the shop and tells us to meet him around the back of the house. We do so and Mr Redig opens the back gate into the garden. There they are ten little puppies squealing and fighting to get to their mother's teats. Their mother lays there in the sunshine patiently while they are all gobbling down milk as fast as they can. Some fall asleep on the job. Mummy asks Mr Redig if they are ready to leave their mother because she doesn't want to be bottle feeding a puppy. Mr Redig assures us in his guttural tone that they are ready to leave and are already eating some solid food from a bowl. He tells us that they just like to nurse as long as their mom is around and that it is very comforting to them. Five of the puppies have been spoken for and are to be picked up this week so we have our pick of the other five. Mum says it has to be a male. I don't want a bitch getting out of the garden onto the street and coming home with puppies in her belly. I wonder to myself, how does being on the street make you have puppies? I make a mental note to myself to ask Mum about that. He tries to point out to us the five that are available but he can only find four of them. Then he kneels down and pulls one out from under its mummies belly, all warm cuddly and black. He is absolutely a smasher. He gives him to me to cuddle. He is so wiggly and fat. I love him right there and then. Mum says, let Rita and Len hold him too and it is love at first sight for them as well. Please Mum, can we have this one and take him home with us. We beg. We want him so bad. Mum asks Mr Redig again if he is very sure that it is a male. He turns the puppy over. Oh, ya ya, he is a goot healthy boy. Mum is satisfied and so it is done, he is ours. We all hug Mummy around the waist tightly; thank you, thank you, thank you. But, of course, none of us think of how he will miss his Mum. It doesn't even cross my mind about him missing his brothers and sisters. But then I myself should know better as I was taken from my Mum and Dad and I know how badly it hurts. It is the worst pain that there is and I cried myself to sleep many nights from home sickness. Mr Redig gives us an old cardboard box with a woolly baby blanket in it for him to sleep in and also a pile of old newspapers. We will learn very fast what they are for. You will need these he says. He tells us to buy a dog collar and a leash so that we can walk him. Mr Redig says that it is very important to walk him every day. I wonder why does he need all of those newspapers? He can't read. We thank Mr Redig and say goodbye. Mummy carries the puppy home and we carry the box and papers. He is so wriggly and he keeps trying to crawl under her coat. When we get home Mum spreads the newspapers all over the scullery floor and puts his box and blanket in the corner by the stove. He isn't to be allowed into the rest of the house until he is trained to wee wee and poop on the papers or outside. So now I know what the papers are for. Mum says we have to take him outside every time after he eats or we will have to clean up after him and of course we all promise that we will. But then promises are meant to be broken, right? The next thing is that we have to decide what we are going to call him. Well, that becomes a heated discussion because we all want to call him something different and my Mum settles it. She comes up with the perfect name. We will call him Bonzo, she says. Why Bonzo we ask? She tells us that Bonzo was a famous dog cartoon character in the newspaper. The most adorable ever, created by Englishman George Studdy in 1921. To us kids that is it and so Bonzo it is. He seems to like his name and very soon comes when he hears it. His first nights at our house are very sad for him. He cries and cries for his Mum. One by one we end up in the scullery trying to comfort him. None of us get much sleep. You can hear his pitiful crying all over the house. Mummy says he is very lonely for his mother. I know how he must feel. I cried many tears for my Mum too. Luckily, my Daddy comes up with a brilliant idea. He wraps up a small wind up ticking clock and tucks it under Bonzo's blanket. Daddy says that the idea is that he will cuddle up to it and think that it is his mother's heart beat that he is hearing and wonder of wonders it actually works. Peace reigns from that night on. If you try it just don't forget to wind the bloody clock. Bonzo grows rapidly and he truly belongs as a member of our family. There is only one in our family who takes offense to him and that is George our cat. This is war. Bonzo is in George's territory and he had better learn his place. If we can't find Bonzo we just look under the copper in the scullery. There he is cowering and shivering with George on guard. Just one swipe from George was all it took to tell Bonzo who was boss. In a few weeks they do co-exist but Bonzo always knows who is in charge. Bonzo has become a member of the dogs' army. When the sirens sounded last night he was the first one down the garden, running, barking and warning everyone. Then into the shelter and he stayed there with us until the all clear sounded. He is no dummy. George, no, he wasn't having any of that togetherness nonsense. He stays in his basket in the kitchen just waiting for us to come back. Just wondering what is wrong with all of us, running out of the house like idiots. Bonzo gives us love, hope and joy during what are some of the darkest days of this war. I hug him tightly during raids in the shelter especially when the bombs are exploding around us and nuzzle my face into his warm black silky coat. He looks at me with those large brown loving eyes, licks and slobbers my face all over. And you know what; it makes everything right with the world at that moment. I thank Bonzo for healing my fear in the many times that I think that I may die. In early summer Bonzo escapes from the garden for a few hours. I can't understand why my Mother is so upset and angry. Then, three months later I understand because Bonzo is obviously going to have puppies. Bonzo is a girl. The puppies arrive, healthy and are soon sent to good homes. Even though Bonzo is a girl we don't change her name because it is not about her name it is all about who she is. She will always be Bonzo to us.

REFLECTIONS:

Bonzo died in 1953 of stomach cancer. She was so very brave and to relieve her of all of her pain and suffering she was mercifully put to sleep. There are tears on my pages as I write this, to never be able to see her ever again or feel her wet kisses on my face is more than I want to bear for I loved her so and miss her to this day. Thank you Bonzo, you always eased my fear and pain. Goodbye my friend. Sleep well. We keep the clock wound for you.

SERVING THEIR COUNTRY

Everyone, men and women alike, are called upon to do their part for our country and everyone wants to serve. My Mum and Dad are no exception. My father joins the ever growing throng of Englishmen lining up to join the army. He wants to serve and make his family proud even though he had been turned down at the beginning of the war for of all things, flat feet. My Mum joins up as a part time air raid warden. She works the daytime shift assisting people that are injured until ambulances can arrive. She also helps find people that are trapped in the bombed out houses. She makes sure that the blackout curtains in homes are hung properly with no holes to let out light as one chink of light can be a matter of life and death. It tells Gerry where we are and where to strike. Air raid wardens are also to report all bomb damage and make sure that everyone is carrying a gas mask. She helps and assists all in need. Mum hands out sandwiches and tea to grateful bombed out residents and helps locate much needed blankets and clothing lost in the bombing. She helps boost morale but I know my Mum is deeply affected by what she witnesses. But with all of that she does her bit. My Dad never gives up. He tries again to get from the Home Guard into the regular army because it is so important to him. He goes for all of his tests and then waits for the postman's knock and for the letter to fall onto the mat. He eagerly anticipates a letter confirming his acceptance into the army. Mum knows how important it is to him to be accepted but I know that she secretly wishes that he won't have to go. As all wives are, she too is frightened that if he goes he won't come back. Maybe they won't take him like the last time when he tried to get in. It is at least two weeks before the letter lands on the mat. It comes one dinner time but we don't dare open it till Dad gets home. It seems like the day will never end. My Dad is out at work boarding windows, fixing broken water pipes, electric and gas lines. There will be no interior decorating work of hanging wallpaper, painting or remodelling for a long time to come. Dad comes home at dinner time. We all sit in the kitchen anxiously waiting to hear him come through the back gate. We hear the gate bang as Bonzo goes running up the side alley barking all the way to greet him. He comes in and says hello to all of us. This is it, the moment of truth. Dad sits down at the kitchen table to a welcome cup of tea. Mum gets his dinner warmed up. We have all eaten earlier. She puts the post by his mug of tea. He picks up the "On His Majesty's Service" envelope and opens it with his dinner knife. The silence is deafening. All of us are hardly breathing; we are all holding our breath. Even Bonzo and George sit there with their ears perked but without a sound. This is so important to my Dad. He doesn't say a word. He finishes reading it, folds the single sheet of paper neatly and puts it back in to the envelope. He places both hands flat onto the kitchen table. We can tell that he is searching for the right words to say to us. He looks tired and drawn. Finally he utters, I am not going, they won't take me. Mum lets out a gasp of relief and the three of us kids shout Hoorah. Well, I should say, Len and Rita do. I don't. He isn't going. He is staying with us through the war. I will say an extra thank you in my prayers tonight. My Dad is bereft. He wants to march off to battle with the rest of our men to serve and protect England. I can't imagine the pain my Dad must be feeling. All my friends Dads have gone or are ready to leave. I am ashamed to say that I am embarrassed that he isn't going off to war. The British Government is saying that my Dad isn't good enough to go. Dad says out loud, do you believe it, again, flat feet. I am no good to them because my feet are flat. The same excuse as last time. I am thinking to myself, what am I going to say to my friends? My Dad can't fight because his feet are flat. I want to be able to boast with the other kids that he is fighting overseas. What will the kids whose Dads are overseas fighting have to say? I am so embarrassed that I want to run away and hide. What I so want is to be proud of my Daddy. I then realize that I am a stupid, selfish, shallow little twerp because I should be feeling lucky to have my Daddy here with me to protect me and proud that he will still be in the Home Guard. Dad is to re-register into the Home Guard immediately and to report to duty on the morrow. The Home Guard is a voluntary army and all who are not fit for the regular army can join. Their main task is to be able to relieve the regular army of many tasks at home so that they can get on with doing the job that they are really trained for. The basic work of the Home Guard is that they should have expert knowledge of our towns and surrounding localities. They are to guard air fields in which enemy gliders or paratroopers might land. They are also to be the first line of defence against invasion by the Germans. The Home Guard is always first on the scene when an enemy fighter plane is shot down and crashes in the gardens or fields. The Home Guard are to hold the pilot if he survives until the regular army arrives to take him away for interrogation. They also have the job of guarding bridges, forming patrols at many of the cities power stations and guarding entrances to many of Britain's railway tunnels. They try to prevent looting of bombed out properties. Mum tells me that the Home Guard number one million one hundred and seventy five thousand volunteers. Whenever we have an air raid people are glad to see the Home Guard who help clear the damage and rescue people. They are doing their bit for Britain. We can't do without them and they are important to our survival. This evening I overhear my Dad telling my Mum that he feels guilty walking the streets in his Home Guard uniform. Some of our neighbours, in cliques, are gossiping why he a healthy British male, is not overseas fighting for us to keep our freedom. He says that as he passes them by they stop their gossiping, shut their mouths and just stare. Some of the neighbours say that only the weaker men are in the Home Guard. What do they know and what are they doing to protect us. At night when the air raid sirens sound and we all run for cover into the shelters or under the kitchen table, just anywhere for safety the sound of the British Ack-Ack guns manned by the Home Guard give us a sense of pride that we are fighting to protect ourselves from the Hun and the destruction of their bombs. Most times the droning of the enemy planes are beyond the reach of the guns but we lay there believing we are defeating them. For most our fear is lessened knowing that the Home Guard is out there to protect us from the Germans, even if they land on our soil to steal our very way of life.

Dad is gone every night and when he has finished his all night duty in Annerly he walks home in his big boots and uniform with military pack. He says he is always deathly afraid to turn the corner onto our road, terrified that the house and the street have been bombed and that we could all be dead. After a couple of hours of sleep, Dad spends his day helping build more shelters, doing lots of plumbing jobs for neighbours by fixing broken pipes from bomb blasts. He helps out wherever he can. It doesn't take too long before all of the gossipy neighbours are thankful for his services to his neighbourhood and his country. We kids bless him for his service and his flat feet and we are proud of how he conducts himself in a time of such adversity. I tell him that I am so sorry that as a stupid child I was embarrassed that he was not going overseas to fight and that I couldn't be more proud of him being with us through it all. The friends I have of whom I was stupidly jealous because their fathers are fighting overseas have often suffered the loss of their fathers who will not come home. How very, very sad, I am so lucky and I thank God for giving my Dad flat feet.

REFLECTIONS:

We need to remember all the children of World War II who lost fathers, mothers and other family members. We thank you for your steadfastness, spirit and bravery, job well done. If it wasn't for your brave loved ones we would not be living free today.

1942 TO 1944

The war continues to invade our lives but we make the best of
it. There are hardly any day raids, just night raids. About two
months ago Dad found two large tins of cine reels and an old
projector in a bombed out house and when nobody claimed
them he was allowed to bring them home. This is Saturday
night so when my Dad came home he put up an old white
sheet on the wall in the kitchen and cranked up the projector
which whirred to life. It is so exciting. He inserts the cine reels
and turns off the overhead light so that it is all dark. We are
over the moon. This is big stuff, great times. We sit on the floor
in our pyjamas, our eyes glued to the white sheet. We are at
the pictures. We are all at the pictures in our own kitchen and
we are all gob smacked. Then, there they are on the white
screen, the two funniest men that I have ever seen, Laurel and
Hardy. We laugh at their antics till our stomachs hurt. The
pictures are silent with just fast funny movements to tell their
story. The projector keeps breaking down and the reels keep
falling off. The picture jerks all over the place but it is the best
entertainment ever. If we don't have to be in the shelter on
Saturdays this is to become the Saturday night ritual. Dad also
has a couple of old silent cowboy movies. He says he thinks it
is Tom Mix. I have never heard of him but it is the best of the
best. Our life is good. It is like we are rich. Cowboys chasing
Indians and Indians chasing cowboys, we are transported to
another world. Suddenly, over the clatter of the projector we
hear the air raid sirens going off. Maybe it won't be a bad raid.
Sometimes they will fly overhead toward another city that is to
be their target for the night but Dad turns off the projector and

we sit in the dark and listen. We then hear the droning of the enemy planes as they approach. It is like a swarming of bees and it gets louder. The bombing starts and that awful whistling as the bombs are released and descend. Where will they hit tonight? There is no time to get down to the shelter and it is dreadfully dangerous to go outside during the raid. Dad goes out into the passageway and opens the front door to see what is happening. Mum makes us get our dressing gowns and slippers on which we hurriedly do. We want to see outside as well. Dad says incendiary bombs are coming down like rain and he pushes us back. Get them under the table, Ruby, he yells. It is just too dangerous to run for the shelter. We are too scared to go under the table so we stand rooted to the spot looking out the front door watching as the incendiaries fall. Across the street at the Barrington's we see a fire. Their beautiful green wooden gate flames up as an incendiary hit it directly. The Barringtons, Florrie and Ernie, are out throwing buckets of water on the gate. They are in their night clothes with tin helmets on their heads. My Dad dashes across the street as do others of our neighbours to help put out the fire. My Dad is screaming at them as he runs over. Look behind you. Turn around you bloody idiots. But with all the noise of fire engines, ambulances, droning planes and exploding bombs they can't hear him and pay no attention but we can see what is going on. Their whole front room is on fire and going up in smoke. It is lit up like a Christmas tree. The curtains are getting licked by the flames. Soon the whole room is on fire. People are throwing buckets of sand and water through the broken window that explodes from the fire. Soon the fire engine arrives and floods their front room to put the fire out. Their beautiful green gate is saved to be walked through another day but their front room and furniture are a total loss. The next day the Barringtons are outside giving their gate a fresh coat of green paint. That is even before they even think of fixing their front room. Oh well, the damaged front room will give Dad some scarce but badly needed work. I guess that it all works out in the end.

THE ODEON CLUB

It is late in October and I have joined the Odeon Club. The Odeon is a big chain of cinemas in and around London and they have decided to open up the doors of the cinemas on Saturday mornings to children ages five through fifteen to give them a break from the on-going war. Needless to say a lot of sixteen and seventeen year olds try to get in as it is free. I have met most the kids on our street and from around the neighbourhood so I have lots of friends to go with. The Odeon is about a twenty minute walk from our street and as I am now seven my Mum and Dad let me go with my new friends without too many admonitions to behave myself. My Mum knows what a terror I can be. My brother will go as well but he will just hang out with his cronies. He won't ever let me be seen with him. My sister prefers to stay in bed and sleep late on Saturdays so she won't be coming. Thank goodness because she can't tell on me to my Mum. I know that it is wartime and often dangerous but life goes on and most of us try to live life as normal as one can expect to. This Saturday we all take sandwiches with us as there are no concessions to buy anything from but we don't have any money anyway so it doesn't matter. We are all happy with what we have. Two of my friends who are sisters, Sheila and Ivy, bring mash potato sandwiches on white bread. I wish my Mum would let me have that but she won't. She tells me that cheese is better for me than mash potatoes. At the cinema they announce that there are to be three hours of cartoons and cowboy pictures today, whoopee. We are having the best time of our young lives. There must be at least three hundred children here today. All descended on the Odeon at once. Noisy isn't the word. Kids are running up and down the aisles chasing one another, screaming and yelling. Fights break out and food becomes the weapon of choice. There are ushers with torches who try their best to control this unruly crowd until the pictures start. We are having such a good time. My mates and I see many kids marched up the aisle by their ears and being told not to come back again but of course the little buggers will. We are anxious for the lights to go down and eventually they do with a gasp from us children for what is to come. All we can see at this moment are the beams from the ushers' torches seating the last few kids. No Mums and Dads here. It is their day off. They must be giving thanks to the Odeon. A hush falls over the audience as the stage lights up and then this huge, magnificent organ rises up from below the stage with a bloke sitting at it and playing music. It is like he is coming up from under the ground. It is truly magic. I have never seen the likes before. We are all spellbound. Well, shall we say, for just a few minutes? The screen lights up behind the bloke at the organ and the words appear for us to sing along and this is where we learn the ever endearing, ever to be remembered, Odeon Club song. "Is everybody Happy" and we all yell, yes, as loud as we can. "Do we ever worry", and no, we yell back. "To the Odeon we have come and now that we are all together we can have some fun". Then as loud as we can we yell, Oy. "Do we help our neighbours". Here we are supposed to say yes but us rotten kids say no just to be obstreperous. "Do we ever worry". Here it is supposed to be no but we change it to yes. "We are a hundred thousand strong, we will fight for right not wrong, we are members of the OCC we stress, is everybody happy". Here we change the yes to no of course. We think that we are so bloody smart. That is our Odeon Club song and do we let off steam with it. We scream our lungs out. Next we sing some more songs; "Johnny Zero is our hero today" is our favourite.

We can really scream out on that one and it feels liberating to scream and let it all out. "The kids all call him *Johnny Zero*" we yell loudly and blimey that feels good. Then at last comes what we have been waiting for, the pictures. We all sit like reformed angels, for five minutes, watching Gene Autry catch the bad man. We cheer for the hero and boo for the bad man. The hero looks longingly into the heroine's eyes and then the girls all say Aahs and the boys all boo and chuck the leftover bits of their sandwiches at the screen. Then our excitement and happiness is broken by the dreaded air raid sirens. Oh why today when we are having fun. Suddenly the screen goes dark and a message in big type appears. There is an air raid in progress, please stay calm, put your gas masks on and get down under the seats. It is scarily dark in the theatre except for the ushers flashing their torches across the cinema to help us with our gas masks. The ushers are telling us that there is not enough time to get this many children out and to the street shelters. There is no noise now just silence as we lay on the dirty, carpeted floor amongst sweet papers, dirty dog ends and who knows what from last night's pictures. Nobody is laughing now we are just scared for our lives. We listen intently for the whistling of the bombs. Fear creeps from the top of your head to the tips of your toes. It is paralyzing and agonizing. You ask yourself, will I die here today? Will Mum and Dad cry when I am gone? Will they miss me? Will anyone miss me? I want to hold somebody's hand for comfort but we are all too embarrassed to reach out and show our fear and need for comfort. We are English and must pull ourselves up by our boot straps. That is what we are told every day. We hear the whistle of the bombs and the thudding sounds as they hit their targets. Please don't hit us I pray, I don't want to have to be dug out of the rubble. I don't want to die, I want to live. I couldn't bring Heather today, she always comforts me in a situation like this but my Mum told me yesterday that I am now too big to be dragging her around with me all the time and that I must leave her on my bed during the day and that I can only cuddle her at night. My Mum doesn't seem to understand that Heather has been the only one in my life to comfort me and give me unconditional love. She has never deserted me as others have. Am I bitter? Maybe, I will have to learn to live without her and it will be the most painful time for me as I never can say goodbye. The all clear sounds. The show will not continue today. We will come again next Saturday. We are allowed to leave the theatre. There is blast damage to the outside of the picture house. We witness the carnage. The train station next to us took a direct hit. The ambulances and fire engines are there. Acrid smoke is rising into the air. I know there are dead people. My stomach feels sick for their pain and suffering. I try not to look, I just want to get home as fast as I can and see Heather and my Mum and Dad. I hope that they are safe. My walk home with my friends is, I think, the quietest that I have ever known with each of us in our own heads. We will get our courage back and I am sure we will go back to the Odeon. Our fear will not defeat us.

REFLECTIONS:

I loved the Odeon club. It was a brief respite from the terrors of war and while we were there we were living like human beings at peace. Thanks Odeon Club. We will always be members of the OCC we stress; is everybody happy and we say, yes.

SIREN SUITS AND WINTER

A new style has arrived on the war scene, the comfortable, warm, practical siren suit. It is usually made out of blankets and old dressing gowns. It is a one piece. You could say much like a jumpsuit that you step into. It has long sleeves and legs with a long zipper plus a warm hood. It is wonderful for quick dressing when you are in bed and the siren sounds for the mad dash to the shelters, hence the name, siren suit. It is also great for weekends when we don't have to wear school uniforms and absolutely super on this absolutely freezing cold day. Betty and her sister Jean, from up the road, knock on the front door. They are not my good friends. Other kids call them bullies with Betty being the worst. They ask if Bonzo and I can go for a walk up to The Woods. It is a public park which at one time had been a private estate but that was years ago. The Woods are full of many very old oaks that are all gnarled and in winter bare of leaves which makes them seem a little scary. We convince ourselves that there are witches and all sort of scary hob goblins hiding and living in the trees waiting to jump out at us. One would never go there by one's self or after dark. We jump out from behind the trees at one another and scare ourselves to death. It is great fun. Bonzo loves it. She is rolling in piles of dead leaves and barks when we jump out at her. We come into a large clearing. This is where the large old majestic mansion is. Some Lord or Lady must have lived there at one time but now the place is boarded up so it looks desolate and lonely. Many kids have tried to break in. Some did and roamed the old place playing the party game, murderers and got up to who knows what. We are way too scared to go in there. We might not ever come out alive. We don't want the house today, it is not our destination. We want the small lake with the stone bridge across it. Other kids have told us that the lake is frozen and that people have been skating on it. What a temptation for us. We have no skates. They would be a terrible expense for our families so you use what you have. You can always push off on your leather soled shoes and get a fun ride. We are the only ones at the lake today. It is so cold and windy that it is keeping others away. They are probably all huddling around their three lump coal fires. Who will be the first to try the ice? Jean says let's let Bonzo go out there first. If she sinks through the ice then we will know that it isn't safe. With that said she picks up a pebble from the side of the lake and throws it, skipping it out across the ice. Bonzo doesn't need to be asked twice. She is gone out on the lake in a flash to get the rock and she doesn't disappear through the ice. Thank goodness, what on earth would I have told my Mum if she had? The three of us lock our arms around each other's waists. Betts being the tallest is the leader. She is always the leader. If Betts goes through the ice we all go. Jean is on the end as she is the smallest. We get safely out to the middle of the lake shuffling along. We are all giggling with nervousness and bravado. Betts can be fun when she is away from her gang of bullies. After a few tumbles we get the idea and are sliding all over the ice. Who needs skates? This is the most fun we have had this winter. We are budding Sonja Henie's or so we think. Bonzo is sitting at the edge of the lake yelping at us as if to say, this isn't good, let's be getting home as it is getting late. The sun is going down but we ignore her. We are warm in our siren suits and I am very proud of mine. It is a beautiful blue from one of my Nana's old dressing gowns that my Mum had kept and made a siren suit from it for me. I love it more because it is from My Nana's gown. We pretend that we have skates and we are trying to do pirouettes but our joy and laughter is interrupted abruptly when we hear a rendering cracking of the ice. Before you can say Jack Flash, we are in shock floundering around in icy cold water. Lummy, what has happened? I haven't learned to swim yet. We are all screaming, trying to keep our heads above water. These bloody wool siren suits are sucking up the water and dragging us down. I can hear Bonzo above it all barking her head off and then suddenly my feet hit something hard, it is the bottom of the lake and my head is still above water. Stand up, stand up, I scream at them. We are all right. Try to get over to the side. My teeth are chattering. It is hard to breathe, being so cold. My whole body is shivering. We all manage to work our way to the edge of the lake but getting out of the water is a big problem. Our clothes are so sodden and heavy but we manage to eventually pull ourselves slowly and agonizingly onto the bank. We all lay there for a brief moment trying to get our breath. We try to ring out our siren suits but we are so bone cold and weak that we don't have the strength to do it. The sun is going down and our breath comes out in a freezing haze. We just have to try to run for home. Luckily, we are only about ten minutes from our street and with luck, perseverance and youthful vigour we will make it. Bonzo is running in front of us barking madly all the way. I don't think that I have ever been or ever will be that cold again. Our clothes are dripping puddles of water as we run, impeding us all the way. We cannot talk to one another for shivering and chattering of teeth has taken precedence over everything else. Betty and Jean's house is the first one we come to on the street. They are up the path and banging on the front door. Hope your Mum won't kill you, Betty yells. Bonzo and I continue without a pause in our steps. I don't go to my front door; I go through the back gate hoping with all my heart that my Mum will be out at the shops. If that is the case she will be gone for quite a long while as the queues are always so long and it takes forever to buy food and a lot of times they are out when you get to the front of the line and you hear, we are all out, come back tomorrow. If that is the case my Mum is going to be in a very bad mood. I drip all the way to the scullery door. Bonzo hides in her dog house outside; she isn't going to witness the punishment that she knows will be meted out very shortly. She is smart. I am sure that she will put her paws over her ears when it starts. I open the scullery door as quietly as I can and there is Rita cleaning her teeth at the sink. I stand on the coconut door mat in front of the door dripping and shivering from cold and fear. Is Mum home, I ask, stuttering with the cold. Rita is gob smacked. She drops her Maclean's tin of toothpaste and doesn't say a word. Then she shakes her head no and utters, what have you done? You have got to be joking Sheila, what did you do? Why do you have to be so cussed? Mum is going to kill you when she sees you. Help me, I say. Well first you had better take off those wet clothes; you are going to catch your death. Luckily for you Mum is out. Please, please, don't tell her I beg as I take off all of my wet clothes, not daring to move off the coconut mat. That would have been adding insult to injury having got the scullery wet with dirty lake water. My clothes lie in a sodden pile on the mat as I stand there shivering with the cold. Rita gives me one of the two family towels to wrap around me. It is thin and rough but it is luxury compared to my soaking wet clothes. I tell my sister what happened. She shakes her head and says, how could you be so stupid and naughty? What are we going to do, I ask? You are going to have to tell Mum what happened, that is what we are going to do. You had better go and get your dressing gown on and put these wet clothes outside in the big bucket. Mum will have to put them through the mangle. We can't hang them outside on the line because they will freeze stiff as a board. I go up to the room that my sister and I share. I am shivering in my dressing gown. I crawl under my eiderdown for warmth. I am so bloody cold. I hate the cold. When I grow up I am going to have a fire in every room. Mum only lights the one fire down in the kitchen in the early evening as coal is so scarce there is never enough to heat another room. It is usually just a three lump fire aided by rolled up newspapers. The problem is that when you have to leave the meagre heat of the kitchen and go upstairs to bed you have to climb up the stairway to the icy linoleum floored bedroom which feels absolutely miserable. We do have our hot water bottles which are good for several hours but then they get cold and clammy in the middle of the night and feel like dead slimy fish on your feet. Right now I don't want to come out from under the eiderdown but I am going to have to. I hear the key turning in the front door and I hear my mother's footfalls in the passageway. I can only hope and pray that she got the food that she was going to queue up for because we need it badly and if not she will be in a bad mood and my punishment will be even more severe. I hear the kitchen door off of the hallway close and I hear muffled voices from below. I know that I am going to get it. A really good-hiding probably but I am thinking that if I work at crying crocodile tears she might feel sorry for me and the punishment may be less but never under estimate your Mum. My Mum is smart. I do get a good hiding on the back of my legs with the hair brush. It stings so very bad and I know that it will hurt for days to come. This time I don't have to try to cry, these are real tears. I think my Mum will be cross with me for the rest of the winter and I hate when she is cross with me. Tonight Rita tells me that it isn't the siren suit or ruined shoes that my Mum is cross about but it is that I could have drowned. You know, I wonder why Mums get so angry that you could have been hurt that they feel that they have to give you something to really cry about. For whenever I fall over, hurt my knees and start to cry she drags me up and says; look where you are going, stop snivelling or I will give you something to really cry about. That shuts you up quick. I haven't the foggiest idea why Mums think like that. I mean, after all you don't go looking for another bloody good hiding.

DOLLY

It is a Saturday morning and it is so bitterly cold and as usual I hate getting out of bed and putting my feet onto the icy linoleum. My bed is cold. There is no more heat from my hot water bottle. I hang my legs and feet over the side of the bed. My feet find my slippers. I hurriedly pull my dressing gown on and pull the cord tightly around me. I mustn't wake Rita or she will be cross with me because she loves to have a lie in on Saturdays. I shuffle down the stairs to the kitchen. There is no fire in the grate yet and there won't be until late this afternoon. My world feels grey. Mum asks; are you ready for breakfast Sheila? I know that I will be getting my usual grey lumpy porridge but at least it is hot and warms me up a little. Wouldn't it be lovely if we had lots of sugar and milk to make it taste better? When I grow up I will have lashings of milk, cream and sugar but we can't so for now I choke it down with a cuppa tea. I mustn't complain. My Dad is home this morning. He asks; what are you going to do this cold morning? I tell him I am meeting my mates up at Easter's bakery and we probably will go to the Odeon Club. Dad says; well at least you will be warm at the pictures but be very careful out of doors. There is thick black ice on the streets this morning. People are having a hard time keeping their footing. It is very dangerous so be careful how you go ducks. I will Dad, I promise. It sounds very exciting to be out on the streets. I want to see what is going on outdoors. One hour later I am washed, teeth cleaned, warmly dressed and I am off to Easter's for the meeting with my mates. There are seven of us. We all lean up against the outside brick wall. There is warmth coming from the bricks due to the big ovens inside baking the bread and rolls. The smell is ever so lovely. It makes us all very hungry. Queues are already forming outside the shop for bread. Queuing for bread is an everyday occurrence and sadly the people in the back of the queue probably won't get any. People are lining up even in the freezing rain that has just started to fall. It is making the black ice worse. People are slipping and falling. Our gang thinks it is funny to watch and we giggle as they fall over. We are so very wicked. Billy Monk, one of the lads in our group of friends, suggests that instead of going to the Odeon Club we find some stout heavy cardboard and go up the steepest hill in our neighbourhood and slide down on our bums but cardboard is scarce. It is always collected by the rag and bone man who pushes an old pram down the streets calling out, Rag and Bone. He takes all of the cardboard and eventually it goes to the war effort. Victor, Billy's friend, comes up with a brilliant idea. Why don't we take the ruddy metal dust bin lids off of the community neighbourhood dust bins and use them. We all cheer. They will make great toboggans. Victor tells everyone what street to go to in order to steal the lids. But be very careful he says; we don't want any of the ruddy neighbours to see us. But luckily for us, as the weather is so bad, not many people are out and about. It takes us just twenty minutes to muster four of the lids. Enough for us to all take turns down the hill. Whoopee! We climb back to the top of the hill. I don't want to say anything but I have to admit that I am really scared to go down that icy hill. I know that the boys will call me scaredy custard but the other two girls say they are scared as well. I then feel better about my fear. We tell the boys and they call us big sissies because we don't want to go. So the boys sit down on the cold metal lids and kick off with their feet. The lids gather speed, kicking up bits of frozen snow and gravel as they fly down the hill. The boys are squealing with fear and delight as the icy rain beats against the bare

408

exposed skin of their faces that are not covered by their balaclavas. We girls watch them with admiration as the four make it to the bottom of the hill. They are screaming up to us to join them. We wave them off. We will walk down very carefully or go down on our bums. Brenda and Janet go on ahead. I decide to stay. I hear the milkman coming around the corner at the top of the hill. I want to wait and greet my friend, Dolly, the milkman's horse. Ernie the milkman always gives me two sugar lumps to give to her when she is on our street. He must give up his sugar rations for her. Dolly pulls a bright orange wagon with a sign on the side that is painted in white and says United Dairies. You can see all of the milk bottles with their bright silver caps in their crates which Ernie delivers to the houses daily. He picks up the washed empty bottles sitting on the door steps and replaces them with the fresh milk. How much milk you get depends on how many people are in your family and how many kids there are. Milk is rationed. There is never enough for cooking only just enough for your cuppa tea and for very young children to drink. My friend Dolly has been pulling the milk wagon for years. She is a real luv. I have only got to know her since coming back from evacuation in Cornwall. Dolly is a dark brown mare with the most beautiful brown soulful eyes. She loves everyone. She is unbelievably patient. Dolly wears a leather harness with shafts on either side of her that attach to the milk wagon. She has leather blinders on either side of her head to keep her from being frightened by motorized traffic. You can't miss our Ernie the milkman. He wears a dark blue peaked cap and a blue and white striped apron but today he also has a warm jacket against the cold wind. Ernie has used her to pull the milk wagon on his route for years. They are the best of friends. Whenever he calls out; Whoa Dolly, she stops. Then Ernie clicks his tongue and she will slowly plod on. It is as if she knows who is to get milk today. She is always here come rain or shine. She is part of my young life in the warm summers and in the icy cold wet winters. My Mum loves Dolly as well but for a different reason than I. For Dolly regularly deposits, either in our street or just around the corner, a wonderful pile of fresh steaming manure. And as I learned very quickly from my Mum's tongue, it is the very best food for your roses. It makes them grow and bloom better than anyone else's. Whenever my Mum sees Dolly pull up on the street she goes into action. She gets out the shovel and the bucket from the cupboard under the stairs, checks the street for deposits and if not there you are dragged around the corner to see if it has happened on another street on Dolly's route. After my Mum collects her valuable prize in the bucket it is returned home and deposited proudly around her prize rose bushes. Sometimes another neighbour is armed with her bucket and shovel ready to try to win the gallant fight against my mother, a formidable foe, who is quick with the shovel and wields it like a weapon if opposed. I fully expect her to yell charge as we run down the street with me in one hand, bucket and shovel in the other. Like the charge of the light brigade. My Mum's roses are her pride and joy. This morning as I wait for Dolly to come around the corner icy winds pick up whipping through the branches of the bare trees along the street. You can hear the branches moaning under the weight of the ice. For anyone to venture out today is a treacherous under taking. Just trying to stay on one's feet is a real feat of sportsmanship. It seems only the young wrapped up in siren suits to insulate them against the cold are able to navigate the frozen streets and they laugh with hilarity at one another when their boot cladded feet go out from underneath them and they land on their backsides. But it isn't fun for everyone, especially for elderly people whose bones are less strong and who are less steady on their feet. My friend, Miss Stone, lives by herself on the hill. She is a very sweet old lady who, if she is out tending her front garden on sunny days and you happen to be walking by she will always greet you with a smile and pass the time of day. She always gives me a pat on the head as she reaches into her apron pocket and produces a bright copper penny which I always look forward to and which I pray she will be out there as I pass by because a penny can go towards a sherbet dab, four or five delicious creamy toffees or a fizzy Tizer drink that goes up your nose and make it go all of a tingle. She isn't very big in stature and is slight in figure with the whitest hair that I have ever seen fashioned in a knot on top of her head. She has the bluest twinkling eyes that welcome you whenever she sees you. Her skin is like porcelain. She is beautiful even at the age of eighty four. That is older than I can ever imagine being. Will I ever be that old? She wears lace collars and cuffs on her dark dresses. Even her white aprons are etched in French lace. She has a quick wit and I wish that if I were allowed to have another grandmother that she could be mine. I just think of all the new copper pennies that I could have.

On this bitterly cold morning I see Miss Stone as she is used to do venture outside of her house wrapped in a shawl against the bitter wind to give Dolly her eagerly awaited daily ration of sugar lumps. I am not the only one who gives Dolly sugar. I am sure that she gets some on every street. Everyone gives up some of their ration for our lovely Dolly. Dolly expects this every day and today is no different. Miss Stone never lets her down and today despite the awful weather Dolly will get her sugar lumps. Ernie slowly comes around the corner to the top of the hill. Ernie is walking alongside Dolly today. They are having trouble keeping their footing. I watch as he struggles to deliver the milk to the Lindsay's at number twenty eight. He is holding on to the low railings surrounding the front garden for support. He has set the brake on the dairy cart. Dolly is turning her head nervously as she tries to maintain her footing. She has an old horse blanket over her back to try to keep out the dank invading cold. As I walk up to her the only warmth emanating from her is the warm air she breathes out of her wide nostrils which then crystalizes into ice. Ernie eventually makes it back to the milk wagon. He hoists the empties on board and refills his metal basket with the next order. Blowing on his chilled fingers which his mittens fail to keep warm he calls out to me, hello ducks, how are you doing, eh, too bloody cold to be outside. You should go home luv. I don't have any sugar lumps for you to give her today, sorry. Sorry, next time. He releases the wheel brake and clicks his tongue for Dolly to continue to his next stop four houses down at the Balls. I follow them down. I see Miss Stone step off the pavement in front of Dolly and reach to give her the daily sugar. Oh, no. Dolly's hooves start slipping on the ice. Sensing that she is losing control she tries to stop herself by trying to rear up on her hind legs, her head and neck pulling against the reins and shafts that constrain her to the cart. Dolly's eyes are wild and filled with fear. Her nostrils are flared as she flails hopelessly to save herself. As her four legs and hooves return to hit the ice in her futile attempt to save herself she knocks Miss Stone to the ground with her front hooves. Miss Stone lies in a crumpled heap with blood trickling from her forehead made ever more crimson against the silver white of her hair that has released from its bun from the blow. Everything is happening so fast. Ernie drops his basket and the milk bottles crash to the pavement. Glass shards lay like diamonds and milk runs in rivulets down the hill. Some of it escaping and trickling into the open drains alongside the street and pavement. Dolly starts sliding down the steep hill. Her legs buckle as the weight of the milk cart and its load push her forward. There is no stopping this catastrophic accident. People stand literally frozen to the spot unable to do anything but trying to grasp the situation, the horror and the futility of it all. Dolly screams in fear. Will I ever forget that cry as there is nothing anyone can do but watch helplessly as she and the wagon careen completely out of control down the ice covered hill? It all ends tragically at the bottom of the hill when Dolly and the cart come to rest. The cart lies on its side with bottles broken and milk in puddles that is freezing in white sheets as fast as it hits the ground. Miraculously some bottles stay intact and just roll to a resting place. Dolly is in a huddled heap. Her front legs splayed out in front of her, her back legs obviously broken from the impact of the wagon that is partially lying across her hind quarters. She struggles pitifully to raise herself up but all she can do is to raise her beautiful head. Her big brown eyes covered in a dark blue haze of pain imploring anyone to help her. Ernie reaches Dolly and kneels down beside her. The crowd that has gathered suddenly are released from their frozen fear and swing into action. Ernie is yelling to anyone to go and get Dr Jones the veterinarian who lives above his practice two streets down and for someone to call Nine Nine Nine from the telephone kiosk on the corner to get an ambulance for Miss Stone who is now being tended by a small group of neighbours from the surrounding houses. Blankets are brought out and the kettles are put on to make tea. They say a cuppa sweet tea is the best thing for shock. This is a crisis of huge proportion and all helpers will be grateful for the tea's warmth and relaxing properties. Ernie kneels down and strokes Dolly's brow to comfort her. I stand to the side with the gathering throng of people. I am so choked up with a sadness that I could never have imagined. Ernie tells Dolly that help is on the way. She whinnies in pain and Ernie covers her body with another blanket. Within minutes Dr Jones arrives. He kneels down by Dolly and examines her carefully. In the distance we can hear the clanging bells of the ambulance coming close. Dr Jones finishes his examination of Dolly he rises and takes Ernie to one side and tells him the painful truth that Dolly will have to be put down straight away. Ernie is shattered and stands there trembling from the shock. A mug of hot sweet tea is thrust into his trembling hand but first he has to say goodbye to his girl, Dolly who has been his friend and partner for many a year and with whom he has shared many a special memory. Dolly was always his stalwart companion. He kneels at her side as tears stream down his cheeks and in a choking voice says goodbye old girl; it is time for you to get some much needed rest. I will be right here. I won't leave you. The vet tells him to stand back. Within seconds a sharp crack like a leather whip renders the icy cold air and it is over. There is not a dry eye in the throng of people. Miss Stone is taken by ambulance to the general hospital where several days later she sadly passes away. Our hearts are broken for Dolly and Miss Stone. We will never forget them. In my heart I know that Miss Stone is still giving Dolly her daily ration of sugar lumps and Dolly is free at last of her cart, shafts and blinders and is grazing in that big warm grassy meadow that she had always dreamed of.

CHRISTMAS AT OUR HOUSE

It is December the twenty fourth, Christmas eve. I am ever so excited because Father Christmas will be coming tonight and that means presents. Rita tells me; don't be so soppy, there is no such thing as Father Christmas and tells me to grow up. I don't believe her but I do believe in him. I do so hope he won't get shot down in an air raid. Tonight at bed time I will pray that Gerry will not come because if he does come over tonight we won't get any presents. I ask you, can Hitler possibly be that mean? Mum told me this morning that Father Christmas won't be bringing much this year because of the rationing and that the war is making it difficult for him to make his deliveries and that he could get shot down before he makes it to England. She laughs that special secret laugh. This year I want a two wheel bike. I have been praying for one for weeks and weeks. I am riding an old three wheeler that used to be my sister's. It is ugly and in need of repair and besides the other kids on the street laugh at me and call names when I ride it. They tease me and call me baby bunting. I am not a baby. I am too old and much too big for a three wheeler. Mum tells me; don't bank on it Sheila. A two wheeler probably won't happen. I want you to be grateful for what we have. We are all together and we are alive as well as having enough to eat unlike so many others who have lost family members, their homes gone and they are suffering greatly. I know that she is right but I can't think about that right now. I still believe that Father Christmas can work miracles and that he will bring me a bicycle.

Our kitchen and front room are looking very pretty. We have been very busy making paper chains to string across the ceilings. No balloons to tie up on them this year. We have made our own Christmas cards that we have coloured with crayons. I have made Mum and Dad a calendar at school for their present. I can't wait to give it to them. I just know that they will love it. Mum brings out a cardboard snowman that she has had for years and sits him on the sideboard in the front room. It is all so very festive. There will be no Christmas tree but we don't mind. Thankfully Mum has been able to get some extra rations as she has been saving our coupons for Christmas so we will eat well tomorrow. She even managed to get a box of dates and some biscuits and some currants and extra sugar to make a Christmas pudding. What a super treat that will be. It makes me so happy just thinking about the food. I am always thinking about food. I didn't dwell on it while we were evacuated as there was always plenty there and I felt guilty for having so much. My Mum has managed to get some kind of meat for Christmas dinner. It is already staying cool in the unheated front room. Also there is a special treat for us children, orange and lemon squash that you mix with water. For the adults there is some kind of booze, whatever Dad could get, lined up in the front room. Mum says that we can even have a fire for heat in the front room on Christmas day. It is all so very exciting. I mean getting orange squash is only a Christmas thing and it gives a feeling of excessive wealth. I pop in and out of the front room so many times just to look at all the bottles of booze, squash and extra food. It makes me feel warm and happy. This is going to be a lovely Christmas. To make it even better my uncles and aunts are coming for Christmas day. I can't wait for it to get here. Daddy makes us children go to bed early this evening. We hang our empty pillowcases at the bottom of our beds. Dad hears our prayers and kisses us good night. I am trembling from excitement. I can't go to sleep so I get up in the dark and stand by the window for as long as I can to see Father Christmas but he doesn't come. Rita says; I am going to tell you like I told you in Cornwall, if you aren't asleep he won't come. Get to bed now or I will tell Mum. Besides, I am so cold and I am shivering. The bedroom windows are frosted on the inside and it becomes very difficult to see out and I am becoming very tired so I finally give in and climb under my eiderdown and put my feet on my hot water bottle. I now feel sleepy and warm. I mutter; please just leave my bike at the bottom of my bed Father Christmas. Thank you and I don't care if my sister says that there is no Father Christmas, I just don't care.

Hours later, when I wake, it is Christmas morning. The sun is pouring in and melting the frost on the windows. Oh gosh it's Christmas day. I sit bolt upright and look at the bottom of my bed. I can't believe my eyes. There is no bike. Father Christmas must be late or he forgot me. How can that be? I look over at Rita's bed. Her pillowcase looks bulky. She must have presents. I get out of bed, look into my pillowcase and I can reach clear to the bottom. There is only one thing in it. It is the last thing that I would have ever asked for, a new gas mask case. I am crushed. Who wants a new gas mask case? I hate it. Even if yours is battered and worn who wants a new one. This is the worst Christmas ever. I climb back into bed to get warm. I try to wake Rita up. If I am awake she has to be too. She grumbles at me and groans. Leave me alone you little blighter and let me sleep but I don't give up. I never do. That is who I am. Besides, I want to see what is in her pillowcase. Did she get more than me? If you don't get up, I tell her, I will play the gramophone very loudly with Richard Tauber singing "Dearly Beloved". I know that she hates that. Sheila you are such a little nuisance. Now that you have woken me up you may as well bring it to me. I get up and drag it over to her. Yes, yes, it is certainly heavier than mine. I dump it on her bed. She sits up, rubbing her sleepy eyes. You never give in, do you she says. I just want to see what you've got. Can you believe it? I only got a tatty old gas mask case. It makes me sad, this bloomin war. Well, it is your own fault Sheila for not going to sleep right away like I told you to. That is why you didn't get anything. You never will do as you are told. I climb into bed with her. This is exciting. Blah, blah, blah I say. Open your pillow case. Do you think Len got anything? How on earth would I know, go and ask him she says. No fear, he will throw me out on my ear if I wake him up. My sister reaches into her pillowcase. She is always so slow. I think that she does it to annoy me. I tell her, impatiently, hurry up, hurry up. I have got to see what you have got. She pulls out a beautiful sewing box. It is embroidered in green and gold. Oh my, she says it is absolutely lovely. I have wanted a new one for so long. Rita likes to sew. She slowly opens the lid. It is lined in dark green velvet. There are scissors, thimbles, cottons and needles, also a measuring tape. She is over the moon. I am happy for her. I wouldn't want it. I don't have the patience that she does for sewing and knitting. I like action like riding a bike as fast as I can. That is if I had one to ride. She reaches back into her pillow case and withdraws a knitting bag with skeins of new wool and knitting needles. Wow. Wool is very scarce. How did Mum come by that? Who does she know? Good old Mum. Rita digs back in again and comes out with a new gas mask case. Now I feel better. At least she got a gas mask case as well. I giggle, don't you love it Rita? Well she says, I got more than you did. I got what I asked for and that's because I went straight to sleep last night. I told you but you never listen. Maybe you will from now on, little wretch. I am not a wretch and I am going to tell Mum you said that. You know that you are not supposed to say that. There is a sharp knock on our bedroom door. Mum comes in. What is all the commotion about? You are waking up the household. Now stop it. Father Christmas didn't bring me a bike and I wanted one so badly and Rita called me a wretch. I start grizzling. All I got is a new gas mask case and I hate it. And a very nice one it is too my Mother says. Stop that grizzling right now my child. You can't always have what you want. But Rita got more than me I complain. It is just not fair. My mother answers me. Sheila stop that moaning right now or I will give you something to really moan about. There it is that hateful saying. I know my limits and I think I have reached them with Mum. Sheila, I want you to put your dressing gown and slippers on straight away and nip down the stairs and get Dad a cuppa tea. There's a good girl. There is tea in the pot. Pour father a cup and bring it up to him as a special Christmas treat. And while you are about it bring me one too. With a naughty glum sulky face I ask why Rita can't do it. My Mum gives me that look. The look that says, if you don't do as you are told you are going to get a thick ear. So I make haste for the stairs. Like I said I know my limits. Coming back up the stairs with two cups of tea that are slopping into the saucers as I climb I feel very hard done by. I reach Mum and Dad's room. They are both sitting up in bed, bundled up in their dressing gowns against the cold. I put their tea down on the tables on either side of their bed. There's my good girl, Dad says, ta Sheila ever so much. That is very nice. I love my Dad. He always makes me feel good about myself. I won't be sad any more. Did you empty your pillow case he asks? I did Dad. I got a lovely new gas mask case. A soft smile creases his face. You are really happy with that then? That is good. I answer yes but Rita got more than I did. Well I'll be blowed he says. She must have been gooder than you he says. I guess so Dad. I should have listened to you and Rita about going to sleep straight away. I ask him, did Father Christmas leave anything for Len? Ruby, do you know if Father Christmas left something for Len? Mum says; I popped into his room earlier to give him a cuppa and he was all chuffed about a new model spitfire, some books and games that he got. I climb up onto the bed and look sadly at my Mum and Dad. I am sorry that I was such a rotten kid. I will really try to do better. Mum says, Sheila, your face looks like a wet weekend. You are such a soppy date. Father Christmas had something more for you but he couldn't get it into your pillow case so he left it with us. Excitedly, I look around the room but I don't see anything that could be for me. Maybe Ducky, Dad says, if you look under the bed you'll find what you are looking for. I get off the bed, kneel down and raise the dark green silk coverlet and there it is next to the big Gerry, a two wheel bike. I squeal with excitement. Father Christmas did come. He didn't forget me. My Dad gets up and helps me bring it out from under the bed. He stands it up. It isn't new. It isn't all red and shiny like the two ugly sisters had in Sussex. It is a dull maroon colour and a little used. It has a new bell on the handle bars which I start ringing and ringing. To me it is the most beautiful bike in the world. Oh my gosh, it is mine, all mine. My own two wheel bike. I love it and can't wait to show it to the kids on the street. Dad tells me to get dressed and he will take it down stairs and put it in the front garden and that when I am dressed I can ride it on the street to get used to it. I know how to ride. I have been borrowing other kids' bikes. I know that my Dad just wants me to be careful. I run into my room yelling, Rita, Rita I got a bike. Father Christmas didn't forget me. Sheila, be quiet and listen to me. As I told you in Cornwall, Father Christmas doesn't exist. There is no such person but you just don't want to believe it but you are now too old to believe in such twaddle. It is Mum and Dad who buy the presents. So grow up and stop being so dopy. Mum and Dad give up so much to try and make our lives as normal as they can. I hate what she is saying. I will always believe in Father Christmas, no matter what, I have to hang on to some normalcy in this war. I want to stay a child and not grow up and disbelieve like my sister. I will just shut it all out of my mind and enjoy the day. I do. I ride my bike and show it to all the kids. They all want to ride it and take turns. Everyone is out to play today showing off their Christmas presents. I believe that mine is the best of the best. Ivy and Sheila Finnegan from over on Upper Clifton Road show up. Ivy's sister Sheila wants to ride my bike. She is so fat that I am afraid that she will break it. My Mum says that she is fat because of all the mashed potato sandwiches that she eats at the Odeon Club. Ivy asks me, where did you get that bike? Suzie Poulter had one just like it and she just got a new one for Christmas. I just rode it. It is a bright shiny red. I have a lump in my throat and I feel like I want to cry so I say I have to go home. I say my Mum wants me. I can't face my friends. This is so wrong. I have to find out the truth. I wheel my bike and park it in the side alley of our house. I open the door to the scullery. My Mum is there busy with our Christmas dinner. The windows are all steamed up. The Christmas pud is boiling on the gas stove. The smell is lovely. Potatoes are peeled. Everything is prepared and ready to go in the oven. She always makes so little taste so good, did you have fun outside she asks? Mum, where did my bike come from, I ask? What do you mean, where did it come from? Well, Ivy Finnegan says that my bike used to be Suzy Poulters but you and Dad said that Father Christmas brought it for me and Rita said that it used to be Suzie's as well. I don't understand. I need to know. Mum sits me down on the steps that lead up to the kitchen. She gives me a digestive biscuit. We don't get biscuits that often so this must be serious. Mum sits on the stair beside me. I turn my head away from her. Look at me Sheila when I talk to you. I don't want to but I do look at her. My child, the time comes for all of us when we have to take a big step forward, stop being a child, and grow up. We have to leave our childhood behind and begin to learn what the world we live in is all about. I think to myself while I listen, I know what the real world is. It is one of pain, loneliness, death, separation and always the question will I or my family die tonight or tomorrow? I see pain in my Mum's dark eyes. She is doing the best she can under the circumstances. Sheila, there is no Father Christmas. He doesn't exist. He is just a figment of our imagination. Children love to believe in him and we as parents let you. It is wonderful to believe but it also hurts when you hear the truth. I don't want to believe her words but I know in my heart that she is telling me the truth. I think I have really known the truth since our last Christmas in Cornwall. Rita had tried to tell me and I thought that she was just being mean. This growing up is so hard. I have had to give up dragging my doll Heather with me everywhere and leave her on my bed all because as Mum said I am too grown up. I don't like this at all and now I am told that there is no Father Christmas. What else will I have to give up by growing up? My child this is what happens at Christmas. Your Dad and I buy the presents, that is when we can afford them, so you could say that your Dad and I are Father Christmas and as that we will always do our best within reason to get you what you ask for. This year money is very scarce and there was no way that we could buy you a new bike. We just couldn't afford it. Your father as you know is an acquaintance of Mr Poulter and found out that he was selling Susie's bike. So your Dad did a lot of extra jobs and was able to make enough money to buy you that bike. I sit there, my face gets red and I am ashamed. I had doubted my Mum and Dad. I look at my Mum. I love my bike Mum. I love it even more than I did this morning. It is cracking. Thank you for telling me the truth. I feel very grown up at this moment and it is not as bad as I thought it would be.

It is dark about five PM. Dinner is over and I even got a threepenny bit in my Christmas pud. Mum is laying out a cold supper for the relatives, leftovers from dinner and a big jar of brown pickled onions in brown vinegar. She has been saving them for months. There is also a Christmas cake made from dried milk, reconstituted eggs and a few currants. She has put a ruffle around it and it looks very Christmassy. I know how much my Mum loves her brothers and wants to make this Christmas extra special for them. She says that my Uncle Eric is a cheeky devil but she says it with much love. He always keeps us laughing with his teasing. My Uncle Ivan is more reserved but when he lets his hair down we have so much fun with him and us kids loved his visits to Cornwall when he was on leave. They meant so much to us. Mum says he is very clever and he is as keen as mustard. I know my Mum has missed my Uncle Ivan and has had much concern for him. He has been serving in Africa and now has a fortnight's leave. We are all grateful that he is safe. My Mum tells me that she is thinking of her younger sister Doris and is very worried for her because she was touring Europe with a large dance troupe before war was declared. She is now living in Naples, Italy where she left the troupe and married a very handsome Italian gentleman. They have two children, Lilliana and Fernando. Being married to a countryman of Italy has kept her relatively safe but two months ago we received information that said that her husband died under mysterious circumstances and that now puts her and the children at risk from Benito Mussolini and his thugs. Anyway, that's what my Dad calls them. On the wireless we hear that Naples is being severely bombed by the Allies. We fear for all of their lives. I will add them to my prayers tonight and ask for God to protect them. They are my cousins and I wonder if in this crazy world I will ever meet them. When will this all end? What a daft world we live in. We are all killing one another, for what?

I can't wait until everyone gets here so the party can start, especially my Uncle Eric because he rides a motor bike. I do so hope that he is going to let us sit on it tonight and toot the horn. Petrol is so hard to get during this war so he fills it with lighter fluid and Mum says that it works great. It gets him to work through the blacked out streets of London. It is a wonder that he doesn't light up like an incendiary. I mean I ask you, he is sitting on the top of a tank of lighter fluid. There it is, I hear the door knocker. We kids run screaming out into the passageway to open the front door. Mum yelling behind us, don't turn the bloody light on and remember the blackout. I don't want the air raid warden coming down here. We open the front door and standing there on the door step is my Uncle Eric and Aunt Madge. We hug and dance up and down calling out in glee and all chatting at once. Oh what a wonderful Christmas this is. I love them both so much. They are full of fun and also they are my God parents of which I am so very proud. My Uncle Eric lets us all take turns sitting on the pillion of his bike. Rita goes first then Len and then finally me. I am jumping up and down waiting for my turn. I think I will wet my knickers I am so excited. Finally it is my turn. My Uncle Eric lifts me up onto the seat. I am trembling and starry eyed. I am going to marry him when I grow up, but what about my Auntie Madge? Oh well, she is old just like my Mum so she will probably be dead when I grow up. Not that I don't love her, I do very much. The three of us kids get to beep on the horn and across the street lace curtains twitch in front of the blackout, especially at the Barringtons, must be those noisy Harveys again, motorbikes, kids and too much company. In the distance we hear someone shout out to us; Oy mind my bike. We can't see who it is. It is pitch black out. There are no street lights due to the black out, just the moon and the stars to light our way. Who goes there we yell back laughingly and then we see a torch light lowered down to the ground and two figures coming up the street. Yes it is him. It is our Uncle Ivan. We kids race to meet him. Happy Christmas, Happy Christmas we yell. Everyone hugs. But who is the pretty lady with him? We walk back to the house. Uncle Eric claps my Uncle Ivan on the back and shakes his hand. It is great to have you back in blighty he says. How is the war and may we ask who this beautiful lady is? My Uncle introduces us to her. Her name is Peggy. Peggy has short curly blonde hair, blue eyes and she is a smasher. I like her immediately. Are you going to marry her, I ask? Rita says Sheila don't be so rude. Don't mind her Peggy she is such a chatterbox. We all go into the house to tell Mum and Dad about Peggy. Tonight the house is full of laughter. We are all happy to be together. Everyone takes to Peggy right away. She is full of fun. I wonder will she be my new Auntie. I hope so. I like her.

My Uncles are always the life of the party and plan all of the party games. They go into the kitchen to set up a game and we all sit in the front room and wait for our turn to be called into the kitchen and for once it is warm in the front room. We are allowed one fire a year in the front room and it makes me feel rich and warm and wonderful. The grownups are sucking up the booze and getting happy. We kids have our orange squash and sit hugging our knees excitedly waiting our turns. We hear screams and laughter. It is exciting and scary. Even so I can't wait for my turn. Finally I am called. My Uncle Eric takes me out into the passageway and blind folds me, holds my hand and I follow him into the kitchen. All the adults are in there having had their turns. They are laughing and chatting. I recognize my Dad's voice saying oh Sheila you are going to love this. You are going on a trip on an aeroplane. I am scared Dad. No don't be it is fun and everyone joins in. You are going to be over the moon Sheila and everyone laughs. My Uncle stands in front of me holding my hands. Sheila step aboard the

425

aeroplane, just a short step up. That is it, careful how you go Ducky. I nervously step up onto a hard surface about four inches off of the floor. Okay luv the plane is taking off. Put your hands onto my shoulders and hang on. My family members are making noises like a plane taking off. I am trembling with delight and fear. Whoa, suddenly whatever it is I am standing on starts to move forward and back and side to side. Being blindfolded I can't see where I am. I scream. I am scared. Everyone yells you are off the ground Sheila, hold on, hold on. You are going higher and higher you are just about up to the ceiling. At this point the top of my head hits something hard. Oh blimey, I am going to die. You've just touched the ceiling I hear my Uncle say. Hold on tight Sheila. Oh Cor Blimey! The plane is conking out. Everyone is making sputtering sounds. You are going to have to jump Sheila before the plane crashes. I can't, I can't, I am way too high I cry. I wish I had never played this game. I am going to die. Jump, jump we will catch you. Just one big jump and you will be safe. Come on ducky you can do it. I will have to jump. Please catch me I cry. We will we promise. One giant step that is all it takes. I will be brave and do it. I take a deep breath more like a gulp then take this huge gigantic leap and instead of falling through the air as I thought I would the floor comes up and meets me immediately. What happened? Everyone is laughing loudly. My blindfold is removed. I am on the kitchen floor all safe. My Uncle Eric shows me what happened. You were standing on a wooden building board about six foot long and one foot wide with an adult on either side. We pick up the board about three inches off the floor and shake it side to side and back and forth. Another adult holds a book above your head and bonks you on the top of the bonce with it. Well I never. No ceiling, three inches off the floor, huge jump, talk about feeling soppy. You've gotta laugh don't ya. We play many games this evening including Murderers, my favourite. I have played it before and

426

it is scary. Everyone gets to pick a card from the deck without anyone knowing what card you have. If you get the jack you are the designated murderer. I always want to get that card. If you get the ace you become the detective who has to solve the crime. Everyone else becomes the victims or suspects but no one in the room knows who is what. The lights all over the house are turned off and everyone runs and hides so the murderer won't find you. There is so much commotion, screams and laughter as everyone bundles around. People are running everywhere bumping into one another in the dark, going up the stairs, hiding behind blackout curtains, under the beds, in the wardrobes, behind doors with much giggling as you bump into someone already in your hiding place. Tonight I find three people under my Mum and Dad's bed all trying not to laugh and give away our hiding place. There are many giggles and much shushing. Suddenly the house becomes eerily quiet. Everyone is in hiding and the murderer is stalking his victim. Will she or he get me? I move closer to the other victims under the bed. Within about one minute there is a long blood curdling scream. The deed is done. Actually the murderer just taps you on the shoulder and tells you that you are dead. If you are the victim you scream and lay on the floor to feign death. The lights are turned on as soon as the victim screams announcing that a murder has been committed. Everyone else assembles around the supposed corpse. Tonight the victim is found in the old bathtub in the scullery. I can't believe it. The victim is my new friend Peggy. What a good sport she is as she lies there in the bath. It turns out the detective tonight is Uncle Eric. He questions all of us and we all come up with hilarious and silly alibis. Somehow I don't think our corpse Peggy is dead. Her cheeks are puffed out as she struggles not to laugh. Suddenly an explosive laugh erupts from her. The detective says that even the dead laugh once in a while. Everyone bursts out laughing. Finally my Dad under much grilling confesses to the murder. Everyone cheers for the detective's mastery and all celebrate with some more of a booze-up. Not my Dad though, he doesn't drink because he had seen too much of it as a child with his Mum being drunk all of the time. My Mum, being just a little squiffy, says oh come on Harry have just a little drink with me. After all it is Christmas and maybe we won't all be here this time next year so let's celebrate. Okay Ruby I will have just a small one because it is Christmas and you are right we don't know what this year will bring. We all move into the front room. Dad sits in the corner by the fireplace and everyone clamours for my Mum to get on the piano and play so we can have a sing along. Before long my Mum is belting out, everyone's favourites and everyone is singing as loud as they can. The candle holders on the front of the piano are vibrating with the noise. My uncle Ivan keeps my Mum's drinks coming. I have only ever seen her drink at Christmas time. She is really belting out the music. People are yelling, Knees up Mother Brown, Knees up Mother Brown. The furniture is pushed back and everyone including us kids is doing the knees up and screaming at the top of our voices as if there is no war and the louder we sing the war seems further away. We all sing out, Knees up Mother Brown your drawers are coming down, under the table you must go, Ei-Ei-Ei-Ei O. If I catch you bending, I will saw your legs right off, Oh, knees up, knees up, gotta get a breeze up, knees up Mother Brown. Everyone is dancing with their knees going up and down. Then comes my favourite part, I have been waiting for this. We all get into a circle and dance with our knees going up and down into the middle thumping away on the floor and we sing, Oh my what a rotten sod, what a rotten sod, oh my, what a rotten sod, what a rotten singer too-o-o-o. This is the best fun of my life being with my family and being able to say the swear word sod instead of song and my Mum and Dad not taking any notice. Everyone is in their cups except us kids.

Even my poor Dad is sitting in his chair blubbering, Oh Rube, Oh Rube with tears coming down his cheeks. That one drink did it for him. By midnight most of the adults are passed out on the floor. My Mum falls off the piano stool with her paper party hat all askew on her head. That is it for her for the night. Us kids help people to bed and mop up sick. No one is going home tonight. This is our Christmas. We manage to block out the war for several hours. It seems so far away right now. We deserve this respite. If we ever lose our ability to laugh at one another we are doomed. We won't ever let that happen.

WE ARE CHANGED

Things have changed in our family. It is about a year since our return to London and our family relationships are strained at times. We each live with our own pain and wounds of war. None of us wanting or daring to talk about them. Talking about them isn't the British way. Try to forget and maybe they will go away. They don't. The separations have caused pain and confusion. My parents have feared for their lives during the Blitz. Day and night for months they have seen death, destruction and suffering all around them. Also there has been the worry of what might happen to us kids. It is always uppermost in their minds. Where will this World War leave all of us they wonder but no one knows the answer? They don't talk about their fear but each of us knows that it is there. We as children had been wrenched away from our parents and felt abandoned. There is a deep rooted unspoken anger within each of us. It dawns on my parents that the responsibility of once again being a family of five instead of being just the two of them is now upon them. After a year of separation living in the shelters night after night and lots of times during the day raids their world is changed. My Uncle Eric and Auntie Madge came to live with them during the blitz as their flat had been bombed and they had no place to live. The four of them were always close. In the shelters they played cards, joined in all of the sing a longs and parties' shutting out the deadly reality of what was happening outside. Everyone in the shelters clung to one another for support. It would seem to an outsider that they were having a rollicking good time during the blitz but it was a façade for underneath all of the bravado they were like

430

anyone else; scared to death wondering if tomorrow would come for them. They adopted the motto of live for today, die tomorrow. I think deep down my Mum and Dad feel guilty for having sent the three of us away to places and people that they didn't know. They did have a choice and their choice was the most painful and heart wrenching decision that they had ever been called on to make as relatively young parents. When we returned to London in 1941 my parents got back three strangers and painfully they were also strangers to us. I try to think about what feels so wrong. Is it my fault? Did I do something to cause this unspoken change in our lives? Did all of us kids cause this? Maybe if we hadn't returned from evacuation this would never have happened. My mother gets very cross with the three of us more often than what I remember and sometimes she and my Dad fall out. I hear them arguing at night while I am in my bed on a night when there is no raid and I am happy to be sleeping away from the spiders. I hear cruel words spoken that cannot be taken back. This war has taken a toll on them both. I want to run downstairs and tell my parents please don't fight, I love you both, but I don't. I sadly bury my face into my pillow, sobbing for a love that is lost and gone. Please God, let this war end soon. Then there is this awkward silence for days. It makes me very uncomfortable. I don't understand it. I want it to feel like it used to before the war began.

The bond with my sister has changed also. I love her but I feel that I am losing her. She is growing up so fast. She is in her teens and has her own friends. I am having trouble with my relationships since coming home. While she and I were evacuated we had our rows and battles but she was always there for me. I could always rely on her and her on me. We were all that each other had. I miss that comforting closeness so much since coming home. I do really love her. I wish I could tell her. If I did she would say; stop being so daft Sheila. I wish we could all tell one another how much we love each other. I think we all want to but we don't know how. It is just not done. I love my brother so much. We were torn apart when we were evacuated and it has been so hard to reunite as brother and sister. We have our moments and I hope that they will grow into what we once had. I love him so very much and I hate the pain he suffers from being sent away and from our separation. He doesn't deserve it. These days we tease one another but we don't really talk. I wish we could go back in time. The world has intruded on our innocence and we can never ever go back to the family closeness that was. Oh well, as my Mum says; Keep a stiff upper lip, don't complain and carry on.

FRIENDS OR BULLIES

I had to leave my best friend Angela behind in Cornwall. We had clung to one another for our mutual support that we could not get from the adults in our lives in that place and time. I think of her often and wonder where she is but I am lucky because I have a new friend, Kathleen. She lives too far away to play with on a daily basis but when at school we spend all of our time together and we can tell one another things that we would not tell anyone else. Then there are the neighbourhood kids who have formed cliques before we moved into the neighbourhood. But I need to fit in as do my brother and sister. I have met Betty and Jean from the other end of our street. We three had nearly drowned together in the pond up at the woods. They had seemed very nice and we had been there for one another on that day. They also have an older sister who is Rita's age and her name is Vera. There is also an older brother, Billy who is a year older than my brother. My sister tells that their family seem to be the bullies of the road. She says that Vera makes her life a misery. Vera and her bully friends pick on her and call her names. They lay in wait for her after school, snatch her school hat and satchel and throw them over a neighbour's fence. And if she has anything that they want like her lunch they take it. Also apparently Billy is the same way to my brother as Rita tells it. He and his cronies, Tony and David, chase him all the way to school, take his milk money and box his ears on the school playground. This goes on for weeks. He doesn't want to tell anyone except for my sister. He hates to go to school and every morning he feigns a stomach ache, sore throat or anything to not to have to go to school. He won't tell Mum and Dad the real reason why he doesn't want to go. He thinks the punishment will be worse if he tells on them but this afternoon after school he runs into my Mum who happens to be home today and he can't get cleaned up from a fight which he always tries to do before she gets home from her warden job. It all comes to a head today. The pocket on his blazer has been partially torn off and his lip and nose are swollen and bloody. She asks him what on earth has happened to you. He tells her he fell off a wall at school but my Mum doesn't believe him so Rita tells my Mum that Billy Biggs has probably beaten him up again just as Vera Biggs does to her and so it all comes out. My Mum is furious. How dare they she says. She takes a very reluctant Len and Rita by the hand, out of the house and walks them up the road. I have to believe that Rita and Len want to die at this moment. Rita tells me later that evening that Mum banged on their front door as loudly as she could. She says I know that a lot of the neighbours must have heard her and were all peering around the lace curtains in their front rooms to see what was going on. To them this was going to be great sport. My Mum was still hanging on the knocker when Mrs Biggs answered the door. My Mum yells at her; I want you to see what your son has done to my child as she thrust Len up the front with his split lip. From now on you keep your hooligans away from my children and tell your loud mouth daughter Vera to leave my daughter alone or she'll have to answer to me. You have to teach them to keep their hands to themselves. Mrs Biggs is used to a good fight. She screams at my Mum calling her a stroppy cow and tells her to take her brats off of her door step and don't be coming up here all posh and proper and toffee nosed. Who the bleedin hell do you think you are with your two goodie two shoe brats. Don't you ever dare darken my door step again. Not to be outdone my Mum calls her nothing but a loud mouth fish wife. Mum turned on her heel and said;

oh I'll be back ducks but next time it will be with a copper. The door was then slammed in Mum's face. Well as if World War II isn't enough the battle lines are now drawn between Mum and Mrs Biggs. That all said, the next week is my turn to experience bullying. Betty Biggs is six months older than I. She goes to the same school as Kathleen and another friend of mine Toby. Toby is a lot of fun. She always makes me laugh. I love her haircut. She has very short straight black hair that just brushes her eyebrows. She is a real tomboy. The three of us play on the playground every day, skipping rope, doing handstands, showing our knickers and we are three complete chatterboxes but Betty Biggs is different. She has her gang of about five girls. In order to play with her you have to be asked to join her pack which includes Pamela, Ivy, Eileen and another Joan. They are all tall, big girls for their ages. All of the other kids at school and on our street are scared of them. They are always punching us and calling bad names. I thought my name was "you little cow" for about a year. I so badly want to be asked to join their gang. It seems strange but it is important for me to belong, to belong to something even if it is wrong for me. Maybe I want to be thought of as tough and in control. Then I can get the respect and fear of other kids. I can make them feel as miserable as I sometimes feel but that would be bullying. Hitler is a bully but I don't make the comparison. I am still too young to learn from all the hell he is causing around the world. Betty and I live on the same street so we come in frequent contact with one another. Today is Saturday. I am outside playing on the street with some neighbourhood children. We are playing hopscotch. We have drawn it out with chalk in the middle of the road. No danger there because so few people have cars and there is no petrol to run them on. The only one that comes down our road these days is Sam the milkman and his new horse. All of us still miss Dolly very much. Betty and her gang come down the street as if looking for trouble. They push us out of the way rudely and start playing our game. The other kids run away telling Betty and her gang that they are going to tell their mothers. Betty and the others chorus, tell her, tell her, kick her up the ol coal cellar. I've heard that rhyme before. I stand there trembling in my shoes. I don't say a word. I don't think I could if I tried. Ivy looks at me and says; you're so ugly. Some mothers have them and they live. Am I really that ugly? Betty approaches me. Do you want to be friends with us? I nod and say yes please, foolishly. But this is what I have secretly been hoping for. Okay she says, if you really want to join our gang you have to give me your shoes to wear any time I ask. I have just got my new shoes that Mum has spent all of her coupons on at Batas and I am so proud of them. They are the nicest shoes that I have ever had. I don't want to hand them over to her but I am so torn. I want to join her group. So foolishly I do take them off and hand them over to her. She sits down on the pavement and takes off her ratty, dirty old plimsolls and forces her feet into my beautiful new sandals. Her feet are bigger than mine so her toes hang over the edge but she doesn't care. She is going to wear them because she has to prove to me that she is in control. She flings her dirty plimsolls at me and tells me to put them on. They are so big I have to shuffle to keep up. She tells me that she will wear mine all day and that I can only have them back in the early evening when I have to go in. She says I have to swear never to tell my Mum and to always let her wear them whenever she wants to and I swear on everything I have never to tell. Then one week later comes that very magic moment. I get to entwine my little finger with Betty's and shake them to the words, make friends, make friends and if you disobey we break friends. I am in. Pamela shakes my pinkie and big fat Ivy reluctantly follows suit. I am then told the rules of the gang. I can never play with my old friends and if I am caught doing so I will be punished and given the thumb. A sign of broken friendship and the taunt will be break friends, break friends never more to make friends. As I am the new kid I am everyone's slave. I have to give them my six pence that I get for sweets every week, hand over games and toys, give them food that I am forced to take from my family's kitchen like cocoa powder and sugar. That is stealing and is so bad especially when I am taking away from my family to give to my so called new friends. Our rations are so short as it is. What is wrong with me? Why am I doing this? I suppose the thought of being bashed and the breakup of our friendship worries me. I am so confused. They take the cocoa powder and sugar and mix them together in the palms of their hands and then lick it up. I am not allowed to have any. This new friendship is not going to last. I have extreme guilt over taking rations from the house and besides my Mum is asking everyone in the house who is taking sugar without asking. She accounts for every granule as it is so very hard to get. If people come over for tea they have to bring their own sugar as there is never enough. Kathleen is crushed as is Toby when I don't play with them or talk to them on the playground. This afternoon big fat Ivy sees me talking with Kathleen in the girls' lav where we think we are safe from prying eyes or big ears so that I can explain to my old friend Kathleen what is happening with me and how sorry I am. But of course Ivy runs to the rest of the gang and as I thought they are waiting for me after school. Going home, they follow behind me calling out, traitor, stupid, ugly, orphan, cry baby, saying my mother is ugly and stupid and that she should be in a lunatic asylum. They continue, everyone hates you and your family. Why did you ever come here? I try to make a run for it but I can't outrun them. They catch up to me and pull me down by my hair, take my ribbons and spit on them. They then take my satchel and empty all of my school stuff out on the road. They smack me around the head. I try not to cry but I can't help it and it just makes it worse. They laugh at me and call me bubble bonce. I am so ashamed. Betty says to her mates, grab her thumbs. They each take turns hooking my thumb with theirs and may I say not very gently. They all chant their mantra, break friends, break friends never more to make friends. They all laugh and clear off. I am so humiliated. I don't belong anywhere. I will have to decide where I do belong. I am smart enough to stay down on the ground till they are gone and out of sight. A lady with her shopping bag comes along and helps me up and asks me how I am and if I am going to be all right. I say, I can't complain and how stupid is that. I am going to be all right I tell her. My knees are grazed and my face is smarting from the blows and my ego is seriously bruised but I will recover. Belonging or being in control of others is not worth this. I am no better than they are but I believe I have been taught to be better than that. My guilt for what I have done to Kathleen, Toby and my family is overwhelming and the only way to get over it is to make it right. Tonight I confess to my Mum that I stole the sugar and cocoa. The whole family has been under suspicion until now. I don't tell my Mum the real reason why I stole the sugar and cocoa. I tell her it was because I was very hungry. I don't want her to be marching up the street again and facing Mrs Biggs. I take my punishment. I get the back of the hair brush on my backside for stealing and for complaining of hunger. Life is far from perfect after the breakup from the gang. They constantly harass me and make fun of me and my family. Some days I think it would be easier if I would go down on my knees to beg them to let me back in to their group just to stop the bullying but I am a stubborn little cuss and I believe that to beg is what they want me to do. I will never give in. I have dug my heels in. Sometimes my stubbornness has gotten me into trouble in my young life but this is the one time it is standing me in good stead for the test of time. My Mum always says sticks and stones can break your bones but words will never hurt you.

But it is not true. Wounds from sticks and stones will eventually heal but hurtful words can intimidate and live with you for the rest of your life.

BUNDLES FOR BRITAIN

There is something new and exciting happening in England. It is called "Bundles for Britain". Last week in school our teacher told us that it originated in 1941 in the USA, created by a New York socialite, Natalie Latham. It started out quite small, knitting gloves, socks and jumpers for British troops serving in the North Sea. Now in 1942 it has become a much bigger operation, clothing, shoes, medical equipment and thousands of other miscellaneous items are being shipped across the dangerous seas of the Atlantic to our war impoverished nation. We are so very grateful for the help of our kind hearted cousins in America. Thousands are benefiting from this program.

Our school has started to receive the parcels. It is such an exciting time. The parcels are passed out for us to take home. You never know what you might get in your parcel but that is all the fun of it. We don't open our parcels till we get home from school and all the family are at home. It doesn't matter what is in it because we are so desperate for everything and anything. We will find a use for all of it and if not for us we can always swap with our neighbours. None of it is ever wasted. Our neighbours are always flogging something. Today is the first time I have brought home a parcel and it is exciting to me and the whole family. After supper Mum opens the parcel. We watch as she slowly unwraps it. It seems like it will take forever for it to come open for us to see what is inside. Blimey, Mum, hurry up I tell her. Then there it is the first thing. It is the most beautiful pair of shoes that I have ever seen. White lace ups with dark blue leather across the arch of the foot. I have seen pictures of American kids wearing these. They are so American and simply smashing. I try one on. They are my size. Hallelujah, they are mine. We are always so desperate for shoes. There is never enough money or coupons to go around for new ones. My Dad repairs our worn shoes. They are rough but it stops the rain and snow from wetting our socks. Sometimes the nails are a bit too long and hurt your feet but it is better than the usual layers of old newspaper stuffed into the insides of your shoes. But now I have new ones. They are so perfect in every way. Well every way but one. When trying on the other shoe I find that they are both left shoes and I have to believe that somewhere in England another child has got a bundle for Britain and has got the two right ones. She has one of mine and me one of hers. But you know what; I am going to wear my two left shoes proudly, my shoes from America. We also get clothes, chocolate bars, soap, toothpaste, tinned food and jam. Such a blessing, we are so lucky. We love these bundles. They lift our spirits high to know that people from America care and are thinking about us. We will never forget this kindness. Thanks America.

HORSEMEAT AND HALT WHO GOES THERE

The war is dragging on. Will it ever end? Food is so hard to come by even if you have enough coupons to buy food there isn't enough on the shelves to feed a hungry family. When there is food at a certain grocers the word goes out and the queues can go on forever. But the English are very patient and no one tries to jump the queue. When the shop runs out the owners come out to tell the rest of us waiting in line, in the pouring rain, sorry we are all out but maybe we will have more tomorrow and you should come back then. People patiently move away. No one really complains. What good would it do? You line up for everything. Bread shops have the longest lines. Bread fills you up fast. As meat is so very scarce they have started selling horsemeat and whales' meat on the high street. The government tells us that it is good for us to eat it. Who would have thought that you would eat horsemeat? I think of my beautiful Dolly the milkman's old horse. How could anyone possibly eat her? Enuf said. This afternoon I go with my Mum to buy some of it. It is so disgusting, large hunks of bright red bloody horsemeat hanging from hooks, dripping blood in pools on the sawdust floor of the butchers. Better than nothing the government says. Well then let the government eat it. My Mum and I leave the butchers never to return. Maybe we can scour up a tin of beans or sardines for dinner. They are always good on toast. After the Butchers Mum lines up for hours for fags that she has to have, her Weights or Woodbines. Tea and a fag keep the grownups going. Without tea and a fag we could lose the bloody war. Everyone fights to keep food on the table. You can see it in their faces in the queue lines, on the buses, trains and in the shops and shelters. Their world is becoming grey. No colour. Some days that is how my world is, no colour, just a depressing greyness but we all know that we can never give up. As the song says; keep your sunny side up. Way down deep we all believe that someday the lights will come back on all over the world and colour will come back into our lives.

It is a Friday night and Dad is on duty tonight in Annerley. We have just had our weekly bath in three inches of water, one after another with all of us using the same water and then for us kids, a dose of castor oil for a good clearing out. We put on our pyjamas and night gowns which Mum has warmed in front of the fire for us. Mum says it is time for me to go to bed. I am about to go up the stairs when the air raid siren goes. Oh, no it is raining cats and dogs outside. Why is Gerry over tonight in this rotten weather? They were just over two nights ago. The ack-ack guns shot down a German plane that came down and crashed into a house in the back of us. It went up in balls of orange and red fire and flame. Tragically none of the family members in that house survived because they had not made it to their shelter. Some nights when the siren goes off you are just so tired and you can tell yourself that well, they may not hit me tonight. It could be another neighbourhood that will get hit or maybe they will not come at all. Many times the sirens will sound followed a minute later by the all clear. Sometimes it is a false alarm for our area. So it is very tempting just to stay in your warm bed and wait and see what happens. My Mum never lets us take that chance. She makes us get up no matter how tired or cold we are or how much we complain. The wardens had searched for bodies in the burning house and for the German pilots of the plane but so far no pilots have been found. The fire was so hot it would have been a miracle if anyone would have survived. Half of the neighbourhood went around to the corner see where the house had once stood. There was a huge crater in the ground and firemen were pulling out the wreckage of the plane. This is a warning to all of us that this could happen to any one of us. Warning notices have been issued throughout the neighbourhoods to be on the watch for any suspicious looking men who could be the German pilots from the downed plane. We are to report anything to the wardens and the police. We are all on edge. Have they by some miracle survived? Could they come into our houses or shelters? We don't want to go down to the shelter tonight; it is so cold and wet. But go we do. Bonzo up the front barking as if to say; we hear you Gerry and we are going. We sit in the shelter shivering and miserable. Rain is coming in through the seams and dripping on us. I think to myself, what if the Germans are alive? They could be right outside the shelter or coming down the garden path ready to jump in on us. My rotten brother keeps saying; they are coming, they are coming, can't you hear their boots on the pathway, they are coming to get you Sheila. I cling to my sister and my Mum for comfort. My Mum gives Len a good telling off. She is really cross with him. Reluctantly he stops. He loves to tease and scare me. But now every little sound we hear we are sure that it is them coming to shoot us. Maybe Len is right. Finally after sixty agonizing minutes the all clear sounds. The fear and worry we are feeling in that damp hole in the ground is over for tonight. We can't wait to get out and breathe some fresh air, but not so fast. Mum opens the shelter door quietly. Mum shushes us. We all hold our breath. Even Bonzo waits patiently, panting with her tongue hanging out. She senses our fear. That is all we can hear except for our own breathing and fast beating hearts. Everything seems okay so we can leave. The rain has stopped. We can see the dark clouds scudding quickly across the sky and the moon is now becoming clear. All of us climb out and start moving stealthily up to the house. I hold on tightly to Mum's hand. The house looks lonely and eerie in the moonlight. We reach the back door. Mum turns the door handle and pushes on it to go in but it won't open very far, certainly not enough for us to go inside. Something seems to be barring the door. It can only be one thing. There is no other excuse for it. It has to be the downed pilots. I start feeling scared. I know that something is very wrong. Bonzo starts barking as she senses our renewed fear. Len starts yelling; Halt, who goes there? Mum tells him to shut up and run. We all run with Mum saying; Hurry, hurry, hurry! We run to our next door neighbours for safety. The wardens are alerted to come and sort it all out and somehow word has spread quickly through the neighbourhood that the downed Germans are in our house. Everyone is gathering to see if it is the pilots. Oh the excitement. We should all be fast asleep in our beds but here we are. The wardens come running, blowing on their whistles and telling everyone to stand back. They put a small ladder up to the kitchen window, open the window, pop their heads in and yell; Oi, you blokes, what's your game, eh? Come out with your hands up. There is silence. No one comes out. The police have shown up and two of them start climbing through the open window followed by the warden. Mum calls out to them. Be careful of my nets. I just put them up yesterday and we don't want them all muddy. We're doing the best we can, mother they reply. Everything goes quiet again and then we hear loud voices and laughter from within and the back door suddenly comes open. The copper says; well mother here is your German pilot. It was just a small cupboard that fell off the wall from the blast of a bomb and wedged itself between the bath and the back door. It is all safe now, you can come in. Everyone is laughing with relief and for some of us, red faces of embarrassment. Mum puts on the kettle and tea is served all around. Finally, the neighbours start to head home while calling out to us Ta-Ta see you tomorrow, hope everything is all right and don't go catching any Germans then. We call back night, night. We have all had a good laugh. It has lifted all of our spirits in these dark days of war. What a story we will have to tell Dad when he gets home in the morning.

COLDER AND QUIETER

It is now January 1943. They said it couldn't last more than a year and then our boys could come home and there would be peace throughout the world. But it isn't to be. We are now five ruddy years into this catastrophic war. The death toll is in the millions, thousands upon thousands are hungry and homeless and people are criminally being punished for their beliefs and for just being a human being. Families and lives are being torn apart and lost forever, with many never to be seen again. How much can the human spirit take? It is winter 1943 and I am going to be nine years old next April. It is the coldest winter that I have ever felt. It is so bleak. The earth is frozen hard as iron. The skies are always grey, threatening freezing rain or snow and the cold north winds blow through the bare trees bowing their branches as if to say, I surrender. Our house is bitterly cold upstairs and down. We all wait for the fire to be lit in the evening to give us a little warmth. Coal is even scarcer now and very dear. To get a few more lumps we kids run after the coal lorry and pick up any pieces that happen to fall out of the bags into the road. We all huddle around the fire in the evening trying to feel the meagre warmth. That little fire in the evening has to do so much. It heats the kettle for hot water for tea, to do the washing up, to wash with and to fill our hot water bottles. We also put bread on long forks to make toast onto which drippings from any roast meat is slathered. That and a hot cup of watered cocoa because there is never enough milk but to us this is a real true treat, toast and dripping, that is living. It is cruelly cold so that none of us ever want to get up in the morning. The linoleum floor is like ice and you feel like your bones are frozen. I hate to take my night clothes off to put my day clothes on. It is truly punishment so I do it as fast as I can. Mum makes Rita and I wear our liberty bodices under our clothes for warmth. I hate those things. I can hear the icy rain hitting and rattling the windows. I must move fast and I shiver a lot. I go down to the scullery to brush my teeth and to wash my face with cold water. Five of us have to use that one cold water scullery sink but we manage and we all finally get off to school or to work. Walking to school in my well-worn shoes lets the cold and damp in and the newspapers that I stuff in them get soaked. My shoes that I got from America are now too small for me. Hopefully Mum will soon have enough coupons and money for new ones. At school we sit in the classroom in our winter coats, knitted pixie hats, scarves and gloves trying to tell ourselves that it is warmer in here than outside. It is hard to pay attention to the teacher and learn even though the teachers try so hard to make it better for us. Our teacher lets up get up every half hour, run in place and thump our arms back and forth across our chests to get our blood flowing and to warm us up. I think this is the coldest year of my young life.

There is good news however to make our lives brighter. The raids are less frequent now and we are sleeping in our own beds instead of in the wet, spider infested shelter. Things are definitely looking up. We are beginning to feel that we have survived it all.

DOWN TO THE SEA

It is spring of 1944 and I am now nine. As things at present are quiet on the home front, Mum and Dad have promised us that they will take us on a holiday to Seasalter in Kent. Dad has a week's leave coming from the Home Guard. A friend of his has a small cottage at the seaside in Seasalter that he is going to let us use for a week. We kids talk about it all the time. It is all so very exciting. We just can't wait. Will the day ever, ever come? And of course, eventually, it does. I have told everyone I know and anyone who will listen to me that we are going on holiday. The day of departure has arrived. It is a Saturday. We all walk to the station dragging our cases. We wait for our train. We are all excited, even my Dad. Finally our train arrives. The porter is calling out the arrival of our train, announcing its stops along the way with the last stop being Whitstable. Our train pulls into the platform. We clamber aboard and find our seats in a third class smoking carriage. We grumble as we kids try to claim the window seats and other passengers glare at us. Mum gets cross and tells us to sit our bums down and be quiet. We do and settle down for the long ride to Whitstable. I am listening to the train as it scurries along the rails. I can hear the whispering in the wheels. It says; we are going away, we are going away, away from the war, away from the war, Sea salter, Sea salter. I never tell anybody what the wheels say to me, that is my secret.

Four hours later we arrive in Whitstable. We are to catch the local bus to Seasalter which only runs once every two hours. We sit on our cases looking glum and wistful. We are all

hungry. Mum is gasping for a cup of tea and a fag. Our
exuberance has waned a little at the long wait. We haven't
eaten since our tinned corn beef sandwiches on the train. The
local bus finally rumbles up to the bus stop. We all climb
aboard for the forty five minute ride to Sea salter. By the time
we get to Seasalter all of our grumbling has subsided. The
driver lets us off at the cottage just across the road from the
ocean. We can see and smell the ocean. It is so fresh and crisp.
We can hear the waves as the tide is coming in. We hear the
singing of the wind as it hums through the telephone wires. It
is like magic. London seems so far away at this time. Right
now I don't want to ever go back. The cottage we are staying in
is called Wye Worrie. The faded sign is hanging over the front
door. The paint on the wood cottage is faded and sun
bleached. It is ever so lovely. We can't wait for our Dad to get
the key from above the door lintel and let us in. I am in love
with the cottage. Inside it is painted white and is very clean. It
is one large room. On the back wall and under two windows
are three camp beds all made up for us kids. There is a back
door between the beds that leads out to the garden. On the
side wall there is a large stone sink. There are no taps just a
large hand pump for pumping the water. Above the sink is an
open window and the curtains are blowing in the afternoon
breeze off the ocean. Next to the sink is a shelf with a brass
primus stove for Mum to cook on. Above the stove there are
three shelves for food. The owner has kindly put in eggs and
gaud love a duck, some bacon. Where on earth did he get it?
Mum says he must be in the black market. There is also a loaf
of bread and a bottle of milk. Dad pumps and lights the primus
and fills the kettle for some tea and some broken biscuits.
Mum has brought a tin of sugar and a bag of tea that she has
packed along with other tins of food and some spuds. This will
help feed us until she can get to the shops in Whitstable. On
the other wall is a couch that opens up into a bed for Mum and

Dad. On the wall by the front door is a sideboard with lots of cups and plates. A kitchen table and four chairs sit in front of it. There is no electricity. We have oil lamps to light up the night. It is all so very cozy. There is no electricity so no wireless and no news from the home front, music or children's hour but we are on holiday. We will read and play board games. We will leave the war behind us for this whole week. The war is now many miles away from us and we all feel the relief. No air raids, no running down to the shelters, just peace. Mum says; I don't know how I am going to do without my gas and electricity but knowing my Mum she will cope. She will feel better about it all after she has her cup of tea and a fag. Dad opens up the back door. You can open just the top and lean out of it and yell to whoever is out in the garden. We go outside with my Dad. There is a loo out there in a corrugated enclosure. You can't pull the chain because there is none. A sign tells us that the honey wagon comes once a week to empty out the sewage ditch. I am going to pinch my nose shut whenever I go in there, especially after a cod liver oil night. It doesn't seem right, not being able to pull a chain. Underneath the back window of the cottage is a wooden bench where we can clean the sand off of our feet after coming back from the beach. The most wonderful part of the back garden is that at the bottom there is a narrow river that runs as far as you can see. It is backed by farmland where cows are grazing. To us this is paradise. I don't want this holiday to ever end.

The following day us kids and my Dad fish in the slow moving river. I wait and wait, there is nothing on my line and I am getting bored but suddenly I feel a tugging on the tackle. Help me Dad, I scream in my excitement. My Dad pulls in my line and on the end is a baby eel. Dad takes the hook out of its mouth. How sad it is to watch. It is wriggling and gasping on the ground. I ask my Dad to please make it stop. My brother runs over to see it and he chops it in half with his knife. That'll stop it he says but the two halves still keep wriggling as if each half is looking for its other half. I don't like this fishing game. It is brutal and I don't want to see dying things.

Most days we are allowed to go over to the beach by ourselves. I am nine now and I am able to go with Rita and Len everywhere. They hate it. It drives them crackers. I like that. We are told by our parents that at all costs not to climb over the iron battlements and barbed wire on the beach put there to keep the planned German invasion from landing on our shores. We were always afraid of the invasion in 1940 but it didn't happen as Hitler decided to invade elsewhere but the beaches are still dangerous. Today Mum and Dad take us to a small beach further up the shore that is too small for a landing of the Germans so there are no barricades. We are going cockling. Our parents tell us to look for two little holes in the wet sand and then dig down deep with your fingers and there it will be the cockle, alive in its two joined shells. We put all of our cockles in buckets filled with sea water and later when our buckets are full we lug them back up the beach to the cottage. My arms feel as if they have grown longer from the weight of the buckets. Mum washes them all very carefully to remove the sand, puts them in a metal bucket on the primus stove and boils them. My rotten brother says; if you listen you can hear them screaming for their mothers as the water comes to a boil. He gets a smack around the head from my Mum. It is murder. We are killing them and I will never eat them. Everyone else enjoys them with malt vinegar. My Mum says; you don't know what you are missing Sheila. That's all right, I'll go without.

Our week seems to be flying by. As a very special treat tonight Mum and Dad take us by bus into the village of Whitstable for fresh fish and chips from the fish and chip shop. To me it is the most wonderful grub in the whole world. Who wants screaming cockles? I can feel the warm package of newspaper in my hands. I dig a hole in it and put in the vinegar from the vinegar bottle on the high counter and salt from a huge salt shaker. I dig in with my fingers and pull out a big beautiful hot greasy chip. It is heaven. After I am full and all through with my dinner the smell of the fish and chips seems to linger forever on my fingers. I don't want it to ever go away. I won't wash them so I can lick them for a week.

We are to leave on Saturday morning to go back to London and as this Friday is our last day the three of us kids go over to the big beach to collect some shells to take home. We are going to make the most of our last day. We look out through and past the barriers. The tide is coming in very quickly. The water is swirling around our ankles but much more than just the tide coming in; the tide has bought in the wreckage of a plane that must have been shot down into the ocean. Is it one of ours or is it a German plane? We can't see the insignia. We know that we must not go to look on the risk of a very good hiding but we just have to go and see. The temptation is strong so we throw all caution to the wind. This is an adventure to be taken, good or bad, whatever the repercussions will be. At this moment that doesn't bother us. It doesn't matter to us at all even though it is very dangerous as well as forbidden. We walk out as far as we can, wading out to the barriers and barbed wire. There are signs warning that going beyond these barriers is very dangerous and forbidden. With the help of my brother I climb up the barrier with him pushing from behind. My sister climbs without any help. We try but we can't squeeze through the barriers. It would take a tank to get through them but we can see enough. Water is sloshing into the wreckage of the empty cockpit and there it is the German insignia, the Iron Cross. Len is so excited. He is into model airplanes and he knows all of the makes. We three cheer loudly. We have shot one down. The pilots must have drowned out at sea. There is no sign of life. Suddenly our jubilation is cut short by a group of uniformed men running toward us, waving their arms and yelling at us not to move. We have fear in our hearts. We are in big trouble. But I couldn't have moved if I had tried because my knuckles are cold and white from holding onto the rusty barrier. They are running through the sea getting their boots all wet. They don't look too happy with us. An officer screams at us; what the hell do you little blighters think you are doing? Get your bleeding backsides off of that barricade there are bloody landmines out there that will blow you to kingdom come. Get back down. Do you bleeding well want to get blown to bits? We three hang on for dear life. What have we done? We three are too scared to move. I can feel the blood draining from my face. This is obviously serious. They shout at us to stay put on the barrier until they can help us off which ultimately they do very carefully, lifting us off and back into the incoming tide. They march us back up the beach in single file. By this time a group of people have gathered. I can see my parents in that small crowd. This is not good. The officer announces to everyone that this beach area is now off limits to all locals. That is until they have investigated the downed Gerry plane. The officer announces that more signs will be posted. If you don't pay attention you could bloody well get killed. He looks at us three and yells; don't you little buggers read? These signs mean you can get killed by playing and climbing the barriers. The beaches on the other side are mined. You could have got blown to bits if you had got through the barriers. Our faces are red and our heads bowed from the telling off. But, he makes his point to us, how dangerous it was to do what we did. I quietly take it all in and wonder why war has to follow me wherever I go, even on holiday. But I have learned today that war has no holiday. It is all I have known since four years of age. If I don't die soon, will it follow me the rest of my life? The officers wrath is nothing compared to what comes next from our parents, a bloody good hiding. Our behinds are tender to the touch for a long time to come. We are told we will never go away on holiday again for the rest of our lives and that the three of us are ungrateful little wretches. We have blotted our copy books for life.

The next morning we are up early, nursing our wounds. We are packed and ready for our return to London. All of us are very quiet on the bus to the station and the silence continues onto the train. We know better than to open our mouths. None of us want another good hiding. It has been a lovely holiday at Wye Worrie and I hope we get to go back some other summer. I don't think my Mum and Dad mean that we will never go on holiday ever again. We have a lot to tell our friends back home. I bet none of them has ever seen a downed German plane floating in the ocean. There will be no lousy "wish you were here" post cards from us. "Wye Worrie" seems like a marvellous motto to live by.

GROWING UP FAST

Back in London I am now attending junior school. Catherine and I are still best of friends. We are very close. Sometimes I think we are closer than sisters could ever be. We share our most private moments, our deepest fears and our happy times. Since the raids have slowed down I don't worry as much as I used to that I won't see her on Monday mornings in class. When the bombings were so frequent and severe I worried all the time. We are lucky that we are alive, so many of our classmates have not survived. It makes us sad. The news tells us that forty three thousand people died in England from August of 1940 to May of 1941 and fifty one thousand have been injured. I only get to see Catherine during the week. I wish I could see her more often. She lives about a twenty five minute walk from my house. My Mum and Dad like me to stay in my own neighbourhood on weekends so that they know where I am. So I hang out with a bunch of local kids, boys and girls, not the gangs anymore. I am finished with that part of my life. Today being Saturday we all meet up to go to the Odeon Club. Mum doesn't expect me home for the rest of the day. Since the air raids have dwindled she doesn't worry about me as much. I am given a sandwich and sent out the door. She tells me not to come home till tea time which will be around five. I think she is glad to be rid of me for a few hours of peace and quiet. As we leave the Odeon Club we chatter all the way home about what was the best part of the pictures and about what we should get up to next. Victor is sort of our ring leader and protector. He is twelve years old. That is old. I don't know why he plays with us kids. He suggests we go into the bombed out neighbourhoods to play. These neighbourhoods have become our weekend playgrounds. We all agree. There are seven of us, three girls and four boys. Our ages range from seven to twelve. We walk over to Dagmar Street where we investigate all of the bombed out houses, row after row of them that are rubble and mortar. There is usually no one around. We have the ruins completely to ourselves today although other kids do sometimes go there to play. The houses or what is left of them are eerily quiet. Normally, you would be hearing children playing, lawnmowers cutting grass, glass milk bottles clinking as they were delivered by the milkmen, Mums calling out to their kids to come in and have their tea. I think about the families who lived here, who laughed, cried and had babies, grandparents, sisters, brothers, aunts and uncles. There were marriages, christenings. There was life but now it is all gone. All that is left to show is a staircase to nowhere, a fireplace still standing and houses completely sliced in half. We see houses that still have an upstairs with a few floor planks still visible from below; there are no roofs, fallen walls, and bathtubs and sinks laying on the lower floors. These houses are posted as extremely dangerous and the signs warn everyone to "enter at your own risk" but being kids of war this doesn't bother us. Nothing can happen to us, we are invincible. We need danger and excitement. We have become street marauders. Victor picks a house for us to go in. There is a front door but no walls. All of us walk through the front door and giggle. We could have walked around it but this is more fun and so silly. The carpeted staircase is still standing that leads to the upper floor. We start to climb, boys in the front and us girls coming up from behind, single file. I have to admit I am scared, supposing it falls down. I whisper to Diane who is right behind me, I want to go home. She says, we can't, the boys will never let us play with them again. The boys reach the top. There is a narrow landing on which we all huddle together.

There are three doors on the landing and maybe they open onto nothing. Victor cautiously opens the door across from us. Perfect he says; there are still three planks of wood going across to the other side of the room. We all peer in. You can see between the planks that there is a clear drop to the floor below. Victor asks; all right who is going to play the dare game? Which of us is going to walk the planks from wall to wall? Of course the boys are all cocky and saying that they will. I don't think that any of them would say no for fear of being called a sissy by Victor. Victor, Freddie and Tommy all agree to play the dare game. They cross on the planks one at a time, teetering with out stretched arms for balance. They cling to the beam on the other side, giggle nervously and look back for our approval, then cautiously turn to come back to the landing. This is bad because now it is our turn. We girls hold our breath. I am even afraid to look. I start mumbling; please God please don't let them make me do it. I will die if they do. Miraculously the boys all survived the walk on the planks to live another day. We beg them to not make us do it? They call us cowardy custards but they decide to not make us walk the planks. We girls sigh with relief then Victor says that they have another dare for us girls. The boys huddle together to discuss our dare. There is a lot of giggling and I hear Freddie say; oh that is beautiful mate, make them do it. Victor tells us to all get down the stairs. We go down to the rubble and bricks in what was once a scullery. There is an old bathtub and a cracked sink, a broken table and lots of debris and broken furniture. Victor says; our dare for you girls is, and you have to do it or we won't let you come with us anymore. We girls look askance at one another. I have been thinking that this isn't a gang but maybe I am wrong. What in the world do they want us to do? Victor, trying not to laugh, says; you ladies are to stand in line, pull up your frocks and hold out your knickers. We want to see what is down there. The boys all snigger and smirk. If you

don't you girls will have to walk the planks. The boys all agree;
yeah, yeah, make them do it Victor. For the life of me I have
never been able to understand why boys are so fascinated with
girls' knickers but they are. They are always trying to pull up
your frock to see your knickers. What is there to see down
there? Even so, I don't want to do it. None of us girls do. We
tell them that we can't because our Mums will be cross. My
Mum always tells me that you never let any boy or man look at
your wee-wee. Diane starts to snivel. Victor tells her to be
quiet. Do you want to walk the planks? I know I will die if I do.
I just can't face walking the planks. So begrudgingly and shyly,
we girls stand in line, hoist our frocks and hold out our
knickers. We girls all have on utility school knickers. There are
only two kinds, navy blue and a lighter blue. Why those two
colours I don't know but in war time London those are your
only choices. I call them my Oxford and Cambridge knickers.
Navy is for Oxford University and lighter blue for Cambridge
University. I always want Oxford to win in the yearly boat race
with Cambridge in April and try to make sure that I am
wearing my navy ones for that event. At the beginning of the
war they had elastic around the waist and legs also with a
pocket for your hanky but as elastic became more scarce they
left off the elastic around the legs and because the elastic is of
such poor quality it becomes easily stretched and gives out
around the waist so you have to use a big old safety pin to hold
them up. I would be ashamed today if I had a safety pin in
mine. Luckily for me last night was weekly bath night and I got
my weekly clean navy ones. Diane also has on navy ones but
Susanne's are the lighter blue and she has a great big nappy
pin in hers. Blimey, I'm glad it isn't me. I just don't know what
they think that they are going to see. The boys line up giggling
and snickering. How daft they are. I don't like boys any more.
They each come by one at a time and look. Dennis, the
youngest boy is shy and tries to avert his eyes when it is his

turn but then cannot resist the urge to look. Victor and Freddie make crude remarks. They say; ooh or that is so disgusting, how do you wee with that. They do seem fascinated. Diane and I smack them around the head for their rotten remarks. They call Susan smelly knickers. Well what do they expect; you only get to change them once a week on bath night. The boys tell us we are finished with our dare. Victor says he has a big surprise for all of us. He says it is a reward for everyone completing their dare. He has pinched a box of fags and matches from his Mum. He will light one and have the first drag and then we can all take turns dragging on the fag. Victor says that he has smoked before and that he pinches fags all the time from his Mum and Dad. Showing my fanny was worth this. I have always wondered what smoking tasted like. It must taste good. Mum and Dad love them. They line up for hours to get them and then smoke them down to the dog end. They even reroll the fag ends in new fag papers. Victor lights a fag and sucks in on it and blows out smoke. Oh it is beautiful he says. He sucks in the smoke deeply and says; Come on then and have a go. I am so excited and feel so grown up. Victor says; when it is your turn suck in on the fag, swallow the smoke and then blow it out. I am up for this. Now it is my turn so I suck on the fag, swallowing the smoke and oh my God I want to die. I can't breathe. I am coughing and gagging. The smoke is choking me. I begin to gag and wretch, coughing my guts up. I have never felt so ill. I am feeling dizzy and sick and I must be the most beautiful shade of green. As each of the other girls takes their turns they too become very sick. We all lay on the floor waiting to die except of course for Victor who is having fits of laughter. Oh, he is truly a stinker. What silly girls we are to let him control us and his mates. His mates ask; what should we do before going home as it is getting late? Victor tells the boys to get behind the bath tub, lower their short trousers, squat down and see who can do the largest Richard the Third (a turd). We

460

girls are to declare the champion. Whoever wins will get a fag. Victor leaves a big brown steaming stinking turd shaped like a large tree stump. He is so very awfully disgusting. The other boys are not able to do a number two. Victor is proud and declares himself the winner. Victor is a lucky beggar. He can keep his ciggies to himself. He is such a cocky bugger and it is time to go home. At night, after I am home, and when it is time to go to bed my Mum comes up to tuck me in. She asks; what did you do today? I lie to her and tell her that after the Odeon my friends and I went to the park and played on the swings. We played a game of rounders. That is nice dear she says. I am so glad that you have made some nice friends. I hate lying to her but she would never understand if I told her the truth. My world is different since 1939. This is war time and I am growing up fast. After my Mum leaves my bedroom I lay and try to go to sleep but I can't. I wonder why kids of my neighbourhood all seem to roam around in cliques and gangs. Most of my friends are past evacuees. I wonder, is it because as evacuees we all clung to one another? We were different and as evacuees people looked at us differently. We felt safer being in groups. We protected one another. We belonged and today I still feel the need to belong to something. My last clique of friends was wrong for me but I do understand their need. They fulfilled their need as best they could and the only way they knew, right or wrong. For reasons unknown to me at this moment, I still miss the girls from my last clique. I see them around. They talk to me. I would, if asked, play with them individually but not as a clique because it then becomes toxic.

JUNE 1944, V1s AND V2s, OH MY

Many things are rumoured during a war and many of them can be frightening and dangerous. I heard a funny rumour from my Dad the other day. A British officer at base camp had sent a message to the fighting front. It said send reinforcements, we are going to advance. But when it finally reached the fighting front it said; send three and four pence we are going to a dance. You gotta laugh. Rumours are especially frightening to us children who hear news on the wireless or who are old enough to read it in the papers like me. The papers headline warnings that say Germany is believed to have secret weapons. There is even foolish talk of long range rockets. How could that possibly be? It is all like a made up story by H. G. Wells or a late nineteen thirty picture called "Things to come" which foresaw our total devastation. But everyone says that this is totally non-fiction.

It is a Thursday evening, June the sixth of nineteen forty four. Jerry hasn't been around and we are enjoying being in our beds all night. We feel that maybe the war for us at home is over. This evening, as usual, Mum is fussing at us to get ready for bed. Being the youngest I have to go to bed first. I hate going to bed. I always want to stay up late but Mum won't have it. These are the rules, half past seven weekdays and half past eight on Friday and Saturday nights. I can come up with every excuse in the book to stay up late but they don't work. Oh well, tomorrow is Friday and I have something to look forward to, an eight thirty bedtime. Dad left earlier for the night to report to his post and I heard him telling Mum that it was probably going to be a very quiet night with not much going on. Maybe

Hitler has finally got our message; "Sling your bloody hook". He kisses us all goodbye and says he will see us in the morning. Have the kettle on when I get home, Ruby. She will of course. Ta Ta Dad we all call out. See you in the morning. I blow him a kiss. After more plaintiff pleading to stay up I finally give in and go on up to bed. I stand in the darkness by the bedroom window and stare out onto the back garden. It is dark now and the moon is partially covered by clouds. Gerry won't visit us tonight. He only likes a bomber's moon, clear and bright. I can see the bomb shelter's outline where the earth covers the corrugated roof. Mum has made such a handsome flower bed out of it. She has told us that she has heard that there may be a contest for best flower beds on a bomb shelter. She thinks that hers could win. But again it could be just another rumour. We aren't going to need you tonight Mr Shelter I whisper triumphantly. We may never need you again but I cross my fingers as I say it. I hear the back door open and bang shut. I see Bonzo bounding down the garden as if to capture an imaginary intruder. She senses that something is out there, but what? I wait to see if she will come back. She doesn't. My feet are getting awfully cold on the bare floor so I reluctantly climb into bed. Mum comes up to tuck me in. She tells me night, night my child, sleep well. She gives me a kiss on the forehead. My Mum doesn't wear scent but she always has that beautiful scent of motherhood. I will probably remember it forever. I struggle to stay awake and for my sister to come to bed. But slumber wins out. I am sure that I am fast asleep and dreaming. I must be because air raid sirens are screaming over and over again and then my Mum is shaking Rita and I awake, calling to us get up, get up and get down stairs. I grab Heather. I don't care if my Mum thinks that I am too old for her. I realize that this isn't a dream. It is a nightmare. We run for the stairs. Mum is getting Len up. She says, children run as fast as you can. We hear the sound of a plane above us but the sound is very different than the sound the usual German bombers make. This plane is different. It sounds like a blow lamp that Dad has out in his shed. Pop. Pop. Pop. The engine is sputtering. It sounds like it is going to conk out any second. Then suddenly it does. We all crouch in the darkened stairwell. Mum turns on her torch so we all can see. The question is, should we run for the shelter or stay where we are? But immediately that decision is made for us. There is a brief uncanny silence. Where has that sputtering plane gone and where are the bombs? Following the brief silence there is an ear splitting ungodly explosion of incredible strength, force and destruction. The house shakes. It feels like we are in a giant cement mixer. Will our house withstand this incredible force? We cling onto the stair railings for dear life trying not to be thrown to the bottom of the now shaking and creaking stairs. There is noise everywhere. It feels like our world is falling apart. Is this the end? We hear glass being blown and shattering out of the window frames and plaster falling from the ceilings. Things are crashing all around us. We can hear our own screams of fear above the fray and then for a few harrowing seconds there is a sudden silence but that is immediately followed by the throbbing engines of other planes slowing down to that sputtering and popping sound of a plane in trouble. Well, that's what we think it is. There is no time to get out of the house and into the shelter. Within five seconds another huge explosion is felt and heard. Mum screams at us; get under the kitchen table. She guides us with the light from the torch. We sit clinging to one another under the table. We all hold hands. Mum says; hold on children, this could be it. Tonight we pray. Tonight we might die. Mum tells us how sorry she is that she and Daddy have brought us back to Southeast London. We should have left you in Cornwall. What is happening? Our world is going crazy. We can hear the engine of another plane shutting off. It sounds like it is right above our house. There is a deathly silence. How can it miss us? How will it feel, to die? We wait for the direct hit and for us to be blown to bits or buried alive. I know I am going to die this night. I have never known such fear in my young life. The deadly ear splitting explosion comes. It feels like the house is being picked up off its foundation and then being thrown back down harshly. We cling tightly to one another, sobbing and laughing in fear. Will this be the last thing I remember? But it isn't us; it isn't our time to die. It must have been the street behind our back garden that was hit. How many homes have gone and how many have died or are dying? They don't stand a chance, poor beggars. Who picks whether you live or die? I don't know. There is a lull in the explosions. Mum says we have to try to take advantage of it and make a run for the shelter. We crawl out from under the table. The top of it is now covered in ceiling plaster. In the beam of light from Mum's torch we can see through the haze of dust some of the damage to the house. We are all shaking from fear and the relief of still being alive. Mum opens the back door and tells us to run for our lives down the garden and into the shelter. It is dark, so very dark outside except for the searchlights criss crossing the skies trying to spot the enemy and shoot them down. Dear old Bonzo leads us down the garden and into the shelter. She is our very own private air raid warden and guide. What a love she is. Even though it is June it is very cold and damp in the shelter. All we have on is our pyjamas and nighties. We are shivering. I have a cuddle with Bonzo and Heather for comfort. It helps make sense of what living is all about. Will I ever stop shivering from the fear and the damp cold? Mum lights the oil lamp and helps wrap us up in the damp quilts and then there they are again. It seems like they are coming over in droves. The air raid sirens are sounding again. What is going on? Tonight sounds so very different from anything we have heard before. The sputtering engines are everywhere and the racket of seemingly every anti-aircraft gun blazing away futilely trying to shoot whatever these things are in the sky. There is explosion after explosion. I liken the deafening noise as to a world gone completely mad. There is no sleep tonight. I cover my ears with a pillow and sing, which annoys my brother. He tells me to shut up. I just sing all the louder. I just want this all to be over whether the outcome is life or death. Will we live to see the morning? Does it really matter anymore? The air raid sirens and the all clears are going off about every fifteen minutes and then the last one we hear is the air raid siren. No all clear is sounded. The night seems like an eternity. Finally the bell of the alarm clock jogs us out of our restless periods of sleep. Dawn has arrived. We are all hungry and thirsty and I have to wee so badly. The bucket finally has its first customer, me. I try to tinkle quietly. I am so awfully embarrassed. I mean, how can you pee into a bucket without making a sound? It sounds like rain on a tin roof. But, oh, it feels so good. My brother giggles nervously. Sheila is taking a wee, wee. But he too finally has to give in, ha, ha. He tells us all to turn our heads on fear of death. Bonzo is whining at the blast door to the shelter. There is nothing for it but to let her out. She too is desperate to go. We wait for her to come back but she doesn't. We eat a few damp biscuits with a little water from a bottle stored in the shelter. Mum says; oh for a lovely cuppa and a fag. We wonder if it is safe for us to go outside. Mum says; we mustn't until the all clear sounds but it doesn't sound, something must be wrong with the system. After about another hour of waiting my Mum looks out the shelter doorway. It is a rainy grey day but everything seems quiet. Mum says; I wonder why Daddy isn't home yet. He usually gets home around eight AM. We are getting worried. Then finally we hear that most beautifully welcome sound, the all clear. We scramble to the surface like rats out of a hole. We stand there in the chill wet of the morning shivering. Other neighbours are also coming out of their rat holes and stand there in the rain in their pyjamas and dressing gowns, their faces showing grief and shock. What a terrible scene. There are houses missing. Just craters and rubble remain. Houses all over the neighbourhood are gone. The screaming sound of ambulances and fire engines is everywhere. The acrid smell of smoke fills the air. Fires are burning all around. What do you say? What do you do? And where do you start, to pick up the pieces. I am sure that men, women and children must have died and are gone forever. Friends and strangers alike, those for whom you fed their cats or dogs when they went on holiday, bought their milk in for them, chatted with over their garden fences, whom you shopped for when they were sick or alone, the list will be long. This is so completely unforgiveable. What will my Dad think when he gets home about all of this? I wish he was here. Before he left to go on duty last night he was telling my Mum that every morning on his way home from his Home Guard duties he is always afraid to turn the corner onto our street. He is afraid that his family and the house will be gone. He says his heart beats faster and faster as he approaches our street and then the relief he feels after he sees the house still there is over whelming. He wants to weep and he thanks God every day for his protection of us.

And so it goes. The V1s have arrived. We hear that they were built and designed to kill thousands and bring England to her knees. Pilotless planes filled with one thousand eight hundred and seventy pound warheads. How can anyone ever have created and designed such monster killing machines and used them on an innocent civilian population? And who in their right minds could have ever given the orders to release them, knowing what carnage and destruction they would bring once released? I don't think I will ever forgive them.

467

The V1s continue their assault day and night. We never go to bed in the house any more. Every day at seven thirty PM, it is still light; I trot off down the garden and call out to all the other kids going off to bed in the shelters. Those of us children that are still fortunate enough to be living in our houses have formed a definite camaraderie similar to the ones we formed as evacuees. When the sirens sound, day or night, everyone dashes down their gardens to their shelters yelling, crying out; doodlebugs, doodlebugs. This is our nickname for them. They doodle up in the sky for seconds before falling into buildings and exploding. Another name we have for them is Buzz Bombs. They are like bees buzzing through the sky until they drop to destroy. Our Bonzo seems to hear the sirens before we do. She barks and barks, her tail wagging furiously while heading for the shelter. She is always first in. She is not daft that girl.

School is still open. We children thought the deadly doodlebugs would mean we wouldn't have to go to school, but no we will have to go until July when the summer holidays begin. We do have the school shelters so there is no excuse. But some school shelters in London have taken direct hits from V1 raids. Children and teachers were incinerated or buried alive. The news in the newspapers is so frightening. Today, while walking to school with a group of kids, the air raid siren sounds. We never know when a doodlebug raid will occur. They come over in all types of weather, rain or shine, day or night. We are told that our big anti-aircraft guns can't seem to shoot them down because they fly so low. That is not very comforting knowledge to us. Today when the siren sounds we kids start to run as fast as we can towards the school, all grouped together, trying to be brave. We are not brave. We are just trying to survive. When we hear the first doodlebugs start to come over us we try to run away from them. We have no idea what their destination is to be, nor do they. They are following us. We look up with extreme fear and yet there is a certain curiosity. We are seeing something so dark and sinister. We see short black pilotless planes with tails on fire spitting out orange flames. On some of them the sputtering engines are shutting down to begin their horrifying plunge to earth to deliver their huge payloads. We try to run from them but when their engines shut off we run in the other direction. I liken it to a cruel game of cat and mouse. We practice to outwit them without really knowing which way they will go. We have a brain and we think we have a chance to fool them. We run until we finally make it to the school shelters with much relief and where today our lessons will be. Much of my education seems to take place here. I have an awful fear of being buried alive in a shelter. I feel I am being trapped and a panic sets in within me. I always worry that if we take a direct hit I could be buried alive and no one will hear me screaming to get me out. I have been having that same panic in our garden shelter. I just want to get out and live. I feel I will die if I stay in a small underground space. I don't tell anyone my fears. They would say; you are being a baby, you are now nine years old so pull your socks up and get on with it. They are right of course; you cannot show fear because fear is contagious. Every day I am anxious to get to school to see if my best friend Catherine is present. All of us children are scared that any day or night we could lose close friends and today is no different. Our numbers have dwindled throughout the school since I started here after returning from evacuation in 1941. Many teachers and pupils have been killed. Also many parents have been re-evacuating their children as the deadly V1s from Hell are taking hundreds more lives with thousands being maimed and many left without homes. The future looks very bleak. Everyone wonders what will come next? It is all so sad. As bad as I fear dying, dying would be quick with a direct hit. But the thought of being re-evacuated again is worse. The pain would be slow and intolerable. I pray every night that my parents won't send me away again. My sister and brother are so emotionally hurt from evacuation. When Rita asked my Mum last week how she and Dad could ever do such a thing to us when they are supposed to love and protect us. My Mum simply answered; when you are faced with a choice of your children living or dying you choose life.

War scars everyone. Scars are not all visible. We all carry some scars that cannot be seen and we will carry them with us the rest of our lives however long or short that is.

GEORGE HAS GONE HOME

Today we are sad. George, our cat, has not come home since the night of the first V1s. Mum thinks that all of the explosions and fires have scared him and that he has run off to hide. We are all so worried for him. Daddy asks the workmen in the builder's yard next to us if he can look for George over there. There are lots of places in that yard where he could be hiding and that is where he is found. Dad finds him hiding under some rubble. He is very ill. He can't walk. We think he has been poisoned by rat poisoning that the workers have put down for the rats. Dad carries him home. We make up a cardboard box for him with some of Mum's old cardigans to keep him warm. Her pink one was always his favourite. She wraps him up in that. He has always been more mum's cat than ours. She has had him since he was six weeks old. She is very attached to him but all of us love him. Mum will stay up all night to be with him and very sadly, he passes away in the very early hours of the next morning. He was not alone. He knew my Mum was there with him to the end. Mum says; George has gone home and is free from pain. Not all orphans of war are human. There are so many orphaned animals, homeless and hungry, roaming the bombed out homes looking for their departed families. They don't understand this bloody war. I know I don't either.

Today as Dad is working with a crew clearing out a bombed house they suddenly hear crying sounds coming from under a collapsed stairway. Dad and the other blokes tear away some stairs he finds six kittens, their eyes barely open, mewing piteously. Their mother is dead from the stairway crushing her. The babies have miraculously escaped death, but what to do. The kittens are voraciously hungry and still trying to feed from the dead mother. If left they will die, they will be just more orphans of this war. The crew can't let that happen. Dad picks out one, an all-black male with a small white bib. The crew adopts the other five. Dad brings him home on the bus, tucked under his coat. He said passengers were wondering where the crying and mewing was coming from. It is a rainy cold day and he had to keep him warm so he could live. I don't think my Mum is ready yet for another cat. It has been just one week, such a short time after George's death. But here he is a ravenous scared little orphan. He is even too young to lap or feed yet and that's where the fun and work begin. He has to be fed every hour with an eye dropper full of warm milk. Poor Mum, she is his adopted mother and she feeds him night and day. She even gives up milk in her tea to give it to him. We help her out when not in school and in the shelter. We cuddle him and feed him. Dad says; don't get too attached to him yet because he might not make it from being left alone at such a young age. But he does make it. He has the will to live and live and thrive he does. The will to survive is strong. We name him Bambi from my favourite picture. He is more attached to my Mum than the rest of us. By nursing and feeding him she has saved him from death. I know he knows it and loves her for it in his own quirky way. He softly growls and threatens the rest of us from underneath the chairs as if we are the enemy but never my Mum. He wraps himself around her feet and protects her. Poor old Bonzo thinks we have brought her a new playmate until she gets her nose mauled. That is the first and I am sure the last time that will happen. Little Bambi has filled the empty void that George has left in Mum's and our hearts. War has many victims. It picks randomly and has no scruples.

MY HEART IS BROKEN

It is a Monday morning in late June. We have spent many hours this past rainy weekend in the shelter with Bonzo and Bambi. Our sanctuary, that hole in the ground that is saving our lives. I wonder, will we have to grow up living like this for the rest of our lives? Surely Hitler will run out of bombs and V1s eventually. The worst part of living in the shelter is that there is always at least an inch of dirty water in the bottom. We spend hours taking turns on the stirrup pump to empty it all out but it won't stay dry no matter how long or hard we pump. Everything in our shelter is so damp and cold. I swear we are all growing green scales over our bodies. I tell Mum we are all going to turn green with mould and then our fingers and toes will start to drop off one by one and we will call ourselves the mouldies. Mum tells me not to be so dramatic. She says; things are bad enough as they are, Sheila without you telling stories. She looks at me, smiles and then laughs. She can't help it. She does have the most beautiful smile. Unfortunately we haven't seen enough of it lately. She has a lot of worries that she keeps to herself but we children understand what some of them are; will we live through another day or night, can she always protect us and feed us. Food is so short, never enough of it. And another worry, will Dad make it back to us in the mornings from duty? And always that nagging question, should she send us away again? The government is advising all parents to do so. She worries about how many dead bodies she will see lying in the rubble and the futile feeling of not being able to help them, only being able to comfort the ones left behind with a few kind words, blankets and a cuppa tea. But that will never be enough. It makes me happy this morning to see that I have given her cause for cheer. We certainly need all the cheer we can get these days.

Today is Monday. Hurray, the all clear has sounded. It is a good day. We crawl out of the shelter and around past the blast wall. We look like people who live under the ground coming up for air. It amuses me to see others crawling out of the ground. It is like a horror picture. I call it zombies rising from the dead. Oh no, there goes my imagination again. Then we all cheer, our house is still standing. It looks very lonely in the rain. We trudge up the garden carrying our bucket. We wave good morning to neighbours who are also making their daily trek back up the garden. We have all survived another night. I liken it to the barker at the fair. House or no house, step up, step up little lady. Now you see it and now you don't. Spin the wheel to see if you still have a house or not. Mum goes into the house to put the kettle on while we bickering kids wait in line at the outside lav to empty the bucket and have the luxury of luxuries when it is our turn to pull the long chain on a flushable loo and hear water sluicing around the bowl. After weeing in a family bucket all night there isn't anything better in this whole world than our loo. Mum is in the house putting on the kettle. We are lucky to still have water. Many people don't. We share what we have. We kids follow her into the scullery with warm thoughts of a cup of tea. Most times there is no sugar or milk but saccharin is on the table. We don't mind it. It is hot and wet. Those tea leaves will have to last all day as tea is so scarce and dear. The first morning cup is the best of all but by suppertime it is well stewed and weak. Mum says that she is fed up to the back teeth with this bloody rationing. Rita, Len and I wait our turns at the scullery sink. Rita being the oldest is first, then Len and finally me. I am always last. We wash in cold water and lifebuoy soap, clean our teeth and brush our hair. We get a cup of tea and a slice of bread and jam if we are lucky. Len and I are then off to school. Rita leaves before us. She has left school and is now working up in the city. She is all grown up. She is fifteen and very beautiful. I am envious of her. I wish I was all grown up. On this Monday morning I meet up with my schoolmates. We believe that there is safety in numbers because we never know whether there will be a buzz bomb raid. We walk slowly down the road collecting shrapnel from last night's raid. My friend Darrel has a big tin of it. The siren sounds. We are close to the school. Should we run for school or head into the street shelter? We hate the street shelters. They smell bad and are dark and scary in the daytime. We decide on the latter and run for the school. The doodlebugs are over us before we know it. They are on our tail. I say to myself; please, please don't let the engines cut out. Let them go on over us but unfortunately for someone else that could mean sudden death but it is all about survival. One V1 stops sputtering. It seems to hover in the sky. We watch in fear as it drifts over us and finally disappears over the roof tops. We crouch down and cover our ears. A deafening explosion ensues. It has hit on Nursery Road, two streets behind us. We have to see what has happened. This is the worst. It has obliterated a small children's home, gone, finished. Life hangs by the finest thread to be cut without warning. Our lives are so very tenuous. We turn away. We cannot watch the rescue. It is too sad. There is death everywhere. It waits for all of us. Our hearts are heavy as we run the rest of the way to school. We go straight away into the shelters, thankful to be there at this time. Not many kids are here today. Some, I am sure are just staying home, scared enough to not want to go out. But who knows when you are going to die? If it is your turn it doesn't matter where you are. Death can seek you out no matter where you hide. Thank God, my best friend Catherine is here today. She is sitting at a long table pasting the letters of the alphabet on cardboard for the little children to learn their letters. My teacher, Ms Ship, gives me permission to help Catherine. There are about ten of us at the table. Everyone loves to paste. Besides, you get to eat the white paste out of the huge jars. So many of us are hungry and even paste tastes good. But if you are caught eating it you are immediately given another assignment. Needless to say we are very careful not to get caught. By lunch time the all clear has been sounded and we are allowed out into the sunshine on the playground. It is beautiful to breathe some fresh clean air after the dark dank shelter. Catherine and I find a quiet corner on the playground to eat our sandwiches. Mine is a dripping sandwich and Catherine has hard cheese. We share what we have with a bottle of milk that is on the turn as it has sat in the crates in the sun. But we are happy to be alive. We talk about getting out of school for the summer this coming Friday and what we are going to do. It is so exciting. We make plans to see one another as much as we can at her house or mine or up at her Dad's allotment where we can pick fresh vegetables and play house in his work shed. It is going to be the best summer that we have ever had. We discuss what we are going to do when and if we grow up and leave school. I want to go to America, be an actress and make lots of money. Then Catherine can come out to see me in Hollywood. Catherine laughs and as is her manner is the practical one. She says that she wants to be a nurse and serve humanity. She will make an excellent nurse. We are as different as chalk and cheese but there is a bond between us that can't be broken. We understand one another even at this tender age of nine. I think we cling to each other out of fear that our lives could be snuffed out in an instant or that we could be sent away, evacuated and not know where the other is. She is my friend forever, in death or absence and we rejoice that both of us have made it through another weekend. We talk about next Friday, our last day at school. All of the kids have planned to form a Congo line on the playground to celebrate getting out of school for three weeks. It is going to be such fun.

It is Thursday. In the playground Catherine and I discuss what we are going to wear for the last day of school. We have been told by the head mistress that we will not have to wear uniform for the last day and that we can wear party dresses. Catherine has a beautiful red satin dress that she wore for her birthday party two weeks ago. I have picked my favourite orange and white sun dress that is a hand me down from my sister that I love. It is my favourite. All the kids are so excited to be going to such a grand occasion.

Tonight is like any other night. We go to bed in the shelters. Mum thinks it best and as usual she is right. It isn't long before Gerry makes his nightly visit. Doodlebugs and more doodlebugs, we put our heads under our pillows and pray. I ask, Oh please God don't let us die tonight. I just have to go to school tomorrow and for the first time in my life I really want to go to school the next day. We hear many explosions and feel much trembling of the earth but morning comes and once again we have survived and it is Friday morning, thank you God. . My schoolmates and I meet up on the corner of our street all dressed in our party clothes. We are all chattering excitedly. Last night has been forgotten quickly as today is our last day of school. What can be better than this? We run all the way to our school in case of another air raid. We pass houses and shops on the High Street that caught it last night. Smoke is still in the air. Debris is everywhere. It doesn't seem right for us children to be so happy when others are suffering and dying. I admit, I do feel somewhat guilty and shameful. But when I get to school I selfishly put it aside. I will think about it some other day, maybe tomorrow. Yes, tomorrow would be a good day to think about it, on Saturday. I can feel sad on Saturday but not today. As there are no air raid warnings this morning we can go directly to our classrooms. Oh, joy we are not going to have lessons today, just games. It is going to be like a big birthday party. The only difference being there will be no cake, jelly or blancmange. As this is war time strict rationing makes things like that inaccessible but we don't care. We each have brought a sandwich from home and we are going to do a Conga line on the playground and scream and yell as much as we want. What could ever be better than that? Everyone is mingling around admiring one another's outfits. The girls look so pretty and the boys so handsome. Ms Ship comes in to call the register. She is so pretty. Catherine and I both are in love with her. She has invited Catherine and me to come over to her house on the bus one afternoon this summer to pick blackberries and to have tea. We are in total awe. Can you believe that our teacher has invited us to her house? This is such a big thing in our young lives. We have been making plans for this big event and we will make a complete day of it. I haven't seen Catherine this morning. I keep watching the door. She is late. Ms Ship tells us to settle down while she calls our names. Where is Catherine? Where is she? She is marked absent as are others. How can she possibly miss today? It is just so important. She didn't seem unwell yesterday. She was as excited as I was. I am sure that she is just late. I know she will come hurrying in the door at any second with that familiar smile that I know so well. I just know that she will. But she doesn't come. She never comes. I don't feel like I want to play games. All the fun and anticipation of the day has gone. I have waited for weeks for Catherine and I to enjoy this day together. Now I just want the bell to ring signalling the end of the school day so that I can walk over to Catherine's to see why she hasn't come to school. Even the thrill of the much anticipated Conga line is no more. I go through the motions but I feel no joy, just a kind of loneliness. There is a fear in my heart but I can't let it come to the surface. I keep pushing it back. It just can't be, I will not allow it. The bell blessedly rings at last. I say good bye to Ms Ship. She asks; are you going to check on Catherine to see if she is all right? I tell her I will go straight away. Have a nice summer Sheila. Don't forget that you and Catherine are coming for tea and black berrying. How could Catherine and I ever forget that? I answer, we won't Ms Ship, we won't, I promise we won't. But even I know that promises are sometimes meant to be broken.

My Mum is waiting for me outside the school. This is very unusual. I always walk home with a bunch of my mates. But today is definitely different. She pulls me aside from all of the screaming kids that have just been let out for the summer holidays, all so exuberant and noisy. We sit on the low school wall. What is going on I wonder? My Mum takes my hands in hers, Sheila I have some very sad news to tell you and I want you to be strong. Catherine died last night during the raid on Braxton Place. A whole row of houses were demolished and unfortunately one of them was Catherine's. It was a direct hit. I am so sorry my child. I was over there this morning working to help with the survivors. Her mother and sister did survive but not Catherine. There is a roaring in my ears. I don't want to hear what she is saying. It can't be true. I don't think I can speak. I find my voice and ask my Mum, maybe she is still alive. She could be buried but still alive. You yourself know how they can dig people out and they can survive. I know that she can't be dead. She can't be. Please Mum tell me she is not. It is all a lie. My darling child I am sorry. They found her body and she was gone. I can't believe this talk. Why, why, why did the others live and not her. I sob, Mum please tell me why and how this happened and how God can allow it. Mum says that according to Catherine's devastated mother they had decided to sleep in their beds last night to get some rest but when things got so bad they headed down the garden to the shelter but Catherine turned back to go get her cat, Matilda. It would only take a minute to go just inside the back door. Her mother had screamed out; no, Catherine no. But Catherine never heard her. Catherine didn't have time to know what hit her. It was over. She was gone. Mum says that last night obliterated most of the row houses on one side of the street. Who knows how many lives are lost. I want to cry but I can't. I have to see. I have to go there to believe. Please, Mum take me there. I have to see. Please, she is my very best friend. My Mum reluctantly agrees to take me. I just have to see it to believe it. When we turn the corner to Braxton Place I want to turn and run away but I have to see where Catherine has died. Nearly one whole side of the street is gone and I can't find where Catherine's house once stood. I should recognize it but I can't. Please help me find it. I have to see. Oh, God help me find it, please. My Mum and I pick our way through the bricks and mortar. It is impossible to recognize any house. Some walls still stand, one with an open clothes cupboard with a few clothes on hangers fluttering in the late afternoon breeze. Wardens are picking through the rubble pulling out broken furniture, personal possessions, toys, bedding and whatever they can retrieve for the few survivors. I hate it all. I hate it so much. I hate Hitler. I hate the people that sent these flying bombs over here. Why, why, why? I now know my friend Catherine is never coming back. All of our hopes and dreams are gone. Please laugh for me Catherine. I try to hear her laugh and I desperately try to see her smile but I can't bring her to me. She has gone away. Come back Catherine. Please come back. My heart is broken. They sing about broken hearts in songs but I now know that it really does break. It is an intense pain that you believe will never leave or heal. Why not me Catherine? Why you? I believe that the whole wide world should stop spinning because of her death, right now, this instant, but it doesn't. It just keeps spinning out of control.

Finally my tears start to fall, uncontrollably and become wracking painful sobs. Nothing will ever be the same. My world has changed from this life changing event. I am nine as was my beautiful friend Catherine. In time I will hear her laugh and see her smile. She will come back to me. I know that it will take time but it will happen.

REFLECTIONS:

A hundred V1s a day are now reaching London. The pilotless planes rain down death and destruction for eighty days. In the first fortnight four hundred thousand homes are either destroyed or damaged and over six thousand are killed in just the V1 attacks. My world is so grey. Will there ever be any colour to it?

LIVING DANGEROUSLY ON THE EDGE

It is a summer of events in August of 1944, three glorious weeks of no school. But what to do, Catherine is gone, dead, and all our summer plans died with her. My Mum and Dad don't want me moping around the house and try to get me to go out to play. I do have to do something. I find Eileen, Thelma, Barbara and some of the boys from the road playing at the end of the street. They kindly ask me to join them. Phyllis and Dorothy have their three year old brother Cecil in the old fashioned pram which everyone calls Cecil's bus. They are trying to build carts to race down Clifton Hill. Everyone is searching in the bomb rubble for planks of wood, any old wheels from scooters, small bicycles and pieces of rope to steer with. I join in and very soon we have a big pile of wood and wheels to work with. Some go home to get hammers, nails and any other tools that they can pilfer without their parents knowing. Within a couple of hours we have assembled three very crude racing carts. The rope is nailed in a loop on the front of the cart to hold onto and to steer with. Our shoes are our brakes. Four assorted wheels are to carry you to your doom at the bottom of the hill. We have three old tin hats borrowed from hall cupboards and from unknowing Home Guard fathers. We all shove off to the top of Clifton Hill. It is really steep. We drag and push the carts to the top. Phyllis and Margaret push the old battered pram with three year old Cecil in it to the top of the hill. We all cheer when we make it to the top and then we realize a group of kids should be at the bottom of the hill to help stop the riders from going into the cross street at the bottom. Four boys volunteer. They will then come back up as the riders reach the bottom. The three carts line up on the wide road with a boy on each one. Michael waves his hanky and they are off. Wheels are going wonky and flying off like missiles and sparks emerge from the nails in the soles of their shoes. Grazed knees and sprained ankles are the order of the day. We girls watch from the top of the hill and say to one another that we can do better than the boys. So we hook Cecil into the old battered pram with his harness, put a tin hat on his head, take the brake off the wheel and the two of us, Phyllis and I, hold onto the handle and we let it start to roll. The rest of the girls are to run alongside to stop any unforeseen posturing of the pram to the right or the left. The old rubber wheel pram gathers speed so fast we can't hold on. We try desperately to hold onto the handle. It is impossible and we have to let go. Cecil is squealing with delight as he whizzes down the hill past the houses. The kid knows no fear. At least he has an old tin hat on. The boys grab onto the sides to try to slow it down. It slows somewhat. As it reaches the bottom of the hill they finally are able to stop it. So we decide that the pram is the way to go from now on. The shade is put down and the boys straddle the pram face down. It is like a buzz bomb bouncing and racing at break neck speed down the hill. It is amazing that nobody is killed. Luckily the pram slows down on the upslope after the crossroad. We are lucky that not many motorists are on the road as they can't get petrol to run their cars. Between the planks with wheels and Cecil's pram we are having terrific though dangerous fun. But we are already living in such dangerous times that to us this afternoon is fun not life threatening. If our parents ever find out they will think very differently about it. The excitement of the day helps ease my pain. I don't think about my loss for a little while.

The doodlebugs continue their raids until about the second week of August. It is like a false lull. Is this it or does Gerry have something else for us? We want to believe that it is over and to sleep in our own beds. We don't believe it. We all laugh and say yes, right and blue birds will be over the white cliffs of Dover. Of course we are just joking but I deeply hope and pray that it will be so.

BIRTHDAY FUN FOR EVERYONE

Phyllis is having her tenth birthday and her Mum is going to have a birthday party for her which is always a difficult thing to do in wartime as there is little extra food for parties and never enough food coupons to buy extra. Everyone in the neighbourhood will muck in and give what they can spare. Parents try to make life as normal as can be for us children. Birthdays are always celebrated come what may. It is more like a celebration of life in that we have survived this war so far. A cake is always made even be it made with condensed milk, powdered milk, dried eggs and margarine. Neighbours save and give up their sugar rations in preparation for the cake. The cakes are never moist and chewy but heavy and dry and take forever to swallow and get down. The thought of icing the top of the cake is never entertained. There isn't enough sugar in all of Britain to do that. You can use saccharin which many people do but it is bitter and better not used. The party is to be this coming Saturday afternoon. All of us local kids are invited. I am going to wear my pink party dress. It is another hand me down from my sister that my Nana had bought her. I think it is the most beautiful dress in the world. It is pink taffeta and pink net. I want to have some nice shoes to wear with it but they are dear and we have no spare money to buy new ones and besides pretty shoes are a thing of the past. Everything in wartime is very basic and utility. Shoes are either black or brown. So, I will wear my black lace up shoes to the party and as Mum would say just be glad that you have shoes. So I do. Saturday morning has arrived. It is sunny and clear. I can't wait to get up and get washed. The party is not until three o'clock this afternoon but I want to be ready way ahead of time. Besides I can't wait to put on my pink party dress. It is only the second happy time for me since Catherine was killed and I feel guilty for my happiness today. I sit on my bed in my vest and knickers and think about her. We had always shared so much. I got my first lesson on the birthing of babies from Catherine. One day at school, on the playground, I had asked her where babies came from. She looked at me with a look of askance, pulled me over into a corner of the playground away from the rest of the kids and in lowered tones gave me the shocking news that they come from the Mum's tummy, silly, and I know that because my Mum has one in her tummy. But how does the baby get in there? I begged her to tell me for she was so knowledgeable on this affair of having babies. I was so impressed. I would never have dared to ask my Mum these questions. That would have been so absolutely mortifying. Catherine whispered to me, you must never tell anyone else. It is a secret between the two of us forever. Swear on your life or I won't tell you how the baby gets into the mother's tummy. I do swear, I do, I will never tell. We linked our little fingers together and swore on it. I waited with baited breath. I was going to learn the biggest secret ever known. Well Sheila it happens when your Dad kisses your Mum on the lips. I think it is something in their spit. It mingles together and that causes the baby to be in the mummy's tummy. Oh how disgusting I said. How do you know that that is what causes a baby to grow in your tummy? Catherine says because I saw my Dad kiss my Mum on the lips and soon after that her tummy began to grow and I asked her why her tummy stuck out and she told me because there was a baby in there. Wow, I said. I have only seen my Dad kiss my Mum on the cheek. She must not want any more babies. Probably not said Catherine, assuredly, otherwise they would kiss on the lips. Believe me I have seen it happen. Then it must be so I answered. All of a sudden I felt very grown up, at nine I now know the ever kept secret of life and it was a secret I was to keep forever. Well, except for telling my doll Heather. She was shocked but she will never tell. Oh, how I miss you Catherine. Why can't you be here? I wish you could go to the party today with me. Life just isn't the same without you. I hear my Mum calling up the stairs; time to get dressed Sheila. Hurry or you will be late. I whisper to Catherine, I'll tell you all about the party tonight when I come to bed. I know that she hears me. I meet the gang at the end of the street outside Easters Bakery. It is closed this afternoon because they only open in the mornings when they have bread which usually runs out in about an hour and if you aren't in the queue at six AM you are out of luck. There are ten of us kids assembled. We all look at one another. We all look so clean and dressed up. I don't think we have ever seen one another so clean. Faces, hands and knees have been scrubbed shiny and the boys hair has been wetted down and flattened though threatening to spring back to its unruly self. Some of the girls have finger ringlets done with curling tongs, held in the flame of the gas ring or embers of the fireplace until hot, hot. This is usually the tool of choice if you can stand the smell of singed hair or maybe a slight burn on your scalp. What we do to be beautiful. The consensus is that everyone looks smashing. We are all carrying small presents. None are bought. We have all scrounged around our homes for something. I am giving a book. A long overdue library book but the library won't miss it as a V1 has made a direct hit on it. It is my favourite, Milly Molly Mandy. I love her and her pink and white striped dress, her straight brown hair with a fringe. She is whimsical and reminds me a lot of Catherine. I have wrapped it in plain brown paper, tied with string. We all start to walk around the corner down to Phyllis's house. She and her family live in an upstairs flat in a big old house. The windows are boarded up from being blown out in explosions. A blackened chimney pot from the top of the house lies in the front garden amongst bricks and broken roof tiles. The party is to be in the back garden. Her Mum thinks it better as it is only a few running steps from a street shelter where we will be safe in case Gerry decides to attend the party. There must be at least twenty five kids at this party. That is a lot of children to be responsible for but we all know the drill for the shelters. Phyllis's Mum has drug out a kitchen table borrowed from the people in the flat below them. It is all laid with an assortment of plates and cups. There is a bunch of daisies in a glass jar in the centre of the table. It all looks very normal. We don't get normal too often. Another one of the neighbours has brought out a wind up gramophone player with some records. This is going to be a real party. What a lovely day this is. Kitchen chairs are set up in rows to play musical chairs. Phyllis comes down from upstairs. She looks so pretty. She even has a ribbon tied around her hair. She is glad to see us with all of our pressies in our hands. We all wish her many happy returns of the day and give her our presents. She says she will open them later, after we eat. We all get paper hats to wear. How did they manage to get those? They must really have scrounged around. We play Oranges and Lemons. You always try to get the stronger person on your side for the big tug of war at the end. Next we play musical chairs. Everyone is running, pushing and shoving to get a chair and many of us ending up on our backsides on the grass. We play Blind Man's Bluff, Egg and Spoon and three legged races. Everyone is screaming with delight and victory. We are young and the world is ours at this moment. No thought of war and death at this party. After the games plates of bread and marge and sandwiches made of fish paste are being loaded onto the table. Best of all there are two jellies, red and green and two pink blancmanges. That must have taken the milk rations for the month. But the most beautiful sight of all is a huge tin of strawberry jam. Her Mum opens it up with the tin opener showing the ragged edges of the ragged tin lid. It is a beautiful sight, that thick incredibly red jam. Everyone claps and cheers. Phyllis's older sister Helen is going out with a Yank who is stationed over here and he has given it to them. My Mum says; Yanks are overpaid, oversexed and over here, whatever that all means. But I love it that they are here. Truly they know the right thing to give for a party. It is said that they can get food things that we can't get any more from a place they call the PX and they are very generous. I might add, in more ways than one. (Mothers guard you daughters was told to all.) Whenever us kids see a Yank in his handsome uniform we all chorus; got any gum chum? Oh boy those sticks of gum are total magic in your mouth. But today the taste of that red strawberry jam is heaven. We line up and each gets a spoonful of it right from the tin. It is sweet and glorious. My tongue is alive with the sweet flavour of the strawberries. This strawberry jam is the hit of the party. This is a super day. Some of the grey of war has gone away. Even the cake with the dried eggs and dried milk is edible. But then you will eat anything when you are hungry. There aren't any candles but we sing extra loud, happy birthday to you, and to end it all on a traditional note we do the traditional birthday bumps. Everyone grabs Phyllis's arms or legs. We lift her up and bump her onto the ground on her backside ten times. She is now officially ten years old. Then there it goes, Waa, Waa, Waa, the bloody air raid warning. Can't Hitler stay away on a birthday? Where are his manners? I don't think his mom ever taught him any. Phyllis's Mum and other neighbours calmly call to us to form two lines. Her mother probably thinking, why has this happened on my watch? They tell us to march quickly to the street shelter. We all want to run but we daren't. If we do then getting all of us into the small doorway to the shelter would cause a big jam up. It is pitch black inside. Some of us are tripping over and banging our knees on the wooden seating forms, all of us trying to find our way. It is so scary. Some kids are making ghost sounds and pretending that they are boogeymen. They are reaching out and touching us and scaring everyone to death. It is just like being on a ghost train at the fair only worse. I stand there rooted to the spot, afraid to move for fear of what is out there and then someone, thank God, has found the light switch and suddenly all is revealed. We are all standing there in our party hats. We all start to laugh nervously at ourselves for our fear. Then we really laugh hard and with much glee as Brian Peebles is marching up and down the aisle with his left forefinger under his nose and his right arm stretched straight out yelling, Heil Hitler, Heil Hitler. What a cheeky monkey he is. We all boo him heartily. It sure takes away much of the previous fear. We all sit huddled on the wooden benches waiting for the doodle bugs which we thought we were finished with. Then they come like swarming bees. I pray they won't conk out over the shelter. I wonder, is my family safe? Then somewhere a huge bomb blast cuts off the electricity as often happens and we are plunged back into total darkness. Soon adults are turning on torches and flashing them across the cement walls and ceiling to see if everyone is all right. Mrs Harris, Phyllis's mother, calls out; it is going to be all right, don't panic. She says; I think we should all have a sing along and sing as loudly as we can so that even old Hitler in Berlin can hear us. It definitely will help to drown out the sounds of Hell. We do a rousing "Daisy, Daisy" and then a riotous "Knees Up Mother Brown" while getting louder and louder. Bobby Miller is sitting next to me. I used to think he was handsome when I was six but now at nine I think he is just plain creepy. He keeps trying to whisper in my ear. I can't hear him. I keep singing louder and louder and then I hear that wonderful concerto, the All Clear. It comes heralding like angels, surrounding the shelter. We all cheer. Bobby tugs at my arm. I am in love with you he says, soppily. I answer back;

you're daft. No he says; you're my piece of crackling. You know what I mean, the best piece of the Sunday roast when the fat all crackles and gets crunchy. I retort; ooh, you're disgusting. I struggle to get away from him and to follow everyone out of the shelter. The air raid warden pokes his head into the doorway and says; gor love a duck, there you all are everyone all right in here then? Let's have you boys and girls. Don't all rush at once! Suddenly Bobby grabs me by the shoulders and pulls me towards him and puts a big sloppy kiss on my lips. It is absolutely the most revolting thing to happen to me in my young life. I hate you Bobby Miller, I hate you. I shove him hard. I remember Catherine's words and spit everything out of my mouth and wipe my tongue on my hanky. Ugh, ugh, I will never forgive you. Bobby gets lost in the shuffle. I come out of the shelter into the bright sunlight shielding my eyes from the blinding light. A group of kids are waiting for me to walk home. The party is officially over. One of the girls says; we thought you were right behind us. What happened? Should I tell them? No, they will just make fun of me. I am sure of it. But on the walk home I come to realize what has happened. I have been kissed by a boy, my first kiss. But then the ramifications of that kiss come swooping over me. I am going to have a baby. Catherine had said that that is what happens and I am only nine and not married. I can't possibly tell my Mum, she will kill me. Nor my sister, she will tell on me, I know it and be happy to do so. What to do? There is nothing for it but to tell someone as soon as possible.

Shirley Harrington, she is the one, she knows everything. She is twelve years old. She knows everything about sex. She is the playground informant. She is boy crazy but she will know what to do.

Very early the following morning I set out on my mission to Townsend Road where Shirley lives. I tell my Mum and Dad that I am going up to the park with some friends. I daren't tell them where I am really going. I pray that Shirley will be home. This is my lucky day, my prayers are answered. She is so surprised to see me as I was never really a friend of hers as she is three years older than I. She is different and has a rotten reputation at school. It is even rumoured around the boys and girls school that Shirley Herrington wears a brassiere. If so, what a hussy she is. But never the less I need her help. We sit on the wall outside her house. What do you want titch, she says? After stuttering to get it out I tell her a boy kissed me yesterday and now I am going to have a baby. My parents will kill me. What can I do? She looks at me. You daft little cow she says that's not how you get a nipper. Oh but it is I say. I thought you above anyone would know that. Catherine told me that if you kiss a boy you are going to have a baby and she would never have told me a lie. Then she is as dopey as you are. I can tell you how it happens but you are too young and stupid for me to tell you right now. If you are still alive in two years come back and I will explain it to you then. Now go home you soppy date. Oh please, I beg, I can't go home until I find out how to get rid of the baby. I am so frightened. I will give you anything, please. She looks at me and sneers. Do you have any money? I have five shillings from a postal order that my auntie sent me. I was going to buy a book with it. She says; that will do give it to me and I will tell you what to do. I sadly hand it over to her. The new book will have to wait as this is so much more important. She pockets the money. Do you have a copper penny she asks? I can get one I say. All right then if you really have to know. When you get home, take the penny and tape it over your belly button and wear it for two weeks and no less. Then the little nipper won't be able to breathe. Now just go away you little wretch and if I hear that you have told anyone else this or that you gave me money I will punch your lights out. It is to remain our secret for life. Now go away you little twerp. I run all the way home. I am so happy and so relieved. I know what to do. I fully believe that Shirley has told me the truth. When I get home I run upstairs and get my remaining penny from my pocket money. It is in a tin under my bed. I find some sticky tape and paste it over my belly button. It is done. I will never ever kiss another boy as long as I live whether it causes babies or not. On the following Friday night while I am taking my bath in my allotted two inches of water my Mum, as usual, comes into the scullery to help me wash my hair and when I stand up to get out of the bath she sees the penny and asks me; Sheila why on earth do you have a penny stuck over your navel? I would very much like to know. I am very curious. I can't hold it in any longer. I have to confess. I burst into tears and confess everything, the kiss, the baby, Shirley Harrington's cure for getting rid of babies, all of it. She closes her eyes and shakes her head in dismay and I think but I am not sure I saw her biting her bottom lip as if to stop a laugh. As I say, I am not sure but I think I did. She says; Sheila, Sheila my dear child. You are not having a baby. Shirley Harrington was telling you a bunch of cod's wallop. Kissing does not make you pregnant. When the time comes I will explain it all to you about babies but until then it doesn't mean you can go around kissing the boys. Time enough for that when you are older. Now finish up your bath and get your nightie on and I will make you a hot cup of cocoa. In that moment I had never loved her more. She went up the steps into the kitchen and shut the door. I could hear my Mum and Dad's muffled talking and laughing and I suddenly knew that everything was right with the world.

CAN PEACE BE FAR BEHIND

The lazy days of summer have come to a close. I never did go to Ms Ship's for tea or black berrying. It somehow didn't seem right to go without Catherine. It would have been a painful reminder of our friendship that was torn apart so sadly. I am ready to return to school. It really has been a summer of events. We are now sleeping in our own beds once again and I mean sleep. It is marvellous. The raids are now few and far between. It is like the war is over for us, at least in London. But Dad still is with the Home Guard and goes on duty every night. Dad says; the war is not over till it is over. People are trying to pick up the broken pieces of their lives, glad for the respite. Food is still very scarce and I am sure it will be for a long time to come but we give three cheers for no more V1s after the eighty days of their reign of terror. Life is sweet. Will our false sense of security be broken? It is. On September the eighth of 1944 another evil machine of death is launched and heads for London, travelling at supersonic speeds of nearly four thousand miles per hour and as high as fifty miles in the sky then smashing its two thousand pound high explosive warhead into London without warning. Unlike the V1s the V2 rockets cannot be intercepted. Over a thousand are fired on London. They don't always meet their mark. It is the first ballistic missile ever launched. Living my young life is hell but some say the V2s are more kind in one way, you don't know when you are going to die because there is no warning, no siren and no time just death arriving out of silence. It is only after it has reached its target that you hear first an explosion and second the rocket motor and then a sonic boom. At least with the V1's we knew that when the engines stopped and those seconds of deathly silence followed you were still in control of your mind and you knew that you would either live, die, be maimed for life or homeless but not so with the V2s. The terror and suspense of it all is unbearable. We are told that Hitler has even another weapon up his sleeve but fortunately for us the last weapon, the V3 is never fired towards London and for that we give our thanks to the heroic men of the Six Hundred and Seventeenth Allied Squadron. Many more lives would have been lost or destroyed if not for the heroic two thousand Allied airmen of that squadron who destroyed the rocket batteries. They sacrificed their lives so that many of ours would be saved. They will never be forgotten. In the V1 and V2 raids nine thousand people were killed and over twenty five thousand seriously maimed and injured. From the start of the bombing in August 1940 to 1945 over sixty seven thousand innocent people died. Fifty four thousand more were seriously injured in England alone. What a price to pay.

It is May 1945. My war is finally over. I have survived to live a month, a year, only God knows but for me it is over. I pray for peace. I will never understand the hate and lust for power in men's minds that leads to the destruction of life. Thousands all over Europe are dead or maimed to never resume a normal life because of war. Family lives were torn apart by the pain of losing their loved ones and their homes. The hurt and the memories will never go away until the very last of us who suffered and survived depart this world and that number of us gets smaller every minute of every day. We must never forget the will of man to survive and triumph over war and the many who gave so much. I am so very lucky that my family and I survived to live another day. I am now ten years old. For six of those years all I knew was war. My family and I have feelings of happiness for being alive and safe and guilt for all who died instead of us. The happiness and guilt will live with us forever. I believe that I was meant to tell the story of what happened in my young life to honour all the children throughout England and Europe, all those who gave their innocent lives and to those who lived through the bloody hell of war and survived. We will all of us rejoice and be reunited one day but before I go home to be with them I would love to see a memorial in London dedicated to all of the children of World War II, to honour them for giving up so much. I do so hope it will come to pass in my life time.

IT IS DONE

May the eighth 1945 and victory in Europe is declared. It is over, it is finally over. People are weeping with joy, grief and relief, relief that it has ended. No more raids. No more killing. The men that survived in battle can come home from the front. Some families will be reunited and others will mourn their lost loved ones. There are to be parties in every corner of the Kingdom to celebrate victory with bonfires on the hillsides, street parties, the gathering of thousands outside Buckingham Palace, parades, flags and buntings flying proudly. England with the help and unbelievable sacrifice of her allies is free. Victory is ours. It is indeed a proud, proud moment for everyone. We did it. Union jack flags are flying from every house left standing. Kitchen tables are drug outdoors and all of our rations and coupons are gathered together to provide for a grand feast. There is music, singing and dancing. It is all so exciting. We feel a huge responsibility has been lifted from us. We are free. What a beautiful word that is, free, free to go to bed at night without the fear of death, free to live our lives with our families, free from tyranny, free to go about our everyday lives and the freedom to believe that there is hope for all of us in this world. Yes it is over but I believe that for all of us who are left behind we will carry through the rest of our lives the silent pain and scars of those six years so very rarely mentioned. It is the British way. Just bury it deep and pretend that it didn't happen. Being strong countrymen, that is what we do but I decided that it is time to speak out for all of the children. I do so hope that you will understand. I ask myself where all the children have gone. Some survived the war but many did not. Some came back from evacuation only to die at home with their families. All of us suffered the pain of separation from home and families. Only we will understand the pain. Some came home from evacuation to find their parents and families dead and their homes no longer standing and are orphans. We all had to be so brave. No one acknowledged us but I salute all of us and we will never be forgotten. I know where the children have gone and someday in the future I shall join them and we will all be together, that great renegade band of evacuees, home at last.

I am part of history and of such catastrophic events for a child which I pray will never, ever be repeated. For children are the most innocent of victims. I pray that mankind has learned from these events and that my prayers for peace will be answered.

ABOUT THE AUTHOR

This is her first and as she says "Her last time" out of the gate with her memoir.

She was born in London, England and is now living in southern California with her husband and their beautiful cat Miss Beasley.

BIO LANG
Lang, Ruby
Faces in the Windows
Paperback

11/16/18

CPSIA information can be obtained
at www.ICGtesting.com
Printed in the USA
LVHW08s1355230918
591103LV00010B/639/P

9 781508 592952